More praise for
SINS OF THE FATHER

"With bestselling author William Wright, Ms. Franklin has written a powerful, poignant, and gripping account of the crime, the memory, and her father's arrest and conviction more than twenty years later."
—*Atlanta Journal & Constitution*

"With Franklin offering her deeply emotional and articulate recollections, and veteran biographer William Wright providing a meticulously researched rendering of the complicated facts of the case, the two make an unbeatable writing team."
—*San Francisco Chronicle*

"[Ms. Franklin] has described the pathos of the haunted victim with unsparing honesty . . . Her honesty in describing how the nightmare of her past has drawn itself over her life leaves the reader devastated."
—*Los Angeles Times*

Also by William Wright:

BALL
THE WASHINGTON GAME
HEIRESS: The Rich Life of Marjorie Merriweather Post
RICH RELATIONS
PAVAROTTI: My Own Story (with Luciano Pavarotti)
THE VON BÜLOW AFFAIR
LILLIAN HELLMAN: The Image, the Woman
ALL THE PAIN THAT MONEY CAN BUY: The Life
    of Christina Onassis

SINS OF THE FATHER

*The Landmark Franklin Case:
A Daughter, a Memory,
and a Murder*

Eileen Franklin and William Wright

FAWCETT CREST • NEW YORK

Sale of this book without a front cover may be unauthorized. If this book is coverless, it may have been reported to the publisher as "unsold or destroyed" and neither the author nor the publisher may have received payment for it.

A Fawcett Crest Book
Published by Ballantine Books
Copyright © 1991 by Eileen Franklin and William Wright

All rights reserved under International and Pan-American Copyright Conventions. Published in the United States by Ballantine Books, a division of Random House, Inc., New York, and simultaneously in Canada by Random House of Canada Limited, Toronto.

No part of this book may be reproduced or transmitted in any form or by any means, electronic or mechanical, including photocopying, recording, or by any information storage and retrieval system, without permission in writing from the publisher.

Library of Congress Catalog Card Number: 91-20504

ISBN 0-449-21999-2

This edition published by arrangement with Crown Publishers, Inc.

Manufactured in the United States of America

First Ballantine Books Edition: September 1993

Cover photo of Eileen Franklin by Vern Fisher.
Cover photo of George Franklin by Michael A. Russell.

At Bill Wright's suggestion, we dedicate this book to my children, Aaron and Jessica Lipsker, who have given me a chance to see how wonderful childhood can be.

EILEEN FRANKLIN

ACKNOWLEDGMENTS

I would like to acknowledge and thank the following people:

Barry Lipsker, who gave me more support and aggravation than any one person deserves.

Bill Wright for his friendship, integrity, and patience. I am most appreciative for the literary skill that he brought into this project and shared, in abundance, with me.

Janice Franklin for her sisterly love, honesty, strength, wit, and devotion to my children.

My Lipsker family: Scott, Fil, Lee, Denise, Shana, Ron, and especially Mom and Dad.

Aunt Sue for her wisdom, caring, and energy.

Sharon Nelson for her beauty, love, and affection, which pulled me through so many times.

Barbara Kontoudakis for her friendship and generosity, especially when I was too weary to give but needed to receive.

Carol Rosemond for years of kindness, sharing, and humor.

Aimee Alotta for her assistance with this book but particularly for her special thoughtfulness.

Binnie Fankhauser-Gun for listening and understanding.

Gina Rubright for her bravery, honesty, and friendship.

Stephen and Julie Wright for their concern and support at a time when I needed it.

James and Maggie Crawford for their words and acts of kindness.

Bill Simon for his guidance, integrity, and protection.

Bob Morse, for always being truthful, just like he promised, and for being an exceptional man.

Elaine Tipton for Everything. Especially for believing in me, allowing me to trust her, and for remembering that I was once a little girl who had a best friend.

There are those among us who live in rooms of experience that you and I cannot enter.

—JOHN STEINBECK, "IN QUEST OF AMERICA"

PROLOGUE

Eileen

On a bright Southern California afternoon in January 1989, my day was going along like the others. The predictability of my life did not bother me, but was something I had worked to achieve. After years of turmoil, I was raising the children I'd always wanted in the way I had always wanted. My future looked promising. I had hoped that my unsteady marriage might have a chance. My life was more settled than it had ever been. Some would call it dull, but to me, it was wonderful.

In a few moments, my two-year-old son, Aaron, would wake from his nap. I would carry him to the family room where my daughter, Sica, was on the floor huddled over a coloring book with two friends. Until then, I would sit on the sofa directly over the girls, waiting for the sound of my son's voice. I would do what I did every day, the banal routine of a young parent, following instinctive dictates that had assumed the appearance of choices. My life was suspended until I heard Aaron's voice call out "Mom."

I loved my children intensely. More than anything else I wanted to be a good mother. I knew I was overprotective. Neighbors made snide remarks about my not letting my children out of my sight. But I knew better than most people that even in the most agreeable neighborhoods, children are not always safe. When I was eight, my best friend, Susan Nason, had been murdered. No one knew why and no murderer was found.

Determined as I was to be a good mother, I refused to let this override other sides of my nature. Although my education was minimal—I never finished high school—I prided myself on having an intellect. Well, not an intellect exactly, but at least a curiosity and a strong desire to improve myself. Since I could remember, I had loved books and read every chance I got. In the few hours I had to myself after the children were asleep and with my husband, Barry, in bed asleep beside me, I would pick up a book and lose myself in the worlds of others.

My father, who *had* finished high school, but only barely, had always encouraged me to read and would boast that once, when I was four, he found me at dawn wrapped up in a book. He had no idea how I had learned to read. For me, reading had always been a way to slip from my existence into the existences of others. My lack of formal education made me feel inadequate and I read as much to improve myself as for pleasure.

Later, in my teens, reading allowed me to leave a bad world and experience snatches of good ones. Now, with my world so improved, the lives I explored in books no longer seemed unobtainable dreams, but rather road maps to future possibilities. I was far better off than I had been growing up, but my life was not yet where I wanted it to be.

I did not think this with bitterness, but rather a soft and pleasant wistfulness. Barry and I had had repeated marital problems—things were all right at the moment, but I had discussed with him my desire for a different future and made clear my intention to go off on my own when the children were grown. He agreed. For many years I did not believe I was capable of a happy, balanced life. I was beginning to think I was.

For the moment, my existence as a young wife and mother was fine. We lived very comfortably in the Los Angeles bedroom community of Canoga Park. I enjoyed most of my daily program and holding Aaron while feeding him with his bottle was one of the more pleasurable parts of it. But more than the benefits of my present life, it was the surprise-free routine that suited my mood and provided a sensible transition from the wild girl of my single years to the mature, self-reliant woman I hoped to become. Barry had given me a safe haven in which to grow up.

But this bargained-for serenity was about to be shattered, but not by an outside force. It would come from knowledge that I had for nearly twenty years carried around inside me, knowledge I had sealed over, perhaps with denial, perhaps fear. It would erupt within me and take over my life—like the chromosome that, after years of quiescence, comes alive as Alzheimer's disease.

Before I left the sofa, I would have an experience that would irrevocably change my life. It would also change my husband's life and the life of every member of my family. I would be hounded by the press, by film companies, by book publishers—all of them wanting to tell the story of *what had happened.* I would be in and out of prosecutors' offices, in and out of courtrooms. Strangers would say I was heroic, others would say I was a treacherous fraud. I would receive death threats, and I would be pitted in a mortal struggle with my father, whose favorite I had always been and whom I had always loved. Above all, I would finally have a chance to confront, then, I fervently hoped, put to rest demons that had been tormenting me since my childhood.

As I warmed Aaron's bottle, I noticed with satisfaction that Daniela, my Austrian *au pair,* had left the kitchen spotless before taking her afternoon break. Passing back into the family room at the rear of our house, I glanced at the ugly curtains on the windows out to the patio and thought of my victory in getting Barry to agree to replace them. I only had to select the new fabric.

I relished all Barry had given me. Even though we could have afforded a much fancier house, it was pleasant and comfortable. Our children attended a first-rate school. Gunning around in my Mercedes, windows down, my long red hair whipping in the breeze, dark glasses, car phone to my ear —trying to inject a little flash of dazzle in the San Fernando Valley's enclave of solid family values. I had grown up thinking myself funny-looking, even ugly. In grade school, the taunts of my classmates had confirmed that opinion. I had trouble believing that others now thought me good-looking.

Most of my life I had lived in middle-class suburbs. I had grown up in one where I had lived until I was eighteen. When I was on my own, I had taken an apartment in another, and I had worked in yet another. Since meeting Barry I had lived in a number of California locations—Foster City, San Jose, Manhattan Beach—but my corner of each of these areas was undeniably a solid middle-class suburb. Aware as I was of the bizarre, even twisted nature of my background, I was not oblivious to the irony that I had spent all my twenty-eight years in the safest, sanest of American residential arrangements, the bedroom communities on the outskirts of big cities.

Now as a young mother, I enjoyed the perks provided by a wealthy husband, but the "things" in my life were not all that important to me. I had rarely envied what other people had. Although, growing up, when almost everyone around me had more than I had, I had plenty of opportunity to be envious. But now the only thing that brought out envy in me was to see a truly happy marriage. It gave me a sensation of being shut out, and made me feel that a big part of life available to many people was eluding me. Yes, the worst thing was to see two people who were in love. I did not feel that Barry and I were.

I knew what I owed Barry. He came along when I badly needed an anchor. When I was single, affairs had come easily to me, but Barry had been so different from the others. He was solid, energetic, ambitious, knew what he wanted. And did he ever want me! I had never met anyone so persistent, so impossible to rebuff. He knew he was going to build a productive, affluent life and he was just as certain I was going to share it with him.

I was flattered and won over by his persistence, but more than that I was intrigued by his don't-take-no attitude that eventually gave a kind of inevitability to our joining forces. His juggernaut determination indicated a strength that answered a deep need in me at the time. On the other hand, I was not oblivious to his drawbacks. He was fourteen years older than I was, he had been married before, and he had been raised Jewish while I was nominally a Catholic. He also refused to communicate on any but the most surface level.

After we got married, we got along pretty well as colleagues in the child-rearing enterprise. In fact, we had some important things in common such as vegetarianism and a hatred of cruelty to all living creatures. I try to avoid leather products and Barry would refuse to kill a beetle that had wandered onto our kitchen floor, instead scooping it into a cup and transporting it outside. He would kill nothing—except mosquitoes, saying "they attack you first."

In our perfunctory marriage, Barry and I were doing what young adults were supposed to do: we were coming together in a contractual arrangement, having children and establishing and supporting a home in which to nurture, protect, and raise them. Barry yelled at me a lot and I had learned to yell back. But most of the time we got along and we both adored our children. Most of all I was grateful to him for the two perfect children he had given me: Aaron, so full of life with his curly brown hair and green eyes, and Sica, so sweet and feminine with her fine reddish-blond hair, her blue eyes, freckles.

The phone rang. Barry from his office. Yes, Aaron was napping, Sica was home from school, Daniela was out or asleep in her room. Everything was fine. See you later. Good-bye.

I went to the kids' room to get Aaron. As I carried him down the stairs, his bottle hung from the rubber nipple, which I clenched between my teeth. I sat in the corner of the sofa, Aaron draped across my lap sucking his bottle. I looked out at the beautiful winter day. It was sunny and warm enough to take the cover off the pool and let the children swim. Holding the bottle to Aaron's mouth, I felt that strange contentment I always felt feeding my children—especially Aaron when he was warm and cuddly before he was fully awake and ready to dismantle the house. The stereo was on—had I turned it on or had Sica?—a tape of one of the children's favorites, Raffi, singing a folk song.

I heard Jessica ask me, "Isn't that right, Mommy?" I had no idea what she was talking about.

I looked down at my daughter, crouched on the floor with her friends, surrounded by crayons and coloring books. It must have been the look in her eyes—quizzical, appealing to me for some response, some action—as I sat looking down at her, the bright sunlight slicing between the curtains and falling in long slabs of light on the carpet—it brought it all back, the scene that had not entered my mind for almost twenty years.

I first felt a wrenching terror, then remembered a wooded setting, my friend Susan sitting below me on a mound or a rock, the looming figure of a man silhouetted against the sun, holding a rock above his head, poised to bring it down on her. The imploring look she gave me held an expression I would first remember as one of betrayal but would later realize was a look of simple terror onto which I projected my own feelings of guilt at my powerlessness to save my friend, to do anything at all to help her. In my memory, the man moved toward her as his arms began to come down. . . .

Inwardly, I screamed "NO!" And then, sitting holding my son to me, immobile with terror, I saw what I had refused to see for two decades, for two-thirds of my life, the terrible knowledge I had known from the moment the memory had returned. The man killing Susan was my father.

PART ONE

Foster City

ONE

On the day that Susan Nason disappeared, September 22, 1969, a series of shock waves pummeled the middle-income suburb of Foster City, eighteen miles south of San Francisco. Her mother, Margaret Nason, a tall, slender woman in her late twenties, first began to think something was wrong when her eight-year-old daughter failed to return home from running an errand. About an hour later, when Susan still hadn't turned up, her mother became alarmed. She went out on her bicycle to look for her daughter around the neighborhood.

Donald Nason was a tall, handsome man with curly dark hair and blue eyes. Originally from Chicago, he had moved to the Bay Area, where he met Margaret, who came from Modesto. When they married, they lived for a time in Seattle, then moved to Foster City, where Donald worked as a salesman for a firm that made movable office interior structures. Like many men in the new neighborhood, he kept mostly to his family, but was well enough liked. Everyone knew that Donald doted on his daughter Susan—a sweet little girl whose spirit and vivacity matched her strawberry-blond hair and freckles. When word got to Nason that Susan was late coming back, he rushed home from work and immediately set out in his truck to look for her. Because he asked all those he met if they had seen Susan, the word spread quickly that the Nason girl was missing.

As each hour passed with no trace of Susan, the more palatable explanations began to seem less and less possible, and the realization that something very bad had happened became inescapable. Perhaps she had had trouble with her bicycle and couldn't get home. No, her bicycle was found in the family garage. Perhaps she had fallen or had some other sort of accident and was hurt. No, enough hours had gone by that surely

9

someone within the small community would have found her and telephoned her parents.

Perhaps she had stayed too long at a friend's house. No, the time had passed when even the most willful and disobedient child would have known she had to return home for supper. If not, surely she would have been sent home by some other child's parents. Foster City was not a social community; there was little visiting back and forth between neighbors, and friendships were mostly the over-the-back-fence variety. But they all looked out for each other's children.

By five o'clock, the Nasons had visited the homes of all of their neighbors seeking whatever information they could. Had they seen her since school let out at three? When? Where? Whom was she with? What was she doing? With no one offering any useful information, Donald called the Foster City police, who took the matter in stride and began routine procedures for tracking missing children. Two officers made the rounds of the same houses Donald Nason had visited, asking the same questions but adding more ominous ones: Was Susan the sort of child who might get into a stranger's car? Was she susceptible to bribes such as candy or a new toy? What was her mood? Additional police were called in from nearby San Mateo, and before long there were police officers throughout the neighborhood.

All evening, telephones rang in the area's ranch-style homes. For a few moments adults would talk in hushed and urgent tones, then return to the family dinner table or television set, waiting until their sons and daughters were distracted to whisper to each other about what had happened. Of course, the children in these houses knew about Susan's disappearance, and began adjusting their views of the world outside to fit half-heard parental admonitions about dangers that lurked beyond the walls of their homes. Later that night, policemen returned to the houses where they had spoken only with the adults to question sleepy and bewildered children, as parents clutched them a little tighter.

Eventually the pretense was abandoned that a minor ripple had momentarily disrupted the community's placid surface, some predictable disturbance to be filed away with other youthful pranks, fights, and fevers—the routine occurrences that earned a few moments' gossip and were forgotten. By nine o'clock that night, Foster City was in a state of all-out panic. Searchlights played over the area's canals and artificial lakes as police dragged them, searching for a body. Helicopters flew low over the rows of modest homes, their spotlights probing into the backyard foliage as their rotor blades noisily slapped the night air, imparting a war zone's clamorous tension to the placid community.

For the next days, volunteer search parties combed the surrounding areas. George Franklin, a fireman who lived around the corner from the Nasons, joined in several of these expeditions, including the massive one the first night. Extensive attention was paid to a stretch of swamp that bordered Foster City's southern flank. Even after the organized search parties abandoned this vast area, Margaret Nason would ride her bicycle to the street that bordered it, and could be seen, in tall rubber boots, wandering alone through the watery grassland.

Rae Alotta, who lived across the street from the Franklins, and whose daughter Aimee went to school with Susan, was unnerved when the police dragged the small fishpond in her back garden. For Rae, the thought was too horrible to contemplate: the body of adorable, blue-eyed Susan—a bit high-strung, but still one of the neighborhood's best-liked children—her straight golden hair matted over her sweet face, being pulled from the tiny pool, the pool itself a symbol of Foster City's prettified, hermetic artificiality. Now this dainty backyard ornament had been twisted into a suspected instrument of child-death.

The realization that one of the neighborhood's children had vanished struck at the heart of Foster City's belief system. Like most suburbs, Foster City was about safety, about humans seeking protection from other humans. The mowed lawns, the swept front walks, the trimmed hedges were signs of shared comforts and values that would be defended against intruders. The neighborhood's very openness—the clear lawns and yards—was a strategy, perhaps unconscious, against stealth and subterfuge. An out-of-place visitor or unwelcome arrival would stand out in the bare, shadowless spaces of Foster City. Evil, as it tried to penetrate the community, would be spotted instantly and stopped before it reached the front door, which could be barred. The assumption was a fundamental one: evil was outside, decency inside. Doors kept evil out. Window curtains were to keep evil from looking in.

The residents had sacrificed much to come here. The young adults who dominated the community were mostly the offspring of blue-collar families, couples setting out into adulthood who had struggled to escape crowded urban neighborhoods by committing themselves to long-term mortgages for the modest homes, ranging in price from $25,000 to $40,000 in 1969 dollars, that lined the planned blocks and circles of the new suburb.

Their aim had been to put as much distance as possible between their families and the resentments and bitter frustrations that festered in the decaying city centers, the meltdown of anger that made life there so dangerous. They were leaving behind the poor, who were unable to achieve a toehold in the burgeoning American economy. The sense of being left behind made those who remained angrier and more menacing, and made the luckier ones more eager to leave.

The move to Foster City gave many of the newcomers a smug sense of accomplishment. They had reached a critical rung on the ladder of social progress. They had left behind the squalid and dangerous streets and achieved the front lawns, backyard barbecues, family rooms, and, above all, *safety*—the promised basic package of the American dream. Their children could walk unattended to and from school. On their bikes and skates, they were given the run of the neighborhood without adult supervision, with the understanding that a concerned adult, a caring member of the tribe, was never more than a shout away.

If you didn't know everyone's name, you certainly knew their faces. The eighteen miles between Foster City's residents and downtown San Francisco was a buffer between good, decent, family-rearing people and *danger*. But Susan's disappearance reminded everyone that you could never totally eliminate the peril of human evil. There was always the possibility of a drifter, one of the deranged misfits and aberrant personalities who roamed the landscape like medieval dragons, preying upon little girls and boys.

It was an oddity of the Susan Nason case that, three days before she disappeared, a schoolgirl of about the same age, Ann Hobbs, had told her parents and later the police that a strange man had tried to lure her into his car, a blue station wagon. Although nothing came of this incident, it had alarmed the entire community, and reminded the residents that even Foster City was not immune from peril. Teachers in the Foster City Elementary School, which Susan Nason and Eileen Franklin attended, immediately gave more forceful warnings to the students not to talk with strangers.

The odd occurrence was like a single storm cloud that drifted over Foster City to remind those Californians that the weather was not always perfect. Although many eventually came to think of Ann Hobbs's experience as either invented or greatly exaggerated, it served as an ominous prelude to the very real disappearance of Susan Nason so shortly afterward. But that was hindsight. At the time, it caused a stir, but did not alarm the community to the degree that doors were locked and children kept at home.

As a serious threat, abduction by a stranger remained on the probability scale at the same level as a lightning strike. Of course it could happen, but it wouldn't—not in Foster City. Where Ann Hobbs's story had shaken that comfortable assumption, Susan's disappearance had destroyed it. A mysterious and malign force had darkened the skies above the community. Until Susan was found—alive or, even if it solved the mystery in a way not threatening to the rest, dead—the terrifying shadow would not go away.

Foster City had been the creation of one T. Jack Foster, a developer who had moved his family to the Bay Area from Texas. Having prospered through routine building projects, Foster had the dream of creating an entire city from a master plan that would take years to implement. He chose for his site an area east of Route 101, one of two major thruways heading south from San Francisco. Most of the established communities in this suburban area known as the Peninsula lay to the west of 101. San Mateo and the affluent communities of Burlingame, Hillsboro, and Millbrae sat between 101 and the Montara mountain range that ran south between San Francisco Bay and the Pacific Ocean.

The swampy land to the east of 101 had been considered useless until population pressures and burgeoning real-estate markets made developers take a second look. Since San Francisco Bay, in this region south of the city, is shallow, landfills were feasible. Indeed, San Francisco International Airport, which also sits on the Bay east of 101, had been constructed mostly on landfill.

Aware of the potential of the Peninsula's Bay side, Jack Foster picked a desolate area known as Brewer's Island, the part of the bay shore at which the San Mateo Bridge hit the Peninsula bringing Route 92, the area's principal east-west artery, across the bay from Hayward. This highway, which would figure importantly in Susan's disappearance, crossed Route 101 at San Mateo, then continued westward up into the mountains, descending to the Pacific Ocean at Half Moon Bay.

To Foster, the site's proximity to the recreational potential of the bay as well as the convenience of the nearby intersection of two major highways, 92 and 101, made Brewer's Island a ripe spot for an extensive residential development. Working with two companies, Centex West and the W. W. Dean Corporation, he bought up the land, much of it owned by the Leslie Salt Company, which had been using it for salt flats, and began mapping out a town that he called Foster City. He began building in 1960, the year Eileen Franklin was born.

In an effort to remove the Levittown machine-stamped stigma from his city, Jack Foster, while keeping his houses simple, made sure that none of them was a duplicate of the house on either side of it. Working with about five basic designs that he allocated randomly along the first streets under development, he further varied the façades with exterior paint and ornamentation. By 1960 his first group of houses was ready for occupancy. He called it "Neighborhood One." Within ten years there were nine such designated neighborhoods. Children arriving at school would be asked which neighborhood they were from, and would respond with a number.

The Alottas claim to have been the twenty-sixth family to move into Foster City. Rae Alotta recalls looking out her window the day she arrived and seeing a moving van unloading furniture across the street at a house she later learned had been purchased by a young couple with an eyebrow-raising *five* little children. The couple were George and Leah Franklin. When Rae caught a glimpse of the couple, she was struck by how good-looking they both were. A few years later the Nason family moved in around the corner.

After Susan's disappearance, some residents would insist that there had always been something askew in Foster City. For all of its sunny, welcome-to-the-middle-class veneer, Foster's dream town, after only a few years of existence, seemed to harbor more than its share of troublesome human behavior. Drinking was heavy and marital infidelity was commonplace, but there were worse problems.

In the first ten years, one family had their children removed and placed in a foster home because of allegations that the mother would get high on marijuana and abuse them. One ten-year-old boy had a propensity for starting fires. Another boy would appear in his parents' bedroom in the middle of the night carrying a knife. A young mother hanged herself in the family garage. Divorce became common; few of the couples who settled in the area during its first years would still be married ten years later.

A young woman who grew up in Foster City during those early years would later theorize about the reasons for Foster City's high rate of problematic behavior, which she felt stemmed from the pressures felt by the young couples who moved there. "Most of them were recent hippies who were trying to move out of the drug culture of the sixties and settle down to raise families. Many were stressed by the responsibilities they had taken on, not to mention the totally different way of living. For many of them it was all new, not just stable family life, but the suburban middle-class version of it. They didn't know if they belonged—or if they wanted to belong."

For all the community's experience with odd events and scandalous behavior, nothing had ever happened that was so profoundly unsettling as Susan's disappearance. The abuse of children that had occurred had been inflicted by parents. Nothing terrible had ever befallen a Foster City child while he or she was playing in the neighborhood. If parents were wobbly and unpredictable, the neighborhood itself was safe. Now that all-important belief was shattered. Doors were locked. Families would no longer allow their children to walk to school; instead they formed car pools. When Susan's fate was later discovered, some families moved from the neighborhood altogether.

In the first days following Susan's disappearance, the memory of most all who knew her was raked for the slightest recollection that might throw light on the case. Margaret Nason was forced to put aside her distress and focus on the precise sequence of her last moments with her daughter. She remembered having been alone in her house, sewing an outfit for Susan's birthday which would be in five days, when her daughter arrived home from school shortly after three in the afternoon. Susan dropped off her school books and asked permission to go out on an errand. Celia Oakley, a classmate who lived nearby, had left a pair of shoes at school, and Susan wanted to take them to her.

When Margaret Nason consented, Susan rushed out of the house carrying the shoes in a brown paper bag. Shortly after four o'clock, when Susan had not returned from her errand, Margaret Nason got her bicycle from the garage, noticing that

Susan's bike was there, and pedaled around the neighborhood looking for her. She never saw her daughter alive again.

Suzanne Banks, a neighbor who had a daughter two years younger than Susan, said that Susan had knocked on her door at around three-thirty. The Bankses lived about six houses up Balclutha Street from the Nasons, at the corner of Balclutha and Matsonia Drive. Susan had asked Mrs. Banks if Celia Oakley lived there. Banks told Susan she had the wrong house and pointed her toward the Oakley house, halfway up Matsonia Drive. For those many people who, years later, would hear of this innocuous encounter, Susan's stop at the wrong house, so near to her own and so near to the house she was seeking, provided an eight-year-old's view of the unwieldy and confusing world she encountered when she ventured more than a few yards from her own home.

The Franklin family lived around the corner from the Nasons, on Harvester Drive. Of the family's four daughters and one son, ten-year-old Janice Franklin was a year older than her sister Eileen and the second oldest of the five Franklin children. When, late that afternoon, she came in from playing, she saw her father sitting silent and alone in the living room. He had a can of beer in his hand and, as he stared straight ahead at nothing, the kind of dark glower on his face that told her some sort of trouble was afoot. As she dawdled with her back to him, closing the door and trying to figure out an alternative to turning and facing him—passing back through the door? disappearing into the air?—he said in a strange, loud voice, "Hello, Janice."

There was something about the tone that she later described as frightening in a way that was quite different from the usual fear of a few hard smacks, verbal abuse, or some other form of punishment he was always ready to hand out. When, twenty years later, every detail of that day was exhumed and examined, Janice could not explain exactly why her father's greeting had been deeply unsettling to her, but she never deviated in her insistence that it had been.

When the police, in the course of their door-to-door investigation, came to the Franklin home, Janice went to the front door and they questioned her about Susan. As with everyone they interrogated, they asked her to tell them anything she could remember about Susan. Was she adventurous? Mischievous? Disobedient? Did she have any reason to fear her mother and father? Had she done anything that might get her into trouble at home, that might make her afraid to return? Did she know anyone who lived outside the neighborhood? No question was too strained or farfetched for the police to ask, but they could turn up nothing that offered so much as a hint of an explanation. Inexplicably, they did not question Eileen, or for that matter Kate, George junior, or Diana.

That night, as the Franklin children were preparing to go to bed, Janice saw that Eileen was crying and trembling. Janice, who was also a friend of Susan's, knew that Susan was her sister's best friend, that the two girls were exceptionally close. Not only did they love each other, but they had the additional bond of both being teased about their freckles and red hair. For an eight-year-old, such harassment is a serious matter, and both girls suffered because of it.

Young as she was, Janice surely could have assumed why her sister was so upset that night. It was the thought of her dearest friend, a little girl of eight lost in the woods or some other frightening place—nothing to eat, no cover, no place to sleep—or, worse, in the hands of some evil kidnapper who would treat her badly, perhaps hurt her. It was enough to make any eight-year-old cry and tremble. Janice did what she could to comfort Eileen until she fell asleep.

In the days that followed, no trace of Susan was found, nor was any information turned up that suggested an explanation. Donald and Margaret Nason were asked repeatedly if their daughter was the trusting sort of child who would respond if a stranger spoke to her. The Nasons insisted that she was not. In fact, Donald Nason added that he had frequently admonished both of his daughters never to talk to strangers. As the police pressed this point, the idea of an abduction was implanted in Donald's mind, and he began to feel guilty that he had not impressed this warning forcefully enough on Susan.

In their desperation the Nasons consulted a psychic, a woman who also hammered away at the possibility of Susan's having been beguiled and lulled into befriending a stranger. Was she generally trusting? Yes, but she knew not to trust strangers, or even speak to them. Was she friendly? Same answer. Were there *any* circumstances under which their daughter might speak with a stranger? Finally Mrs. Nason admitted that perhaps if the stranger had offered Susan a puppy or a particularly beautiful doll, she might have forgotten the warnings and

spoken with him, even gotten into a car with him. Commenting
on this later, Margaret Nason said, "I was in such a distraught
condition I had no idea what to think, no idea what could have
happened. It all made so little sense, I could not rule out any
possibility."

When a child is missing and the police fear foul play the
father is automatically a suspect, and the police returned again
and again to talk with Donald Nason. "I told him he was a
suspect," said Detective William Hensel of the Foster City
Police. "I was up front with him. We tore the house apart, went
through the attic, the area under the house. Nason was drinking
heavily, hardly knew what was going on." Rumors of this
suspicion leaked out, so that Donald Nason, in addition to the
devastation of suddenly and inexplicably losing a beloved child,
had to live with the awareness that, in the eyes of some of his
neighbors, he might have killed his own daughter.

A few days later, George Franklin called out to Janice that
the police were on the phone and had another question to ask
her. As she headed down the hall from the bedroom to the
telephone, her father came up behind her and gave her a hard
kick in the back. Even at ten, Janice was used to sudden and
surprising attacks from her father. Usually there was some sort
of reason, however improbable or unjustified, for his violence.
This time, however, she could see no possible reason, nor did he
give any. She continued to the phone and spoke with the police,
trying to concentrate on what they were saying while feeling
excruciating pain. Over the years, this incident stood out in her
memory above all the many bursts of violent anger from her
father. One reason was that the kick would plague her with
painful lower-back problems for the rest of her life, and for
many years she had to wear a brace.

An important change came over Eileen Franklin in the days
following Susan's disappearance: she stopped doing well in
school. She had always been a better-than-average student—
quick, curious, eager to learn. Now she sat morosely in class,
taking in nothing that was happening around her. To the extent
that this was noticed in the emotional turmoil everyone felt
after Susan's disappearance, Eileen's change from a good student to a nonfunctioning one was assumed to be a result of her
grief. She and Susan had been best friends, after all. By the time
things returned to as close to normal as they would ever be, the
teachers and other people around Eileen had grown accus-

tomed to her new performance as a low-achiever and may have forgotten that she had once been quite different.

Rarely in any case had the local police been besieged with so many tips, clues, and proffered testimony, and rarely had this sort of assistance led to so little. Someone remembered seeing Susan in a red dress, talking with a young male adult. Another saw her in a blue dress, talking with an old woman. This sort of thing went on for weeks. Invariably the police followed up the information, and just as invariably they were able to refute it. ("But, ma'am, it couldn't have been Susan Nason you saw in the shopping center parking lot at two P.M. She was in school until three.")

Usually the informants believed their observations were relevant, but there were some bored or lonely people who invented potentially useful information in an effort to inject themselves into a heady drama. As the fliers with Susan's picture began circulating around the country, the calls increased and the police honed their skills at quickly detecting the patently bogus.

As the days became weeks without a trace of Susan, the possibility that she had run away was ruled out. People who knew her had never considered that a possibility, and most others were aware that in the unlikely event that an eight-year-old girl ran away, she would either change her mind and voluntarily return home, or be delivered home by adults concerned about a child so young being on her own.

For days, Susan Nason's fate was the number-one topic with both children and adults. In conversations everyone gradually began referring to Susan's "kidnapping" as though that were the only remaining explanation of what had happened. But of course everyone really thought kidnapping was just one of two possibilities. The other was, of course, that she was dead.

After a few weeks, with the mystery still in the news, the Nasons began receiving extortion letters and calls. One said that if a large amount of money was not delivered to a site in San Francisco, they would start sending Susan's fingers to the Nasons. The FBI was brought in, a ransom drop-off was set up and the extortionist, one Joseph Rudy, was arrested.

Eileen

I remember being on the sidewalk not far from Susie's house before school one day. I saw a classmate, Beth Weber, walking toward the Nason house carrying a bunch of garden flowers. I knew that Beth Weber had always been mean to Susan. I was only eight, but I got mad and thought how fake this was of Beth.

For years my memory of all the events following Susan's disappearance would be hazy, but eventually I did remember being ignored at the time, and I felt this was not right. She was my best friend, but no one paid any attention to me at all.

What I remember most about playing with Susan is her wonderful and frequent laugh. I remember the sound of that laugh and the good feeling of laughing with her. I don't recall anything special that she and I found so funny; I think we both acted silly and ridiculous—one of the freedoms of childhood.

Susan had a bright, sunny bedroom that I loved. We played with her toys there and made up stories and games. Sometimes her little dog would jump on her bed and wag his tail. I was afraid of dogs, but Susie knew just how to play with him. She would playfully poke at him and spin her fingers above him and we would laugh. I also remember playing at my house, which I think she found exciting because it was so loud, disorganized, and filled with kids. Sometimes we played with other neighborhood children, but the best times were when it was the two of us.

At school we would take a corner of the playground and play imaginary games about being grown up. We would wander through the field next to the school because sometimes a treasure could be found in the weeds. Susie was adventurous and curious, and I followed her more than I led.

When I think about Susie, it is hard for me to believe that the sound of her laugh and her bright, freckled, smiling face are gone. I have had to learn not to think about her, which hurts. When I think about the sound of her laugh, eventually the other sound comes.

As Route 92 leaves the suburban lowlands of San Mateo and begins its ascent into the Montara Mountains, the houses, as they become fewer, become larger, until finally the only indications of habitation are occasional driveways trailing off into the hills. Eventually such signs cease altogether as the highway reaches a crest and starts down into a scenic valley surrounding a long lake that, on a bright day, provides a sparkling contrast to the dark sequoias and other pines that line its banks. The lake is the Crystal Springs Reservoir, and most of the unspoiled scenery surrounding it, some 23,000 acres, is owned by the San Francisco Water Department. Because of this public ownership, in the high ground that runs down the center of the Peninsula there is no sign of the suburban sprawl that otherwise characterizes that region.

For twenty years, since his discharge from the armed forces in the years following World War II, Ephe Bottimore had worked for the water department as a watershed groundskeeper, as his father had before him. Bottimore's job was to patrol the vast acreage, primarily to keep people out of it— campers, poachers, and vagrants—as well as to check for natural developments that might create problems. To monitor the area, he was able to cover much of the land in his truck, but he frequently got out and hiked through the woods and brush, often in areas where there were no trails.

On December 2, 1969—a cool, brisk day—Bottimore decided to check out the hills west of the reservoir. He drove his truck up 92 where it left the reservoir and started the twisting climb to the final ridge. About a mile and a half past the reservoir he pulled over at a turnoff, one he liked for its sweeping view of the valley. Shimmering below him, Crystal Springs Lake made a stunning focal point for the vista of undulating mountains stretching off to the north and south.

Bottimore paused a moment to take in the fine panorama spread out before him, knowing that as soon as he climbed down the bank to start his hike, the tall brush that covered this area of the hills would block out the scenery. As he started to ease his way down the steep bank, he noticed the trash and pieces of furniture that had been dumped here. Area residents often used these highway pull-offs for discarding unwanted large objects. This pull-off was particularly popular for that purpose, since the items could be dropped with little effort and would slide down the bank, coming to rest out of sight of the highway. But not out of sight of *me,* Bottimore thought, as he cursed the inconsiderate SOB's who were trashing his land.

As he arrived at the bottom of the twenty-foot bank, he passed a discarded box spring, partially concealed by some branches, resting on others at a forty-five-degree angle. Most of its fabric had rotted off, and the springs that protruded were orange with rust. As Bottimore walked past the springs, his eye was caught by some bright blue fabric on the ground under the springs. As he looked closer, he saw, among the rusting metal and other debris, what looked like the remains of a body.

He looked through the box spring and could see that the body was, or had been, that of a little girl, now mostly a skeleton. Much of what little flesh remained had dried and separated from the bones, while other parts appeared to have been eaten by animals. There were some scraps of clothing on the corpse. One foot was bare and had a discolored white sock on it; a child's brown shoe was nearby. Ten to fifteen feet away, another white sock was found hanging at eye level on a bush.

Like everyone else in the Bay Area, Bottimore had heard about the disappearance of Susan Nason. He had followed the story in the newspapers and knew that the mystery had never been solved. Returning to his truck, he called his office on his CB radio and reported what he had found, adding that he thought the body might be that of the Nason girl. Within a half hour the San Mateo sheriff's deputies were at the sight. A preliminary, on-site examination showed that the girl's skull had been crushed with a large object, probably a rock. There was no doubt that she had been murdered.

Horrified as the area's residents were at this news, there was also a sense of relief. The terrible feeling that the child was alive somewhere and needed help—terrible for the Nasons and a cause of anguish to everyone else—was now, after ten agonizing weeks, put to rest. Susan's story was concluded, with only one piece missing. The focus of the drama now shifted from finding Susan to finding her murderer.

TWO

GEORGE THOMAS FRANKLIN GREW UP IN FRANKLIN COUNTY, Virginia, an area south of Roanoke, in the foothills of the Blue Ridge Mountains, which lay to the west of his hometown of Bassett. As the county name suggests, his father's family had once been prominent people in the area. While they had lost their founding-father distinction, his branch of the Franklins could still boast of their relationship to a rich Franklin, George's great-uncle, who owned an important highway-construction business.

The Franklins he was one of were poor and had, in recent generations, given up any pretenses or ambitions, including any education beyond the most rudimentary. Although they were perilously close to white trash, they clung to their legends of past prominence as a talisman to ward off the dreaded designation.

George's father, Onis Franklin, had a reputation as the ugliest man in Franklin County. He somehow lured into matrimony Hattie Jarrett, who had once been voted the county's most beautiful woman. Since Onis showed no interest in making a living and Hattie brought no money to the marriage, they set out to have four children with few prospects for feeding and clothing them. Aside from making love to his wife, the only activities that interested Onis were drinking and making whiskey. When things grew desperate, he would take a job with his uncle's construction company.

If Onis made money from his moonshine, he drank up the profits. While George and his three sisters grew up in near-poverty, Onis stayed drunk most of the time. Years later, when his own children complained, George would remind them that he had sometimes had to go to school without shoes. Hattie

23

Franklin came to view her good-for-nothing husband with amused contempt that extended to his indefatigable ardor. After her husband's death, Hattie, with a laugh, told her teen-aged granddaughter Eileen, who had gone east for a visit, "I told Onis to go play with his own thing and leave my monkey alone."

Not only was Onis Franklin a drunk, but he was a mean drunk. It took little to send him into a rage, and his temper was often directed at his only son. Probably exacerbating the friction between father and son was that young George, with strong features and thick, wavy, dark red hair, was growing up to be as handsome as his father was ugly. The family's financial situation improved when Onis's father died and left him enough money to support his family, but the drinking continued, as well as the friction with his son.

In later years, George's sisters would not talk about the extent of their father's violence against him, but it must have been severe. When he was seventeen, his mother said to him, "You better get out of this house, Georgie, before your father kills you." Hattie had learned how to deal with her husband when he was drunk and feeling mean; she would maneuver him to bed. Because none of the children was as resourceful, it was also decided to get the sisters still at home out of the house. Dipping into some of the inheritance, two of the three girls were sent to a Baptist boarding school. Forty years later, when George Franklin was discussing his father's violence toward him, he was asked if his mother interceded to protect him. "She didn't have to," he said. "I protected myself."

Others were less impressed with young George's ability to handle the drunken Onis, so the decision was made to remove George from his father's wrath. Hattie and Onis's oldest daughter, Isis, had married and moved to San Bruno, a town south of San Francisco. It was decided that George should be sent west to live with her. In 1956 he got himself to California, moved in with his sister, and enrolled in Capuchino High School, where he played on the football team. His brother-in-law remembers him as being a quiet, courteous, and helpful addition to the household.

For pocket money while he was attending school, George worked as a bagger at a Safeway Supermarket. At the checkout counter one day, George looked up to see a striking young woman in front of him, paying for a pack of gum. She had dark brown hair, and a good figure, but it was her face that had the greatest impact on him—a well-formed mouth and large hazel eyes, soft and sympathetic. He was in love.

When the young woman passed through the lane without looking his way, he stopped her by reaching for her chewing gum. "Here," he said, "I'll carry this to your car for you."

Surprised, and with a nervous half-laugh, she said, "That's not necessary. I can manage it."

"It's my job," he said seriously. "If I don't, I'll be fired."

She shrugged and started walking to her car, with George trailing behind her, carrying her gum, asking, "What's your name? Where do you live? Can I call you?"

She told him her name was Leah, but would tell him nothing else before getting into her car and driving off.

Back in the store, George was moaning to the cashier about his failure to get a phone number. "You're in luck," the woman told him. "She filled out an entry form for the contest the store's having. It should be on top of that pile there." George lunged for the forms. On top of the pile he found the form which had her full name, Leah DeBernardi, her address, and— praise heaven—her phone number. When he called, she was impressed by his cleverness in finding her. She bantered with him for a few phone calls, then finally agreed to go out with him. He found Leah as smart as she was pretty. She, in turn, liked his bright humor, his energy, and his looks. She was as attracted to him as he was to her.

Leah's father, Leo DeBernardi, was born and raised in San Francisco, California, where his mother ran a boardinghouse. The Depression had been hard on the DeBernardi family, and there had been no money for college. After marrying, Leo had settled down in the wealthy San Francisco suburb of Burlingame, where he took a job at the post office. He would work there until he retired. He and his wife, Marie, raised two more daughters, one three years younger than Leah, and one thirteen years younger. Both Leo and his wife were devout Catholics. Marie DeBernardi played the organ at their parish church and taught piano lessons at home to help with the cost of raising Leah and her two sisters. In spite of the tight finances, all three girls attended private schools.

When George had been seeing Leah for only a few months, she discovered that she was pregnant. Since she was also staunchly Catholic, there was only one thing to do: marry George. This was fine with him, although he still had not finished high school and could not possibly support a wife and child on a bagger's pay. He had joined the Marine Corps reserves in the hope of eventually getting admitted to the U.S. Naval Academy, but matrimony would end that dream. Still, he was passionately in love and was certain he could work things out.

Leah's parents were dismayed. In spite of their modest situation in the world, they felt that George was far beneath them. A bagger in a supermarket! And wasn't he from some sort of hillbilly family from the South. His treatment of Leah now confirmed his bad blood. Leo always regretted his lack of a college education and he was delighted that Leah had just won a scholarship to Lone Mountain College. As ambitious for herself as her parents were for her, Leah had been thrilled at the prospect of graduating from college and having a career.

Capping the arguments against marriage, everyone but George agreed that they were too young. None of these considerations could stand up to the Catholicism of the DeBernardis, or Leah's need for a husband. Or the desire of George and Leah to continue sleeping together. Without a quibble, George converted and agreed to bring his children up Catholic. Leah was resigned to this shift in her plans. At least she was enthusiastic about him.

On the tenth of November, 1957, George Franklin, age eighteen, married Leah DeBernardi, age seventeen. Leah's parents, having fulfilled their obligation to the Church by acquiescing to their daughter's marriage, felt no obligation to the marriage itself. They always viewed it askance, considering it a liaison from which nothing good would come. Relations between George and his in-laws rarely got beyond the level of chilly civility. Although they eventually made an effort, George made little and there would be frequent stretches of not speaking.

Once he was married, George dropped out of high school and began to work full-time for the supermarket. He continued his education through a correspondence course. As a Marine reservist, he enjoyed a number of benefits that helped considerably with the expense of having a child. In the spring of 1958, Leah gave birth to a baby daughter who they named Cathleen and who would later be called Kate. When George went off for six months' active duty at Camp Pendleton in Southern California, he wrote Leah long letters telling her how much he loved her and their baby daughter. Two months after delivering Kate, Leah was pregnant again, with a second daughter, who would be named Janice. The medical and other benefits from the

Marine reserves impressed George. He looked about for another form of benefit-rich public service to enter on a full-time basis. He was drawn to firefighting work because of the hours: three alternating twenty-four-hour stretches at the firehouse, followed by four days of free time. While in the Marines, George had undertaken to complete high school by mail. When he got his diploma, he joined the San Mateo Fire Department.

Firefighters' hours were particularly appealing to him in that he had a long-range goal he wanted to pursue to make a fortune in real estate. His intention was to buy properties cheaply and fix them up as rentals or sell them for fat profits. Leah went along with the plan, even though it meant putting much energy and every available penny into buying or refurbishing small suburban houses.

"It will make us rich one day," he would tell her. "Then we'll have money to send the kids to college, do whatever we want."

It sounded all right to Leah, but she was too busy having children to think about much else. In the third year of their marriage—on November 25, 1960—another daughter, Eileen, was born. When George was shown his new child, he was delighted to see that she had red hair like his. "Isn't she beautiful!" he gushed. "Just look at that gorgeous red hair!" When, years later, Eileen was being tormented at school for her unusual hair, George told her about his first reaction. She treasured this sign of his special feeling for her. "He desperately wanted a son," she said, "and here he was being shown his third daughter in a row and he was thrilled by me!"

Eileen was followed by a son, George junior, then another daughter, Diana. One evening when Leah was pregnant with Diana, she and George sat up drinking after the children were in bed. His drink was beer, hers Chianti. Some minor disagreement flared into a fight, and George, in a rage, started beating Leah. She screamed that she was pregnant and he stopped. Although they had been married six years, he had never before been violent toward her. This marked the beginning of a new order.

By the time Leah was twenty-three, she had given birth to five children. It probably would have been more if George hadn't shrugged off his new Catholicism and had a vasectomy. When it was later learned that Leah was unenthusiastic about motherhood, that in fact she seemed to lack the most fundamental parental instincts, the question arose as to why she had had so many children so fast. The answer family members gave was that she was an ardent Catholic. She also felt it was expected of her and it was what all her friends were doing.

For the first months of their marriage, George and Leah lived in a small apartment in San Mateo. Then they moved into their first house, also in San Mateo, which, to raise its market value, George spent his free time working to refurbish. They moved out and rented the house at a profit, and in 1964, when Eileen Franklin was about to turn four, they moved to the house that would become the family's home for the next seven years, 678 Harvester Drive in Foster City.

The one-story house had four bedrooms, two of them facing the street. The living room and family room opened onto the backyard, and the kitchen was to the right of the front door. The house to the right was so close it was difficult to see to which house the Franklins' garage belonged. The street was well laid out, and in a few years, when the new neighborhood planting had grown up and the raw newness of the houses had worn off, it would appear an attractive place to raise a family.

T. Jack Foster's community had a number of idyllic features. Two blocks away from the Franklins' house, a pretty canal ran behind the houses on one side of Matsonia. The playground of the Foster City Elementary School, which the Franklin children attended, backed up to the houses on the south side of Balclutha. A shortcut between the gardens of two homes made the school a five-minute walk from their home. Also within walking distance was a man-made sand beach—complete with lifeguard—on the man-made lagoon. That such a pleasant style of living was possible on a fireman's salary, in a community with year-round moderate weather and a view of mountains to the west, made the California dream more than just a fantasy of blue-collar easterners.

An innovative feature in Foster City was a serpentine brick walk that snaked through a landscaped strip separating the back fences of some houses. This afforded a communal, traffic-free place for children to play. Janice Franklin loved to rollerskate along the winding path and was the one Leah most often sent to the store since she was the fastest. Swings, seesaws, and other diversions were placed at intervals along the strip.

Janice recalls that an early issue of the local newspaper, now called the *Foster City Progress,* had a photograph on the front page of two little girls going down a sliding board. The caption extolled Foster City as "a great place for kids." Because of subsequent events, it is unfortunate that this issue has disappeared since the two girls were Eileen Franklin and Susan Nason.

Eileen

My first memory of my father is from the time when I was about three or four. It was in the earliest hours of the morning. I don't know what I heard or smelled that woke me and made me climb out of bed where I shared a room with Diana. The floor was carpeted, but the house was cold and I felt chilled in my flannel nightgown. The house was very still. I walked down the hallway toward the kitchen, where I could see the lights on. My dad was up, alone. He was making a cup of coffee, I think. I walked over to him and lightly touched his back. He didn't jump, but he smiled down at me and patted my head.

"Honey, what are you doing out of bed? Go on back to bed." He still had his Southern drawl then.

I turned from him and made my way back through the quiet house to my bed, which was still warm. I felt so safe and so in love with my daddy. I felt happy, and satisfied that I had shared this private, sweet moment of early morning and absolute quiet.

I was only a few years older when my dad became my hero. Diana, George junior, and I were playing in front of a neighbor's house. George had climbed up high in a tree, Diana was below him in the tree, and I was on the ground. Somehow George stepped on Diana's head, she slipped, and a branch tore the flesh on her leg.

I told her to stay where she was, and I ran home as fast as I could. My dad, in white painter's pants and a paint-spattered T-shirt, was in our driveway, rinsing his paint equipment. When I raced up to him, I was completely out of breath. I gasped that Diana was hurt, and pointed in her direction.

As he took off, I ran after him and watched him run so fast, so strongly, so surely. Before I could reach the tree again, my dad, carrying Diana, was running back to our house. As I watched him carrying my little sister in his arms —so confidently and kindly, and running faster than I had ever seen anyone run—I felt very proud of him, really in awe of him.

As Leah emerged from her childbearing marathon, she began to realize all that her teenaged marriage had caused her to miss. This was the mid-1960s, the Age of Aquarius, when it was a splendid time to be young, good-looking, and spirited—but not if you had a fireman husband and five children crying for attention. With Franklin's increasing black moods and the onset of violence, Leah looked at her situation, as if for the first time, and was dashed by what she saw: the endless toil for a large family and, for recreation, painting walls and mowing lawns at her husband's investment properties. She also saw that she had not lost the weight she had put on during her last two pregnancies; she was now over 180 pounds. In exchange for an enormous load of unwanted responsibilities, she had handed over her youth and her looks. She became increasingly dispirited and bitter.

In 1967, George Franklin was driving alone one night and ran his car into the pylon of an overhead expressway. The car was totaled and he was almost killed. With his right arm paralyzed and his jaw wired shut, he was at home for three months. Leah remembers this as the period when the situation in the household deteriorated drastically. "Something about the accident," Leah recalled many years later, "made him a lot more angry, a lot more violent, and he took it out on me and the children."

Many years later, when the San Mateo authorities were seeking all the information that they could about George Franklin, they found two sisters who had been baby-sitters when they were twelve and thirteen, in the Harvester Drive house shortly after George's accident. Both gave statements that when they were alone with him, he made sexual advances to them. The experience was made even more terrifying for the girls by his wired jaw.

To make such advances to the young daughters of neighbors shows a remarkable degree of recklessness on George's part. Leah may well have been right about the accident's role in the changes, but by then he may have had more on his conscience than hitting his children. Leah would later tell them that the car crash was not an accident, but a suicide attempt. She said George had expressed to her a desire to end his life, saying that he "had done terrible things, things you can't even imagine."

In discussing the beating of her children in later years, Leah speculated that her husband's abuse of them all may have made him hate himself and the hatred resulted in more abuse. She also said that she was unaware of how brutally her husband treated her five offspring. She would later say that child abuse was not discussed at the time, and it did not occur to her to ask her children if they were being abused.

By way of reconciling her memory of this period with her daughters' very different ones, she would say that the children were unaware of all she was enduring—some physical abuse, but endless verbal abuse. She would maintain that in her own struggle for survival, she didn't notice what they were suffering. But Eileen and Janice don't believe this. They feel that whatever Leah was experiencing may have made her less concerned about her children's problems, but they reject her claim that she didn't know what was happening.

There is no doubt, however, that the accident made Leah's life very difficult. With five children between the ages of three and nine and a disabled and violent husband in the house all day, not knowing if he would be able to work again, she buckled under the strain. In 1968, long after George had returned to work, she had a nervous breakdown. He came home from the firehouse one day to find his wife crying uncontrollably, and he took her to a doctor, who placed her in a hospital under a psychiatrist's care. She was diagnosed as severely depressed.

In the weeks she was away, her duties had been delegated to the children. Each night Janice and Kate, in the third and fourth grades, made the next day's school lunches for all five children. Eileen was put in charge of five-year-old Diana and made totally responsible for her welfare—and responsible, too, for her misdemeanors. When Diana's Barbie doll was left on the living room floor, Eileen got punished.

Partly because of their similar appearance, the two little red-heads adored and doted on each other, Diana, puppylike, following her seven-year-old sister around the house while Eileen found her things to wear or something to eat. Her fondness for her baby sister, Eileen later recalled, was almost a physical thing: "I used to love holding her fat little fingers. They were incredibly soft." As adults, the two good-looking women would startle strangers by holding hands in restaurants and other public places.

Leah began to change from an indifferent mother to an openly hostile one. Immediately following her return, she remained in bed for a few weeks, the children continuing to run the house. This became a permanent arrangement. When Leah

was on her feet again, she would do the things she liked—she
particularly enjoyed sewing—but she avoided doing chores she
found distasteful, such as preparing meals.

This would include most of the nights when her husband was
at the firehouse. When he was home, she would fix dinner for
the family; when he was working, she would tell her children to
fix themselves something. Since she had little interest in shopping, they would look in the cupboards and usually find nothing they were capable of making and so would eat dry cereal.
For many years this was a standard dinner for the Franklin
children. A running joke with them was that, when their mother
was given shock therapy, "the doctors must have fried her
brain's cooking center."

When Eileen was in the second grade, she was given the job
of making all five lunches for herself and her brother and sisters
to take to school the next day. A hard enough chore for a
seven-year-old, it was made considerably more difficult by the
dearth of food in the house. "I would somehow get something
together for each of us," she said, "and if there was anything
special lying around, like an apple or an orange, I would slip it
into Diana's bag."

Janice can remember having to pull a chair up to the counter
and stepping onto it, then onto the counter, in order to reach
the cereal box. Although Leah expected her kids to wash the
dishes, she never showed them how, and the effort of four- and
five-year-olds to lift heavy frying pans into a sink they could
barely reach led to many broken dishes, which in turn led to
punishments. Sometimes Leah would make an effort for her
children, but more often she made it clear to them that she
regretted having them, that they were a source of nothing but
aggravation and trouble, and were the primary obstacles to her
having a life that gave her any pleasure.

There was another abnormality in the Franklin household
that Eileen Franklin, at least, did not understand until she was
a teenager. Both Leah and George drank regularly and were
frequently drunk in the evenings. The drunkenness often led, on
George's part, to violence against the children. He would lash
out at one child on whatever pretext—toys left around, too
much noise—then all the children would be brought together
and beaten.

On one occasion they were all thrashed because one of them
had neglected to flush a toilet, and, at another time, when

George found dust on a baseboard. Anything could set him off, and although only one was guilty of a particular incident, all five were punished. These beatings were so much a matter of course that Eileen assumed that such outbursts occurred in all families, that beatings were part of being a child. When friends would later deny they were hit by their parents, Eileen assumed they were lying.

The one to suffer the worst beatings was George junior, who was growing up to be a handsome boy with curly blond hair and the good features that marked all the Franklins. As the only male child, he was adored by his sisters, but was alienated from them and spent what time he was allowed out of the house with neighborhood boys his age. A spirited child, he got into the pranks and scrapes of other little boys, and sometimes more imaginative ones. He invented the game of riding trash chutes in a nearby apartment and was once caught dancing naked on top of the fence that separated the Franklins' yard from their neighbors'. Unlike other boys, however, George, the much-wanted son, would be brutally beaten for his mischief.

The punishment routine with George junior was that he would be taken into a bedroom, the door closed, and then he would be thrashed with a belt until he was released, a whimpering and sometimes bloody heap of a child. Eileen can remember one of these beatings that was so long and so severe that she risked her father's rage by entering the room after it was over to look after her younger brother.

"I knew that if my dad came back," she said, "I'd get beaten as badly as Georgie."

Although he had no problem making friends, young George frequently was picked on by other boys who were quick to spot his insecurities. At an early age he showed a keen intelligence. According to Lois Shannon, who lived across the street, "Even as a little kid he would make remarks that went right over the heads of the rest of us."

The second most abused was Janice Franklin, who had a sassy, rebellious attitude that she now thinks she concealed from her parents but may have caused her more pain than she realized. A typical episode was when she was "knocked around" for having broken a flower stalk of one of the agapanthus plants that lined the front walk. Knowing she had not done it, she tried to convince her incensed father that the paperboy had probably accidentally broken the flower. She often found the newspaper in among the agapanthus, she said imploringly. This plausible story only confirmed her guilt in his eyes, and she was thrashed.

Incensed at the injustice, she made a point of breaking one stalk each day as she came in from school. "They didn't notice," she said years later. "That was typical of them. One minute something was the most important thing in the world. Important enough to beat us over. Then they would completely forget about it. They'd be on to something different."

The evenings when George and Leah sat up drinking inevitably led to the kind of trouble the children feared the most, another beating. The pattern was that George would start fighting with Leah—yelling, swearing, sometimes striking her. Heated combat between parents is in itself frightening for most children, but the Franklin children, supposedly asleep in their rooms, knew these outbursts were only a prelude to their becoming targets of their father's fury.

The dreaded warning signal was often a Hank Williams record, the album containing the song "Why Don't You Love Me Like You Used to Do?" which was a particular favorite of George's. When that record went on, they knew their father's level of drunkenness was at the danger level and that he could soon be moving their way. Invariably the lights would be snapped on in their bedrooms and a snarling, out-of-his-senses George Franklin would haul his five children into the living room, excoriate them incoherently for some failing or transgression, then beat them.

On the day following one of his explosions, George would appear to be unaware of his actions of the preceding night. Once, seeing some bruises on Janice, he asked Eileen how they had occurred. Eileen told him. "After that," she said, "he'd see one or more of us bruised, and he'd kind of look at me imploringly. I'd say 'yeah' or just with my eyes and a slight nod let him know what had happened. We were that close."

George Franklin's abuse of his children was not always physical. His verbal abuse of them was constant. "Why do you have that stupid look on your face?" "Why are you dragging your feet?" "Look at your shitty posture." Such remarks spewed from him without letup. According to Janice, years later when he was living with various girlfriends, he would carp at their children in the same way. "He had this curious thing against kids. It baffles me now, and it sure as hell baffled us all then."

He did not have to be drinking to lash out. His rages might be sudden and without provocation. Although he was almost never violent with Eileen after Susan's murder, one incident that took place when she was in her early teens and they had moved to a two-story house typifies his irrational impulses to punish. One evening, Eileen could see her father was in a black mood and was conversing with him cautiously, avoiding disagreeable subjects and promoting ones calculated to lighten his mood. As they watched a television discussion of an upcoming election, she heard a term she didn't understand. Knowing he was pleased by her efforts to learn and better herself, she asked, "What is that expression they use, 'electrical vote'?"

George shot her a venomous look, then sprang out of his chair and came at her. She ran and made it to the staircase. As she scrambled up the steps to escape, he caught her ankle and pulled her down onto a tile floor so he could hit her. Between blows he raved, "Don't you ever say that again! It's electoral vote, not 'electrical vote.'"

Adding to the twisted injustice of this sort of outburst was Eileen's status, undisputed by her siblings, as George's favorite child. A household ritual when Eileen was an infant, was his dressing her and singing, as he put on her shoes and socks:

> *"Shoe, shoe—stocking, stocking.*
> *Pooh, pooh—pocking, pocking."*

"Pooh" became a nickname for her, which he invariably used unless he was angry. From the time of the earliest group punishments, he would sometimes maneuver Eileen out of the way, or hit her fewer times than he hit the others. One reason for the favoritism was Eileen's looks. All of the Franklin kids were good-looking, but Eileen was exceptionally pretty. She had golden red hair, large eyes, and a pert face dappled with reddish-brown freckles. To adults and to her sisters, this made her adorable. To children in school, it made her weird, a physical oddball. Eileen was unpopular in school, was teased mercilessly by the other children about her freckles and red hair, and says she was "too much of a wimp to do anything about it." Born in November, she was at the low end of the age level for her class, and was smaller than most of her classmates. This added to her general insignificance in their eyes.

With such a terror-filled home life, Eileen Franklin found little consolation outside her home. In addition to being unpopular in school, she considered Foster City an unfriendly, perilous place. "As I walked to and from school," she recalls, "neighborhood boys used to lie in wait in a narrow path that cut between two houses to reach the school playground. They would wait behind bushes, then jump out and grab me. I'd be terrified. It wasn't me particularly. They'd do it to any defense-less child. They were just rotten kids, bored, looking for something to do."

She can also recall, when she was about ten, walking a dog on a leash, a large and shaggy English sheepdog her father had brought home on a whim. The dog, attracted by some boys sitting in the park, bolted toward them, dragging Eileen behind. Alarmed to see the large dog heading for them, the boys got angry and chased Eileen and kicked the dog. Such incidents implanted in her the idea that Foster City was especially dangerous. When she visited her grandmother in Burlingame and played outside on similar streets, no such calamities occurred. Nor did anyone beat her in the house. The trouble, she began to think, was Foster City.

When George Franklin was sober, he could be a good and caring parent, but he swung erratically between extremes that left his children confused; for Christmas the girls would be given expensive Madame Alexander dolls, but the rest of the year had no toys at all. In an effort to augment his children's education, he would occasionally organize outings to a museum or an exhibit. A big event was the annual expedition to the rural areas west of San Mateo on Route 92 to find, in the wild, the family Christmas tree. Eileen remembers this as a particularly happy outing, one in which her father's good spirits were likely to hold. As a rule, however, his good moods or his sobriety were no guarantee against a sudden explosion of anger toward his children.

When Leah was alone with her children, she expected them to stay out of her way. If they angered her, she rarely punished them herself. A far more effective curb on bad behavior was to threaten to call the firehouse. This struck terror into the Franklin children, since it invariably meant a beating when their father got home. George didn't concern himself with Leah's reasons, but fell immediately to the job. Although he seemed to relish the role of disciplinarian, the punishments were, more often than not, instigated by Leah, who would sometimes absent herself, but not always, so she could not have been unaware of what was happening.

In some ways, more hurtful to her children was Leah's coldness to them when she wasn't angry. Janice Franklin recalls, "If you asked her a question, she wouldn't answer it, just ignore you. She never explained anything, or did anything to help you develop." By way of contrast, Janice found some good words to say about her father. "For all his rages, black moods, drunken rampages, we always knew that our father cared. Leah never cared. She had her own van, but if it was pouring rain, she would never pick us up at school. If he was home when it rained, he always drove over to get us, and lifted our bikes in the back of his van." Janice and her brother George had a joke: "What's worse than Mom on a bad day? Mom on a good day."

The five Franklin children had different ways of dealing with their grim situation. Eileen and Janice had a sense of solidarity with their siblings and would contrive, usually unsuccessfully, to spare not just themselves, but all of them, a punishment or a deprivation. Kate tended to look out for herself. If Eileen sensed a benevolent mood in her father, she would plead for a half-gallon of ice cream for them all; Kate, on the other hand, would try to wheedle him into buying her a cone. Janice would get into trouble trying to argue her mother out of making a firehouse call. As the youngest, Diana was in no way an instigator either for herself or for the group, but rather took whatever was being handed out at the time, ice cream or beatings.

Basically they all saw their household as being divided between a mercurially tempestuous father—caring and fatherly one minute, a raging monster the next—and a mother who was perpetually indifferent, generally neglectful, and frequently hostile. Twenty years later, Eileen would be asked in court to characterize Leah's mothering. She replied with one word: "Nonexistent."

Leah had skills that she used at times for her children's benefit. She was an excellent seamstress and would frequently make clothes for her children. She resisted spending money, especially on her children. If she did so, it was in odd ways. When Eileen was about seven, Leah enrolled her daughters in a dancing class that had been organized by a neighbor, Fay Munier, whose husband, Ron, was also a firefighter and who had known George and Leah Franklin since the Muniers had been their neighbors in a seedy section of San Mateo shortly after the Franklins were married. Years later, Fay Munier would recall Leah, whom she admits she did not know well, as being a good mother, "very supportive of her kids." Hadn't she given her daughters dancing lessons? Fay Munier also recalled that "Leah made light of everything. She was a bit of a Pollyanna—things are going to be fine. She was very optimistic and pleasant to be around. She dreamed of everything being perfect."

The children worked hard on their dancing. One year Fay had all four Franklin girls work up a dance routine for a Christmas show. Leah made them identical outfits in different colors and Eileen had a candy-striped cane that honked when you tapped it on the floor. Fay Munier remembers Kate as being pretty, Janice as sad, Eileen as shy, and Diana as clingy: "She'd grab hold of your leg and not let go."

A Foster City woman who lived across the street said that, as a neighbor, Leah had been friendly, but only up to a point. "She'd stop by and chat in front of the house," she said, "but she would never come in for coffee. I remember her as being very heavy, and kind of a hippie. She'd wear loose muumuus, bare feet, long hair—and she read all the time. She always had a book in her hand. Her kids would come over and I'd give them cookies. I could tell they weren't getting fed at home. I knew she was a lousy housekeeper. The place was a mess all the time."

Leah's contradictions are difficult to unravel. She would spend many nights sewing dance costumes for her children, but not bother to prepare them meals. She complained about all the work of running her home, but when George offered to get her a maid, she refused.

In the children's roster of anxieties, however, Leah's hostility and neglect took second place to the shadow that hung constantly over the Harvester Drive house: the dread of George Franklin's rages.

A next-door neighbor, Earline Douglas, a young married woman with two sons, was fond of the Franklin children, particularly the inseparable Eileen and Diana. "I used to love it when they would come over—I always had a treat for them, a cookie or something. I didn't know about any trouble in that house, but I remember Eileen once saying to me that she wished I was her mother. I was young and I only heard the flattery. Now, when I think back, I realize how strange it was. If one of my boys said to some other woman that he wished she was his mother, I'd kill him. If there was trouble in the Franklin home, I didn't know about it, but I will say one thing: I'd often go out my front door, and there on the front step I'd find Eileen and Diana, just sitting there waiting for me to come out. They wouldn't ring the bell, just be sitting there waiting. . . ."

As a very young child, Eileen had a strong fantasy life which was drawn from favorite books and characters like Pippi Long-stocking. One of her favorite television programs as she got a little older was "I Dream of Jeannie," in which the main character could materialize or dematerialize at will. When she was about six, Eileen developed a fantasy that she was able to make herself invisible. She took to hiding with no particular motive. She would crawl behind the living room sofa and wait quietly for as long as an hour, until someone entered the room. She would then be thrilled at hearing or seeing what was going on without being "visible." She was there and not there. Sometimes her disappearances seemed more of an effort at total escape; she can remember crawling into the huge pile of dirty laundry that sat perpetually in the garage and, with little likelihood of anyone coming, just hiding there for hours.

THREE

Eileen

As we kids grew old enough to hold a mop or a brush, we were put to work on our father's investment properties. His moneymaking plan was thriving. In ten years he owned a number of houses, and we lived in the nicest. Years later, another firefighter, Bob Galbraith, said that my dad could be "very ballsy" about real estate, that he bought "way-out places that no one else would touch." Others may not have had his free work force to make the places less "way out." He used to call us his "niggers."

Many evenings and weekends he marched us to one of the houses. It might be a new purchase or a rental that had just lost its tenants. We were put to work pulling weeds, prepping walls, hauling trash—whatever needed to be done to make the houses more rentable. There was never any talk of payment; instead we were promised college educations, which the properties would pay for.

Because I was my dad's pet, I sometimes got a break from the work to go with him on an errand. One day he took me with him to the paint store in San Mateo. When we entered the store, the man behind the counter made a comment to my father about his little helper. Smiling, my father answered that, to carry some of the supplies, he had brought along one of his niggers.

The man looked startled by the word. These were the late 1960s. Civil rights and African-American consciousness were growing strong, but I was too young to understand any of that. Still, my dad calling us that word had always made me uncomfortable. But now the paint-store man's reaction—the look of surprise and disgust on his face—told me that other people besides me did not think such mean talk was funny or clever, and that it was not right. I'll never see this man again, but I walked out of that paint store with a new strength. So much of my thinking and my emerging sense of self was dominated by my father, but someone—another adult— had finally affirmed a belief of mine that went against his.

While George Franklin pushed his children hard, he worked even harder himself. When he was not refurbishing one of his own properties, he, along with two firefighter friends, took painting jobs in the area, some of them quite large, like shopping-mall renovations or new houses. "He would set a price for the job," a man who painted with him said, "then work like a demon to finish in the four days we had off." On other days, he would put on a suit and tie to sell life insurance. The money George earned from his outside jobs went into his investments while life on Harvester remained austere. He seems to have been driven by a belief that wealth would be his salvation.

When on duty as a firefighter, he did what was expected of him, and was never considered either a hero or a malingerer. Firefighter Ron Munier remembers him as being "as well liked as anyone." Others thought of him as too much of a wiseguy, always having the final word on any subject. "He was abrasive with others," recalls Bob Galbraith, "and had an air of superiority that rubbed the guys the wrong way. He was also a master actor—he must have been, to keep all his other sides hidden from us. At the firehouse he was as easygoing as the rest of us."

In the late sixties George got a reputation as a troublemaker quick to challenge the rules. In one such skirmish he made a conspicuous stand on the issue of facial hair. He wanted to grow a mustache, but fire department regulations forbade it. Joined by a few other men, he threatened legal action. Franklin and his rebels won. To celebrate, he grew an Afro hairstyle to go with his new mustache.

"His attitude about our work was very different from the rest of us," said Galbraith. "We all knew it was a quasi-military organization, you had to give up some privileges, but he always fought that idea—wanted to wear his hair long, wear an earring—anything to buck the rules. He left on disability for a back problem, and got a good pension deal."

In 1968, George bought one in a series of Volkswagen vans, which he used to transport equipment for his moonlighting painting jobs. He also used it for recreational trips, and for this he had a platform installed in the rear, on which he placed a mattress. He also put curtains on the windows. When the van was used for a painting job, the mattress was easily removed to make room for his equipment.

On his four-day breaks, George would drive off on solitary rambles, in search of adventure, starting a nomadic pattern that would increase in later years. Sometimes he would wake up at three in the morning and suddenly decide to spend a day or two in Sacramento or Monterey. His family was unaware of what kind of adventures went on in their good-looking father's motorized bedroom.

Eileen

Although we knew our father could be cruel, we also knew that if anything good was going to happen to us, it would be because of him. He would suddenly announce a trip to the zoo or a baseball game or some other treat, but, more important than that, most of the love and affection I received came from him, not from my mother.

When I was about twelve years old, I asked my father about my Franklin grandfather. He told me that I didn't want to hear stories about Onis Franklin, who was a mean old drunk. This shocked me, squashing my visions of a courtly old gentleman of the romantic South, but piqued my curiosity. I could be persuasive with my father, and coaxed him into telling me about his early life.

The story I got was one of drunkenness and violent, unprovoked beatings. I learned about his sisters and his mother, who all lived in terror. He told me about winters without enough heat and about owning only one pair of pants to wear to school. He told me of a childhood of fear and pain and abuse. He told me that Onis had threatened to kill him if he did not leave their home.

I felt truly sad for my father. I was convinced that, compared with his own father, my father was a good father. The physical abuse and fear in my home paled in comparison to the beatings my dad described. I felt deep sympathy for my poor, suffering dad, and felt bad that I had not known what he had gone through as a child.

As I thought about his stories, I grew sadder and sadder. I felt I wanted to do something to ease his pain from so long ago. I decided I owed it to him to be an exceptionally good daughter, causing him no trouble. I thought hard about how to persuade my sisters and brother to treat him well and behave perfectly. Now, when my father became angry and was cruel to us kids, I immediately forgave him because I knew of his suffering.

I spent a few days trying to make the world a perfect place for him, though he probably never noticed. After trying for a while to make his life better, I saw that nothing had changed, and he hadn't changed. Pretty soon I gave up trying to make his life better. I realized I could not change the world and make it perfect for him.

My fascination with my father approached adulation. I hung on him, climbed his legs. Years later, when we were all-out adversaries, I would think about how strong my feelings were for him. When he and Leah got dressed up to go out, he'd come out all spiffed up and reeking of Old Spice cologne. "Don't I smell *purdy*?" he'd ask. We used to call it "foo-foo." "Daddy's wearing foo-foo," we'd say. I was in love with him. He was so handsome. Even as an adult, when I'd run into a man wearing Old Spice, it would melt me, but only for an instant."

Two incidents when I was little gave me a strong dislike for policemen, for all men in uniform. It lasted right up until years later, when I had to work with law enforcement on my father's trial. One time, as my oldest sister, Kate, was leaving for school, Leah told her of discovering some transgression for which she would be punished by our father when she got home that afternoon.

Having all day to think about what was waiting for her at home, Kate did something very daring. She told her teacher that she was to be beaten by our father after school, and appealed for help. After asking a few questions about our family's punishment routines, the teacher grew so alarmed that she called the police. When Kate arrived home that afternoon, she was accompanied by a policeman—which amazed me.

My father was waiting for Kate and was geared up for brutal action. When he saw the policeman, he turned his anger on him. "I'll raise my children any way I see fit," he bellowed, then announced he was a firefighter. The officer backed off. The message seemed to be that it was okay to beat your children if you wore a uniform.

Another time, my father was on one of his worst rampages, roaring at us kids and beating us. One of our neighbors, we never knew which one, called the police. Whoever it was must have been familiar with this sort of noise from our house, but must also have felt that this time it was getting out of hand. Cries and other sounds of violence could still be heard from our house when two policemen arrived. When my father opened the door and saw the police, his mood changed abruptly. Calm and steady, he said, "It's okay. I'm a fireman, officers. I've got the situation in hand."

That was all it took. I couldn't believe it. Our condition made it obvious to the two officers how badly we were being beaten, and my mother was bleeding from her face in front of them, but they simply accepted my father's assurance that everything was okay. This convinced me that police and firemen were horrible people who would wink at anything done by one of their own. I believed that for years.

One spring evening, when we kids came in from playing outdoors, we found our parents sitting somberly in the living room. In his most authoritarian tone, my father told us to come stand before him. "We've got a real problem here," he said in that grim voice that meant major trouble. "I want you to go around the house and come back and tell me what you see."

Like prisoners on our way to the guillotine, we trooped through the house. We returned to the living room and reported that we could find nothing unusual. We knew it was the wrong conclusion. "Think again," he said more forcefully. "Is this the way a house is supposed to look? This house is unfit for anyone to live in. Now, all of you are going to go through it and straighten it up. Then report back to me."

We knew that no matter how tidy we got our house, we would still be punished. We went through the house like condemned robots, picking up toys, stray articles of clothing, wet towels. When everything was put away, floors vacuumed and bedspreads smoothed, we returned to our parents, who were still sitting tribunal-style in the living room. Without moving to check the results, our father imposed his sentence.

"No one can live with the kind of mess you've been making. Your mother can't take it, and I won't take it. To make sure that it doesn't happen again, we are grounding you for the summer. When you come in from school, you will go right to your rooms. You can come out to eat, but then you go back to your rooms till bedtime. Got it?"

We were dumbfounded. With summer coming on, we were looking forward, like any schoolchildren, to the freedom from classes, to the opportunity to play until dark, to long days given over to nothing but good times. The rest of the year was spent obliging adults; summer was for us. Now, during this part of the year that we spent the rest of the year yearning for, we would be locked in our bedrooms, where there was little to do and where we would be able to hear our neighborhood friends playing outside.

It's to our credit, I think, that our will and spirits were not demolished by our parents' heavy-handed punishments, that we did not become cringing, obedient wimps. We continued to get in trouble, because we knew we would be punished whether or not we misbehaved. No matter how bad things got, we never lost our ability to joke about our situation.

The severe decision to keep the Franklin children in their rooms all summer may have been prompted by the threat of Leah having another emotional collapse. She wanted her house to become, in appearances at least, a child-free zone. In addition, there seems to have been a link, twisted and symbiotic, between Leah's exasperation with mothering and George's need to brutalize his children. For this troubled woman, he was her in-house pit bull who needed only the slightest encouragement to lash out —both to deal with whatever had upset her and, at the same time, to vent his own inner anger. What upset Leah—invariably, perpetually—was her children. As parents, George and Leah were a two-headed hydra: she snarled and he bit.

For interested people outside the family, grandparents and aunts, the summer grounding was their first unequivocal indication that George and Leah were using extreme measures to discipline their kids. Beatings were done in private and were over quickly. Confining five children to their bedrooms for three months inevitably became known. To some members of Leah's family, it didn't sound so much like raising children as like dealing with them in the easiest way possible. It also sounded exceptionally cruel.

Leo and Marie DeBernardi doted on their grandchildren, but felt powerless to do anything because of the bad feeling that already existed between them and their son-in-law. (Leo DeBernardi was particularly fond of Eileen. Two decades later he could recall his wife taking their grandchildren to Cost Plus where she gave them each a dollar. As expected, all of them got something for themselves, except Eileen, who bought a gift for her grandmother.)

Leah had two younger sisters, Jean and Sue. Sue had finished college, married a rising corporate executive, and settled in the upscale Peninsula community of Portola Valley. A warm, out-going woman, Sue was fond of her good-looking nieces and nephew. When she questioned Leah about keeping her children indoors all summer, Leah's angry response threatened to break off relations entirely. Like many in Sue's position, she felt she could do the children little good if she was shut from their lives altogether.

The Franklins, particularly George, resented Sue's rising social position, which made it more difficult for her to help her nieces and nephew. George and Leah felt that Sue, with her college degrees and successful husband, considered herself superior to the Franklins. A bitter sense of rivalry erupted in odd ways. One Christmas, Sue gave her nieces necklaces from Saks Fifth Avenue. Seeing this, Leah and George, who rarely bought their children any kind of clothes, took them all to Saks, where they bought them expensive leather boots. The girls found their stylish new footwear far too fragile for tramping the often muddy route to school.

In his calmer moments, George told his children that if they ever needed anything, they should ask for it. When they tried this a few times with Leah—requests for new jeans, a special book for school—her reaction was invariably irate. They learned never to ask for anything. A curious manifestation of Leah's unhappy restlessness was her taking a volunteer job manning a switchboard in the evenings at a center dedicated to helping—ironically—youths in trouble. Perhaps she did this out of a desire to escape her children and husband, or just from a desire to interact with others closer to her age. Whatever the reason, Leah, with five young children at home, spent her evenings for a time working without pay for a charitable organization.

Outside his home, George Franklin kept to himself. He would occasionally drink beer with his firehouse cronies, but he had no close friends. When he took off on one of his four-day Volkswagen prowls, he went alone. Although he wasn't particularly friendly with the men he worked with, he was not belligerent either. His firefighting colleagues never saw his violent side. "He only hit women and children," Janice later remarked bitterly.

In spite of his outside diversions—moonlighting jobs, real-estate properties, trips in the van—at home he continued to terrorize his children. Except for the two calls to the police, the world outside the Franklin house had no knowledge of the beatings going on inside. In part, this was due to a lower awareness about child abuse than exists today. Neighbors were ignorant about abuse, and insensitive to the signs. Further guarding his secrecy, the children, like many other abused children, kept silent. They were ashamed of the rages in which they put their father. They were also frightened of greater punishments from him if they sought help.

On rare occasions, outsiders sensed a problem. Bob Galbraith remembers going on a firefighters' muster with George to Columbia, California, an old mining town popular with tourists. "My wife came along," Galbraith said. "She was Estonian and, as a child in the years following World War II, had some very rough experiences. George had brought along Eileen and Janice, and my wife took the two girls off for a long walk in the woods. They really hit it off, and when they came back it was as though they shared some secret knowledge. Later she said to me, 'Those girls really have a problem.'"

Many years later, in a statement to a law-enforcement officer, Kate Franklin said that as a child she often thought about how much better off they would all be if her father was dead. She fantasized about this often and remembered sitting in front of a mirror practicing expressions of grief for his funeral.

Eileen

By the time I was ten, life at home was extremely violent. My father's beatings and the mean way in which he spoke to us were terrifying. There was no way to predict his outbursts. Most evenings my father would become enraged over something real or imagined. Hours of shouting, violence, name-calling, and threats were routine. Always, I received much less physical abuse than did Kate, Janice, or George. After Susan's death, the violence directed toward me nearly disappeared.

Being at school was not much better than being at home. I was physically much smaller than the other children. My red hair cried out to the other students, "Pick on me, tease

me." My face was covered with ever-multiplying freckles.
My front teeth were bucked. I knew I was the ugliest child in
the class. I was ridiculed and badgered continuously.

In first, third, fourth, and fifth grades I loved all of my
teachers. I thought that my teachers didn't hate me, even if
all of my classmates did. Worshipping my teachers made
school tolerable. I was particularly fond of my fifth-grade
teacher, a sweet, grandmotherly woman named Mrs.
Walker. She read the most wonderful stories to the class,
stories I liked so much I would search them out later at the
public libraries to reread. She complimented me frequently
on my creative writing and my poetry, even submitting several of my stories to the local newspaper for their junior
section. I adored her.

She lived in Burlingame, close to my grandparents. At the
time I considered Burlingame to be near heaven. It had all
sorts of treats: nickel candies from Adeline Market; huge
trees lining the streets; Our Lady of Angels Church, with its
elaborate stained-glass windows; a park where no one ever
teased or bullied me; and a beautiful old library I could walk
to from my grandparents' home. In Burlingame the ladies I
met through my grandmother were always nice, which I
attributed to their churchgoing. In my mind, Mrs. Walker
was almost as wonderful as my grandmother, and, because
she lived in Burlingame, at least as nice as the other ladies.

At the time, Kate and Janice were already in junior high
school and were experimenting with makeup. One of them
discarded a compact of blue eye shadow, which I quickly fell
in love with. Using my fingertips, I applied the bright color
to my eyelids each morning before leaving for school. I
thought at the time that the blue was rather striking, particularly next to my bright red hair, and I enjoyed the mature
fashion statement I thought I was making.

One afternoon, after a particularly nasty time with the boys
in my class, I sat on the classroom steps and cried. The
boys had called me mean names and tried to drag me into
the boys' bathroom. Several kids had walked by as the group
of boys yanked and pulled on me, but no one had tried to
help, though I screamed for help.

Mrs. Walker approached me as I sat sobbing on the classroom steps and told me that I was being "oversensitive." She
told me that I cried too often about insignificant teasing and
taunting from the other children. I had heard from teachers

in previous years that I was "sensitive," but "oversensitive" was a new term, and her tone told me it was not a good thing to be.

For the first time I wondered if Mrs. Walker did not reciprocate my adoring feelings. She went on to tell me that I was cynical, a word I did not know, but she repeated it twice, which convinced me she was serious. She then asked me what "that blue gunk" was on my eyes, and said it made me look terrible. She felt certain that I received plenty of attention at home, she added, and that I should not do anything to gain extra attention. She told me to be happy with the life I had. She finished with the pronouncement that she did not want to see me at school again with the eye shadow on. I was devastated.

When I got home I took the dictionary to my room and searched for *cynical*. Having no idea how to spell the word, and no luck in guessing, I asked my father how to spell it. He asked why I wanted to know. I told him what Mrs. Walker had said. He hugged me and said, "Oh, honey, that's not true." But I insisted he tell me how to spell *cynical*.

I then asked him what a "faggot" was. The boys in my class called me "faggot" constantly. "Franklin the faggot" was the daily chant across the playground, and it sent me in search of new hiding places. My dad became angry and told me that I did not need to know what this word meant, and that I was not to use it again. He told me that only boys could be faggots—not much defense against my bully classmates.

I went back to my bedroom to read the definition of *cynical*. Two thoughts crossed my mind after I read the definition. The first was that this was not a good description for a ten-year-old child. Second, I realized that my teacher must not like me or she would not have called me cynical. I thought that Mrs. Walker must be stupid to use such a word to describe any child, especially me. My feelings of hurt, rejection, and confusion were compounded even more by Mrs. Walker's insulting my appearance with my wonderful blue eye shadow.

Until this time I had loved being in school. I dreaded recess and the walk home because of the teasing and bullying. But the time spent in the classroom had been my comfort. I loved to read and write, and I loved learning, especially from Mrs. Walker. But now I was forced to acknowledge that Mrs. Walker did not adore me. I already knew that my classmates and my parents did not. I stopped adoring Mrs. Walker, and life at school became a constant hell, which in my mind mirrored the misery at home. Now there was nothing left at school to balance out the cruelties at home. My eye shadow gone, I began biting my fingernails, and withdrew into myself and my world of books.

After Susan's murder, major changes occurred in the Franklin household. Eileen became withdrawn, began doing poorly in school, and became more fearful than previously. She avoided dark places. A badly lighted hallway, a heavily shaded path, an unlit room all held unfocused terrors for her. If she passed the boys' washroom at school, a chronic trouble spot, she was sure someone was going to jump out and grab her. She threw herself into Girl Scout activities, remaining with the group until she was twelve, long after most of her classmates had dropped out. "Anything to stay out of the house," she later said.

In everyday dealings with others, she became even shyer than she had been before. She also developed some nervous habits, pulling at her hair in certain spots until they were bald; there would be sores, many self-inflicted, that she picked at and scratched until they bled. Looking back from many years later she recalled a curious fatalism that enveloped her. "I didn't think about my future, because I didn't think I'd have one. I always had this vague feeling that I would be killed. I didn't know why."

Psychologists know that children who are exposed to continuous verbal and physical abuse come to feel themselves powerless and worthless. This makes them highly susceptible to demands from the abuser to keep quiet about what they have experienced. With the constant use of terror, abusers gain control of their victims' minds. To report the misdeeds of their terrorizers would be a forceful assertion of selfhood, and with abuse victims, the sense of self has been crippled.

For the abusers, this is a fortuitous by-product of whatever the primary agendas of their behavior might be. This natural mechanism to ensure secrecy is often given added reinforcement with threats. When the acts being hidden are criminal and could lead to jail, the threats can be dire: if the child tells anyone, he or she will be killed, her pets will be killed, people she loves will be killed.

Eileen would never know when she repressed witnessing the murder. The process may well have begun the night it happened. Years later she would recall that her father, at the scene of his crime, had threatened to kill her if she told anyone. She would remember his telling her that if she told what she saw she would be thought crazy and be put away as her mother had been. He also said that Eileen would be blamed because it was her idea for Susan to get in the van. All of these threats were buried in her mind along with the horrendous scene she had witnessed.

Even without specific threats, George Franklin may well have felt confident that his eight-year-old daughter would remain silent about what she had seen that September afternoon. He knew that, like her brother and sisters, Eileen lived in constant fear of him. Like most child abusers, Franklin had plenty of evidence that his victims were so intimidated and emotionally battered, they were unlikely to report any of his actions to outsiders. Except for Kate, none of the Franklin children ever did.

Eileen certainly did not. She never opposed him or defied him in any way. Her moment of insurrection in the paint store over his use of the word *nigger* was an inward, unspoken victory, one that she would remain proud of for years. Openly confronting him over even the smallest matter was unthinkable. When added to the fear Eileen and her siblings constantly felt, he threatened Eileen with murder, a crime she now knew he was capable of, she was certain to react as she always had and obey him.

Many psychologists who work with traumatized children have observed that children who are subjected to traumas outside their homes—a fire at school, a car accident, a friend drowning—take their anguish and confusion to their parents for comfort, reassurance, and healing. When, however, parents have caused the traumas, or for some other reason the children are blocked from telling their parents, the children may well find themselves disenfranchised, with nowhere to turn. Unable to carry such burdens alone, they often repress them.

Unlike forgetting, which is a passive action, repression requires an effort, a determination to push the unbearable experience from the mind. But since the effort is invariably unconscious (or repressed along with the painful memory), people experiencing this phenomenon are unaware that anything has occurred. They usually have no awareness of a blank or a gap in their memory. They also do not know they played a role in burying the memory. Repression is a coping mechanism, as automatic as passing out from pain.

During Sigmund Freud's lifetime, he changed his mind on a

central point of his system of psychoanalytical thought that concerned repressed childhood memory. He at first believed that the traumatic childhood episodes of parental abuse that he unearthed from his patients' subconscious were real. He later came to believe they were mostly fantasies. The argument continued long after Freud's death, but today there are few bona fide psychologists or psychiatrists who do not accept the reality of the majority of accounts of parentally induced trauma and accept as well the high incidence of repression of such traumas.

Those most familiar with this phenomenon also know that it is very common for individuals who have repressed such memories to have them resurface when they are in their late twenties or early thirties, a time in their lives when they have usually escaped the tyranny of the abuser or have achieved a level of maturity that enables them to accept and integrate into their consciousness the forbidden memory.

While, for Eileen, the fear of her father and the horrifying nature of what she had seen were more than sufficient to bring about repression, it was undoubtedly reinforced by the public furor surrounding Susan's disappearance. Eileen had to proceed with her life among people who were obsessed by the mystery of Susan Nason's disappearance. The psychological pressure of knowing the answer to the question that gripped everyone around her—playmates, adults, teachers, parents—may have been more than she could bear. The weight of her terrible knowledge may have broken something inside her and, with little conscious or unconscious effort from her, collapsed into an unreachable area. If the memory was already buried, the public clamor must surely have forced it deeper.

Although Eileen was not consciously aware of her father's threats, this inner knowledge may have translated to the more acceptable notion that she would one day be murdered by "someone." At the same time, she had contradictory feelings of invincibility. "I once broke a glass in the kitchen," she recalled, "and as I cleaned it up I was sure that the pieces couldn't hurt me. I could walk barefoot through them, and none of the glass would touch me. I don't know what was behind this. Maybe, after all I'd been through, a broken glass was nothing."

Although Eileen was not aware of all she'd been through, there were other signs of the buried memory pressing against her consciousness. Many years later she recalled attending a slumber party when she was about ten. The other girls began talking about Susan Nason's murder. One of the girls said that her father owned land in the hills not far from where Susan's body was found.

Eileen was swept with a sickening wave of anxiety. Without knowing the reason, she had an intense feeling that this subject was absolutely forbidden and must never be discussed. She said nothing to stop the girls' chatter, but she can remember having a fearful feeling that her father might be looking in the window.

The biggest changes in the household after Susan's disappearance were in George Franklin, who was thirty when Susan was murdered. He began sexually abusing some of his daughters. As long as any of them could remember, the family had been very free about nakedness; modesty was not encouraged in the household. When in a good mood, George enjoyed taking baths with his daughters. This sometimes led to sexual acts that were frequently ambiguous.

When one of the girls was about six, he asked her to stand naked in front of him so he could examine her thoroughly. If modesty was not part of the household, it *was* part of the small girl's genetic responses. She was distraught, and tried to cover herself with her hands. George ordered her angrily to hold her hands behind her. If, as many authorities agree, child sexual abuse is not about sex so much as about power, this episode would seem strong corroboration.

One daughter would later insist she had no recollection of sexual abuse by Franklin, but does not deny that it happened. Eileen repressed any awareness of such abuse for years, but would eventually remember a number of incidents. Another daughter remembers her father having intercourse so regularly with the sister with whom she shared a room, he kept a jar of Vaseline in a bedside drawer.

When Eileen later became aware of her father's crimes against his own children, she hoped they were impulsive lapses, sudden dictates of twisted lust that, in his normal moments, he would recoil from as much as others would. When she learned of his planting the jar of Vaseline by one sister's bed, it put an end to this explanation that on occasion he lost control. This evidence of advance planning established that the sexual acts against his daughters were carried out with cool premeditation. And those daughters who were aware of the abuse and who would discuss it agree that it became worse after September 22, 1969. In the words of one of them, "After Susan's murder, all hell broke loose."

FOUR

WHEN ONE FOSTER CITY NEIGHBOR OF THE FRANKLINS learned years later about George Franklin's predilection for little girls, she was surprised. "George hit on every wife in Foster City," she said. "When did he have time for little girls?" His colleagues at the firehouse confirmed this picture of sexual prowess. In fact, they expanded on it with such locker-room tributes as "George would screw anything you held down." On his solitary excursions in his van, the mattress in the back was put to frequent use.

Even if Leah had not let herself go physically—her weight rarely got below 180 pounds—George would undoubtedly have been a womanizer. He thought about sex constantly, and, for him, seduction was a reflex. A young woman who lived with her husband next door to the Franklins for a time on Harvester recalls his relentless efforts. "He used to work up on the roof of his house. It seems like he was always up on that roof. Maybe he was casing the neighborhood. If he'd see me in the garden or coming up the walk, he'd call down and make some insinuating remark. I used to call him 'Mr. Flirty-flirty.' " In spite of the cute nickname, the woman made clear her disgust at George's constant passes. Many women were not disgusted.

The studies of child abusers conducted by Drs. Ann Burgess and Nicholas Groth point to the secondary role that sexual desire plays in child molestation, and the dominant need on the part of the molesters to feel powerful and in control. In addition, sex with a child is free of performance anxiety and of the array of threats to ego, self-esteem, and authority that go with adult intercourse. Sex with a child is an act of total dominance, woefully easy to achieve. While there is good reason to think that George Franklin was impelled by many of the psychological pressures that typify child molesters, his exceptional sex drive undoubtedly contributed to the frequency of his acts.

In an essay on incest offenders in Dr. Suzanne Sgroi's *Handbook of Clinical Intervention in Child Sexual Abuse,* Dr. Groth writes that there are two basic types of child abusers: fixated and regressive. Fixated molesters are adults, usually male, who have always been attracted to children and who have little interest in sex with adults. With almost no exceptions, Groth writes, these men molest only boys.

Regressive molesters, also male in most cases, are primarily interested in adult members of the opposite sex, but in moments of anxiety or low self-esteem they regress to children. With long histories of relations with adult women, these men suddenly find themselves sexually attracted to children. Unlike fixated molesters, regressive molesters are attracted to children of the opposite sex. When the emotional crisis passes, they return to sex with other adults.

There is no evidence that George Franklin ever had any interest in his own sex, adult or child, so he fits the regressive pattern in that regard. As for being a man of anxieties and low self-image, he appears, at first glance, quite the opposite—cocky, self-assured, in charge. With closer scrutiny, however, he shows signs of deeply entrenched self-doubt. One example would be his hypersensitivity to slights and putdowns, as with his prickly dealings with Leah's college-graduate sister, Sue, and her husband. His tyrannical rule over his family would be another, especially when coupled with his docile manner with his firefighter colleagues. Even his fondness for reading—Civil War history was his main interest—could be seen as another concern about his sparse education.

In his book on child abuse, *By Silence Betrayed,* John Crewdson speaks of a recently recognized third category of abusers: "cross-over" pedophiles, adults who initially seek partners their own age, but who increasingly shift their focus, until children become their exclusive interest. From the materials found in George Franklin's apartment in November of 1989, this appeared to have been his pattern. The materials also suggested he had a specific erotic obsession with father-daughter incest.

Child molesters are generally people with no close relationships with lovers, friends, or family. This would also fit George Franklin. Whatever kinship had existed between Leah and himself had long since faded, and their marriage was reduced to fights and bickering. The person closest to him was probably

Eileen, but that intimacy fluctuated with his mood and schedule —and she was a child. Nor did he have any close male friends, either at the firehouse or in the neighborhood, and he maintained little contact with his family. No one around him, including his daughters, thought much about this, but it is unusual for anyone with Franklin's social assets—good looks, humor, and gift of gab—to be so alone in the world.

Dr. Groth writes that conflict in a marriage and pressure from the burdens of adulthood can turn an otherwise normal heterosexual man toward children for sexual gratification. Speaking of such adult areas of anxiety as job, marriage, fatherhood, money problems, illness, Dr. Groth writes, "The sum of these responsibilities, demands and misfortunes prove more than these men can cope with, and they find themselves becoming sexually attracted to children. Such sexual interest in children appears to be a departure from their more customary and conventional sexual orientation toward agemates activated by some precipitating stress or combination of stresses."

In addition to the anxiety-free allure of very young sex partners, children seem to hold for the molester another somewhat amorphous attraction, one that the psychologists only touch on: a desire to escape the adult world entirely. If this is so, it would appear that the child molester uses a child for sex to lessen his anxieties about being an adult and, at the same time, uses his adulthood to gain mastery over the child.

While many may feel such aberrant impulses, acting on them requires a high level of ruthlessness. Sadly, such levels abound. A landmark 1985 survey by the *Los Angeles Times* found that twenty-two percent of 2,627 men and women questioned across the country (twenty-seven percent of the women and sixteen percent of the men) had been sexually abused as children.

Many years later, when Eileen was about twenty and she and her father were enjoying one of their periods of closeness, Eileen asked him about the problems between him and Leah. The picture he painted was some distance from the image of Leah as the perpetual victim. "I was constantly criticized," he said, "and she never missed an opportunity to put me down." He also spoke bitterly about her opposition to the dream of real-estate wealth that had dominated his young adulthood. "She never worked as a partner with me. If I wanted to make any progress at all, it always meant a fight with her first—even something I wanted to do with you kids—it was always a battle with Leah. You can't imagine what it was like," he said, "when you are working so hard on something big like my property deals, to have someone fighting you every step of the way."

It is not difficult to imagine the pressures weighing on George Franklin during the first decade of his marriage. Five unruly children at home, a wife indifferent to child-rearing and house-keeping who obstructed his real-estate dreams and who was given to nervous breakdowns and stays in the hospital, eight or ten mortgages to meet each month as well as the countless bills of raising a family, a number of complaining tenants to keep happy or evict, and a regular job that was not free of danger.

If adult pressures and low self-esteem drove George Franklin into the beds of some of his daughters, the chances are good that his powerful sex drive brought him there frequently. All four girls were growing up to be exceptionally good-looking. For a womanizer, it may have been akin to living in a clutch of Playboy bunnies, all dancing around him scantily clad, traces of their blossoming femininity strewn around, innocently showing him physical signs of affection. When such incitements are placed before a man who has smashed the ultimate moral barrier by molesting, then murdering a child, sex with his daughters may have been moved from the complex area of a psychological symptom into the area of basic gratification.

It is quite common for abused children to feel more resentment toward the non-abusing parent than toward the one who abused them. The underlying supposition is that the abusive parent was an anomaly and out of control, while the other parent could have protected them. This reaction was apparently true of both Janice and Eileen Franklin, but their negative appraisal of Leah was based on more than just her passive assent to George Franklin's abuses.

Eileen

Even though our father always told us that if we needed anything we should just ask for it, we kids knew better. Requests always irritated Mom. When I was ten, I wanted something so badly, I broke our own rule and went to my father. Through the school, I heard about a nature camp an hour west of Foster City that lasted only a week. It cost thirty-six dollars, and I desperately wanted to go. I think my brother and sisters were amazed that I went to our father and asked for the money, and were even more surprised when I got it.

I loved the camp and was thrilled the following year, when they let me go again. I had only been at the camp two days the second year when I got sick with violent stomach pains. The head counselor decided I was too sick for their rudimentary facilities, and phoned my parents to come for me. Leah was at home when the call was made, and refused to come. She said that if I just stayed in bed for a while, I'd be all right.

After a time my temperature rose to above 104 degrees, which brought the camp director into the crisis. He phoned Leah and emphasized the seriousness of the situation. Again she argued against making the trip. The camp counselors had brought me to the director's office and stretched me out on a sofa in the waiting room. As I faded in and out of consciousness, I could hear the director arguing with my mother. In the end he convinced her that my health was in danger, and that unless she came and found proper medical help for me, he could not be responsible for the consequences. Leah agreed to come.

When she finally arrived at the camp that evening, my mother was furious. Seeing the terrible condition I was in did nothing to soften her mood. Not wanting to leave the other children alone at the house, she had brought along Janice, Diana, and George junior. Without saying a word, my mother hustled me into the backseat and started the return trip to Foster City. For the entire drive, she complained about having been forced to come for me. The roads were bad. She wasn't used to driving in the mountains. She'd had trouble arranging for someone else to pick up Kate at dancing class. She never asked how I felt, or held a hand to my forehead.

When we arrived home, she was still in her fury. She got out of the van, slammed the door, and stormed into the house, leaving me in the backseat. I was semiconscious and had broken out in fever blisters. I half-walked, half-crawled into the house and got myself into bed.

The following morning my father arrived home and was astounded to find that I was so sick. He couldn't believe my mother had allowed things to get this far. I had never seen my father so angry with her, especially sober, as he was now. While screaming at her, he picked me up and gently carried me to his van and drove me to the hospital. Leah came as well.

I was diagnosed as having acute appendicitis, and had to

be operated on immediately. As nurses shaved my stomach in preparation for surgery, my father stood over me, speaking to me comfortingly and lovingly while my mother leaned against the wall, looking away from the bed, just staring at the wall.

Years later, when my family was embroiled in a far more devastating crisis and some of us were trying to resuscitate family relationships that had never really existed, I asked Leah about the camp incident, hoping my memory had exaggerated the horror of the recollection. At first she denied having been neglectful that night, but after a time she fell back into all the old complaints—how far camp was, how tricky the roads were, how she had the other kids on her hands. She also claimed because I was a child I exaggerated the delay, but a neighbor and her mother were also at the camp and remember I became very ill before breakfast and it was growing dark when she arrived. I almost died that night and Leah knew it, but twenty years later I was still the nuisance in the backseat of the car. Leah was the victim.

My father's real-estate properties did well, and in 1971 we moved to a larger home on Beach Park Boulevard, a more prestigious Foster City neighborhood along the bay shore. A levee, ideal for strolls and bike-riding, blocked the view of the water from the street or ground floor, but from the house's second story we could look out over the water. Looking to the left, we could see the seemingly endless span of the San Mateo Bridge, which carried Route 92 across the bay to Hayward. For all the added comforts, the family situation was as bad as it had ever been and Janice quickly dubbed our new house "Auschwitz."

My mother and father seemed to fight more than ever, and he turned his rages just as frequently on the rest of us. When he wasn't making life a hell for us at home, my father threw himself into a fight the firemen were waging against the city of San Mateo to establish a union. Although he held no official position among the unionists, he worked hard for the cause. There was a bitter strike, and my father's side won. Within a few more years my father would leave the fire department.

My brother and sisters and I had moved from the elementary school to Bowditch Middle School, which was a much greater distance to walk each day. My ability to make friends had not improved, nor had the harassment over my red hair and freckles lessened. From fourth grade until eleventh grade, I had almost no friends.

When I was eleven I decided it might be fun if I joined the school band. My mother's interest in the arts stopped with dance, and I felt certain she wouldn't buy me a musical instrument. Since no one at the school wanted to play the French horn, the music teacher offered to supply one to any student willing to learn it. Seeing my chance to play in the band, and become part of a group, I threw myself into lessons. Each day I would lug that instrument, which was as big as I was, down Beach Park Boulevard to and from school.

The children's allowance in our family was a quarter a week, regardless of how much we worked on our father's properties. Even then, he often forgot to give us the money, and we were afraid that asking for it might set him off. To earn pocket money, I began baby-sitting in the neighborhood. A family I worked for regularly, the Diricksons, brought about a major change in my view of the world.

The Diricksons had grown-up children and had a number of foster children whom I would look after for an evening or two a week. I had always regarded with total skepticism my classmates' claims that their families were happy, even when I saw them firsthand. I was convinced that, when no outsiders were present, the same ugliness I experienced at home would break out in their homes as well. I thought beating was what fathers did. But as I began to get to know the Dirickson family, this assumption fell apart.

I loved being at their house. They were so kind, and they all got along. There was plenty of food, and they were very generous with me. I fell in love with these people, so I began studying them with a very critical eye. After only a few evenings in their house, I decided that the father, Jack Dirickson, *never hit his children*. I could see that his kids had no fear of him, and some of them had come out of really bad environments. I never would have dreamed of asking the kids if he ever hit them, but I just knew that he didn't. This was a major awakening for me. When you are constantly yelled at, put down and punished, you come to believe that *all* kids are a pain in the neck to *all* adults. Maybe believing that helps you deal with your own situation.

I also found that I had a strong maternal streak. I discovered that I loved kids. I loved taking care of them—cooking for them, cleaning up afterward, all of it. It surprised and delighted me that the adult Diricksons appeared to love kids too. It was something totally new for me. They treated me so warmly. When my work was done, I felt welcome to remain with them. I never felt they were shoving me out the door.

The unaccustomed warmth and acceptance I felt from the Diricksons may have led to another new development in my life. I experienced my first crush. It was on one of the Diricksons' sons, Michael, who I thought was extremely handsome. Many years later, Michael Dirickson would turn up in my life in an ironic way.

While I was discovering that anger and violence were not part of all families, the situation between my mother and father deteriorated. Their fighting increased and took ever more ugly turns: they fought about her inadequacies as a mother, about his black moods, rages, and about which of them drank more. Finally, divorce proceedings were begun. This merely shifted the subject of the fights from each other's failings as human beings to nasty wrangles over who would get what at the settlement.

Things got so tense, my father moved out. The development made Leah no easier on us kids, but improved the general atmosphere in the home enormously, with the threat of beatings removed. I can remember no incidence of violence by him against any of us, anywhere, after he separated from Leah.

Religion had never been an element in my life, since my parents were not churchgoers and never encouraged us to go. The only link to my Catholic background were my visits to my DeBernardi grandparents. When my grandmother Marie played at services, she'd let me sit up with her in the organ loft. I used to love it. So calm, so peaceful, so safe. It was like sitting up there with God.

Just before entering high school, I became interested in religion and began attending a nondenominational church with Leah, who also was reaching out for improvement in her life. For a time I joined a Christian youth group. I really was into it, and took the religious part very seriously.

I made a new friend a few months later who would have a large influence in my life. Diana and a classmate had taken after-school jobs in a doughnut shop. An older man came in regularly who had befriended the teenaged girls. His name was John Dorick, and he was a retired widower in his sixties, with time on his hands. During slow periods in the doughnut shop, he would sit at the counter and chat with the two girls. They all became very friendly.

John had an attractive apartment close by the shop. When I was taken to meet him, he immediately took an interest in me, and a solid, completely platonic friendship developed between us. Several years later, after I had moved out of Leah's house, I lived with John for a while. He never behaved inappropriately with me, but instead gave me the kind of lessons on poise, manners, and polish that I had never received at home.

I entered San Mateo High School, and for the first year I was as unpopular and miserable as I had been at Bowditch. One day a rich boy in my class asked me why I always wore the same clothes to school every day. I asked what he meant. Nastily, he said that I never wore anything but the same dirty jeans and shirt. "Why don't you get some decent clothes?" he asked.

I was humiliated. I had never thought about my clothes. When things wore out, Leah would find something for me that Kate or Janice had outgrown, or I would buy replacements with baby-sitting money. I was always dressed; it never occurred to me that other people might concern themselves with *how* I dressed. I started noticing the clothes others wore, and to my surprise I saw that most of the students came to school in different outfits every day, some quite nice. I suddenly realized how shabby I was, and had always been. I was so embarrassed, I stopped going to school for a period.

When I returned, I asked to be put in an experimental section called Small School. It was a voluntary education program for students who were often brighter, but were rebellious or had emotional problems, or problems with attention or attendance. The curriculum stressed more humanistic subjects, and performance was not measured by tests and work projects, but by a once-weekly meeting with the teachers. Students worked at their own pace. It had a reputation in the school as being for the "stoners"—the pot smokers—and there were a lot of hippie types. But there were a lot of bright kids as well. Still, it was a lot more relaxed than the other school, and it worked well for many of us—particularly for me, because I began to make friends.

The first was a cheerful boy named Ricky Mendelson, then a girl named Regina Chin became my best friend. Ricky and I enjoyed spending time together and would often go roller-skating in the evening, or to see a movie. I also became friends with another student, a handsome boy named Todd Kirk, who had brown hair and enormous green eyes, and lived not far from me in Foster City. Ricky had a car and began picking me up in the mornings along with Todd, Regina, and a pretty blond girl named Lisa Silverstein, also in Small School, whom I had known at Bowditch.

We all hit it off very well and the drives to and from school became the high points of my days. For the first time in my life, I had a group of friends. Todd was dating Aimee Alotta, my Harvester Drive neighbor, who had developed into a pretty and lively young woman.

Lisa Silverstein remembers Eileen as funny, honest, and totally open about herself, except in one regard. "All of us had problems with our parents from time to time, and we'd tell the others. I mean, I had a great family, very loving and all that, but sometimes I'd have a fight with my mother or father—we all would—and I'd give the others a play-by-play. Todd and Ricky did too. But not Eileen. I knew she was having problems at home. One morning I got in the car to go to school, and I could see she had been crying. But she never talked about it, not even when I asked her what the trouble was."

When the Franklins' divorce became final, Leah did well financially. She got title to over half of George's houses, then nearly twenty, with the understanding that a good part of the money was to go for the children's college education. Leah had other ideas. The first thing she did was to begin an energetic program to lose her excess weight, then fit herself out with a new wardrobe. She bought herself a new car, a Volkswagen Rabbit that could only seat three passengers, which was an odd choice for a mother with five children living at home.

Leah also invested some of her new affluence in group psychotherapy, but, according to Janice, was "thrown out for not leveling with them." She was told to come back when she was "ready to tell the truth." In 1978, Janice recalled, "I told Leah about the sexual abuse I had suffered at the hands of my father. She took me immediately to a therapist and seemed annoyed when she was told that it would take more than one session to undo whatever damage had been done to me."

Leah started traveling, first taking a cruise to Mexico, then trips to Asia and Europe. "I really admired that," said her neighborhood friend Fay Munier. "After a nasty divorce a lot of women sit around feeling sorry for themselves, but not Leah. She got herself up and out, did something positive." To others it was less admirable. Her financial settlement had been for herself *and the children*. The children needed education and clothes and, when they started working, cars. She spent almost nothing on them, but she spent a great deal on herself. The household larder, which would be stocked on George Franklin's days off, was now almost always bare.

To the surprise of many people, including her children, Leah enrolled in law school, and worked feverishly for four years. She graduated and was admitted to the bar. Her story would be a triumph for oppressed wives if it had not been for the pesky existence of her five children. By the time Leah had paid for her new car, the trips, and law school, there was little of her divorce settlement left, and the kids were informed that college was out of the question.

Some of the children saw their father regularly. He began living with a young woman named Karen, who was tall and had almond-shaped green eyes and a good sense of humor. They got an apartment in Mountain View, a town south of Palo Alto. Karen, who had a blind daughter and a son named Manuel, went out of her way to be kind to her lover's children. "All of my father's girlfriends were nice to me," Eileen later recalled, "certainly a lot nicer than Leah. When they broke up, I was crushed because I had come to love Karen so much."

When she turned eighteen, Janice was suddenly told by Leah that she had to leave the house and go off on her own. Janice was particularly helpless, since she didn't know how to drive, a necessity in California for getting a job. Janice always suspected that Leah had continued to keep her immobile so that she would become dependent on George Franklin and his girlfriend, thus putting a strain on that love affair. As expected, Janice moved in with George and Karen, but any such plan of Leah's was foiled by Karen, who taught Janice to drive and helped her get a license.

Eileen

When I was about seventeen, I underwent a major change. From the attention I was getting from boys, I realized I must be getting attractive. For someone who had adjusted to being forever funny-looking, the possibility that this might be changing was fantastic. I was so thrilled, I thought of it as divine intervention. The fact is, when I was involved with the church, I used to pray every night that God would make me beautiful. So people would stop teasing me. But I knew it had to be nothing less than God to bring this about. I never used makeup. I thought, "There's no hope so why bother?"

In my junior year, Todd asked me to go with him to the homecoming dance after the big San Mateo–Burlingame football game. Many thought Todd was the best-looking guy in the school. My mother actually took me to buy a dress— a white halter dress, like the one worn by Marilyn Monroe in that photo with her skirt blowing up. I thought it the most elegant, feminine thing I had ever owned.

I decided to try makeup. Kate was working at Macy's then, and had beautiful clothes and one of those huge makeup boxes, six shades of everything. I asked if I could use her makeup, and she said I could help myself. I told her I knew nothing and needed help. She grew impatient. "There's the makeup—just put it on. How wrong can you get it?"

I didn't know where to begin. I started to cry. It was this wonderful, exciting day—the big dance of the year. Janice and her friend Joanne Lutz came in. When they saw how upset I was, they leaned on Kate to help me. She said okay, but just for a few minutes. She helped me a little: "Put this there, put that there." So I put some on, and I was stunned by how great it made me look. All I wore was eye shadow and blush. I don't think I even put on lipstick. It made all the difference in the world! My God, I thought, I look so much better!

I was totally thrilled. One of them told me to spray hairspray on my face so my makeup would last. At the dance, we were sitting at a table with Ricky Mendelson and his date. Ricky kept staring at me.

"Why are you staring?" I asked.

"Because you look so beautiful," he said, as if he were dazed. "I can't believe it, Eileen, you really look fantastic!"

He said it about five times, over and over. I remember lying in bed that night, thanking God for answering my prayers. After a few days I thought to myself, "Okay, I'm good-looking. Now I've got to work on not being stupid."

My father and I maintained our close relationship after he

moved out of the house, which angered my mother a great deal. He told us, "If you kids want to see me, you call me." He did not want to call and ask us to come visit, because my mother would answer the phone and a fight would ensue. Just like my grandparents' house on my weekend escapes when I was younger, my father's home became a safe haven for me, which infuriated my mother. She hated my visiting my father so frequently. She and I had not become any closer when my father moved out; in fact, we had become enemies. She verbally attacked me after every telephone call from my father and every visit. I was starting to get rebellious, so I'm sure I wasn't any prize daughter for her either.

My father knew of the hostility between my mother and me, and suggested that I might be happier living elsewhere. My mother agreed, so my father sent me to spend the summer with his mother, sisters, and nieces in Florida. I enjoyed this, and became spoiled with home-cooked meals, car trips, and Southern hospitality. No one ever yelled at me. Life was for once peaceful. Except for missing Diana, I had little desire to go home. At the end of the summer, my father asked me if I would like to stay longer. I told him I didn't want to go back to Leah, so I was enrolled in the local high school. I felt very loved by my father because he was protecting me from the hostility at home.

Shortly after school began, I received a telephone call from my mother. She told me that she missed me very much. She wished that I would reconsider my decision and come home. I told her that I felt she hated me. She told me that she loved me, missed me, and wanted me—words I was starved to hear. I decided to return to Foster City.

My mother had agreed to pick me up at the San Francisco airport, but when I arrived, no one was there. I felt betrayed and started crying. I wondered if my mother had persuaded me to come home, then left me stranded at the airport to show that she truly did hate me. When I called home and Janice told me that Mom was sleeping, I cried even harder.

My mother said that she had forgotten about my arrival and would come pick me up. Waiting at the airport, I realized that I had made a huge mistake. My father would have never forgotten me at an airport. My father had sent me away to shield me from this type of treatment, yet, after one kind phone call from my mother, I had run home to her.

* * *

In a relatively short period in her mid-teens, Eileen underwent a series of major changes that improved her life enormously. Not only did she change from funny-looking to pretty,
but she acquired her first group of friends, and the constant
menace of an explosive father was removed from her daily life.
Deliverance from the loneliness, self-doubt, and pain of her
childhood brought out a number of facets of her personality,
not all of them admirable.

As if making up for her years of miserable shyness, she moved
quite rapidly into the opposite camp of self-assured cockiness. A
spirited and adventurous side emerged as she made known her
willingness to try whatever others were doing in terms of alcohol,
drugs, and sex. Her young male friends, many of whom were
turning out to be gay, relished this freewheeling side of her, and
egged her on. The first sexual experiences she can recall were not
pleasant, but frenzied, uncomfortable encounters, totally lack-
ing in affection or tenderness.

Some of Eileen's close school friends were unaware that she
did not graduate from San Mateo High School. She had lost
too many credits from cutting classes because of her wardrobe.
Another element of her new assertiveness was the absence of
any adult in her life who cared much what she did. Shunning
school, she chose night life as her arena. Curiously, since her
appetites were exclusively heterosexual, the night life she pre-
ferred was gay.

While still in high school, Eileen and some gay friends would
go to the Answer, a gay bar in Redwood City, a sprawling
suburban community a few miles south of Foster City. With all
that Eileen had gone through in her upbringing, whether or not
the affecting experiences were in her conscious memory, it is not
surprising that she would emerge into adulthood with some
unusual facets. Her affinity for male homosexuals came early
and grew throughout the years she was on her own.

There would come a time a few years later when Eileen would
openly declare that she distrusted heterosexual men. This
sweeping declaration was based, in her mind, on her real-life
experiences with them. It was undoubtedly fueled as well by the
male brutality she had experienced as a child, a great deal of
which was still beyond the reach of her conscious memory. Her
dilemma was that she only enjoyed sex with men. She felt most
comfortable socializing in gay bars, but frequently went to
straight bars with her gay friends. Because of the strong and

caring friendships she formed with her gay friends, this was one
of the best periods of her life. For the first time, Eileen felt she
was part of a supportive and loving family.

With gay men as her friends, she could enjoy the companionship of men without the ingredient of male lust that made men
threatening to her. Her gay friends' permissiveness matched her
own mood of unbridled experimentation and thrill-seeking. She
applauded their feisty defiance of the bigoted, unfair straight
world, and this gave her an outlet for the usual late-teenage
urge to strike out at injustice. The shy, funny-looking Eileen
had disappeared and been replaced by a self-assured, ready-for-
anything young woman.

She had a strikingly pretty face, stunning long red hair, and
a good figure. Since she was often the only straight woman in
the crowded bar, if one heterosexual male happened to be there,
he would quickly find his way to her. While she was coming to
appear brash on the surface, none who knew her ever doubted
her good-heartedness and her underlying sensitivity. The men
in her group found her to be a devoted and doggedly loyal
friend.

Later, as she became more experienced on the man-woman
playing fields, she found other aspects of the gay milieu that
appealed to her. "I never liked the atmosphere in straight bars.
If you asked a guy to dance, that meant you wanted to sleep
with him. Everybody was so uptight and self-conscious. In gay
bars I didn't have the feeling that every guy was sizing me up
all the time, trying to decide whether to hit on me or not, trying
to decide if I'd let him. For me, gay bars were completely
relaxed. I could have fun. If I felt like shooting a game of pool,
I could do it without feeling I was offering myself up for God
knows what."

One night Eileen came home from an evening at the Answer
and was told by Leah that, since she was about to be eighteen,
she had to move out. Eileen was stunned. She later admitted she
had been out late a number of nights in a row. Also, she had
been involved in a minor motorcycle accident about that time,
an accident that Leah was convinced, wrongly according to
Eileen, resulted from pot smoking. "Whatever her real reason
for throwing me out," Eileen said, "there had been no buildup,
no warning. Not a word. Just 'Get out.' " Her father helped her
find a job in property management, and demanded that Leah
give Eileen her share of child-support payments. For a time she
moved in with her friend Todd, then later Janice.

Eileen

For my nineteenth birthday my father took me to Mexico. In his Volkswagen van we drove south from San Francisco to Ensenada. We admired the fabulous views along our way and enjoyed each other's company. We had Thanksgiving dinner in Santa Barbara in a restaurant on the ocean, then proceeded to San Diego where we drank keoki-coffee in a bar until quite late. In Mexico I had my first margarita. My dad is an adventurous and interesting traveler, and it was a terrific trip, one of my best birthdays ever.

A short time after this, he moved to Sacramento, where he bought a run-down apartment building. He asked me to join him to help out. I left my second job, also in a real-estate office, and moved to Sacramento. I was happy to help him with the office work, but the manual labor in the dry heat of Sacramento was not high on my list of favorite things to do. I'd done enough manual labor on rental properties as a child to feel no guilt about my refusal to work on the buildings.

My dad had a part-time job as a courier of documents. We regularly drove from San Francisco to Sacramento, collecting or delivering bank documents. With his back injury, it was one of the few jobs he could easily manage. He had a favorite town where he liked to stop, called Bolinas. He told me that twenty-six times the state of California had put up a road sign announcing the limits of Bolinas, and that twenty-six times the sign had disappeared because the residents did not want visitors. We sometimes stopped for a drink in Bolinas. Being outsiders, we received the cold shoulder from everyone, which was just what we expected. For some reason this delighted my father.

One of his finer traits was his ability to scout out the best restaurants. He knew exactly where to stop when traveling for a perfect cup of coffee or a piece of warm pie. Just the mention of hand-made tortillas would send him twenty miles out of the way to find me a good one. We both loved to eat on the road, and he knew where to get delicious food in unconventional settings. Living in Sacramento with him was an experience. At first we lived in a house he had just bought, sleeping on the floor in sleeping bags. Eventually I went back to the Bay Area.

FIVE

In the first years of living on her own, Eileen had a number of jobs and apartments, always with roommates, and most of those were gay men. She had a number of affairs, but never lived with any of these men. Having made her triumphant escape from her own fears and hangups, she was happy to pass along the secrets of her new-found strength. Eileen met a young man named Bob Albright, who had moved to the Bay Area from the East to pursue, somewhat timorously and, as far from his family as the continent allowed, a homosexual life.

"I was a mess," Albright recalls. "I didn't know who I was or what I wanted. Eileen decided to make me her project. She sized me up as a blank canvas she could turn into anything she wanted. Boy, did she turn me around! I was so shy, I couldn't ask directions from a stranger. She gave me pep talks, yelled at me, told me to take myself in hand. She gave me commonsense lectures, told me I was driven by emotion rather than logic. She would do that sort of thing with everybody. She worried that her friend Todd used to drink too much. Eileen would torture him about it. With me, her campaign worked. She turned me from someone who never spoke into a loudmouth.

"Most of our group had problems with our families. My father used to beat the shit out of me. If I saw him take off his watch, that was the sign I was in for it. Eileen didn't talk about it, but we knew that her childhood had been rough, too."

Eileen's strong mothering impulses, which she first showed as a child with her sister Diana and later with the Dirickson children, now took an odd turn when she became a loving mother for a group of young gay men. "When she lived with us," Albright recalled, "Eileen looked after us all. She was very caring and concerned about us, but she wanted to be in charge. Our other roommate used to fight with Eileen a lot; they both wanted to run things. They really locked horns. But you can't intimidate her, and she knew better than anyone how to work us. She could usually get us to see things her way.

"She was protective of us, too. One time, my mother was on the phone giving me hell about being gay. Eileen listened to the conversation for as long as she could, then she grabbed the phone and started yelling at my mother! 'How dare you give Bob this kind of trouble? He is a wonderful person, and you're trying to make him feel terrible. Life is hard enough without your putting guilt on him!' My mother didn't know what hit her. Who was that masked lady who just rode off? Eileen handled herself well in tight situations. She had a good mouth."

Eileen

I had no definite plans or belief in my future. I did not want to get married, although I had always wanted children. With no career plans and little education, I never envisioned a normal life for myself—or a long one. A couple of my friends were attending Stanford University, and I envied them. Their lives were my impossible dream. I was impressed with the education they were getting, but also with their intelligence and social skills. I fantasized that one day I would attend Stanford and receive an excellent education, but I knew it was a futile dream.

My father gave me a cat that he named Twinkle Toes. One night, one of my roommates let the cat outside and he ran into the street and was killed. I started crying. Without hesitating, I telephoned my father. He came right over. There had been no decision process; he was simply the first one I thought to call.

About a year after leaving home, I again needed a place to live, so I accepted the offer of my older friend, John Dorick, to move into his apartment, which happened to be within walking distance from my job in Foster City. John had been a successful businessman and was very knowledgeable about the world. He felt I had a lot of potential, and set out to hone my rough edges and give me some polish. I had always wanted to improve myself, but never before had anyone offered to help me do this. I was thrilled.

At first John limited himself to advising me how to dress

—this looked well on me, that didn't—but when he saw how grateful I was for the advice, he stepped up his program and told me such things as to show less gum when I smiled; it would make me more attractive. Even then, I thought it was a very loving thing for him to have told me.

Through my gay friends I met Chris Lydon, a tall, good-looking gay man who at first I didn't much like, he seemed so sarcastic and cutting. But when I heard he was looking for a roommate just when I needed a place, I accepted his offer to join forces. We took a place together in San Mateo.

Chris was six years older than I was, and had an unusual past that included extensive travel and a stint with the circus. He wasn't effeminate, but he didn't care if anyone knew he was gay. He's not the kind of person to try ingratiating himself, but I soon became very fond of him. I had a king-sized water bed that we both liked, so we started sleeping together, even though there were two bedrooms. We'd sit up late, watching T.V. I'd help him iron his clothes, and he'd help with mine. It was wonderful. We never were physical, but it was like being married. Chris would remain one of my closest friends.

Like my father, I lived with an ugly secret for many years. Unlike him, I have lived in shame and with the fear of being discovered. I knew that, should my secret become known, my life and the lives of my children would be damaged. One reason I waited so many months before I reported having witnessed Susan Nason's murder was my fear that my secret would be brought out if his crime went to trial. It was primarily to avoid this that I tried to go to the authorities anonymously.

Ultimately I realized that, in order to do the right thing for Susan, I had to stop worrying about my secret. While I have not regretted the decision to tell the truth about Susan's murder, this added humiliation has increased my sadness about the personal cost of justice.

In 1980, after living in Hawaii for several months, I returned to California and moved in with Chris. I got a job as a waitress in an Italian restaurant, and it turned out to be a great deal of fun. I liked the owners very much, joked with the cook, and flirted and partied with the bartender. Business, however, was slow and I made very little money. I worked as many hours as I could, and whatever of my pay that was not necessary for living expenses went for recreation, specifically cocaine.

I had used cocaine off and on during my first years on my own. By the time I became a waitress I was more deeply involved in it, and would probably be considered a habitual user. I made friends with some of the restaurant's regular customers, even did coke with a few. One older couple I became friendly with mentioned that they had a good friend who ran an escort service. They claimed that a girl like me could earn very good extra money working part-time as an escort. They told me that because of my looks, I would do well. They asked if I would like to meet their friend. I understood that *escort* was a euphemism for *prostitute*.

Given my small income, the expense of cocaine, and, in retrospect, my very low self-esteem at that time, I considered their proposition. I had already had a lot of experience with being manipulated into bed against my wishes, so I was not a stranger to loveless sex. Although I was still interested in men, my view of them had grown jaded. Since both parties were consenting in the escort game, I saw nothing wrong with it. I agreed to meet their friend.

One afternoon I went to the home of the older couple to meet a man I'll call Ray Black. He told me how successful his escort service was, and how much fun it was to work for, that most of the girls had regular jobs, but turned occasional tricks for extra money. Ray explained that I would not have to have sex with any customer I did not want to have sex with. He assured me that none of his girls had ever been hurt or killed. He explained that as a safety measure, telephone contact was always maintained when an escort was out on call. He insisted that he did not sleep with, beat, or rob his girls. He was not a pimp, he said, but a businessman.

Ray Black got his customers through advertisements in newspapers and the phone book. The girls were hired out on an hourly basis, for which he charged fifty dollars. Sex was not advertised, as that would be flagrantly illegal; the fifty dollars was merely an "introduction fee." Ray kept the majority of that money (to cover his expenses, of course). Any additional services were privately negotiated, and the girl kept the money. Ray Black knew that the escorts earned great "tips," because his wife was one of the escorts.

I decided to try working for Ray. While continuing my job at the restaurant, I started taking jobs. Most of the time the sex was numbing and boring. I felt like a disinterested observer watching the clock until the time was up. Occasionally customers were perverse or threatening, and then the situation was quite frightening.

One afternoon when I'd been working for Ray Black for six or seven weeks, I was asked to do a call at a motel in San Jose. This particular day I was in a rush because I had plans for the evening. I asked Ray to find someone else for the call, but he was in a bind, so I agreed to go. Because I wanted to get in and out of the motel room as quickly as possible, I was very careless in the way I handled myself.

I met the customer in the motel room. I was in a hurry, and disrobed as we negotiated the price. That was forbidden in the business. Since police usually don't like getting out of their clothes, you let the customer undress first. Once the man in the room and I had agreed on a price, the door slammed open, a man rushed in with a camera flashing away, and I was under arrest for prostitution.

I knew almost nothing about how our legal system worked. My mother was an attorney, but bringing her into this was out of the question. I was terrified of going to jail. I had no idea how bail worked, or even if I was eligible. I was terribly confused and frightened. I was apprehensive about a number of things in this kind of work, but had not anticipated this.

In the ride to the police station, my wrists were handcuffed behind my back. The police officer who had taken the pictures of me at the motel was driving, and he offered me a cigarette as we drove through San Jose. I asked him how he proposed that I smoke a cigarette with handcuffs on and my arms behind my back. He shrugged.

I was escorted to an inner office where the vice squad was housed. As I entered the office I was told to close my eyes to prevent my seeing any undercover agents. I remember thinking, "What an absurd security measure." Naturally, I peeked so that I wouldn't trip over the furniture. My cop-date proved to be an unpleasant individual. He was disappointed that I had no criminal record or outstanding warrants. He repeatedly asked me to tell him the aliases I had been arrested under. When I insisted that I had never before been arrested, he ignored my response and demanded that I provide the information he wanted.

After a while he left the office for a few minutes and

returned with a new accusation. I had previously been arrested, he told me, under the name *Elaine* Franklin, in San Francisco. No amount of denial by me could convince him I was not Elaine Franklin. I suggested that he compare our fingerprints, or do something to settle the matter. He left the room abruptly. Another officer later told me that Elaine Franklin was a black woman.

The arresting officer showed me a photograph of Ray Black and asked me to identify him as the man I worked for. I'd seen movies where people, especially prostitutes, ended up dead for identifying other criminals, so I was afraid. But I was not a good liar, so I said that I had met this man, but only once.

While they questioned me, my car was being searched, and a small amount of cocaine was found in a purse in the trunk. Now there were two charges against me: soliciting with the intent of prostitution, a misdemeanor, and possession of cocaine, a felony.

I was booked into Elmwood, the women's jail outside San Jose. My few hours behind bars were frightening and dehumanizing. A very masculine female prisoner with large tattoos on her arms stood in the doorway of the bathroom where I was strip-searched. She was supposed to be mopping the floor, but she was leaning against her mop, staring at me in the nude. The guard was slow, but after her search and a brief conversation, she told me, "You don't belong here." I almost cried because I knew that she was right. I swore to myself that I would give up cocaine and never be involved in prostitution again.

I realized that I needed an attorney, because I wanted to get out of jail—permanently. After calling several lawyers, I found one who claimed he could keep me from serving any time in jail, particularly since this was my first offense. Naturally he wanted a retainer, so I paid him half of his fifteen-hundred-dollar fee, with the other half due if the case went to trial several months later. This attorney attended one hearing with me, at which a second hearing was scheduled.

When the time for the second hearing arrived, he refused to attend without full payment. Since this was not what we had agreed on, and I did not have the money yet, I was in a terrible situation. To make things worse, he refused to refund the unused portion of the retainer money.

I was now without a lawyer and out several hundred dollars to a true criminal, my attorney. I knew that I could not hire another on my earnings as a waitress. As I grew desperate to find the money, I considered going back to work for Ray Black. When I called him he was impatient with my situation, telling me that criminal attorneys were notorious for robbing prostitutes. He assured me that I could come back to work for him any time. I was determined to get out of this in some other way than going back to prostitution.

In what seemed like a lucky break for me, a girlfriend suggested I speak with a criminal attorney who she knew socially. She said he was a really nice person and thought he would be financially reasonable. When I met attorney number two, he seemed knowledgeable and nice. He wanted a much smaller retainer, and agreed to let me pay off the balance of fees over time. I was relieved to have an attorney handling my case and thrilled that I could afford his fee, so I retained his legal services. As the court date neared, my attorney suggested that I have sex with him in order to ensure his appearance in court. I declined and was, once again, without an attorney.

I was clearly incapable of handling this problem on my own. Even if I could find an attorney who wasn't an SOB, I had no money to pay him or her. Admitting defeat and very ashamed, I called my Aunt Sue and asked her if I could come talk to her, that I was in deep trouble and needed help.

When I drove up to my aunt's house, I was extremely nervous. Aunt Sue was shocked when I revealed my situation to her. She gave me a wonderful lecture, unlike anything I'd ever heard. She told me that I needed to take responsibility for my life. She said that I must admit that most of the people in my life did not care about me, and advised me to break off contact with everyone who was a negative influence in my life. Our lives are made up of choices, she said, and my choices had been very bad.

For the first time I opened up and told my aunt of the terrible environment I had grown up in. I told her of the routine violence and fear. I confessed that my use of drugs was clearly out of control. I even blurted out how much I had always hated having red hair. So much of the advice she gave me would appear obvious to most people, yet I was light-years behind most people when it came to comprehending life. I had received so little guidance and attention from my parents that I was unprepared for adulthood and overwhelmed by it. I was twenty years old, yet I was starved for the type of guidance a parent would offer a teenager. For the first time I was getting it. I resolved to live my life responsibly, maturely, normally.

Once she was sure I wanted to change, Sue told me she knew a prominent criminal attorney. She contacted him and he agreed to oversee my case and have a junior associate represent me. He would let me pay off the fees by doing secretarial work. I was elated! Not only did I have a top attorney, an aunt to attend court with me, and arrangements for paying, but I felt as if someone actually cared how I came through this.

The junior associate was a brilliant woman who had recently become an attorney. The felony charge of possession of cocaine was dropped owing to an illegal search and seizure, which was a tremendous relief, since that charge carried the heaviest penalty. I pleaded guilty to solicitation, because I was guilty. A fine was imposed and I was released.

With my aunt's help, I cut back greatly on cocaine and all recreational drugs, and within a few weeks I stopped using drugs altogether. I will always be indebted to my Aunt Sue, not only for rescuing me from a nasty situation, but for making me see what a mess I was making of my life.

Eager as I was to start over, I now had this nasty, nagging secret. I found out that, if I lived five years without another criminal conviction, the record of my arrest could be legally sealed. I mentally clocked off the time, believing that when the five years had passed, my mistake would be wiped out.

For the time being, however, Eileen's arrest was the rude jolt she needed to stop her slide into depravity. She resolved to straighten herself out. She gave up cocaine, cut down on her partying, and found a job in the management office of a Foster City apartment complex. She occasionally made the bar rounds with Chris and pursued desultory romances with three men, all considerably older than she and all wealthy. ("I always thought Eileen had self-esteem problems," Bob Albright said years later, "because all the guys she dated were older and rich.")

To this coterie she added another lover, also middle-aged, Sam Nolde, who was even wealthier than the others and, to Eileen, a lot nicer. Nolde, whom she started dating only a week after her arrest, treated Eileen with the same kindness and consideration that had marked her platonic friendship with

John Dorick. For her, it was the first time one of her erotic involvements included, along with the fun and sex, tenderness and feeling. For Eileen, it was a new experience and a wonderful one.

Just when she believed that she was finally in love and had found the salvation from her self-destructive binge, Nolde told Eileen that he was not yet free of a previous involvement. He wanted to stop seeing Eileen until he had a chance to terminate the other relationship, and then he would return to her. To some of her friends it sounded suspiciously like a variation on the usual married-man put-offs—we must wait till the children are older, until my wife finishes her typing course, until Venus is in the ascendant.

Even if Nolde was sincere in his intentions, his cool announcement shattered Eileen, in that he had assured her that he was as committed to their affair as she was. To put her on hold so blithely made painfully clear his ability to walk away from their relationship, something she knew she could not have done. Eileen's period of exuberant promiscuity had given her some high good times, but it had not improved her opinion of the male character. The man she thought was different from the others began to look very much like them. On the evening of their last meeting, he gave her a necklace with four small diamonds. For all her feeling of abandonment and betrayal, she was deeply touched.

The apartment complex that Eileen worked for in Foster City in 1981 was, like a number of others recently built in the area, aimed at young, single people with good jobs and on their way up. In the fifteen years of its existence, Foster City had established itself solidly as a desirable place for families; more recently, developers had expanded their sights and had tried, with substantial success, to attract affluent young unmarried people as well.

On a regular basis the different apartment complexes organized social and sporting activities whose purpose was to introduce the residents to one another and to lure others to join the fun by buying a one-bedroom apartment for around $90,000. "It was great," one young condo owner said, "it was like living in a retirement community, but everyone was young. Kind of a Leisure Village for the BMW set."

A typical resident of the condo where Eileen worked was a computer programmer in his mid-thirties named Barry Lipsker.

Lipsker was an intense, personable fellow with a fiercely logical mind that he imposed on the world around him with a huckster's zeal. About five feet eight inches tall, and on the stocky side, Lipsker would be considered handsome by few, but he had the kind of agreeable looks that complemented his affable, outgoing manner. On meeting Barry, people tended to like him.

When he met Eileen, Lipsker immediately made his interest clear, and she was just as quick to discourage him. She was dating three men already, she said, and didn't need a fourth. If she needed three, he countered, none of them could be too wonderful. In the days after they met, Lipsker found endless reasons to phone or drop by the condo office. When he knew Eileen was going to be on duty alone there, he might suddenly appear with bagels and lox for two, or with two crystal wineglasses and a bottle of good Chardonnay. After a considerable time—she says it was months; he says "maybe a month or two" —she finally gave in and agreed to go out with him.

Compared with the men she was dating, Lipsker was not rich, but he seemed a lot more interested in her and attentive to her than they were. She had just turned twenty-one, however, and was not unimpressed by his obvious intelligence—always an admirable attribute to Eileen—his knowledge of the world, and his white Mercedes. But more than anything else, she was impressed by his dogged persistence.

She was pleased to see that they shared a sense of humor and enjoyed doing the same things. They became regulars at comedy clubs and attended the area's zany sporting events, which often included boating games that usually ended up with large groups of overstimulated singles falling screaming into the artificial lake. They enjoyed taking walks around Foster City's man-made charms, would take paddleboat rides and feed the ducks—they had a favorite duck that they named Seymour.

As she learned more about Barry, her interest grew. She was pleased to find he had a strong sense of right and wrong and never flinched from acting on it. Although Eileen's recent history would seem to deny it, she too had a strong ethical sense that occasionally moved her to audacious action, like the time she grabbed the phone from Bob Albright and blasted his mother for imposing guilt on him.

Barry had an altruistic streak, and had enrolled as a medical technician and worked as a volunteer fireman. He had once delivered a baby, and had on another occasion worked feverishly, though unsuccessfully, to resuscitate a child who had been hit by a car. Both Eileen and Barry dismissed the coincidence with her father's line of work, but neither of them considered the large numbers of men who do *not* get up in the middle of the night to rescue strangers in trouble.

Eileen was most drawn to a dogged, focused quality he projected, the kind of pigheaded determination he had aimed at her until she agreed to go out with him, but with Barry it came into play with everything he did. She was not accustomed to this sort of singleminded purposefulness in the men she had known. Possessing the trait to a degree herself, she liked it very much in him. She felt comforted and protected by his strength. Eileen and Barry were soon living together.

Barry Lipsker was born in Los Angeles in 1947, the son of Aaron Lipsker and his wife, whose first name, coincidentally, was Lea. When he was a child, his family moved to Billings, Montana, where his father bought a sporting-goods store and his parents became popular and active members of the city's sizable Jewish community and were energetic supporters of a number of artistic and charitable organizations. Barry and his younger brothers and sister grew up in a life of solid affluence, in a loving and supportive household.

When Barry was a teenager, a rival sporting-goods store opened in a shopping mall outside of town, and his father's business plummeted. Lucky to have found a buyer for the failing store, the Lipskers, in greatly reduced circumstances, moved back to the Los Angeles area. This financial calamity had a lasting effect on Barry. Aaron Lipsker invested his modest capital badly, and ended up taking a job selling life insurance to American soldiers stationed in England. The family found themselves living in a large eighteenth-century house outside Cambridge. His father hated his work, but Barry remembers this as a good period for him and his brothers and sister: "We had a big room for nothing but Monopoly."

Barry and his brother Scott formed a rock band and, after they moved to Europe, got jobs playing in Germany; then toured American bases in Vietnam. For several months Barry and his band traveled from base to base, playing to fervidly appreciative audiences and, in the bargain, enjoying themselves enormously as patriotic morale boosters, mini-celebrities, and civilian, free-agent bon vivants. After joining the Air Force, Barry met and fell in love with a German girl and got married.

During his military service he received extensive training in computers. After his discharge, he enrolled in Orange Coast Junior College on the GI Bill, and later transferred to California State University in Fullerton. After twelve years of marriage, he and his wife were finally divorced. They had no children.

Convinced that his future was in computers, he did everything possible in and out of school to advance his knowledge of this burgeoning field, and after graduating he did exceptionally well in various computer jobs. By the time Eileen met Barry in 1981, he was on course for a brilliant future in the field. Although he relished this sort of work, he had a strong nostalgia for the rollicking, footloose adventures with his rock band, which would remain the high point of his life, one from which, for all his subsequent success and wealth, he never quite recovered.

Although Eileen had straightened herself out considerably since her encounter with the law, she would later tell Barry that, had she not met him when she did, she would probably have been "either dead or in jail." An instinctive nag, he badgered her to give up partying and drinking. He so deplored her smoking that he promised to give her his Mercedes if she would quit. She promptly did.

Like many couples, when Eileen and Barry later ran into problems in their relationship, they overlooked entirely the many attributes they shared. Both were strong-willed, controlling people. Both had quick, logical minds and a no-nonsense approach to communicating that often included heated arguments. Both were compassionate toward others, including animals. Both had a strong sense of justice and hated to see people get away with things.

Eileen's family was unenthusiastic about Barry. Her friends were not much more supportive. After meeting Barry, Chris Lydon said to Eileen, "You left me for him?" Her gay friends had been hoping for a more spectacular match for her, especially after the richer, more dashing men she had been dating. Eileen did not feel herself to be in love with Barry, but his obsession with her and his forcefulness gave her a feeling of security that answered her needs. In 1982, at twenty-one, Eileen moved in with Barry, and her life changed completely.

SIX

Eileen

When I learned I was pregnant, I was thrilled. I didn't know how much of a future Barry and I had together—his efforts to ingratiate himself had dropped noticeably since we had been living together—but I knew I very much wanted a child. Externally at least, our life was picture-perfect. Barry was working in Silicon Valley, and we bought a pretty house with a pool in San Jose. I wasn't working, just concentrating on having the baby I had always wanted to have. Barry was anxious to become a father and was ready for it financially.

A great advantage of my new leisure and Barry's generosity was the chance to broaden myself. For the first time in my life, I traveled extensively—Europe and all over the United States. Barry was so smart, had a more cultured background than I did, and had such a broad range of knowledge, I was stimulated to keep up with him. I read eagerly—world affairs, child-rearing, geography, computers, and, because I felt I still needed polish, books on etiquette, which I would sometimes read two and three times.

Another positive change for me was that I began making friendships with women. I had never had many women friends, and think I may have had trouble along these lines because of my bad relationship with Leah. But now I was meeting some very nice women with whom I shared a major interest, motherhood. I was very pleased to be so readily accepted by them and I learned how supportive and strengthening good women friends can be.

When Jessica was born, most of my family weren't speaking to me. They were unhappy about my having a child out of wedlock, and by a Jew, that sort of thing. Even though I had given her her first grandchild, Leah wrote me a letter disowning me. My Aunt Sue came to the hospital and my grandparents wanted to come, but my grandmother was very sick with cancer. The rest of my family kept their distance. I was thrilled by Jessica's entry into the world, but I was also stung by my family's reaction.

I wanted someone to tell me how beautiful she was, what a great job I'd done delivering her without medication, how wonderful it was that I was breast-feeding her, how wise I was to read books on pregnancy, childbirth, and infant care. I wanted someone to acknowledge that I could be a wonderful mother. Like all mothers, I thought my daughter was the most incredibly beautiful baby the world had ever seen. I'd say that to Barry, and he'd say, "She looks like a baby." I wanted someone to fawn over Jessica and, at the same time, give me a pat on the back. That's why I was elated when my dad called and said, "I want to see my first grandchild."

I had not spoken with my father in several years. He had learned of Jessica's birth from family members, and he showed up with the most beautiful, tiny, lacy, green-and-red Christmas dress for Jessica. He held her and told me how pretty she was. I could see the pride in his face when he held my daughter. I felt as if he loved me and he loved her, which was what I needed.

He expressed pride that I had given birth without drugs. Patiently, and with a smile, he listened to me ramble on about the benefits of breast-feeding. He congratulated me on that, too. I told him that, although I loved him, I was not going to repeat the upbringing he had given us. I would never let anyone physically harm my child. I let him know how strongly I believed in gentle, caring child-rearing. He listened without comment. When I finished my speech, he told me he believed in my commitment.

A few days later he returned, bringing Sica a large red truck. "You don't want her to be too girly, do you?" he said. It was wonderful that he was so involved.

Barry had been pressuring me to marry him, and used the birth of a child as the final lever to get me to go through with it. A few weeks after Jessica's birth, Barry and I were married. The only member of my family to attend the ceremony was my father, who arrived with his girlfriend at the time,

Carolyn Mount, who would return to my life years later as Carolyn Adams.

Once we were married I began to feel that Barry saw me as a not-very-important possession. Communication was minimal, and our love life was perfunctory. He was nowhere near as involved with Sica as I was. His attention was taken up with his plan to start his own consulting business. His idea was to go into a company and design their entire computer operation, creating software that fit their requirements, recommending hardware he felt was needed. He would have a number of specialists on call to implement the plans and service the systems he devised. Having accurately anticipated a real need, Barry had, from the outset, more clients than he could handle, and his name began to become known in his field.

Of the various women friends I was making, one became particularly close. She was a married woman, slightly older than I was, named Sharon Nelson, who had a child about the same time I had Sica. We met when I volunteered to supply milk to a local charitable organization, the Mothers' Milk Bank, which Sharon had helped organize. Sharon saw me through my early marital problems with Barry, and would remain a devoted friend after I left San Jose. Years later, when I had become controversial, Sharon would tell anyone who would listen that I had a heart of gold. That's a friend.

I grew fond of Barry's parents, Aaron and Lea Lipsker, who had moved back to California. I also liked Barry's brothers, Scott and Lee. Lee was a psychologist, and I was particularly fond of his wife, Denise, who was a nuclear physicist. I made a concentrated effort to win my in-laws' approval, and taught myself to cook Jewish specialties like matzoh balls. I resolved to observe both the Christian and Jewish holidays in raising Sica, so that my daughter could decide for herself which religion to adopt when she was old enough. With my enthusiasm for my in-laws, as well as my natural instincts for mothering, I liked everything about my marriage, except the deteriorating relationship between Barry and me.

In viewing this strange marriage, it was natural for friends and relatives to consider the negative aspects—and conclude that it was as joyless as it was loveless. Actually, Barry and I had periods of relative tranquillity, even some good times.

It was not that I changed my negative feelings about him—certainly I never felt he had changed his attitude toward me—or that I came to believe that the good outweighed the bad. I was frozen into inaction, into making the best of my situation, for the same reason a lot of women are—a complete lack of alternatives.

Because things were not going well in my marriage I was delighted when my father reentered my life and we became as close as we had ever been. The new grandchild may have been the occasion of his first visits to San Jose, but I felt his affection for me was the reason he continued to visit. We both needed someone, and we enjoyed each other's company. I was thrilled to have my status as the favorite child reinstated; also, he filled a serious need for the mutual caring that I felt my marriage lacked.

By July of 1984, Barry's manner toward me had grown worse, and I decided I could not live with him another day, so I packed my things and fled with seven-month-old Jessica. Barry went on a rampage. For several days I refused to respond to his pleas, passed through my friends, to call him.

Finally, when Sharon Nelson urged me to contact Barry, I relented and telephoned him. If I didn't come home at once, he told me, he would divorce me and sue for the custody of Sica. He told me he had learned about my arrest. Devastated that he now knew my secret, I immediately returned home.

Barry got this information through one of those roundabout paths of communication that would become so common in my family in the difficult period to come. When my mother attended law school, she became friends with a student named Mike. In the evenings, Leah and Mike met to study their law courses. This led to eating occasional meals together. Leah was more than a decade older than Mike, but since losing her excess weight, she looked well—and not much older than he did. Just when their friendship seemed about to develop into something more, Mike met my sister Kate, and fell in love with her. Kate and Mike eventually married with my mother's good wishes. Barry and I saw a lot of Mike and Kate.

Aside from my aunts Sue and Jean the only member of my family who knew of my police record was Diana. On one occasion Diana and Mike drove alone to Jackson Hole, Wyoming, where his parents had a vacation home. They were on

their way to join Kate for a week of vacation. Diana later
denied vehemently that she had told Mike my secret. However he learned, Mike came away from the Wyoming trip
knowing about my stained history. Barry, when making his
frantic phone calls to track me down, naturally called Kate
and Mike. Mike told Barry about my past. I had never
worried about my vulnerability in this area, but I now realized it had been there all the time.

My blindness to this danger was not due so much to a
belief that Barry would never stoop so low to break me, but
to my not thinking of that part of my life at all. That had
been a different me. What did *her* mistake have to do with
anything? But of course, it really was *my* past, and it was now
in the open between us. It would always be there, a permanent shackle. I would do anything to keep Sica. He was Sica's
father. I was an unfit mother. Checkmate. Nothing had to be
said, I knew he had me.

Late in 1984, Barry, who now had clients up and down the
West Coast, decided that Los Angeles would be a better
place to base his business, so we moved to Manhattan Beach,
in the southern end of the city. About this time, my father
went through an alcohol recovery program, moved to Hawaii, then bought four condos there, which he managed. He
wrote me cheerful, upbeat cards and letters with an underlying current of loneliness:

                                                    8/1/85
Dearest Ylyn [phonetic spelling of Eileen],
    Woke early this A.M. wondering how/where you two are.
[Jessica and me. He had little use for Barry.] *I'm living a
day at a time doing what has to be done. I've been thinking
of you a lot lately, knowing you are very much my daughter
with many similar traits and I am happy the good traits are
winning out. Have been thinking a lot about the 11 western
states and am enthusiastic about working and playing with
you. About time we spent some time together.*

                                                Love, Dad

    Another reads:

*I was with a 42 year old granny last P.M. — tattoos and all
— and she was telling me about the unique relationship between her and her grandson, so different than being a parent.*

The one-generation removal adds an extra dimension to things. Sounds fun to me.

The picture is of a cartoon tiger cub hanging from a branch, with the caption, HANG IN THERE BABY—FRIDAY'S COMING. Another letter, dated July 11, 1985, had enclosed in it a card printed, GIVE ME A HUG. He had addressed one letter by using a rubber stamp he had made for a post-office box he had taken in Manhattan Beach. I had agreed to pick up and forward any mail that might come for him. More for convenience than secrecy, he used it to send his letters to me.

Hi Pooh and Pooh II, too.

Now that I have a real 100% genuine rubber stamp, just watch my bureaucratic mentality go ape-shit. Just a note to say I love you. Drop me a line and let me know you are OK. These are the times that try men and women's souls. Hang in there.

Love, Dad

Because I had commented on his rubber-stamp address, his next letter reads:

What do you mean my rubber stamp is tacky? The post office has just voted me a commendation because they can now read the address.

Eileen, I mailed to you an application for an AA convention in Las Vegas. I had not necessarily planned to attend it unless you chose to also. I had planned to attend the Honolulu conference instead. However, things have changed, eh? I do now want to attend the Las Vegas conference. So, if you will kindly decide if you want to attend with me as an Al-Anon, please send in application for me with remittance, etc. I trust your judgment. Enclosed is an envelope to mail and a stamped and addressed return envelope to immediately notify me as to the status of your decision. Let me know at that time the amount you sent and I shall send you a check to cover. I suggest you make copies of everything before mailing because after all, sweetie, you are dealing with a bunch of scatterbrained drunks. These conventions are really UP, so you may wish to attend, also know you will enjoy it. Jessica will also be OK there. Let me know.

Love, Pappy.

In another letter he enclosed an almost blank postcard. At the top he had written "Dear Mr. Wonderful," and at the bottom, "Love, Ylyn." In the space between, I was to have filled in a message and mailed the card back to him. The printed picture on the reverse is the words "I love you" repeated hundreds of times in different colors.

Several years later, in the months before I was to go into court to do battle with my father, I showed these letters to a friend and said, "See. You didn't think he loved me, did you?" My friend replied with amazement that after all I had been through because of him, I hadn't said instead, "You didn't think I could have loved him, did you?" My friend had a point.

With his letters, my father, aware that I was struggling to find a way to wrest financial independence from Barry— learn a profession or start a business—would often send me articles and brochures that contained ideas and messages of self-help inspiration. If I got divorced, he didn't want me to be a fish out of water. In one letter he wrote out a quote from the writer Paul McElroy that is a strong argument for people helping each other. It draws a parallel between humans who try accomplishing things alone, and a log trying to burn alone. It concludes: "Alone we may be as dying embers, but together we may set the world on fire." At the bottom of this, my father had written "AMEN!!"

A long letter from me to my father that was among the things he left with me sums up the sorry state of my marriage and concludes with me urging my father to visit.

Barry is sincere about going to counseling. OK, this sounds great, except that I've heard it a dozen times before. Barry plays by Barry's rules, which change as needed. Agreed? So I suggest (1) he sees who I say, such as someone who sees through his walls, and (2) that he see this person alone, and (3) that he shut up about the cost. After four sessions I will know which way to go. This is reasonable.

The counselor that I suggested read right through him before, and she does not believe in long-term counseling where short-term effective counseling is available. Wherever the marriage goes, I can handle it. Barry knows that he really has to prove his intentions, not with words, bribes, or BS.

There are some real good reasons to make my marriage work, but there are more reasons to give up. My guts are balanced—not afraid, not hopeful, not in dreamland. I have learned to see who I am, and I am not anyone's doormat or punching bag. I could leave today and do very well, but my guts are feeling secure. Cautious and secure. This all came about through prayer and talks. I can make it alone, but I can also wait a few weeks when I am making that choice as a strong, well woman. I love you.

Barry has now agreed to go to ACA. He thinks it's for me, but I think it will help him. Daddy, there are lots of things I need to see happening before this marriage is permanent. I know what I am looking for and I know when to walk away. There won't be a miraculous change in him overnight. If there is, it's faith, but I won't wait forever. I love you. Trust my judgment. My mistakes make me learn, just as forgiveness makes me grow. I'll try. I haven't looked back, but I'm watching closely. Pray for me to see God's will. Onward.

Your stuff [belongings he left with me] will be fine. I can settle things here for your belongings. You can stay with me in a serene environment here or a serene environment with me and Barry. No more battle zones. OK? You have a place in L.A. that welcomes you with open arms, open hearts and peace. Whether Barry's in the picture or not, I won't settle for less than peace, respect and serenity. OK? MAYBE YOU COULD QUIT SMOKING. NO PUSH, JUST A LOVING SUGGESTION.

Another letter from me:

If Barry and I stay together, we'll be buying a home soon with a room for you. I thought you wouldn't mind staying with us, if it's peaceful. Trust me. I love you. Pooh to you.

The letters show that in 1984 and 1985 I was looking to my father to provide the emotional anchor that was missing from my life. Although he had had a series of girlfriends in the years since leaving my mother, living with a number of them, he now was alone and was turning to me to fill the same gap I tried to fill with him. The bond that had always been there throughout my childhood and that, in those turbulent years, then had been twisted and periodically shattered because of his drunken rages, was now, with his quitting drinking, coming through with a fresh intensity. I was almost twenty-five and he was, at last, loving me as a father should.

One incident with my father jarred the closeness that had returned to our relationship. Visiting me in San Jose one day, he was playing with Sica in the living room as he chatted with me. Leaving the room for a moment, I returned to find my father holding my daughter on the coffee table in front of him, carefully scrutinizing her sexual organs, pushing the labia open with his finger. I was stunned. "What are you doing?" was all I could say.

"Can't I admire my beautiful granddaughter if I want to?" he asked, and quickly began talking of something else. I said nothing more, but for days the incident bothered me.

Another thing occurred during this period that I forgot about until several years after I knew enough to understand it. One day when my father and I were talking I began thinking about Susan Nason. "Why is it," I asked him, "when Susie died, I was not allowed to go to her funeral? I was her best friend, but no one paid any attention to me. Why?"

He switched to his own reminiscences of Susan. "Do you remember how much Susie liked me? How she used to love to play with me? She'd climb on me, try to tickle me. I'd tickle her. She loved that."

I felt the room starting to spin, then I became dizzy. I had no idea why I was having such a strong reaction; I knew only that the conversation had to end immediately, and that I had to escape. "I just remembered," I mumbled, "I forgot to buy milk when I was at the store." I rushed out the door, knowing that if I didn't get to my car quickly, I would faint.

SEVEN

WHILE EILEEN'S MARRIAGE WITH BARRY SETTLED INTO A DISPIR-
ited but ever more affluent routine, Janice Franklin, who had
also turned out to be stunning, had been enjoying her freedom
from "Auschwitz" with a series of love affairs. Even though she
had a near-genius-level IQ, she had shown no strong career
inclinations and had moved through a number of indifferent
jobs. Traces of her bruised childhood were discernible in her
high-strung, sensitive nature, but her good looks and outgoing
nature made it easy for her to attract friends and lovers.

She thought often of Susan Nason's murder and always
dreaded driving over Route 92, not so much because it had been
the murder site, but more because it passed Susan's grave at
Skylawn Cemetery. Ever since she was a child she felt a fear of
the cemetery and believed if she entered it, the whole story
would be revealed to her. Yet the idea of entering the grounds
filled her with fear. Even driving by the entrance made her
anxious.

In 1984, when Janice had not seen her father in several years,
he turned up one day and took her out for lunch. While walking
away from the restaurant, Janice suddenly had a strong sense
that her father had murdered Susan. The feeling was not based
on anything said at lunch; she thinks it may have been nothing
more than an intuition arising from her knowledge of his violence, his sexual ruthlessness, and her memory of her father's
odd behavior on the night Susan disappeared.

At the time, Janice was sharing an apartment in the Peninsula community of San Carlos with a friend named Mary Hartford. One evening the two young women were discussing their
backgrounds, and Janice told Mary the story of Susan Nason's
murder. Janice then added that she believed her father was the

murderer. When Mary expressed amazement, Janice went on to describe his history of violence, his strange greeting to her the evening Susan disappeared, and his kicking her when she went to answer the police's questions.

Mary was amazed that her roommate might hold the key to the famous unsolved mystery. She urged Janice to go to the police, but Janice was terrified of the idea. A friend of Mary Hartford's was married to a San Carlos police officer, Bruce Potts. Mary contacted Potts and told him that her roommate had information concerning an unsolved homicide, but was fearful of coming forward. Mary suggested that if Potts dropped by casually one evening and met Janice and put her at ease, she might tell him her story. He agreed.

When Potts showed up, Janice was reading in her bedroom. After chatting with him for a while, Mary went to Janice and told her who was visiting in the living room. Mary emphasized that he was a sympathetic friend and urged Janice to come out to meet him, if only to size him up. If Janice felt comfortable with Potts, she could tell him what she knew about Susan Nason's murder. Janice met him and, after speaking with him for a while, decided to make her accusation.

When Potts heard everything she had to say, he knew that Janice's story was not sufficient for an arrest, but he felt her information was certainly significant enough to justify reopening the investigation, this time targeting George Franklin. Perhaps, he thought, other members of the Franklin family could add to what Janice had told him. Potts also realized, however, that the crime had been committed outside his jurisdiction, so he asked Janice's permission to pass her information along to the proper authorities, the Investigative Unit of the Foster City police. Emboldened by Potts's supportive reaction, Janice said to go ahead.

Very soon after this meeting, Janice received a call from a Sergeant Richie of the Foster City Police Department, who had been told she had some information on a homicide and wanted to take a statement from her. When they met, Richie made clear from the outset that he was skeptical. How did Janice know her father had committed the murder? Just a hunch? They couldn't take action on hunches, he said. When he questioned her, he zeroed in on the time she had seen her father on the afternoon of the killing. Janice wasn't sure. Had she seen him at 3:00 P.M.? No. At three-thirty? She didn't think so. At four? Maybe.

Richie had apparently briefed himself on the known details

of the crime, and it was equally obvious that Janice had not. When she hesitatingly said that she may have seen her father at four, Richie dismissed Janice's accusation, since Susan had been seen by her mother around three-fifteen. Forty-five minutes was not enough time for George Franklin to have picked up Susan, driven the twenty minutes to the spot on Route 92 where she was found, and returned home to Harvester Drive in time to encounter Janice at four.

Potts, who sat in on the meeting between Janice and Richie, later said he felt Richie had been predisposed to reject Janice as having any relevant evidence to bring to the case. Potts also felt Richie's line of questioning about the time she had seen her father had been improperly conducted. Instead of throwing out times to her, Potts said, he should have simply asked her what time she had seen her father. His questions "led" her to making a statement about which she was far from certain. "I could see," Potts said, "he had kissed off the whole thing before he finished the interview."

That was the end of Janice's attempt to bring her father to justice, and for almost two years thereafter she never told any members of her family what she had done.

Ambivalence toward the abuser, which is common among abuse victims, ran high among the Franklins. Eileen could live with, and even have good times with, a man she believed would not hesitate to blackmail her into staying with him. Janice could spend a day at the beach pouring out to a friend a catalog of Leah's misdemeanors as a mother, then, the same evening, finish a phone conversation with Leah by saying, "Love ya." In years to come, George junior would testify in the defense of a father he avoided and had not spoken to in many years.

Such contradictory relationships help to explain Janice's offering to house her father when he returned from Hawaii not long after she had told the police she believed him to be a murderer. If Janice was willing to put out of her mind not only suspicions of past crimes, against Susan Nason but also against herself and her siblings, she was not able to forgive his behavior while in her apartment when he made a number of physical advances to her.

Janice gave up trying to analyze her father's strange behavior toward her; she knew only that it disgusted her. Shortly after these two incidents, Janice was driving with her father, and she noticed him staring at a little girl who was standing close by on the sidewalk as they waited for a traffic light to change. On an impulse, Janice said as naturally as possible, "Aren't little girls sexy? Don't they have the sexiest little bodies?"

Her father looked at her in surprise, then agreed enthusiastically. As if delighted to have someone to whom he could speak frankly, he added some observations of his own, which Janice later forgot. It didn't matter. In her mind she had heard and remembered enough. She believed she had tricked him into admitting what a monster he was, that he had a taste for molesting little girls, and that he had probably molested Susan, then murdered her. For Janice Franklin, all of the courtroom proceedings that followed in the years to come were superfluous. She had caught her father, tried him, and convicted him. She now knew he was a dangerous man, but, having already gone to the police, she was at a loss what to do about it.

An opportunity soon arose. Eileen and Barry had been fighting more than usual, and once again Eileen's desperation had reached the point where she had to escape, regardless of consequences. When Barry left for work one morning, Eileen drove to the bank and withdrew half their balance. Upon returning home, she packed up herself and Sica. She hadn't decided where she was going, just *that* she was going. The front doorbell rang. She opened it to see her father. He was on his way to Las Vegas, he said, and he had stopped by to see his daughter and granddaughter.

Stunned by the propitious timing, Eileen asked him if he would take her and Sica with him. She explained her situation, and he said he would be delighted to provide the means of escape. He had been given the use of a condo in Las Vegas, and there was plenty of room for them all. In the state of confusion and desperation that Eileen always felt when she had to break away, her father's turning up at that precise moment seemed like divine intervention. Franklin loaded Eileen and Jessica into his van and they set out for Las Vegas.

Whenever Eileen left Barry, he took to the telephones, and shock waves roiled the entire Franklin family. Inevitably, when communications ran at feverish heights, new information was added to the family data base. On the occasion of Eileen's flight to Las Vegas, Barry learned something that would have just as far-reaching ramifications as the discovery of Eileen's arrest. Janice, who was still wrestling with her confirmation of George Franklin's attraction to little girls, was genuinely alarmed when she heard that Eileen had gone to Las Vegas with him, had taken the infant Jessica, and that they were all staying in one apartment. This meant that if Eileen went out on an errand, Franklin would be alone with his granddaughter.

Not knowing how to reach Eileen and frantic to tell someone, Janice phoned Barry and blurted out what was now her conviction about her father's sexual taste and Jessica's danger. To substantiate her strong accusation, she told Barry of incidents of the sexual abuse she had suffered from her father. Up to that time, Barry had known nothing of this. Already in a state of high emotion because of Eileen's defection, Barry, when he learned that his infant daughter was in the hands of a child molester, became hysterical.

In so much of the saga that would unfold in the next few years, a major factor governing Barry's actions, actions many people found overly aggressive if not berserk, was his genuine fear for his daughter and, later, for Eileen and himself. While others were trying to comprehend the unwieldy ramifications of Eileen's accusations against her father, Barry remained focused on the fact that there was a dangerous man at large who had a number of reasons to target him and his family. At the moment, the man was in possession of Barry's daughter.

While his distress was obviously sincere, Barry could now flaunt his usual frenzy to get his wife back as a moral crusade. This time his exertions were not aimed at repairing a damaged ego, apprehending an AWOL housekeeper, or recapturing a missed bed partner, but rather at rescuing loved ones in peril. Barry had already shown that he could play tough when thwarted; he now enlisted the most expensive professionals to play tough for him. He retained the noted attorney Marvin Mitchelson to file charges against Eileen for taking half of their money, which was in a corporate account and thus was not hers to take, and for transporting Sica across a state line. Eileen had not realized that either action was against the law, so she quickly sent up the white flag. When she agreed to return, Barry had Mitchelson drop the charges.

Eileen

Once Barry and I were back together he issued an edict: George Franklin was not to be allowed around Sica ever again. Disturbed by Janice's new information, I agreed.

A week or so after I learned about my father's abnormalities, our front doorbell rang. I was home alone with Jessica and had just washed my hair and wrapped it in a towel. I opened the door to see my father standing before me. He was beaming, ready for a grandfatherly visit. With my voice very steady, I told him he could not come in, that we did not want him visiting anymore. He looked stunned, then, without a word, turned and walked back to his van.

On October 7, 1986, I gave birth to a son. Barry and I wanted to name him after his father, Aaron. Although Barry was excited about the birth of a son, the problems that I believed undermined our marriage were still in place. They were merely pushed aside by more immediate demands on our attention, primarily our new baby, and our daughter who was about to turn three.

About this time, Janice and I fell into a conversation about our father. On an impulse, Janice broke her silence and spoke of having told the police her suspicions about his having murdered Susan Nason. I asked Janice what evidence she had. When she said she didn't really have anything definite, I scoffed at the idea, and it was not mentioned between us again.

When Barry became exasperated with the growing amount of time he spent on the Los Angeles freeways each day, he decided we should move to Canoga Park, one of the newer suburbs in the San Fernando Valley. Canoga Park was predominantly a middle-class grid of attractive homes, punctuated with an occasional church, shopping mall, or landscaped office complex. The straight, flat streets were broad and flower-lined, and had views of the Santa Monica Mountains to the south and the San Gabriel Mountains to the north.

The house was a two-story ranch-style building at the end of a cul-de-sac street, which meant little danger from traffic. Across the back of the house was a long, open space—the kitchen to the left, dining area in the middle, then a large family room with a fireplace and sliding doors opening onto a walled patio, much of which was taken up with a kidney-shaped pool. As Barry's business kept growing, I became more and more involved. He trained me in various aspects, including the tricky contract negotiations with new clients. I found enormous satisfaction in raising my children.

I was determined not to turn out like my parents. All the

time I was growing up, they complained about us constantly; there was never a letup from the harangues and blame. In my naïveté, I came to accept what they said, that we five children had driven them to their extreme behavior. Hearing this so often, I became convinced that, prior to giving birth to us, Leah DeBernardi and George Franklin were both wonderful, happy, fulfilled people. I believed that the arrival of five children had ruined their lives.

When I became a mother, I swore that I would not be like them. I decided that at any time I was uncertain how to handle one of my children, I would figure out what my parents would have done, then I would do something different, if not the complete opposite. What I have tried to do with my children is nurture them. As a child I wanted so badly to be important to someone, to be loved and nurtured.

My children have known where to come for a kiss, a hug, a story, or a warm bed on a scary or rainy night. In return, my children have let me into their childhoods, not just as their parent, but as one sharing their experience. They have allowed me to transcend time and stand beside them as their equal when they are playing, or pursuing new adventures. Although they don't know it, they have given me my first glimpse of a childhood without terrifying night rages, severe physical abuse, humiliating verbal abuse, and outright don't-give-a-damn neglect. Raising my children has allowed me to have the childhood I so passionately desired when I was their age. I feel indebted to my children for allowing me the pleasure of their childhoods.

Barry shared my passion for our kids. We took them on frequent expeditions—rock climbing, pony rides, train rides, animal farms. He taught them songs from his band days and was energetic about educating them in practical skills. He encouraged me to enroll the children in a variety of classes—swimming, gymnastics, tae kwon do—anything Southern California could dream up for children. His thoughtfulness and affection for Aaron and Sica was one of the things I most admired about him. Still, I knew there were underlying problems between him and me.

Throughout this period we saw a number of marriage counselors. As usual, Barry didn't see that we had a problem, but sometimes, when he was also feeling optimistic about the marriage, he would agree to attend a session. Invariably, after a couple of sessions he would make an excuse and not go. Undaunted, I plugged on alone with the therapists.

I knew I had developed into some kind of responsible adult, but with my subjugation to Barry's wants and needs, I had no idea what sort of person might emerge if I finally broke free, if I ceased being an extension of Barry's will and lived for myself and my children. In my late teens, when I had done that, it had gotten me in serious trouble. That was six years ago. I was a very different person now, but what sort of person? Without Barry, who would I be?

Late in 1988, a recollection came to me that shocked and distressed me. I was very young, around six, and I was saying good night to my father at bedtime. Suddenly he penetrated me with his finger. I tried to shake off the repulsive image.

I knew he had done things to some of my sisters, but until this moment, I had no memory of his doing anything sexual to me. In fact, I was quite certain he had not, believing that my status as his favorite had spared me. But this memory of being molested was clear and unequivocal.

PART TWO

Memory and Decision

EIGHT

Eileen

If, as I believe, the return of my repressed memories was part of an evolutionary process, then I think I would place the beginning at my ten-year high school reunion, in September 1988. Since I had not been popular with my classmates, I had mixed feelings about going, but decided I would. I was proud of the changes in myself and in my life that had come about since high school. It is possible that going to the reunion and, from the safe distance of my present life, seeing the faces of Foster City classmates, stirred my deepest memories and allowed them to start their climb to the surface. It was not long after the reunion that I had my first recollection of being molested by my father.

The next step in the process may have been a miscarriage I had about two months later. I was shattered, and couldn't believe it when Barry said he was relieved I had miscarried, because he did not want more children. My mother-in-law, instead of expressing sympathy, was hurt that I had never told her I was pregnant. When I told my mother, she seemed distracted and reminded me that I already had two kids. Everyone I reached out to for compassion had plenty to say, but no sympathy. Although I did not make the connection at the time, my feelings of aloneness were similar to my feelings when Susan died when no one acknowledged my loss or my right to feel pain. Subconsciously, the similar emotions may have brought Susan closer to the surface.

In December 1988 I filed for divorce from Barry. For some time I had felt this was inevitable, but after his callous reaction to my miscarriage, I was certain the time had come. I did not know exactly how he would react, but the one thing I did not expect was that our relationship would improve once divorce papers were served. We had some long talks, and I agreed to postpone the divorce until Barry had given marriage counseling another try. He promised to begin in several weeks, as soon as he completed a major computer project. This time, he assured me, he would stick with the counseling.

As 1989 began, things got a lot better between us, and I was beginning to think my marriage could be saved. Daniela, my children's nanny, had recently joined our family. I had never had a helper I liked so well. Jessica was five, Aaron two, and they were beginning to play games with each other. Barry was working extremely long hours on the computer system at the *Los Angeles Times,* but was exhilarated to be at the helm of an important project. The biggest threat to my peace of mind was the fifteen pounds I had put on during the pregnancy, and that would not come off. I suspected this was a result of the shock and depression I felt after the miscarriage. And then the memory returned.

When, that January afternoon, I remembered seeing my father murder Susan, the floor seemed to collapse, my gravitational center careened wildly. My immediate reaction was to summon forth all the denial in my being and inwardly shout *No!* No, no, no—it was the sole reaction my brain could muster. I felt terrified and confused. I didn't want this recollection. I wanted it to go away, or melt into a dream. But all my power of will was pitiful against the force of the scene that had reentered my mind. It was out, released, disgorged. It was with me. It would always be with me.

Even when the memory itself passed, I was still gripped by terror. It wasn't the dread of some imminent danger, but rather a wrenching sense of an all-enveloping, uncontrollable evil. It was also the terror of knowing something I should not know, the kind of unwanted and forbidden knowledge from which you can never retreat, that you can never shed. You can only hope no one discovers that you know it.

I remember setting Aaron on the sofa after he finished his bottle, then getting up and going into the kitchen and putting his bottle in the sink. For a few moments I stood there steadying myself, clutching the counter, trying to gather my thoughts. I felt terribly claustrophobic, and told myself there was no logical reason to remember this. I thought I must be going crazy.

"If I go crazy, who will take care of the kids?" I thought. "My God, I don't want to lose my kids!"

I grew determined to make the memory of Susan's murder go away, to force it back wherever it had come from, but had no idea how. I was reeling from a profound shock, and it would be many days before I would be able to think about what I should do with the terrible information that had crashed in on me. For the moment, trying to assimilate it into my own consciousness, my own store of knowledge, finding a place to put it, took all the strength and determination I possessed.

The most painful aspects of my memory involved sound. When I first remembered Susie saying, "No, don't!" when my father was on top of her, those words would torment me for many days. The sound of him digging, striking his trencher into the hard, gravely ground confused me; I could never figure out what he had been digging. I remember the exact sound of my father saying, "God damn it Eileen," which was doubly frightening because he almost never called me Eileen.

I tried to avoid the memory by keeping busy—frantically running errands, walking on my exercise treadmill, involving myself more with my children. I also overate. But inevitably a quiet moment would come and just as inevitably I would have thoughts of the memory, which, in spite of my efforts to push it away, had grown; more pieces continued to surface.

Everything pointed toward keeping this to myself, probably forever. I would have to struggle with it alone. As this thought penetrated, I felt gripped by the agonizing loneliness of someone who has committed a terrible crime. An important element of my life, perhaps the most important, might never be known. If I was forced to smother such overwhelming information, it would be as if I, not my father, had murdered Susan.

During the next few days I stumbled through the routines of the young Canoga Park wife and mother as if microchip controlled. At night, as I tried to sleep, I would envision the terrible scene. In the morning, it would be my first thought. As the days became weeks, the awareness of what I had seen settled in and became a permanent part of my being—a constant, indelible pain, like the awareness of an incurable illness.

Gradually, I thought more and more about telling the police, but then asked myself what would be the point. It happened too long ago. It would probably be my word against his. And did I really want my father to go to jail for the rest of his life? Then, too, everything was going right with me and Barry. The last thing I wanted to inject into my marriage was a question about my sanity. In addition to giving Barry cause to worry about me, I was a little concerned that he might use it against me.

I had to admit an even graver fear. I was afraid of my father. What if he was accused, learned I was the accuser, and was then released? I was not naïve about the criminal-justice system. You only had to watch a little television to get an education in the system's technicalities, loopholes, and legal tricks—all the devices for getting guilty people acquitted. If my father should get off, would he then come after me and my children? He had threatened me at the time of the murder, and so far I believed I was alive because my mind had kept me silent.

I began to be plagued with thoughts of the Nasons. How they must have suffered for twenty years! I should bring out my information, if only for their sake. I wanted to tell the Nasons and let them decide what I should do. But that thought also made me hesitate for the same reason I had rejected other people I might have confided in: once I told them, they would want to inform the police. I would no longer have anything to say about any of it and I knew it was my life that would be ripped apart. More and more, I began to see my only option was to keep the discovery to myself.

For several months before my recollection, I had been seeing a therapist, Katherine Rieder, to work on issues relating to adult children of alcoholics and to determine the underlying cause of my marital problems. In the course of our talks, Rieder induced me to discuss my childhood. We discussed the alcoholism and abuse in my home. I also spoke of my best friend having been murdered. At one point in our talks, I mentioned the brief episode of having been sexually abused. She saw nothing strange about my not having thought of this for years and we passed quickly on to other topics.

In one session with Katherine, I was speaking of the embarrassment I had felt as a child concerning the squalor of our home. I told of the piles of dirty laundry, of having to put bad-smelling socks on each morning. When I said this, Rieder put her hand to her mouth and made an exclamation of what I took to be disgust. Talking about such humiliating matters with a person I trusted but did not know well had been difficult for me. For Rieder to react with disgust was mortifying to me. I later realized Rieder's reaction was probably an attempt to show sympathy for what I had endured, but I was feeling so sensitive and vulnerable, I took it as revulsion and decided she was not the therapist for me.

I've always had great difficulty disappointing or wounding others. For weeks I pondered how to sever my connection with Rieder. What was the protocol for quitting one therapist and taking another? Did you just stop going? Were you obliged to explain why you wanted to leave? I ruled that out in this case; it would be too embarrassing to bring up the smelly socks again. I would think of something.

In the meantime, Barry and I had started marriage counseling with another therapist, a man named Kirk Barrett, who had been recommended by a friend of mine. Kirk was a mild-mannered and handsome man in his late forties, with a sincere voice and a gentle manner. I soon felt completely at ease with him. Barry began skipping our appointments, but I continued going to Kirk and soon developed a trusting relationship.

For a while, I went through the motions of continuing to visit Rieder. When, months later in court, I was badgered about my failure to tell her about my recollection of Susan Nason's murder, the defense attorneys might have had less trouble accepting this omission if they knew how much difficulty I had in telling Katherine something as routine as my desire to discontinue our counseling relationship.

In the months after the memory returned, I gained more than thirty pounds. I now know it was from the turmoil I felt about the memories, and the horrible fear that there might be more. In May, Barry and I took a short vacation to the Club Mediterranee in Ixtapa, Mexico. I was miserable being so fat at a beach resort, but far more upsetting was that I thought about the damned murder every day. No matter where I was or what I was doing, my mind went to Susan Nason and my father. Murder, murder, murder—I prayed to God that it would go away.

One day I went into Zihuatanejo to shop. In an art gallery I saw a picture of white flowers on a blue field. As I looked at the peaceful scene, the horrible memories came spilling in. I nearly burst into tears because I was so confused and scared. I bought the daisy picture. I thought maybe in some way it might help make the memories go away. Desperate woman, desperate measures.

Barry and I made friends with some other couples and socialized with them. When we got together for a meal or a drink, I thought, "If these people knew what was going through my mind, they would think I was crazy and never come near me."

I felt as though I were being punished by life. I was afraid of the memories. I was still afraid they were signs I was going crazy. I had to pretend that I was normal in order to exist, because I knew this memory stuff was not normal. I was overwhelmed by the pressure of pretending that the memory didn't exist. I thought, if I am going crazy, maybe I should just do it and get it over with. I felt as if I were living dishonestly, and I hated that.

After I had been seeing Kirk Barrett for about three months I began considering telling him about my memory of Susan's murder. The more I had come to know him and felt his compassion for my tormented childhood—and also saw the caring yet professional way he listened to my horrible scenes from my past, the more the idea grew in me that if I was ever to tell anyone, it would be him.

Even with my growing trust in Kirk, it was not until June that I finally decided to tell my story. Was it possible, I first asked him, to have a memory of something important that you had not remembered before? He assured me that it was. I then asked what his legal obligations were if the memory involved a crime. What were the rules governing this sort of revelation? He told me that, as my therapist, he could keep anything I told him confidential. My final question showed my fear of being thought crazy. If I told him my secret, would he promise to believe me?

My main motive in telling Kirk was to learn if it was possible to forget such a powerful event. I also wanted his help in dealing with the memory, perhaps reducing its hold over me. As I told him the story, I began to cry and couldn't stop until I finished. As I expected, Kirk was soothing and understanding. He told me that now that I'd brought the memory into my consciousness, it could no longer hurt me. He urged me to believe that I had made a sizable step toward psychic health.

After pouring out all my thoughts about the murder, I felt the weight of this knowledge lighten. It still caused constant pain and anxiety, but the simple act of telling another person made it no longer my own private torment. It was now a fact and, however horrible, it was not now mine alone. I had also come through the dreaded ordeal without seeing my two biggest fears materialize: Kirk did not think me crazy, and he did not promptly call the police. My relief was enormous. I had spoken out—and the whole ugly business was still controllable.

A few weeks later, I was rocked by another memory. I suddenly saw myself in a strange house with my father and another man. I was about eight or nine. I was on something like a table. My father was holding down my left shoulder with one hand, his other hand over my mouth. I saw the face of a black man. I heard laughing. I felt a horrible, searing pain in my lower body. I tried to scream but couldn't because of my father's hand. Now in the present, I could still feel that pain. It was unendurable. I had believed that the worst memories buried inside me had come out. I was not to be so lucky.

As time went by, I felt more certain that I should take legal action about Susan's murder. But I needed help in figuring out how to go about this. I decided that I would tell Kate about my memory and ask her advice, since she was the eldest of my siblings. I invited her to visit. When she accepted, I arranged for her plane ticket. I told her that there were some things about our childhood I needed to discuss. She replied that there were things that she would like to discuss with me as well.

Kate arrived in Canoga Park and stayed a few days. After

our long estrangement, I was delighted to see her. Each time I brought up our childhood, however, she dismissed the subject impatiently, saying that our parents had done the best they could. I was surprised at the thought, and even more surprised at the number of times she said it. I didn't see how Kate or anyone else could believe that sexual and physical abuse was part of the best-our-parents-could-do category. I could see that Kate had changed her mind about having things to discuss with me. Kate was obviously not the one to tell.

As I got closer to deciding to go to the police, I still had many reasons for not going. I did not want to disrupt the lives of my family by being publicly identified. I did not want my father to feel that I had betrayed his confidence, though I naïvely believed that if he was arrested, he would confess. I was afraid that everyone would think I was insane and I would lose my children. I was concerned that the police would mishandle the investigation and that my father would remain free and seek revenge. I had little confidence that the police-firefighter brotherhood bond would make for a fair investigation or prosecution. And what about my arrest? Was I ready to expose my past?

I had so many conflicting feelings about going forward. But each day when I looked into the faces of Jessica and Aaron, I knew that I had my children and that the Nasons did not have Susan. This made me feel guilty and partly responsible for the Nasons' pain. It was my fault that the murder had never been solved.

When George junior came to visit me in August, I had no intention of discussing the murder with him. I was overwhelmed with the memories and with trying to decide what to do, but I did not want to involve him. He had just lost his job, and I hoped that some home-cooked meals and a change of scenery would brighten his mood. George and I had a great visit together. He could make me laugh harder and think more deeply than anyone else.

George, who did not resemble any of his sisters, had grown into a good-looking young man—six feet tall, with light, curly hair and a broad face, he also had a genius-level IQ. He was fun to be around, and all of us enjoyed his cynical sense of humor and his sharp tongue.

I felt that George junior had suffered the most at our father's hands, certainly in terms of physical abuse. Although George had avoided seeing our father for years, his fear of him was so great, he told me, he had slept with a baseball bat under his bed. He also told me he would not put his name on the mailbox of his apartment so that our father could not find him.

One evening during his visit, George and I were chatting in the kitchen as I was warming up the popcorn popper. I decided to tell him what I had witnessed. His initial reaction was shock; his mouth dropped open and he backed away from me as if recoiling from something repugnant. His reaction brought to the surface all my fears of being considered insane. In a moment of panic and stupidity, I asked him what he would think if I told him I had been hypnotized, and that had caused the memories to return.

The word *hypnosis,* which I uttered in desperate reaction to my brother's disbelief and the look on his face that suggested he thought I had lost my mind, would haunt me. In the preliminary hearing it would be the central issue, since California does not admit testimony derived from hypnosis. Such legal considerations, however, were the farthest thing from my mind at that time, and my grasping at hypnosis as a prop to believability was a major mistake, one that came very close to relieving my father from ever standing trial.

George, whom I considered very well read and wise on a variety of subjects, accepted the hypnosis statement and went on to say how credible he thought hypnosis was. He compared the human mind to an onion that could be peeled back to uncover hidden layers. Upset as he was at first, he did not reject the idea that our father might be a murderer.

I felt very unsettled after our conversation. I did not know which bothered me more, that I had lied to him, or that my secret was no longer a secret in our family. He asked me what I was planning to do about my memory. I told him that I was not going to do anything, which was the truth at that time.

George's initial reaction to my disclosure confirmed my greatest fears. If my own brother was going to back away from me in shock or disgust, how would the police react? Logically, I became more certain that I should not pursue a resolution to Susan's murder. But emotionally I felt guilty and loathsome for not going to the authorities.

I later learned that George had said to others that I believed I had seen the murder, but it was a delusion, adding that "the mind is a powerful instrument and can play strange tricks." If he said this, he was ignoring the possibility that his own powerful mind might have been trickily attempting to reconcile his complex feelings toward our father and me, or, even more likely, attempting to reconcile his revulsion at finding himself the son of a murderer with his revulsion at having a sister who would lie about something so important.

In the months to come when George junior spoke to the authorities, he presented them with a new theory. If our father had really murdered Susan, he said, he would have waited a few months until the whole thing "blew over," then murdered *me* to ensure my silence. For all of George's high IQ, I would grow more and more amazed at how illogically he seemed to be struggling to dismiss my recollection.

Every day I felt more horrible about the murder. I decided that I would discuss it with my mother. If she could remember my changing after Susan's murder, she would be more apt to accept the truth. I phoned and asked if she could remember changes in me at that time. This seemed like an innocuous question; surely any child would change if her best friend was murdered, whether she had witnessed the murder or not. My mother told me that she remembered changes in Diana, but could not remember my changing at all. I was astonished. She told me that my father had changed and become more distant and violent. She said she would look through the family photographs. This might help jog her memory.

The next time I spoke with her, she said she still could remember no change in me. Later in the conversation, I finally told her that I had been present when Susan was murdered by Dad. She was shocked and exclaimed, "No!" so vehemently that I immediately started arguing with her that, yes, it had happened that way.

She explained that her exclamation had not been from disbelief, but rather from horror at what I had witnessed. I told her I was trying to decide what to do about it legally. She said that she would stand behind me one hundred per cent, whatever I decided to do. She promised me that she would not discuss my memory with anyone for any reason, and we ended the conversation. In a phone conversation a day or two later, my mother startled me by saying that for a long time she had suspected my father of murdering Susan.

When I telephoned Janice to tell her of my recollection, she reminded me that she had expressed the same belief to the police five years earlier. Janice encouraged me in my growing feeling that I should tell the authorities.

Much later when I told Kate, her reaction was nearly hysterical. For me to go to the police with my story would accomplish nothing, Kate insisted, but to bring scandal and disgrace on us all. For the first time, she told me, she had achieved some sort of a normal, stable situation in her life. She had a pleasant home in a good suburb, a lawyer husband, and a social position. My stirring up a major scandal would destroy all that. Unprepared for such a selfish reaction, I was dumbfounded by my oldest sister's indifference to Susan's fate or to our father's terrible crime, which might go unpunished.

A few hours after my first conversation with Kate on the subject, she phoned me back, even more upset. "Eileen," she said with older-sister certainty, "you haven't thought this through. Do you realize that if our father is convicted of this murder, your children will never be able to enter the foreign service or run for public office?" Both of these fears were false, I was later told. I had not expected all the turmoil and ridiculous behavior my moral dilemma was causing my family.

When my mother saw that I was intent on going to the police, she suggested that I speak with a criminal attorney. She thought that if I wanted information about pursuing this matter legally, a criminal attorney could best advise me. My top priority was to remain anonymous. I dreaded the notoriety that might result from press coverage, which I assumed would be local. A criminal attorney, Jay Jaffe, was recommended to me, and, early in November of 1989 when Barry was in Switzerland, I made an appointment.

I told Jaffe what I had witnessed, and that I did not know how to pursue the situation legally. I told him that my highest priority was to remain anonymous. He suggested that, through him, I give a statement to the Los Angeles Police Department. If they were able to match what I said to the events surrounding the murder, we could proceed. If, however, I was unable to give verifiable information, my anonymity would remain intact and I could walk away from the case satisfied that I had tried my best. That sounded perfect.

Jaffe warned me that if the police gave me any information or attempted to assist my memory, it would make me an unreliable or invalid witness. He impressed upon me the importance, in order to maintain the integrity of my memory, of not receiving any information from the police. He also said that he would investigate the possibility of my being considered an accomplice in the murder. That was something I had never considered and the mention of it made me quite nervous. While that would be unlikely, he informed me, it was certainly a possibility that should be researched.

Jaffe explained that if my statement contained information that only an eyewitness could know, I would have to decide whether to proceed. If my statement was given to the police through him, my legal privilege to privacy would protect my identity as long as I was deciding what to do. He explained to me that if the case was to be pursued with my cooperation, I could not remain anonymous very long. I appreciated his honesty.

In order to retain his services to keep me anonymous only for a while, I would need to pay him $10,000, which was more than I could spend without consulting Barry and I had not yet decided to involve him in this.

When I left Jaffe's office I felt that there was no point in delaying longer, and that I should proceed immediately. When I told my mother I had decided to go forward, she grew alarmed and insisted I would be making a mistake. This was quite a change from her vow of support, but consistent with our relationship. I also told her that I would have to tell Barry. My mother also reacted very strongly against this, insisting that I do no such thing. My mother, the lawyer, told me that once Barry knew of my involvement in the murder, he would divorce me and have legal grounds to take my children.

I was floored. Instead of having my children taken from me because I had an arrest record or was insane, I was going to lose them because I was pursuing justice. I told my mother that I did not believe Barry would divorce me over this, or try to take Jessica and Aaron from me. On the other hand, I had no idea how he would react; he hated it when I discussed my childhood. I decided to wait.

* * *

Ever since moving to Canoga Park, Barry had been having second thoughts about Los Angeles as a place to live. Since he and I were both vegetarians and highly health conscious, we were more and more unhappy about the frightening levels of pollution that were becoming routine. Some brazen crimes in Canoga Park further soured both of us on Los Angeles as a place to raise children.

Thinking of alternatives, Barry decided Switzerland might be a good place to escape the problems of Los Angeles. He also considered Holland, but his first choice was Switzerland. As might be expected, he learned that the major Swiss cities —primarily Geneva and Zurich—were unenthusiastic about foreigners immigrating to make money. But with his incredible resourcefulness, Barry persevered and discovered that several smaller Swiss cities were not only eager for skilled foreigners, but offered them tax concessions and other inducements.

He made contact with the Swiss Consul in Los Angeles and learned that a representative of the town of St. Gallen was coming to Southern California in a few weeks to persuade promising candidates to move to Switzerland. A dinner was arranged for Barry and me to meet the Swiss recruiter. Everything went beautifully, and Barry and I began making plans to move.

Many months later, when the Franklin murder case had become national news and I was the family member most sought after by the media, it was assumed by many that Barry and I had moved to Europe to avoid the notoriety. We admitted that could have been the reason—had we not already made our decision many months earlier, for reasons that had nothing to do with my legal battle with my father.

In the late summer of 1989, Janice was having health problems so Barry and I asked her to come live with us until she was feeling better. In October, Janice moved to Canoga Park to become part of our family and Barry and I flew to Switzerland to explore St. Gallen and set up a base. When I returned to Los Angeles I was very happy to have Janice living with us. She provided me with a housemate whom I loved and with whom I could enjoy a relaxed, lighthearted companionship.

For both Barry and me, the trip to St. Gallen had been a success. We were delighted by the small Swiss city which was in the foothills of the Alps, close to Lake Constance and the Austrian border. With much to see and learn about our future home, I managed to push from my mind the constant worry over my recollection and the racking decision as to what to do. Not only had the murder occurred in another time; it had now happened in another country. It was, however, waiting for me back in Canoga Park. My knowledge of an unsolved murder was now as much a part of my life as Sica and Aaron.

With the move to Switzerland drawing closer, I felt an added pressure to take action on my memory. I knew that if I still had done nothing when I moved abroad, I never would. With this on my mind, and with a number of others now knowing my secret, I could not put off much longer telling Barry. Perhaps the time had come.

I was more and more certain that I would come forward with my information. The frivolousness and self-interest behind the protests of some of my family had pointed up for me the moral issue and hastened my decision. Barry would be affected as much as anyone by my going to the authorities, provided we stayed together. It was not right for others to know the momentous decision I was approaching while keeping him ignorant.

That was another problem. Going forward meant remaining with Barry. I knew that once I told my story to the police, my life would be in the hands of others until the trial ended. That could be a year, maybe two. Once I committed myself to the prosecution of my father, I would be trapped in a nightmare of legal and family battles. To add to all this a divorce, or even a separation, was out of the question.

If I went ahead and became the main witness in a murder trial, I would be committing myself to my marriage until the trial was over. That could be years. I was almost twenty-nine. If I wanted to have another life, I could not put off the break with Barry indefinitely. This added an altogether different consideration to the many I was weighing.

With all of this going through my mind, I decided that when Barry returned from Switzerland I was going to tell him about the murder, whatever the result. In spite of my strong misgivings, he was my husband and I felt I owed it to him. To test Barry's reaction, I started with a different revelation. I told him about the rape, emphasizing I had had no memory of it until recently.

His response was to say my father was a real bastard, but he advised me to forget about it and get on with my life. While he hadn't tried to comfort me in any way, neither had he yelled or blamed me, so his reaction was better than I expected. I was worried, however, that if all he could suggest was that I simply forget about being raped, would that be his advice on my witnessing a murder also?

A few days later, Barry and I were both working in our upstairs office. He was finishing some work and seemed to be in a calm frame of mind. As he got up to leave the room, I said I wanted him to sit down, I had something of great importance to tell him. I added that it was something that would affect my own life, his life, and our children's lives for many years to come. I also asked that he not interrupt until I finished what I had to tell him.

Barry, who had just heard of my father's assisting in my rape, did not hesitate in believing that I had witnessed him murdering a child. To commit acts of sexual depravity on your own daughters was so far from Barry's understanding of human behavioral limits that he saw my father as a dangerous monster for whom murder was just another facet of his villainy. He said that we had to go to the authorities immediately. Informing the police was the only moral thing to do. And since there was no way of knowing when my father might turn his sights on me and our children, it was the safe thing to do as well.

I felt a sense of relief and enormous gratitude to Barry. I had been so disheartened by the strange reactions of my family. Ever since having the recollection, I had had a strong sense that something should be done; I just didn't know what, how, or when. Their attitudes of disbelief or "let's forget it" bothered me deeply. For Barry to see so quickly and clearly the moral issue and feel there was no choice but to act on it, made me very proud of him. At last I had an ally and I felt closer to him than I had in some time.

I apologized to Barry for not telling him sooner and for going behind his back to speak to a lawyer. He didn't see why I went to a lawyer; I was not guilty of anything. I also told him of my conversations with my mother. He was very upset that she had tried to dissuade me from pursuing justice. But he was more angry with me. He told me that it was going to take him a long time to forgive me for not coming to him first.

I told him I had more or less decided to speak out, but first needed to get more definite information about my legal risk and the best way to proceed. I pleaded with Barry to let me move ahead at my own pace. He felt the reasons for acting immediately outweighed the reasons for delay, but he promised to respect my wishes.

NINE

"DISTRICT ATTORNEY'S OFFICE. ETTER SPEAKING."

"Yes, hello. My wife just gave me some information that she has been living with for some time. When she was eight years old, she saw a murder."

"I see."

"Pardon?"

"Yes. Go ahead."

After Eileen told Barry her story, they discussed it for hours, weighing all the reasons against involving the police. Eileen was well aware of the reasons in favor of going forward—seeing justice done, bringing resolution to the Nason family, removing a dangerous man from society. For these reasons, Barry felt she had little choice but to speak out. To him, a more viable option than doing nothing was to have his father-in-law disposed of.

He acknowledged that Eileen's fears were well grounded. He also felt that neither of them had enough information to gauge the validity of these fears. As they argued, it became more and more apparent to him that they both lacked the knowledge they needed to make a sound decision. Barry decided to phone the San Mateo District Attorney's office anonymously to ask the questions that had come up repeatedly between him and Eileen.

A few days after they had talked, Barry, without saying anything to Eileen, ducked into his bedroom and placed a call to the San Mateo County District Attorney's office, and was put through to Inspector Charles Etter. When she learned that Barry had done this, Eileen was furious. They spent the entire weekend arguing about his belief she should go forward immediately. He badgered her endlessly about how dangerous her father was, reminding her of her rape, of the threat to them all that he represented, and that she was allowing a murderer to walk free. She reiterated her fears that her testimony would be disbelieved or would be insufficient for a conviction. She would be dismissed as crazy. She needed time to convince her family she was doing the right thing. Barry brushed all her reservations aside. She had to go forward *now*.

Months later she would say that when Barry made his call, she knew she would go forward eventually, but because of his goading she did so perhaps a month earlier. Although she knew it was not too late to retreat, she could still avert the shattering of their lives, but she was overcome with a heavy sense of inevitability, the sharp but sweet dread that comes from knowing you are committed to something at one time disruptive, painful, dangerous—and right.

Barry told Inspector Etter that the murderer and the victim were both people his wife knew well, and that the murderer had threatened her. In the first minutes of the conversation he added that his wife had been seeing psychiatrists, a worrisome implication of mental disturbance to inject into a phone call that, in itself, was bizarre. His throwing out this untrue and damaging information was an attempt to address the troublesome issue of why his wife was coming forward so long after the fact. Before Etter made any comment, Barry said, "I guess she can't live with it anymore, so she told me for the first time today."

Eileen

At first I was extremely angry with Barry when I found out that he had contacted the district attorney's office. Then for three days he was my hero. I was very proud of him. He listened to all of my fears and concerns, then expressed them rather accurately to Mr. Etter.

Barry and I had put our heads together in a way we had never done before. We really communicated on the issues that went along with my going to the police. We had similar questions about statute of limitations, prison terms, the likelihood of a conviction twenty years after the fact. But for both of us the main concern was the impact it would have on our family, especially our safety.

Barry was really looking out for me. He was clearly trying to protect me and my anonymity. He respected my not wanting my name made public. Not since those initial seventy-two hours have I felt the closeness with Barry and the admiration for the sensitive way he supported my fears and worked to protect my anonymity and shelter me from the sad, frightening facts.

As I expressed my trepidations and concerns about coming forward, Barry listened carefully. My first fear jibed with his own, that my father might react in such a way as to endanger my family. But while I saw this as a reason for *not* immediately going to the police, he saw it as the opposite.

How could I be certain that he would get a long sentence, or even go to jail at all, for a crime that occurred so long ago and on which the prosecution would be based on the long-buried memory of an eight-year-old child? I might be stirring up a great deal of trouble, perhaps danger, for nothing. I also knew that as the accuser, I would be put on trial as much as my father. My arrest for prostitution put me in a different category from most witnesses to crimes. For me it was bad enough that it might come out, but it also might destroy my credibility.

Barry acknowledged my points, but found it difficult to believe that eyewitness testimony would not be sufficient to put my father away forever. As we argued the pros and cons, Barry kept returning to his belief that my father was a heinous criminal, as dangerous now as ever, and had trouble mustering sympathy for my hesitations and fears about going to the authorities.

In the ensuing conversations, both Barry and Eileen showed an above-average awareness of police procedures and a sophisticated apprehension of the hazards involved in bringing serious criminal charges. It is surprising, therefore, that they were unaware, and did not suspect, that this sort of phone call to the authorities was routinely tape-recorded, and that the tapes of the conversations would eventually be made available to the defense.

Every word that Barry, and later Eileen, said in these "anonymous" phone conversations would be meticulously scrutinized by George Franklin's lawyers for any suggestion of a discrepancy or inconsistency, which would later be paraded before the jury. Barry provided the defense with many such statements, but Eileen did not. It is unlikely that this was due to Eileen's greater legal acuity, but rather to the fact that she had a firmer grasp of her memory, which she had been mulling over for ten months.

Barry, on the other hand, had only days earlier been told the most astounding story ever to touch his life; he had clearly not assimilated all of the details, nor had he given himself a chance to weigh its complexities. Since he would say a number of things to Etter that contradicted Eileen's account and almost brought about what he most dreaded, his much-feared father-in-law going free, his hastiness in calling the police for information can be seen as a warning to any who might contact law enforcement to help in the decision of whether or not to come forward with information about a crime.

His reasons for calling anonymously for guidance are readily understood, but so are law-enforcement reasons for recording calls of this nature. It is curious that the law does not require the authorities to announce to callers that such conversations are being taped. On the other hand, had they told Barry this, he might very well have ended the call. Strangely, neither Leah nor the other lawyer consulted by Eileen and later by Barry warned them of this likelihood.

When Etter asked why Barry's wife had waited so long, his response that he guessed she couldn't live with it anymore would cause considerable trouble in the litigation to come. There would later be much disagreement among the five people Eileen had told before she told Barry about how Eileen's memory had come back into her consciousness. None disputed her assertion that it had been lost to her for many years. It is inconceivable that Eileen did not also tell Barry this crucially significant fact. But defense attorneys could point to Barry's conjecture about why she had waited so long as proof that, as of her first call to the authorities, she had not yet "invented" the repression story.

Barry would later express bafflement as to why he said this, but he does not reject the suggestion that he was so concerned about the concrete dangers to his family, and about the all-too-real legal snarls and pitfalls he and Eileen faced, that such an abstruse concept as repression seemed inconsequential. It was a psychological nicety, when he was seeking hard information. He may not have absorbed it himself at this point, or he may have felt the police would not believe it.

Among the early points he raised in the ensuing conversations with Etter was the scrutiny Eileen would be subjected to if she was forced to take the witness stand. Barry wanted to know how much of her personal history they could evoke, a worry Eileen had discussed with him at length. Etter said he doubted that defense attorneys could introduce everything they wished. He then asked Barry what his last name was.

"At this point in time," Barry replied, "I would just rather get some information. I mean . . . we're considering how to proceed." This was one of the few instances in which Inspector Etter tried to coax Barry a bit more into the light. Throughout the conversation, which lasted thirty minutes, Etter just let Barry talk, throwing in an occasional "I see" or "uh-huh."

Understandably, Barry felt under pressure. He rambled and repeated himself so much that the actual exchange of information could be reduced to a few sentences. Never once did Etter show the slightest impatience or skepticism. If rebuffed in his occasional attempts to elicit information, he immediately retreated and let Barry tell him once again that the murdered girl had been eight years old and had been his wife's best friend, that the crime had occurred in San Mateo County, and that his wife had done some things in her past she would not be "thrilled" to have made public.

Reducing these concerns to a mere warm-up routine, Barry finally moved into what would be the dominant theme of this and the five subsequent phone calls. "Here's my worry," he said. "My guess is that if it happened a long time ago and there was nothing at the time, no evidence they could relate to the person who did it, that probably the primary evidence at this time would be her eyewitness testimony. First of all, would that stand up in court? I don't know, is that enough?"

"Well, it certainly is quite possible. . . ."

"[My wife] can describe all kinds of details about where it was, things . . . that were not brought out, apparently."

"Well," Etter said, "that would certainly be a credit to her statements when she got into court. . . ." Then, as though fearing he might have frightened his caller, he added, "If it ever got that far. . . . It may not ever get that far."

Etter's rare intrusion into Barry's flow managed only to shift it into a new area of concern. "Okay. That's another worry of mine. Why go through all this if it won't go anywhere?"

With admirable deftness, Etter recovered by saying that he had not meant to imply it wouldn't go anywhere, but "there are many steps in this process. At one of those steps the suspect could come in and say 'I did it. I'm guilty.' "

"Oh, I see."

"Therefore there would be no trial and no court appearances."

Mollified, Barry admitted the possibility of a confession, if an unlikely one. He repeated that his greatest dread was that the accused would be made aware of his accuser's identity, then be released for insufficient evidence. Without knowing any details of the crime under discussion, Etter was forced to allay Barry's anxieties with anything valid that came to mind. Barry bemoaned the American criminal-justice system and pointed to the countless blatantly guilty criminals who got off on technicalities.

Barry subsequently expanded on this notion by telling Etter that the murderer had some money and could afford sharp lawyers, the kind who claim to be able to get anyone off. Etter replied that occasionally guilty felons got off, but they were the ones who got attention; the countless others who went to jail were less noticed. Etter stressed that the police might have substantial additional evidence already, "and maybe it would just take your wife's testimony to swing the thing."

Not deflected, Barry asked, hypothetically, if there were no other evidence, "would the eyewitness testimony of an eight-year-old girl twenty years ago be enough?" Etter said that it might be. In an attempt to minimize the disruption in witnesses' lives, Etter said, citizens came in all the time, testified for one or two hours, then went on about their lives. Although Etter at this point had no idea of the drama and newsworthiness of the situation he was blindly discussing, his humdrum appraisal of an accusation of rape and murder based on a child's twenty-year-old recollection was one of the only times he strayed from either candor or sound judgment.

As if summing up his position, Barry said that he wanted his wife to come forward because he believed it was "the right thing to do."

"It is," Etter agreed.

"Secondly," Barry went on, "the guy needs to be put away, or at least gotten help." For him, this was an uncharacteristic excursion into compassion; a number of times elsewhere he said that he would like to see "the guy dead, off this earth." His third point in favor of Eileen's coming forward was that in doing so she might save another child's life. Always coming back to his and Eileen's fears, Barry asked if his wife would have to be identified when they opened the investigation. Etter said not necessarily, but at some point, under the laws of disclosure, her name would have to be revealed to the accused. Before it came to trial? Barry asked. Etter said it would.

When Barry went back to the danger to his entire family and the threats the man had made to his wife, Etter pointed out that the suspect had had twenty years to make good on those threats, but had not done so. Barry took the point, but added that the man was not stable. At the end of the conversation, Barry deflected Etter's attempts to get him to reveal his name and phone number, and said that he had an appointment to speak to an attorney in a few minutes and would phone Etter again that day. "I'd like to get the ball rolling on this very soon," Barry concluded.

"Yes, now that it's out," Etter said with more optimism than accuracy, "it should be done as quickly as possible."

"I agree, I agree."

"All right, sir, thanks for calling. We appreciate that."

Two hours later, Barry phoned Etter again and said that his wife wanted to engage an attorney. She feared that she would be put on trial rather than the accused. Barry didn't see the necessity of an attorney, he told his new confidant, then added that his wife was "really quite confused."

"Why don't you put her on the phone and we'll see what we can do."

Barry agreed. "What's her name, first?" Etter asked.

"I don't want to give you her name because right now she feels too upset about it. . . . If she wants to, she can."

Eileen took the phone and—shyly, quietly—said, "Hello."

"Hello. My name is Inspector Etter and I'm with the district attorney's office up in San Mateo County, as you probably know. Your husband wanted me to talk with you. What do you think about this whole thing?"

"I just want to make sure that I do it right," Eileen said. Then she introduced a new concern, "that I don't give a statement to someone . . . then you say, 'I'm not really the one for you to talk to. Go talk to the police.' Then I talk to the police and they say, 'Well, we're not really the ones to talk to, go talk to so-and-so.' I don't want to get involved in a whole chain of having to go through this because emotionally it's draining. It's very difficult."

Etter pointed out that she might eventually have to talk to the police in the town where the crime occurred, but then argued astutely that her husband had already mentioned going first to the Los Angeles police before coming north; in other words, he had considered creating a chain of his own. He asked if she would be willing to give some sort of statement over the phone so that "we can get working on it at this end. However, I want you to do what you think is right." He then added, "It might save some other child's life."

"Oh, I know," Eileen said. "That's why I'm pursuing it now. I would just like to have the weekend to think about it, then I will contact you or Barry will contact you—or I'll decide to have an attorney and I'll have him contact you, because I think you've been really helpful. Then we'll take it from there. I definitely want to pursue this."

They discussed the way in which Eileen might come forward, with an attorney or without. She said she wanted to discuss the decision once more with her family. She asked how soon after making her statement the case would become public knowledge. Etter answered that it might be a week or so, so she had ample time to tell her family. "You know," he added, "it's not going to make tomorrow morning's headlines."

No!" she said emphatically. "I hope it doesn't make any, but I'm afraid that it might." Eileen asked him about the location of his office, then said, "What are you, exactly?" He told her he was an investigator for the district attorney's office, in the Bureau of Investigation.

"What does that mean?" Eileen asked, her usual bluntness undiminished by the tense situation. Etter told her he investigated crimes, often homicides, committed in San Mateo County.

"So would you personally do any investigation on this if I talked to you?"

He explained that he could not give her that kind of assurance until he knew more of the facts of the case.

"Right," she said. "But that was my fear, that I'd talk to one person and then they'd say, 'Oh, no, I'm not the right person.' " Etter held firm that he could not promise how the case would be handled, or by whom, until he had more facts.

"Okay," she said. "How long have you been with the DA?"

"Nineteen years."

Eileen's posture of the wary, in-control adult had been slipping since she started asking Etter about himself. For a moment she abandoned it altogether. "Wow!" she exclaimed. "So you probably *do* know what you're talking about."

With his unfailing tact, Etter told Eileen that most of his colleagues had as much experience as he had. Before the conversation ended, Etter made a final try for an identification.

"What's your first name?" When she was silent, he said, "You don't want to tell me?"

"No, I'm sorry."

"Okay."

"Okay?" she asked. He told her to call him again when she was ready to tell him more, and that he appreciated their calls so far.

At one-fifteen on the afternoon of Monday, November 20, Barry telephoned Inspector Etter and again launched into his and his in-laws' fear of the man his wife was accusing. When Barry started in for the seventh or eighth time on the probability of a light sentence ("I've got two little kids.") or acquittal on a technicality, Etter tried a different tack. "You know," he said, "you've got this on your conscience. Apparently it's bothered you. . . ."

Back and forth they went in a conversation that lasted another thirty minutes and, for the ever-patient Etter, produced only such snippets of new information as that the accused was a relative, that he had beaten a girlfriend, and that he was "an alcohol and drug addict." Repeatedly, Barry raised the same three or four fears, and Etter tried to smooth them down, like stubborn cowlicks, with the same generalities. Then Barry would return to his primary quandary: "I don't know how to proceed, and you can't tell me he's going to jail for twenty years."

Etter would be forced to say yet again, "No, I can't at this point. It's very difficult to say. . . ."

"Well, I understand that," Barry said, "but all I can say is that a little girl was raped and murdered, okay? I don't know the details . . . my wife does. . . . This guy should be put to death. Well, nobody gets put to death in our state, which is too bad, but worse, they get out on ridiculously short sentences. . . ." Although they had clearly arrived at an impasse, Barry forged on, perhaps hoping Etter would volunteer something previously unmentioned that would facilitate the decision to go ahead.

When Barry got back to the family's fear of the accused, he suddenly blurted to the police officer, "They're all saying, 'Why don't we just go hire a hit man and kill him ourselves?' Obviously we can't do that. We could, but, you know . . ."

"No," Etter said, "I wouldn't suggest that. . . ."

"But I mean that would be the easier thing to do, but we're

law-abiding people, we're not going to do that, but our system of justice at times tends not to work the way people would like it to work."

Finally switching to fresh territory, Barry asked Etter if he could obtain any statistics on the length of sentences received by people accused of committing murders twenty years ago. Politely, Etter said he doubted such statistics existed, since there were few, if any, such cases. Barry was interrupted by a call on his other line. When he returned to Etter he said, "More concerned people," referring to anxious relatives, and laughed, then added that his wife's family was highly agitated by the development.

After further reworking of his themes, Barry told Etter of the accused having "raped his own children." Returning to his theme of the facility with which the most blatantly guilty can get off, he illustrated this point by saying, "If John DeLorean can get off when he's on videotape with cocaine in a case, you know anybody can get off anything."

Every so often Barry would come home to his basic fact—that a little girl was raped and murdered, and his wife saw who did it. Then he made his first mention of Eileen's reason for not having come forward sooner: "And for the longest time she blocked it out of her mind."

What Etter said next was undoubtedly a coincidence, because there was nothing in the record to link the Nason case with repression. "Did this happen in Foster City? Seems to me they had that type of homicide in Foster City twenty years ago." Barry was noncommittal. He shifted the conversation by telling Etter that, for business reasons, he and his family were moving to Switzerland. Barry elaborated about the molestations and other vile things the murderer had perpetrated on his own daughters. He mentioned that his wife's mother was a lawyer and that she was "deathly afraid of him, too." Later he said it had been ten years since she divorced him. Etter picked up on this new information.

"Your wife's mother was married to this man?"

"Yes. I'm giving you more information than I want to."

Barry told Etter what a wonderful person his wife was, that he had a very successful business that she ran for him, but that she was arrested "ten years ago when she was seventeen or something . . . she had a small amount of cocaine . . . she said the records were sealed and everything was fine . . . but I would guess in a murder trial, somebody can get access to these things, my wife said she'd be willing to go through that, but not if in the end it makes her a noncredible witness. . . ."

Etter tried to convince Barry that his wife's record probably would not affect her credibility. They moved into a long discussion of the likelihood of forensic evidence still existing after so many years. If his wife identified herself, Barry asked, could she then be forced to testify? Reluctantly, Etter admitted this could happen. When Barry's other phone rang, he told Etter he would call him later. In the entire thirty-minute conversation, Etter learned a few new things, but failed to get the most elementary information he needed: the identification of the crime. For his part, Barry had done most of the talking—further venting his and Eileen's concerns—but had learned nothing new.

The next morning, just before eleven o'clock, Barry called Etter and told him that he and his wife had decided how they wanted to proceed. She would identify the crime for Etter, then they would ask him to dig out whatever information the police already had on the case and let them know if, combined with her testimony, a conviction could be assured. Etter said it might take him a week to get the information. Barry said he hadn't thought it would be sitting on top of someone's file cabinet, but they had to allow for the possibility that evidence might have been lost, burned up in a fire—or never existed in the first place. They wanted to know in advance what evidence was available to reinforce his wife's testimony.

Eileen came on the phone. (She would be identified in the transcripts of these conversations as "unidentified female.") Her first words were tinged with the jaunty coquettishness she often affected when she felt intimidated.

"Well, have you figured out what case this is yet?" she said.

"No, we haven't."

"Okay. It was in Foster City and her name was Susan Nason."

"Susan . . . ?"

"Nason. N-A-S-O-N."

Etter asked when the crime took place. Eileen responded that she thought it was in the fall of 1969. He then asked her to tell him what had happened. Because Barry had assured her she only had to give Susan's name, Eileen resisted. Etter said her husband had told him she was going to supply details. She turned to Barry and said, "Why did you tell him I was going to give details?" In the background, Barry could be heard talking excitedly. Eileen said to Etter, "Are you listening to all this?" Etter said he understood that her husband was talking, but he couldn't hear what he was saying. Eileen asked, "Can I just give it to you briefly?"

She began. "I was in the car with the person who committed the crime. We picked Susan up . . . across the street from her house. There was an empty field there. She was on a sidewalk . . . in Foster City. We went out to, uh, the woods, I mean that sounds strange . . . I think it was like out toward Half Moon Bay, that way. . . . The person who committed the crime raped her and I was right there when it happened . . . I was in the car . . . [they were] in the back of the car . . . after that we were all out of the car . . . and Susan was sitting down and I was standing by the car and she was sitting—I can't give the exact distance . . . like maybe fifteen feet, twenty feet from the car, and she was sitting on like a little tiny hill, or maybe it was a rock. She was sitting on something that was slightly elevated. And he, uh, hit her on the head and he hit her again and she had a—blood went everywhere. She had a ring on her hand and it crushed the ring on her hand."

"I see," Etter said. "Go ahead."

"Isn't that enough?"

"Isn't there anything you'd like to add at this point?"

"If this goes along with what you find, then I'll talk more. I mean, this isn't real easy for me to discuss."

"Did Susan have her clothes on at the time?"

"As far as I remember, yes. Yes, she did."

"She was fully clothed?"

"Yes."

"And what was she dressed in? Do you remember?"

"I'm sorry, my other phone is ringing. . . . I'm sorry. What did you ask me?"

"What was she dressed in at the time?"

"Let me think a minute, okay? It's just so unclear, because I want to say it was a dress. . . ."

"We certainly don't want you to guess."

"No, that's why I'm saying I don't want to and . . . I don't know. My inclination was that there was a sweater or a jacket, either lavender or blue . . . but I can't remember the exact clothes."

When Eileen seemed to be running down, Etter asked if there was anything else she wanted to add. Eileen asked when they could expect to see the file on the case. Etter calculated aloud, concluding that it would probably be the end of the week. "And your husband said he would call every day?"

"Yes," she said distractedly, "he wanted to . . ." Then suddenly, "Yes, she had to be wearing a dress, actually, because he didn't take her clothes off when he raped her, he just pushed her dress up."

"And you witnessed the actual rape?"

"Well, I just didn't stand and stare. I put my head down after a while and just cried. . . . This is really terrifying for a child. I hope you can realize that."

"Oh, I know definitely," Etter said. "Being an adult, and you're talking to adults. Do you feel . . . that he actually made penetration of the young girl?"

"My feeling is no, which is really strange. I don't know why I feel that way. Maybe it's because I don't want to believe that it really happened, or maybe it just didn't happen." After a long discussion of how they would next make contact, they concluded the conversation.

At one-thirty the next afternoon, Eileen phoned Etter and said, "Hi. This is Mrs. Barry speaking . . . how did it go, did you get anything?"

"We did," Etter said, "and I am personally very excited about it. Very seldom do I get excited."

"Excited about it and you seldom get excited! Barry! Get on the extension. My husband wants to hear this. Okay?"

Remembering Jay Jaffe's warning, Eileen quickly added, "I don't want you to give me any details or anything that would impair my memory in any way . . . that would make me an invalid witness."

"We're not going to do that," Etter said, and told them that he had with him a deputy district attorney who was very interested in the case. "Your wife has some excellent information. It connects with everything we know about the case currently, and—"

Barry started to interject, "You were able to—"

Etter cut him off. "She couldn't be anything but an eyewitness," he said, firmly stating the underpinning to the state's commitment to Eileen and the case. Barry started asking what they knew. Again, Etter cut him off to say he wanted them to talk to the district attorney, a man of twelve years' experience who would be in charge of the prosecution, and who "wants to do everything he can for you."

"What about the evidence?" Barry asked. "Was there any physical evidence?"

"There is evidence," Etter replied, "but I can't tell you what it is, because we'd be prompting your wife." Eileen and Barry said they understood. Etter introduced them to Martin Murray, who was in charge of the homicide unit.

Murray was a man in his early forties who had been handling homicide cases since 1981; during three of those years he had been head of the child-molestation unit and was experienced in the testimony of children. He had a reputation for calmness, thoroughness, and dogged tenacity in pursuing the cases he handled. He also had a reputation for integrity and for refusing to cut corners to win convictions.

Clearly, Murray had been briefed on Eileen and Barry's qualms, and he assured them he understood their hesitancy. His office would launch an investigation with all the resources at their disposal, and would "not contact the suspect until we make a determination this is a prosecutable case. We won't divulge your name until the last possible minute. And that basically means your name doesn't even get mentioned until we make a decision that this man is going to prison. Okay?"

Eileen asked what charges would be brought. Murray told her that the charge would be first-degree murder, explaining that under the felony murder law any murder, premeditated or not, that is committed during the commission of a felony, in this case child molestation, is automatically first-degree. Murray said he did not want to mislead Eileen and Barry. He could not guarantee a conviction, but his ethical duty was to file a criminal charge only if he believed he could win a conviction.

Barry replayed his fears about George Franklin's threats to Eileen, repeating George's claim that, if she told, no one would believe her and he would kill her. Murray, picking up on the less ominous of those two threats, confused Barry by saying, "She's going to be believed."

Eileen and Barry both began saying that they feared revenge more than that Eileen would not be believed, but Murray cut them off with a reiteration of the one element in all the information exchanged so far that would harness the full power of the California criminal-justice system to put George Franklin in jail. "There are facts," Murray said, "that she knows that no one else could know."

Eileen asked if she had told Etter anything that wasn't public knowledge. Murray said, "I don't want to confirm any of the facts that you have given us . . . because I don't want to be accused of having fed you information that you simply fed right back to us."

"But," Eileen persisted, "if everything I told you yesterday was stuff that was in the paper, then it doesn't mean anything."

From the very start of the state's allegiance to Eileen's accusation against her father, the exclusivity of her information was a key ingredient, largely because it was important to her for external validation of her mind's strange behavior, but even more because the law enforcers made so much of it. Clearly it would be helpful in establishing the credibility of her recollection. Over the months ahead, however, this claim of exclusivity grew into an *essential* aspect of her story, one always mentioned in press accounts to give her instant credibility. At the trial, however, it nearly sabotaged the prosecution when the defense lawyers challenged it and insisted that everything she remembered could have been learned elsewhere. The prosecutors involved never wavered in their insistence on the firsthand-only quality of Eileen's information.

Staunchly refusing to pass along the evidence in the records, Murray assured Barry and Eileen that there was extensive information, that the case had been "fairly meticulously preserved." Suddenly Barry asked, "Was there penetration on the rape?"

Eileen almost screamed, *"Don't say that!"*

Murray said he would not talk about such things. Again Eileen said, "Don't say that!"

"Why?" Barry asked. "I was just interested."

"Because," Eileen said, "I don't want you to change my memory, to suggest anything."

"Okay, fine," he said, "I won't. Sorry."

They talked on for a while, then Murray, after assuring them that if they found they did not have enough to convict, they would tell them, said he wanted to turn them over to the detective who would be investigating the case, Robert Morse. He first told of Morse's outstanding seventeen-year record with the department, that he headed the sheriff's office for investigating homicides. He added that "it's a little-known but grisly fact that San Mateo is used as a repository for dumping bodies. We get bodies dumped from all over the Bay Area, because it's a rural area fairly close to San Francisco." Morse had a reputation, Murray said, of solving unsolvable homicides, and was "the best investigator in the county."

Murray said he wanted to send Morse and his partner, Bryan Cassandro, to Los Angeles to speak with Eileen. Although it was Thanksgiving weekend, he wanted to send them on Saturday. Eileen said she needed time to think about it. Drawing on her old attitudes about the police, Eileen asked, "They're not going to try and push me around or anything?" Then she added, "I have a general mistrust of police officers, not from anything I've done, I just don't like them."

With anticipation of this initial face-to-face contact with the police, all of Eileen and Barry's fears came flooding back, including a few that had seemed too farfetched to bring up earlier. Would she be in legal jeopardy for waiting so long? Would she be seen as an accomplice? Would her name be kept private until the last possible minute? Murray reassured them on all points, but was firm in his insistence that he would go no further with the investigation until his men had spoken with Eileen.

One reason for this, he told them, was the necessity of establishing that Eileen had no personal motive for bringing action against the suspect. Evoking the kinds of domestic battles the police have learned to avoid, Murray asked, "You don't have a lawsuit against him? You're not trying to get money from him? No custody battle over children?" Gently but forcefully, Murray made it clear that the time had come for Eileen to trust his office with her identity. He then turned them over to Detective Robert Morse. When he came on the phone, Morse said, "Hi." Her voice flat and mistrustful, Eileen said "Hi" in return.

Robert Morse would become a major figure in Eileen's drama. He was fifty-two, had been born in Utah, and had grown up in San Francisco, then had served in the air force for eight years. During three of those years he was stationed in London, where he played drums in a band that was an outgrowth of the Glenn Miller Orchestra and married an English girl by whom he had two sons. For another three years he worked with guided missiles in Germany. After getting out of the service in 1963, he got divorced, then he went to work for the San Mateo police in Menlo Park. In 1972 he joined the County Sheriff's Office where he ultimately became the Detective Sergeant in charge of the homicide unit. One of his two sons by his first marriage worked for the FBI in San Antonio. He has a son and a daughter by his second wife and is known by his colleagues to be an unusually proud and loving father.

Morse was of average height and slender, which may have explained his nickname, "Bones." The sobriquet also might have had something to do with all the dumped corpses he had encountered. He and his colleagues all claim not to know where the name came from, but all of them smile when they say this. His slightly hooded eyes gave him a sleepy or bored look, but he was passionate about his work, which he approached with an odd mixture of dedication and cynicism. He had a knack for the unexpected remark as when he emerged from hours of psychiatric testimony at the preliminary hearing and said to a nearby journalist, "Thank God for repression!"

The journalist asked what he meant. "If I remembered all the body bags and other horrors I've seen," he said, "I'd go nuts."

When Bob Morse came on the phone with Eileen and Barry, communications between Canoga Park and the San Mateo District Attorney's office took a bullish turn. Until now the officials' tone had been one of sympathy, patience, and reassurance. Morse introduced a gung-ho quality totally absent from the long discussions with Etter and Murray. He began by complimenting them, not only on their decision to come forward, but on the way in which they were doing it.

"I just want to let you guys know who I am, okay? . . . I've been doing this for a long time, way over two hundred homicides . . . we've never lost a case. I'm telling you flat out. Check it out, you'll find that it's true. The other thing is we've never lied to anybody. We have a good reputation, and you can ask any lawyer, any judge, or any district attorney around here: we have never lied to anyone. I have never had a witness intimidated or hurt. We have never once burned somebody in the newspapers or not kept our promises. . . . I'm not a lawyer, but I've worked with these guys on hundreds of cases, believe me, this sounds like a case that the guy's going to prison on. And you are impressive. You are asking all the right questions. I can tell you're intelligent, and you're doing this right."

After assuring them that he understood their fears, he said, "The bottom line here is that you are our bread and butter. Without you, this case is unsolvable. We would be really stupid if we were to jeopardize our relationship with you in any fashion at all." This made sense to Eileen and she began to trust him.

Now really warmed up, Morse said that "the safest thing for you is to let us find this guy and book his butt right into jail."

When Barry mentioned the money the suspect had for lawyers, Morse was ready. "We've dealt with many, many people that have lots and lots of money. I'm not impressed with any of that. Doesn't bother me one, stinking bit. . . . You've got one of the best attorneys they've ever had in this county representing the case right now."

Barry brought up the possibility that the suspect would make bail. Morse said there would either be no bail or it would be "astronomical." As he went into his windup, Morse pulled out everything he could to inspire their trust and confidence, to allay their fears. "We're a team, we operate like a team. Marty's the quarterback. . . . Anyone messes with you, we mess with them," Morse added. "We're good friends to have, but we're shitty enemies. And we know what we're doing. We've got a lot of influence and a lot of friends. Believe me, no matter how much money this guy's got, we got more. No matter how many friends he's got, we got more. . . . We're more powerful than he is. He wouldn't make a pimple on our butt."

Almost as if from fear of where Morse's accelerating passion would lead, Barry and Eileen both told him they would discuss it for ten minutes, then call him back.

Twenty-five minutes later, Etter's phone rang and "Mrs. Barry's" voice said, "Hi, this is Eileen."

"Irene?"

"No, Eileen. E-I-L-E-E-N."

"Eileen. And this is Mrs. Barry?"

"Yep."

She gave her last name, her birth date ("You have to say happy birthday to me on Saturday."), her address and phone number. Morse came on the line and they made arrangements for his visit to the Lipskers on the coming Saturday. He then asked if he could have the suspect's name so that they could start working up a computer background on him. Eileen got so choked up she had to hand the phone to Barry.

There was a silence. Morse said, "Hello?"

"You want the information now. . . ." Barry asked. "You're not going to contact him until you're sure you've got a case?"

"You have my word of honor," Morse said.

" 'Cause otherwise we're—"

"You have my word of honor."

"His name is George Franklin." Barry paused. "It's her father."

TEN

Eileen

November 17, the day that Barry first spoke with Inspector Etter, was a Friday, the day that his parents always played bridge nearby and stopped in afterward for a visit. Barry thought we should tell them about the murder. I did not want anyone else involved, and was still upset that Barry had called the district attorney's office without consulting me first. He said that if I did not want to tell his parents, he was going to. Again, I felt stripped of any choice.

Barry asked his parents to come to our bedroom, where we could talk in private. He started out by telling them what a horrible childhood I had survived. He said that my father had been extremely violent and my mother neglectful. Barry told them that I had recently remembered something from my childhood that we were considering pursuing through legal channels.

I felt very uncomfortable. Barry was dragging out the disclosure, and each minute was causing me more embarrassment. His parents sat on the edge of our bed, looking at Barry and me, not knowing where the conversation was leading. I wanted to disappear. Finally, I could not stand to listen to any more adjectives describing my horrible childhood, saying, in effect, how damaged I was. I pleaded with Barry to skip the buildup and just tell his parents.

They were very surprised. Barry said he intended to pursue the matter and had spoken anonymously to the San Mateo County district attorney's office. Heatedly, my father-in-law advised Barry to go no further, pointing out the number of times our legal system did not work. Aaron is a very mild-mannered man. He is extremely intelligent, but rarely speaks out emphatically against Barry. "Don't do it," he said. "Eileen's father will get out of jail in a couple of years, and you'll both spend the rest of your lives watching your backs!"

Lea rejected her husband's fears and insisted that if a child had been murdered, we had to try to get justice. After a lot of discussion, Aaron agreed. When our meeting broke up, Barry and his father left the room before Lea and I. She put her arm around my shoulder and told me that whatever my father had done and whatever had happened in the past did not matter; she and Aaron considered me their daughter. I was part of their family, and they loved me.

For Thanksgiving of 1989, Barry had asked Eileen to cook a large turkey dinner for his family. At the party were the older Lipskers, Barry's brothers, Scott and Lee, and their wives, his sister, Shana Lipsker-Jennings, and her husband. During the meal, Barry stunned Eileen by telling the group that something of great importance was happening to him and Eileen, and he believed the others should be informed about it.

Eileen was very upset. She had kept her shocking information clamped inside her for months; in a few days Barry had already told his parents and was now telling more people. She knew that having revealed her name to the police, everything could become public. But that excruciating decision was the culmination of ten months of torment for her. It now controlled their lives and would control it for a long time to come.

It was perhaps unreasonable of Eileen to expect her volatile husband to remain silent about such powerful news. She felt strongly, however, that this was *her* problem, with far greater ramifications for herself and her family than for anyone else. The last thing she wanted was for the information to be widespread or to become public before it was certain an arrest would be made. Why tell everyone right now? Why spoil a family party? Now that she'd made the long-dreaded step of telling the police, all of Eileen's resistance came down on the far less consequential matter of timing.

Barry insisted on telling them. This development, he said, would impose a major change in all their lives, the Lipskers' as well as the Franklins'. Now that the authorities knew, the whole matter would become public in a matter of weeks. If she would not inform his family, he would. Seeing she could not stop him, Eileen left the room in tears, as Barry told his version of her story.

A short time later, Leah, who had remarried, gathered at her house in the Portola Valley all the members of her family who lived in the Bay Area—Diana, George junior, Kate, and her husband, Mike. Little else was discussed but Eileen's rash call to the police. Family members differed on the validity of her memory—George junior now maintained it was a delusion— but the truth or falsity of her claim was less important to the group than the consequences of her having reported it. On this point, the consensus was strongly negative.

Every one of them agreed that Eileen's involving the police was a calamity for the family. The matter could still be dropped for insufficient evidence or on a technicality, but most of them felt that a criminal trial with full-blown publicity was all but inevitable. Other ramifications were weighed and argued. The moral implications of the situation were barely touched. When they were, they were hastily brushed aside, as when Kate repeated her belief that the Nasons had "probably forgotten all about it."

As if to fan the panic, Leah passed around two photos, one, a newspaper photo of Susan Nason, and the other of Eileen's daughter, Sica. She asked them to note the resemblance, and told them she believed this was behind the entire matter. This theory may have been advanced with more hope than conviction. Leah's later statements—as well as her testimony at the trial—took the position that Eileen's memory was true.

In the early afternoon of Saturday, November 25, on Eileen's twenty-ninth birthday, detectives Robert Morse and Bryan Cassandro arrived at the front door of Eileen and Barry's house. Cassandro was a handsome man of Italian extraction, who, despite considerable gray in his hair, looked younger than his forty-eight years. He had been born in Vancouver, but had lived in the San Francisco area since he was a teenager. Athletic and an enthusiastic outdoorsman, he made frequent trips to Yosemite Park, skiing in the winter, backpacking in the fall. He was less outgoing than his longtime partner Morse, but had a quiet sense of humor that contributed to his popularity with his sheriff's office colleagues.

The two officers had flown that morning from San Francisco, rented a car at the Los Angeles airport, and found their way to the Canoga Park address. Finally seeing the mysterious "Mrs.

Barry" for the first time, they were both struck by Eileen's poise and her looks. Barry and Eileen were cordial, the detectives civil and correct, never attempting "to push around" Eileen. The atmosphere was stiff but tranquil. Aaron and Sica had been taken off by Denise and Lee to see *The Little Mermaid.* When they were ready to record Eileen's statement, the two detectives asked Barry to leave the room. He offered no objection. Swearing to tell only the truth and with the tape recorder going, Eileen answered their questions convincingly. She forcefully denied any ulterior motive for animosity toward her father.

With that out of the way, they led her through the description she had given over the phone of the events of September 22, 1969, the only difference being that this time instead of referring to "the suspect" or "this guy," she called him "my father." She told them of other episodes with her father, including the rape by her father's friend who she thought had been black.

When they finished, they asked Eileen to leave the room, and took a statement from Barry. Morse later commented, "We came away believing that Eileen was telling the truth. When we talk to people making accusations like that, we generally try to maintain a positive attitude, yet skeptical, too. If someone's going to turn out to be a time-waster, we'd rather find out sooner than later."

In reflecting on his several interviews with Eileen, Morse later said, "She remembered so many details which fit exactly. For me the clincher was her remembering her father *throwing something* brown, possibly Susan's shoe. I am certain that it never appeared in the press that one of Susan Nason's socks had been found hanging on a bush *at eye level,* or that one of her shoes was never found. My impression of Barry was that he was a hero, that he had a good moral sense. He was fully cooperative." Although Morse would have his disagreements with Barry, he never changed his firm belief that Barry had acted heroically in the entire matter. Before leaving Canoga Park, Morse and Cassandro elicited whatever information the Lipskers could offer on the whereabouts of George Franklin, saying that the next step was to arrest him.

Eileen

The morning I was to give my statement—I woke up around five in the morning, feeling extremely nervous. I was very much afraid of talking to the police, especially male officers. I was certain of specific details about my memory, but I was still afraid that this whole thing might blow up in my face. What if Inspector Etter was lying to me? What if they made an arrest, then my father was released on bail and came after me? What if he was arrested and then they dropped the charges? What if there was no evidence tying my memories to the crime? What if the Nasons didn't want me to come forward, or weren't even alive anymore?

I lay in bed thinking about what I was about to do. I knew that Kate would betray me, that she would try to discredit me. She boasted that she had already dealt with her past, implying that to deal with mine effectively, I should forget everything about it. She had asked me, "What exactly do you hope to gain from this exercise?" I didn't understand how reporting a murder could be considered an exercise. I could appreciate that this was shocking to Kate and Leah, but how long would it take them to accept facts as facts? They were behaving so irrationally, with no concern for Susan or me— or the truth.

Susan must have thought that I betrayed her. For the small moment after I screamed, then again after the first crack, she must have thought that I was somehow involved. I hoped that she understood and forgave me. I could not protect her, I could not stop him, I did not know that it was going to happen.

Barry tried to help. He worked to convince Leah, Kate, and Mike that I was doing the right thing. After talking with them, he was very frustrated and repeatedly told me what idiots and assholes he thought they were. Barry rarely swears, but they really were pushing hard for me to stay silent. Talking to them upset him, but not nearly to the degree it upset me. Every conversation started my stomach aching. Even listening to Barry talk to them sickened me.

I hated having to do this today, but none of the other options were available anymore. It was too late for me to go to my dad and plead with him to confess. Maybe it would have worked. It was too late for me to call the Nasons and ask their advice. The suggestion one of my sisters made that we hire a professional killer to deal with him was, of course, impossible. I had to make a horrible choice; there simply were no winners in this situation. Susan wouldn't get to come back even if there was a conviction. Perhaps my mind would rest easier once I was no longer living with my secret. I forced myself to get out of bed to start the day, the day I was to defy my father.

I went through the morning pretending it was like any other until Inspectors Morse and Cassandro arrived. Bob Morse looked and spoke very "coplike." He was factual and businesslike, but also sensitive, an unexpected quality. Bryan Cassandro didn't talk very much; he made me nervous because he was so silent. I wondered if he was bored. I thought he had great-looking eyes.

Barry watched television upstairs while I gave my statement. I think that Bob and Bryan expected me to say that I hated my father, but I didn't. I wondered if they thought I was nuts because it took me so many years to come forward. They promised me that they wouldn't make an arrest unless they believed he was going to be convicted. Bob was a very convincing person; I believed that he was telling me the truth.

After giving my statement, I went upstairs to read, but paced the floor while Barry gave his. I couldn't imagine what his statement would be. Giving my statement had left me in shock. I felt numb. I thought that I had made a mistake in what I told the detectives. It's horrible to try to be totally, absolutely accurate about something that happened twenty years ago. My dad was a silhouette, not a person. I needed to trust my memories better. I hoped that I hadn't messed up too badly. Please, Susan, forgive me.

After Barry and I had each given our statements, Kate called, now very sweet. She asked if I would wait until Tuesday to give my statement to the investigators. She said she wanted to get a post-office box that I could then pass on to the investigators as her address. When I apologetically said it was too late, the sweetness vanished and she hung up on me.

When the officers returned to Redwood City, Eileen's statement was put together with all the other information on file about the case. Martin Murray agreed that no more time should be wasted before arresting George Franklin. He knew of the many family members who were now aware that Eileen had contacted the police, and feared that with further delay, George Franklin might hear of the forces assembling against him and flee. They were aware that Eileen dreaded more than anything her father learning that she was his accuser, but they also felt that once he was in jail, that worry would diminish, and she could concentrate on her testimony.

Morse and Cassandro knew only that Franklin lived in the Sacramento area. A check with the Department of Motor Vehicles confirmed this, but did not produce a street address, since Franklin operated out of post-office boxes. Working through the Sacramento police, they had a computer check run on him. To their surprise, Franklin's name and address were on file with the Sacramento police—for a complaint *he* had filed about malicious mischief against an apartment complex he owned and managed. He now lived in Carmichael, a large community just west of Sacramento.

At Morse and Cassandro's request, Sergeant Harry Macon of the Sacramento police drove out to the apartment. Finding Franklin not at home, he left his card with a written message asking Franklin to phone the police at his convenience. Considering the enormity of the crime the police were now convinced Franklin had committed—and gotten away with for twenty years—the calling card was an odd social nicety that might have afforded a more guilt-ridden and paranoid criminal a chance to escape. The police were relying on his ignorance of their new information.

Worries of losing him began to eat at Morse and Cassandro, who disliked just sitting in Redwood City waiting for their prey to RSVP the Sacramento police. They decided to proceed immediately to Carmichael. At around four o'clock on the afternoon of November 27, 1989, two days after their visit to Canoga Park, the detectives drove to George Franklin's apartment. Finding him still not home, they went to the police station to wait and plan their next move.

While they were there, to their amazement, George Franklin telephoned Sargent Macon in response to the note left in his door. Now feeling secure that he was not planning to flee, they decided to get a night's sleep, then arrest him early the next morning. Aware that he had again left his apartment, they arranged with their colleagues in the local police to have Franklin's place watched—"not a full stakeout," Morse said, "just to see when he showed up again."

Eileen and Barry were extremely anxious about this phase of the program, and were being kept briefed by telephone. When, at a late hour, they were told that Franklin had still not returned home, they were convinced he had learned what was happening and had either fled—or was heading toward them, bent on revenge. It was a very bad night in Canoga Park.

When, in the early hours of the morning, Franklin was spotted entering his apartment, the police proceeded with their plan. Morse and Cassandro arose at five-thirty and drove to the police station, where they picked up two other officers and proceeded in two unmarked cars to Franklin's apartment. The complex was a nondescript, two-story building surrounding a modest swimming pool and some indifferent planting—"like hundreds of others in California," Morse said. They noted that Franklin's vehicle, a black pickup truck, was parked in the building's lot, then walked to his unit, which was on the second level and reached by a building-length balcony. The other two officers kept a lookout below.

It was about six-thirty when they rang Franklin's bell. The door was opened by a totally disheveled man with a mass of curly gray hair, a thick, scraggly beard, and the strong, diabolic features of a B-film villain. He was dressed in a wrinkled sweatsuit and gave the general appearance, not so much of someone who had just awakened, but of someone who had been up all night.

"Mr. George Franklin?"

"Yes?"

"We're from the San Mateo County Sheriff's Office. We have a new captain who is going over all the old, unsolved cases. Your name is on a list. We want to talk to you about the Susan Nason case. We'd like to take a statement from you," Morse said. "It will only take a little while."

"But why me?" Before Morse could answer, Franklin asked, "Have you talked to my daughter?"

In the trial to come, Franklin's question was trumpeted by the prosecution as evidence of guilt and strong corroboration of Eileen's story. They were overlooking, or choosing to ignore, another possible interpretation: that Franklin might have believed an hysterical daughter was making wild accusations against him. Janice in fact had. His awareness that the police visit probably stemmed from something a daughter told them didn't carry with it an acknowledgment that what the daughter was saying was true. While it was certainly a suspicious thing for him to say, it was not necessarily incriminating.

Franklin told the detectives he would be willing to make a statement, but added, "I'd rather not have you come in," as he stood blocking them. In that case, Morse said, would he be willing to accompany them to the station? He said he would, but asked that they wait a minute until he got himself together. When he turned and reentered the apartment, Cassandro followed him in, providing the first indication that this was not a merely routine fact-seeking visit. Cassandro later said, "You never know what they are going to come back at you with, or if they are going to jump out a second-story window."

Cassandro described what he saw inside. "The apartment was filthy, a real mess—papers, clothes, trash, and Styrofoam food containers everywhere, on the floor, on the furniture. As I stood waiting for him in the living room, I could see Franklin sitting on the bed in the bedroom, talking on the phone to someone named Gladys."

On the drive to the police station, Franklin was silent. When they arrived, he told Morse and Cassandro that he had changed his mind about giving a statement. Without further preliminaries, they told him he was under arrest for the murder of Susan Nason and read him his rights. Franklin said he did not understand the rights, and asked that they be read a second time. Morse read them again.

Franklin's first comment was, "I am really shocked by this." In Morse's opinion, however, his prisoner did not sound or appear shocked. He observed that there was nothing about Franklin's body language, a major form of communication in California, to suggest shock. He asked if the two detectives thought he should get an attorney. That was his choice, they told him. "Well, in that case," he said, "I will get an attorney and say nothing else."

A state law dating from frontier days prohibits the police of one county from arresting a suspect outside their jurisdiction and transporting him without the permission of the local authorities. Although Morse and Cassandro assured Franklin this required the merest formalities, and that no one in any county would quickly grant him bail on a murder charge, they suggested he waive this right so they could set out immediately for Redwood City. He refused, as if hoping for an extradition battle between Sacramento and San Mateo county law-enforcement authorities. "He was a real jackass about it," Morse said.

Morse and Cassandro got a search warrant and returned to Franklin's apartment. They found what one of them called a "boiler-room operation" of sexual depravity: piles of child pornography, paperback books about incest, bestiality, and sex with children, a file folder containing a great many articles about father-daughter incest, another of personal dating ads with one ad underlined that said, "Woman seeks man who loves children." In a storage locker Franklin rented in the area, the detectives found a large amount of similar material. None of it was permissible evidence in the upcoming trial, having no direct bearing on the murder of Susan Nason. It would be included in the probation report, which also had letters from Sacramento friends of George Franklin, all of whom made the point that they had not the slightest reason to think he had unusual proclivities.

Morse and Cassandro also found Franklin's address book, which contained a phone number for "Gladys," who turned out to live close by with her husband and son. All three refused to talk with the detectives. When several other names in the address book were called, the people were shocked and surprised, were sure the officers were making a mistake, and could offer no relevant information.

That night, Morse and Cassandro returned to their motel and Franklin spent the night in the Sacramento jail. By the next morning the necessary permissions had been obtained, and the three men set out for Redwood City. Franklin slept during the drive, speaking only once to ask Cassandro to turn down the classical music that he always played when he drove.

Both detectives knew that when word of their passenger's arrest got out, it would cause a sensation—with the public and, even more, with the police. Heinous but unsolved crimes torment communities for years, remaining perpetual wounds in the body politic's sense of security and well-being. Closing one of these open sores is a major cause for rejoicing for all citizens, but for no one more than the men and women whose job it is to treat them. "By the time we got back to Redwood City," Morse said, "word had gotten around the department that something big was going down about a famous unsolved case."

Neither Morse nor Cassandro felt they had done anything extraordinary in arresting George Franklin. Nevertheless, having brought in the alleged perpetrator of a famous, long-unsolved crime carried with it a certain amount of glory, and glory, in police work, frequently carries with it a degree of peril from superiors. Men who risk their lives making the world safer for their fellow man can be notoriously jealous and petty when praise is being passed out. Robert Morse, rather than being decorated for his exemplary work, was hauled into the office of his boss, Sheriff Leonard Cardoza, and removed from the Franklin case.

When Franklin was arrested, Morse had telephoned the news to Martin Murray, the Assistant District Attorney overseeing the case. Murray had reported the development to his boss, District Attorney James Fox, who was quick to phone the news to a friend of his, Rudy Siemssen, a retired inspector from the sheriff's department, who had worked on the case twenty years earlier. Morse had also told his superior, the lieutenant, who had told the captain, but he had failed to tell the sheriff. When Rudy Siemssen called his old colleague the sheriff later that day to discuss the arrest in the case, Cardoza had not yet learned of it. Sheriff Cardoza was infuriated to learn that Siemssen had gotten this news before he had gotten it from his own men.

When, after being relieved, Morse asked if he was still in charge of the homicide unit, Cardoza said that he was. Morse then said he wanted Bryan Cassandro to take over his duties on the Franklin murder case. Since the two men worked closely together, the net result was nil. Because of this and other tensions that had been accumulating, Morse shortly left the sheriff's office and walked down the hall to take up the same work, only now for the district attorney's office. He and Bryan Cassandro would work side by side on the Franklin case until a verdict was reached, a year later.

Eileen

Bob Morse called me to tell me that he had arrested my father. I was stunned; it had only been four days since I gave my statement. It felt like someone punched me in the stomach. My dad was in jail. I asked Bob to make sure no one hurt my father in jail. I know it was contradictory, but all my feelings were tangled beyond logic.

Janice tried to hug me because I was upset, but I was too tense and had to move away. I paced the floor. She and I each had to deal with our pain on our own, because I had nothing to give and didn't want to take. I was glad she was there with me. Even not communicating, we understood each other's pain.

Martin Murray called and surprised me by talking with me for fifteen minutes. He said that many of his seasoned colleagues were amazed that I had come forward. He was feeling victorious about the arrest, but I felt devastated.

I called my grandfather to tell him. He seemed to understand, and told me that he thought I was doing the right thing. I disliked having to tell him; I did not want this to upset his life at eighty-two years of age. My Aunt Sue was wonderful. She took the news calmly and was very supportive, which was what I needed. She told me that this whole business made her very angry toward her sister Leah for having stayed in the marriage for so many years. She told me Leah should ask forgiveness from all of us children.

When I phoned the news to my Aunt Jean, she was stunned. Jean told me about a diary my father had kept, and which he had buried. She said it might have something in it to prove he had murdered Susan. I had no idea what she was talking about. She thought Leah might know where it was buried. Why had Leah not told me about this?

I apologized to Diana for calling her at work, but told her I did not want her to hear about the arrest on the news before she heard it from me. My information came as a complete shock to her, and she grew highly upset, which made me feel terrible, I have always loved her so much. Before the day was over, she and I talked four times. During her last call, she told me that our father had been sexually abusive with her. I became incensed. *That bastard!* I thought. I had tried so hard to protect her as a child, but I had let her down. Diana had been such a pretty, shy, quiet little girl. He had no right to damage her, too. Poor Diana was going to have to deal with a lot of pain—like the rest of us.

I called George junior, and left repeated messages on his answering machine asking him to call me before he spoke to anyone else. I did not want him hearing from Kate or Leah. George told me that if I was sure I was doing the right thing, he would back me one hundred percent. Thank God, I thought.

I asked Barry to call the Nasons and tell them how very sorry I was, and to explain to them how scared I was to come forward, and that I had not wanted to prolong their pain. After calling, Barry said that Mr. Nason was glad I was doing this.

I had a talk with my children, telling them that a bad man had done something wrong, that I had told the police, and that this might take a lot of my attention. I wanted to keep the discussion truthful, but as vague as possible. I did not want them to become afraid of what daddies or granddaddies could do to little children.

By the time of George Franklin's first arraignment, on November 30, 1989, almost a year after Eileen's recollection, word had gotten out to the local press that an arrest had been made in the twenty-year-old Susan Nason case, and that the suspect had been accused of the crime by one of his four daughters. When Franklin was brought manacled before the judge, the courtroom was full of television and newspaper reporters who saw an untamed-looking, middle-aged man dressed in prison-issue orange T-shirt and pants, his jaw and well-developed chest thrust out defiantly, his long, steely hair still unkempt, a full beard, his dark eyebrows twisted into a fierce scowl. He might have been a mountain man brought in for bar brawling. He looked like an artist's unsubtle vision of a child molester and murderer. The judge ordered Franklin held on two million dollars' bail, considerably less than the ten or twenty million Morse had assured Eileen and Barry a judge would impose. Since only ten percent of the actual amount had to be produced in cash, Franklin could quite conceivably raise $200,000 and be released. Barry felt betrayed by the district attorney's office.

Press efforts to learn the name of the daughter who had brought the charges were firmly rebuffed by the district attorney's office. To most reporters, secrets with such brief life expectancies are the greatest challenge, so the refusal to divulge the accuser's name was the starting gun of a reportorial race to discover the identity of the mystery daughter and track her down.

Dan Morain of the *Los Angeles Times*, learning that Franklin had divorced the mother of his five children, checked the divorce records and obtained the names of all the children. He then ran the daughters' names through the computers at the Department of Motor Vehicles, which at that time cooperated in such searches even to the point of providing married names and addresses when only birth names were available. Based on Susan's age, Morain figured Eileen must be the daughter who had witnessed the murder—a lucky shot, since Janice was only a year older and had frequently played with Susan as well. Morain did not remember, as Eileen recalled his telling her, how he knew she lived in Southern California. (Morse inadvertently said it in a statement.)

Three days after the arraignment, Eileen's phone rang. It was

Morain, asking if she was the daughter who had recalled witnessing Susan Nason's murder. She told him she would not comment. Morain belittles his achievement, because Eileen would not talk to him—"Anyone can get a name, the interview is what we all want"—but to Eileen his finding her was of enormous significance in that it signaled the end of her privacy and the beginning of she knew not what horrors from the press. Within minutes of Morain's call, she answered the door to a reporter from the *San Jose Mercury News*, saying, "We know you're the one." Eileen, knowing exposure was unavoidable and hoping to spare her sisters similar intrusions, admitted they were right.

Apprehensive as Eileen and Barry had been about press curiosity that would focus on her and her strange story, they were totally astonished by the onslaught that now hit them. As the first news stories began appearing, mostly in the Bay Area papers and television news shows, their lives were held hostage to the public curiosity about the twenty-nine-year-old mother who had recently recalled seeing her father murder her best friend twenty years before.

Starting as early as six in the morning, and continuing until late at night, their phones would ring with reporters asking for information, an interview, a photo, the name of a friend who might talk. Other journalists took a more direct approach and simply showed up at their front door. Within a few days, film and television producers joined the pack and telephoned relentlessly.

Eileen refused to talk to any of them, not only because the district attorney's office had advised her not to, but because she had no desire to. She made one exception. She was so amused by a producer from "A Current Affair" who appeared at her door holding out a tin of Mrs. Field's cookies, she let her in for a few minutes, but still would not speak about the case.

Eileen felt strongly that this entire matter was between her, her father, the legal system—and Susan. She hated the idea of its becoming the world's property. Her family had warned her that this could happen, she feared that it would get into the news, but she was totally unprepared for the national attention it was attracting. She was becoming a celebrity, not because of anything she had done, but because of Susan's death, and the idea disgusted her. This feeling intensified as film and book offers began arriving; she was repelled by the idea of making money from her best friend's murder.

Eileen was equally unprepared for the response the media attention brought forth from Barry. Rather than being angered at the disruption in their lives, Barry relished the attention. He was proud of Eileen and was eager to talk about her courageous action. He also felt that publicizing her story might encourage others with related experiences to speak out. He overlooked, however, the legal pitfalls of public statements and the enormous dangers of making assertions that differed from Eileen's.

Eileen would come in from picking up the children at school and find Barry chatting on the phone with a newspaper or television reporter. Even more upsetting was that Barry, with breezy inaccuracy, would quote Eileen, discuss her recollection, her reasons for not coming forward sooner, how she felt about her father. These were all matters that would be important issues in the trial. For that reason she was forbidden to discuss them. And she had not discussed them, even with Barry, who was now presenting himself as an authority.

She was relieved that the court had imposed a gag order on her and other potential witnesses; it provided her with a quick and inarguable excuse to the reporters. The district attorney's office had also insisted that all potential witnesses form a wall of silence while they assembled their case. Eileen was dismayed to find her own husband providing such a willing chink through which reporters could extract information which they assumed to be, if not from the horse's mouth, certainly from the next stall. They had no reason to think that his information might be inaccurate.

After one article appeared in which Barry had discussed at some length his wife's "flashbacks," Martin Murray called and berated Eileen for the damage Barry's statements were doing to the case. Neither Murray nor Eileen knew exactly what a "flashback" was, but they felt quite certain it was not what Eileen had experienced and sworn to in her statement. Murray did not want to be required to build his case on some made-for-television term concocted by Barry. Murray suggested that a way to choke off the informational flow from Barry was for Eileen simply to stop telling him things. "I *haven't* told him anything," Eileen said plaintively. "It doesn't matter. He just improvises." It was essential, Murray told Eileen, that, one way or another, she silence her husband.

When Eileen appealed directly to him to stop, Barry refused. His respect for the San Mateo County District Attorney's office had plunged a few days earlier when bail had been set so much lower than the detectives had predicted. He had seized on the police's miscalculation as proof of either the deviousness or the ineptitude of Martin Murray and his team. Barry took their exaggerated bail expectations as a license to disregard the law enforcers' demands and admonitions and to do as he wished.

From then on, when Eileen quoted Murray's injunctions to Barry, as she would now do increasingly, he dismissed them with a stock line: "They don't know everything, Eileen. Remember what they told you about the bail." Or an angrier version: "Why listen to them, Eileen? They *lied* to you!" This adversarial relationship between Barry Lipsker and the district attorney's office was one of the most unusual developments of the Franklin case. Attorneys prosecuting a difficult case expect to be given complete control. It was not in Barry Lipsker's nature to step aside and hand over control of a matter that so directly affected his life and that of his family. The friction would escalate.

Eileen

Just before Christmas 1989, I had a telephone conversation with George junior, which was the beginning of his turning against me. I told George that I planned to visit our father in jail and ask him to confess. George replied that he did not consider me a cruel person, but that this would be cruel. I was surprised. Asking our father to tell the truth was cruel?

George told me that he had gone to visit our father a week earlier and found him in shock. He also denied having committed the murder. I asked him if he didn't believe that I had seen our father do it. He replied that he had not seen the crime I claimed to have witnessed, so he could not say who was telling the truth. This would also become Diana's exact response when queried. George junior and Diana were close.

George proceeded to tell me that he advised our father to "fight like hell any conviction." I asked him why he had said that if he did not disbelieve me. "Leah and you four girls are ready to hang Dad," he said. Given the lack of female unity in the family, this was an incredible statement. He added that Dad deserved a fighting chance. Bitterly I reminded him that Susan had not had a fighting chance.

George asked me if I didn't think that Dad had been punished enough by the absence of his five children from his life. How would I feel if Jessica and Aaron were to avoid me for ten years? I told George that I had not done anything to cause my children to reject me. I reminded him that even without the murder, Dad was an extremely violent and sexually abusive person. It was clear that George was trying to view the arrest as a punishment of our father by me; he said to me, "Someone has to be on Dad's side." It was hard to follow his reasoning.

George added that if our father was convicted of the murder, then he would believe me. He began a verbal assault against Barry. He told me that he had heard Barry on the radio, and he demanded that I stop Barry from giving interviews. I informed him that I had repeatedly asked Barry to stop but that he wouldn't.

Our conversation ended with George attacking the integrity of Martin Murray. George told me that he was convinced that the only reason this case was being pursued was to provide a springboard into politics for Marty. I began to sense how desperately George was grasping at straws, to find any reason for the arrest other than the truth.

If his theory about Marty were true, I asked George, how did the sheriff's department and the judge fit into his fantasy scenario? He answered very bitterly, as if he were stating facts, not a prime-time scenario he had dreamed up. The sheriff's officers would receive bigger pensions, he said, and the judge's career would flourish if they got a conviction. I told George his theory was absurd.

I had tried to be rational with George. I had answered his irrational questions and his accusations without becoming emotional or angry. I had listened to theory after imaginary theory as to how the arrest came about. It was clear that George was deeply entangled in his father's lie.

While the press attention seemed to stimulate Barry, it was depressing Eileen more and more. She hated the way the public curiosity was upsetting her family, and she hated even more what it promised for the next year, if not longer. The entire prospect of a long, highly publicized trial grew increasingly abhorrent to her, and she began plotting ways it might be avoided.

When Eileen's Aunt Jean, and later Leah, told her of a diary her father had mysteriously buried, Eileen seized on this as a possible shortcut to justice. If she could find the diary and it contained a confession of his having murdered Susan, the trial would be unnecessary. Eileen had recently remembered, years earlier, going with her father into the woods and helping him conceal something. Could it have been the diary? She concentrated and described a possible location, a wooded area. Uncertain as to what the diary's contents might be—if there was one —Eileen and Barry flew from Los Angeles to San Francisco and set out with Bob Morse on a diary hunt to Starhill Road where Leah had said the diary was buried.

The bizarre expedition was fruitless. Eileen was unsure of the general location, and even less sure about a specific spot. She had hoped that if they could find the area, the surroundings would trigger her recollection of exactly where the book had been buried. Nothing like that occurred, and they gave up after a few hours. That she had grasped at such a slim chance, however, was a good indication not only of her conviction that her father had killed Susan, but of her desperation to avoid a trial.

Martin Murray and his detectives were not the only ones irate about Barry's indiscretions to the press. After reading one news article in which he was quoted, George junior called Eileen, outraged that she had allowed Barry to talk so freely about their ugly childhood and other highly personal matters. "Listen, George," Eileen said, "I am telling you right here and now, I have not only asked Barry not to give these interviews, I have *begged* him. Then I walk into the room and he's doing it."

When Barry heard this, he grabbed the phone from Eileen and started yelling. "Listen, George, it's about time you grew the fuck up and realized how brave Eileen was for doing what she did. People are interested in this. This is how news is made. If I want to talk about it, I have a right to. There's no gag order on me."

Without waiting to hear what George replied, Barry handed the phone back to Eileen. Eileen tried to convince her brother she was as unhappy about Barry talking to the press as he was. Exasperated, she turned to Barry and said, "Isn't it true? I don't like it?" Barry said it was true, and again started listing his reasons for ignoring her wishes.

Even Barry was stunned at the aggressiveness of the press when a reporter from CBS intercepted one of Leah's clients as she emerged from Leah's San Mateo law office. The reporter placed a microphone under the startled woman's mouth and asked, "What do you think about the murder?" Barry was furious at this intrusion. He phoned the CBS San Francisco offices and lambasted the producer, who had already called the Lipskers many times. In the conversation, the man asked Barry if there was a CBS news personality that Barry admired. Barry said that he had always thought highly of Charles Kuralt. A few minutes later Barry received a phone call from Kuralt asking if Eileen would relent and give an interview to CBS. Barry gave them a long interview, which CBS shelved when Eileen refused to talk with them. Barry also talked at length to CNN.

Consistent with his press cooperation, Barry was even more stimulated when screen and book offers began arriving. Eileen would overhear him talking to a would-be producer of "The Eileen Franklin Story," saying, "My wife and I want this, we want that...." Eileen was furious because she did not want *any* of it, and felt her own husband was creating the impression she was interested in making money from her friend's murder. Sometimes Eileen yelled at Barry, then they would yell back and forth, but eventually she grew tired of the futile wrangling and retreated into the knowledge that, while Barry might claim to talk for her, he could not sign anything for her.

One of the members of Barry Lipsker's old rock band was a television cameraman, Jeff Scarborough, whose brother was the well-known anchor of the local NBC news in New York, Chuck Scarborough. Every year around Christmas, Jeff would call Barry to catch up on his life during the past year and find out how he, Eileen, and their children were doing. This year Barry had real news to report, the extraordinary event that had caused such upheaval in his and Eileen's life. When Scarborough heard the story, he grew excited and said it was astounding, a fantastic news story.

When he learned that Eileen had refused all interview requests, Scarborough grew even more excited at the prospect of snagging a major scoop for his brother. Would Eileen allow his brother Chuck to interview her? Jeff could guarantee that Chuck would be sympathetic and sensitive, and would abide by whatever ground rules Eileen cared to impose. He also said that if Eileen granted this one interview, the other contenders would back off, that they would stop arriving on her front steps with bags of cookies.

Barry was enthusiastic about the idea. Eileen was intrigued by the prospect of stemming the endless flow of calls and intrusions. She asked several people if they thought that would really be the result. Most thought it would, particularly the now media-sophisticated Barry; they all want an exclusive, a scoop, he explained. Once that possibility is gone, they will lose interest and stop bothering us. Barry's eagerness for the NBC interview—probably nothing more than a desire to do a friend a favor—gave Eileen another idea. If she did the Scarborough interview, she asked Barry, would he promise to stop talking to the press? He agreed.

She had another reason for considering Barry's urgings. Having feared from the first moments of the recollection that the twenty-year repression of such a momentous event might be viewed, even by her therapist, as a sign of mental disorder, she was now doubly concerned that an unfriendly, distant public might be quick to assume this. She began to see the wisdom in doing a single interview on national television to show the world that, on the surface at least, she was normal.

When Chuck Scarborough had heard Eileen's story from his brother and learned that she was considering giving him an exclusive interview, he immediately saw the chance for a journalistic coup. He told them that the piece would be aired, not just on his local news show, but on one of NBC's national shows as well—"The Today Show" or the NBC evening news, perhaps both. He had no trouble accepting her conditions that they not discuss the details of the crime or the plans for the prosecution.

A date was set for the interview and Scarborough went to work to create a full-blown news piece on the case. He obtained the agreement of Donald Nason for an interview, also of Janice Franklin, and tracked down a retired sheriff who had worked on the case. He also found a leading expert on childhood trauma, a psychiatrist named Dr. Lenore Terr, to talk about the phenomenon of repression.

NBC flew Barry and Eileen to New York for the interview and gave them star treatment, with limousines at the airport and a room at the Omni Berkshire. For the interview, Eileen wore a simple green turtleneck that set off her good features and her long red hair. She sat on a sofa, with Barry at her side. The nervousness she felt about talking on camera came across as thoughtful reserve, a care in choosing her words that added to her credibility and appeal. Her succinct and unembellished account of her fantastic experience, set against Scarborough's thorough and skillful scene-setting, was mesmerizing and totally persuasive. This was no Los Angeles loony with a bizarre tale of bloody visions, but a mature, articulate, and beautiful young mother, telling, with just the right mixture of resolute control and quavery emotion, an astounding story of having witnessed her own father commit a murder and of then having repressed the horrendous memory for twenty years.

Talking to Scarborough, Donald Nason, with great difficulty and close to tears, described his vivacious daughter. The piece included a brief statement from psychiatrist Lenore Terr, who explained the sort of things that could trigger a repressed memory. Terr ended her list of examples by saying that such a stimulus as having her daughter reach the same age as the victim had been when murdered might well have brought forth Eileen's buried recollection. There were two film clips of the sheriff, one taken at the time of the murder, another shot recently. The jarring change in the man's appearance deftly underscored the twenty-year interval between the murder and the arrest. The piece was a succinct yet thorough presentation of a complicated and haunting story.

When Eileen returned to Canoga Park after taping the interview, she received another irate phone call from her brother, who had heard about her efforts to obtain a family photo for the NBC piece. He warned Eileen that if she dared show "his likeness" on television, or discussed him in any way, he would sue her and NBC. Eileen was stunned by the legalese. He demanded to know what NBC had asked about him, what indignities she had already exposed him to that would soon be aired on national television. Eileen replied, "No, George, you will be disappointed to learn that they didn't ask about you at all."

Eileen would eventually conclude that it had been shortsighted of her brother and sister to be so confrontational with her. "If Kate and George hadn't been so nasty about it," she said, "they could have influenced me. But because they acted so tough and threatening, I decided to ignore them and do what I thought right."

Eileen

A few days after my father's arrest, a movie producer called me at home, inquiring about my life rights—a term I had never heard before. I thanked the man for calling and informed him that I had no interest in a movie involving me or my family. More producers began to call, and within a couple of weeks I had received over a dozen requests for my life story.

Finally, producers were calling me day and night, sending letters, videotapes, and press kits. My home was being invaded from all sides until I dreaded answering the telephone, opening the mail, or answering the door. I was contacted by agents wanting to oversee the movie, personal managers wanting to "package" me, TV writers who promised sensitive scripts, film directors considering me as their next project, literary agents on both coasts, a network representative, and several actresses. I was constantly picking up the phone to a secretary instructing me to hold for someone I had never heard of.

I had naïvely believed that if I said no, politely but firmly, all offers and interest would disappear. Instead, I learned that a movie about my involvement in Susan's murder would be made with or without my cooperation, using my name regardless of accuracy or of my feelings about the matter. Once I testified in court, everything I said would become public domain, meaning an unauthorized movie could easily be made.

Barry suggested that we get a lawyer, if for no other reason than to handle the telephone calls so that I could live my life and raise our children. Martin Murray, who had also received calls about me from the media and producers, was not pleased with our decision to speak with an attorney, but he understood that I felt under siege in my own home.

Barry and I got the name of an attorney specializing in entertainment law. I made clear my lack of interest in a movie deal. The attorney, Bill Simon, told us to direct all calls to his office, where any progress on a film could be stalled or halted. This took care of the producers, but the press was still hounding me, which was why I agreed to do the Chuck Scarborough interview for NBC.

Although the press left us alone after that interview aired, as Scarborough had promised, it brought forth a new flood of movie offers that finally peaked at thirty-five different production companies trying to buy my story. Our lawyer, who was offered bribes to arrange an introduction, said that he had never in all his years in Hollywood seen such a frenzy over a story. Eventually, he advised me to commit to a production company before my life story became public domain and was pirated by an unscrupulous producer who had little interest in the truth.

I felt completely conflicted. Martin Murray claimed that my involvement in a movie could endanger the prosecution of the case. On the other hand, I was afraid that my siblings would blame me, and reject me even more, if a sensational, torrid depiction of their lives was released only because I refused to authorize my life rights to a reputable production company. The reverse, I felt sure, would also be true. If I did agree to a film, my siblings would think I was exploiting a sensitive family situation. Also, I was extremely concerned that my prostitution arrest would be discovered and that I would be publicly humiliated by a film depiction of that episode in my life. I was very much afraid of the effect that might have on my children's lives.

To add to my uneasiness, a number of authors had contacted me, claiming they were ready to start writing a book about my life. They claimed that while they hoped to meet me, enough information would come out in court about me to make for an interesting book. I also learned that these authors, to get the material they needed, intended to interview former friends and classmates of mine. The invasion of my privacy seemed unstoppable.

The issues were spelled out for me. According to Marty, if I agreed to cooperate with a film and a book, I would be endangering the prosecution of a murderer. I thought I would also be compromising my integrity, putting a price tag on Susan's death, and risking long-term rejection by my family. If I did not agree to cooperate, however, I would be portrayed in any way the filmmaker or author wished. I could be publicly humiliated, my family would get the same treatment, and Susan's murder would be sensationalized.

Both choices were grim. I hated being responsible for making a decision that would affect my siblings when some of them, by now, were not speaking to me. I decided to decide nothing. It wasn't until I was lied to by an author that I realized that I was indeed about to be publicly raped. I learned very painfully that a book was being written about me by someone who had claimed he would not proceed with a book unless I agreed to cooperate. Suddenly I saw that among all of the "nice producers" and "nice writers" who had called me, there were people waiting to make a financial profit from the murder of Susan Nason and my freakish repressed memory, regardless of what it did to my life.

With this lesson, I realized that I needed to take control of the public aspect of my life, decide on a film company and an author, and hope that I could explain to a jury what living under siege, being betrayed, and being threatened with dishonest exploitation was like.

The idea of visiting my father grew stronger. Ever since I'd had the recollection, I had been carrying on a dialogue with him in my mind. Why not say some of these things to his face? But, more important, if I could persuade him to confess, to make him see it was the only thing to do, everyone—my family, the Nasons, and I—would be spared the grim ordeal of a sensational trial.

Knowing, as I did, not just about Susan's murder, but about all the misery my father had caused so many people for so many years, I saw confessing as an opportunity for him to atone, to compensate in a small way for the enormous harm he had done. He had always stressed to us kids the importance of being honest. With all that would result if he continued to lie about his crime—when was there ever a greater need for honesty?

Two weeks after the arrest, I told Martin Murray about my wish to go see my father—and why. He said that he could not ask me to do that. *He* was not asking me, I said, it was entirely my idea. I also assured him I did not want to do anything that would hurt the case. Marty seemed surprised at my determination, but said that he didn't think it was such a bad idea. He repeated that he could not ask me to do it.

I waited until the beginning of the new year, after I'd gotten my family through Christmas, and Barry had left for Europe. The whole idea of facing my father made me very anxious. Every time I tried to plan what to say, I felt like crying, so I stopped thinking about it.

I called the jail to arrange the meeting. The officer who answered the telephone seemed surprised that I was requesting a meeting with that particular prisoner. I was informed of regular visiting hours and told to come on one of those days and wait in line. I explained that I was traveling from Southern California on a particular day, and had only a short time. Couldn't an exception be made to fit with my schedule? The duty officer asked my name. When I told him,

I was immediately put through to the man in charge, Sergeant Cuneo.

I explained to Sergeant Cuneo that I was flying up to meet with Martin Murray, but wanted a brief visit with my father. I told him that, because of all the press attention, I wanted to come when no one else was around. Cuneo offered to make the prisoner available at two o'clock on the day I requested. He then added that I had better not make a habit of scheduling visits outside of regular hours. Gruff, but helpful. My kind of cop.

Because I had a number of things I wanted to accomplish in my one-day visit, I hired a car to pick me up at the airport and take me to Redwood City. My first stop was the DA's office. Martin Murray impressed me right away as a decent person. He also had a calm, businesslike manner. I didn't feel threatened at all, which was surprising, given his importance in my life. I thought that working with him would be fine.

Among the things I wanted to discuss were my reasons for agreeing to the NBC interview with Chuck Scarborough. I told Marty of the constant harassment by the press. If one interview would end all that, I wanted to do it. Marty was not pleased at the idea. I understood his reasons for wanting me to remain out of sight. Too much pretrial publicity could cause a change of venue or even jeopardize the conviction if I made an inconsistent statement during an interview. We were at an impasse but he said he could not forbid the interview.

As two o'clock approached, I took the elevator up to the jail and met Sergeant Cuneo. He told me to take a seat in the visiting room, and the prisoner would be brought in. I was thankful that I was going to have a few minutes to compose myself. The visiting room was ugly—a cracked linoleum floor, orange trim on the walls, a row of four metal stools facing corresponding stools on the other side of heavy glass.

I was startled to see my father seated waiting for me. So much for composure time. At his first glance, his expression seemed to say, "Oh, so this is my visitor," with mild interest. He looked a second time, and his expression changed to a quizzical, "Who is this?" Then he showed complete shock and disbelief as he realized that it was me.

On the bare shelf in front of him he had placed a brown flexible folder and a book by Clarence Darrow on courtroom procedure. I thought he looked very handsome, but I had always thought my father was extremely good-looking. For what seemed like several minutes we sat across from each other, staring through the glass. Finally I picked up the telephone hanging in front of me.

"Is it really you?" he asked. I smiled sadly and told him that it really was. I said that I had some things I wanted to say, and that I would appreciate his letting me speak without interruption. When I was finished I would listen to anything that he had to say. He told me that was fine.

My emotions surging in my chest, I started by telling how much I had always loved him. I told him that so many of the good qualities I found in myself I attributed to him. I said I did not hate him and probably never could, because of how much I had loved him.

I said I understood what it felt like to panic and do something rash. I did not believe that what he had done to Susan was premeditated. I believed that he had let the situation get out of control, then, in a moment of fear and panic, he had killed her. Everyone has done regrettable things in moments of panic, I said; the problem was that what he had done carried a heavy penalty.

I reminded him that he had always told me that "the truth shall set you free," and that perhaps by telling what I saw, I was giving him freedom. I told him I believed that freedom could be attained in many ways, and that perhaps his freedom was being in jail—freedom from sexual compulsion, freedom from hurting people.

I told him I remembered all of the wonderful things he had done for me, how he had saved my life when I had appendicitis. I told him I felt deep appreciation for that, and that I had never forgotten all of the extras I had received because I had been treated as his favorite child.

I felt completely overwhelmed emotionally. I came close to tears several times, and so did he. Seeing him sitting there stripped of everything, I felt all of the old love that I had for him swell up inside me, and I felt enormous compassion for my father, who was hurting and alone behind a plate-glass window.

Even so, I pushed on to say what I had come to say. I asked him to do the right thing and confess. If he told the truth about the murder, I could maintain some respect for him. If he insisted upon fighting the charges against him when we both knew that they were true, then I could no longer respect him. "The murder is bad enough," I told him, "but don't be a hypocrite and a liar." I pleaded with him not to put the family through the tremendous pain of a public trial.

When I was finished, I asked my father if there was anything he wanted to say. Without speaking, he pointed to a sign hanging behind him on the wall, which said that conversations may be monitored. I then asked if there was anything that I could do for him, thinking he might need cigarette money or to have telephone calls made for him. He responded by saying, "There is one thing that only you can do for me." From the heavy, slightly sarcastic way he said it, I knew he meant I could recant my accusation. He asked if I would come to see him again. I felt an enormous sadness that he was not going to tell the truth, but would persist in dragging us all through a trial. Without a backward glance, and twenty-two minutes after I had entered the visiting room, I left.

Deep inside myself, I had hoped that my father would claim not to remember committing the murder, just as I had not remembered witnessing it, like one of those times when he had blacked out from drinking, then asked me to piece events together for him. I so wanted to hear that he had done it during a drunken blackout, a mental lapse, a time of incapacity; that would be easier to understand. But I didn't hear it, so I would have to work hard to stop loving him.

ELEVEN

For months before the Franklin case arrived at the district attorney's office, Martin Murray had been contemplating leaving his job and entering private practice. Most of the elements of his career shift came together shortly after he assumed the case, and he alerted his superiors of his plans. Another attorney, a thirty-seven-year-old woman named Elaine Tipton, announced that, if Murray left, she would be willing to take over the Franklin case.

Tipton had been a deputy district attorney like Murray, but had recently been promoted to the purely administrative post of assistant district attorney, where she oversaw the work of twenty-two prosecutors. For a number of reasons, Murray changed his mind about leaving, but, because of a conflict with another case to which he was previously committed, he decided to turn the Franklin case over to Tipton anyway.

"From day one, Eileen had said she did not want to be passed from one person to another," Tipton recalled, "so we did not tell her right out that Marty was handing her case over to me. We kind of eased her into it. We felt she needed a lot of reassurance. She also wanted to feel she had one person, a knight who would avenge her cause. She feared being thrown to the wolves, being churned up by an impersonal criminal-justice system. This possibility was a major concern, but more than anything else, she was terrified of the whole thing."

Over the four months leading up to the preliminary hearing, Tipton became increasingly involved in the case. She did not meet Eileen face to face, however, until she, Murray, and Robert Morse made a formal visit to Eileen on May 5, 1990, three weeks before the start of the preliminary hearings. The purpose of the visit was to take another statement from Eileen, who had remembered additional details and had been told not to offer them over the phone. Perhaps an even stronger motive behind the visit was to introduce Eileen to Tipton and to tell her officially that Tipton would be prosecuting the case.

Eileen

The first time I met Elaine Tipton was with Marty Murray and Bob Morse at my house in southern California. Marty had mentioned Elaine's name to me a few times over the telephone. He had suggested that she might become involved in the prosecution of this case. I didn't think much about this, believing that Marty would not hand the case over to anyone. I would have considered it a breach of our "team" agreement.

Shortly after they arrived, Elaine picked up a framed picture of my children that was on the mantel in the family room. I could tell that she was looking at Jessica much more intently than at Aaron. I felt uncomfortable and very sad that my children were being brought into this trial. I felt like I had let Jessica down, failed to protect her.

When we first sat down in the kitchen to talk, the telephone rang. I picked it up to hear the voice of Barry's father, Aaron Lipsker. Without thinking, I said, "Oh, hi, Dad." Hearing that, Bob Morse jerked his body bolt upright and Elaine's mouth dropped open. I realized what they thought. I told them that it was *Barry's* dad. They all laughed with relief.

When I was told Elaine might be assigned the case, my first reaction was one of skepticism. Why was she being put on the case if Marty was the best, as I'd been told in the beginning? I felt mistrustful and could not understand why Marty would not prosecute the case himself.

This meeting was the first time I was allowed to discuss any details of the crime with the district attorney and the investigators. I had been warned repeatedly not to disclose any pertinent information over the telephone, but only in the presence of a witness. I felt a delightful thrill that I could finally tell them all the things that had grown, evolved, changed, or become more clear during the past months. I was ready with a mental list of details and events to disclose, and started volunteering information as soon as I could. Talking about my bottled-up memories after months of enforced silence was a great relief.

I explained why I had lied to George, telling him that I had been hypnotized. I also told them that I did not feel badly about initially lying to George. I had been frightened by his reaction, but I had been truthful in telling him I had seen my father murder Susan. I finally got to explain why I believed that the crime could not have happened in the morning, because of the silhouette the sun had made of my father when I first looked up at him that day.

Because I saw no reactions as I told my horrific story, I began to feel really stupid. I was afraid I was wasting the investigators' time with trivia. That was how I felt when I disclosed that I had remembered seeing my father throw something brown, maybe her shoes. I could remember the angle he stood at, the arc of his arm, the grunt as he threw the object, but I could not definitely say what the object was that he was throwing, so I thought it would be of no use to them.

I told them I was still cloudy about whether Janice had been in the van or not. I was certain I had seen her in the field when I was in the van, but I was not certain about whether she had gotten in with us. Once again, I was completely frustrated about that missing piece in my memory.

When I was describing the murder scene, I had trouble verbalizing my visual scope and the physical location of the van, Susan, my dad, and me. I reached across the table for one of their notepads and drew a primitive stick drawing of the scene I remembered. Several weeks later, when I was given a copy of the report of our meeting, I was embarrassed to discover that my crude drawing had not only been seized as evidence and duplicated for the report, but had been sent to the defense attorneys.

I needed to explain to them on the record why I had initially described my rape as having been committed by a black man, then realized it had been my parents' friend and my godfather Stew Smith, who was white. I told them there had been a poster of Jimi Hendrix on the wall in the room where I had been raped. And my head was held in such a way that I was forced to look at it throughout the entire ordeal. I was speaking directly to Elaine, and I asked her, "Do you know how if you stare at something for a long time then look away, you can still see the reflection of the object in your vision?"

She looked at me without expression for a moment, then replied, "No."

How much more clearly did this woman want me to describe it? I thought she wasn't even trying to understand what I was saying. I decided that I did not want to work with her. I launched into a more detailed and lengthy description. I tried to describe how the face of Stew Smith became clear to me through the radiating colors and superimposed image of Jimi Hendrix. In my frustration I hoped that Elaine Tipton would not be assigned to this case.

Some time later, when I came to know her better, I realized she had been completely professional, yet uncharacteristically abrupt. With her blunt "No," she forced me to explain, with as much clarity and patience as I could muster, something that was both painful and difficult to describe. I think she may have been evaluating me as a witness. At the time I thought she was just being impossible.

Elaine Tipton had grown up on the Peninsula, the fourth of five children. She had a younger brother and an older brother, and two older sisters. Her family were Californians for many generations and had, several generations back, been people of wealth and prominence in San Francisco. Her grandfather had been a lawyer for the Southern Pacific Railroad and had argued two cases before the U.S. Supreme Court. Tipton also came from a line of high-achieving women. Her great-grandfather and his sister had been practicing physicians at the turn of the century, she being the first woman to graduate from the medical school at the University of California at Berkeley.

Tipton's grandmother, who was a major influence in her life and with whom she was still very close, had also wanted to be a doctor. She had taken an undergraduate premed course at Stanford and, around 1910, entered that university's medical school. In her final year before becoming a doctor, she met Tipton's grandfather, who was already a lawyer. They fell in love and planned to marry. He insisted, however, that she abandon medical school. It would not be enough that she agree not to practice medicine; he stated unabashedly that he did not want a wife with a degree higher than his. With only months remaining before graduating, Tipton's grandmother quit medical school to become the mother of five children, and, eventually, the grandmother of sixteen devoted grandchildren.

Education had always been important to the Tiptons, but to none of them more than to Elaine Tipton's generation. Since there was not much money in the family, Elaine and her brothers and sisters had to put themselves through school. Even so, after graduating, they all went on to get advanced degrees.

"We had a very strong sense of our parents loving us unconditionally. They wanted us to do well and to them education was the key," Tipton said. "It wasn't a matter of 'Are you going to college?' but rather, 'Where are you going to graduate school?' It was just assumed. But it was also understood we had to do it on our own. We were a bunch of little Horatio Algers." Her older brother obtained two doctorates from Harvard, and was a professor of theology and sociology at Emory University, in Georgia. One sister was a physician, the other had a master's in education from Harvard. Her younger brother held an MPA from USC, and works in civic administration.

As a teenager Tipton considered herself the least intellectual of her family, and at one point was thinking of attending only junior college. Ever since she was a young girl, her interests had been less scholastic and more social and gregarious. At the Catholic girls' school she attended, she was president of her class and was active in a number of school organizations. She values having had an all-female education, feeling that it helped develop her leadership abilities and potential.

Following the family tradition of graduate school, Tipton went to law school and graduated uncertain of what she would do with her degree. An old friend who worked for the San Mateo District Attorney's office suggested she apply there. At that time she had no particular predisposition for a career in law enforcement, but, having no firm alternative plans, took his advice and went with the district attorney's office at the age of twenty-six. Happy as she was to have landed the job, she had nagging misgivings about whether or not she had what it took to be a trial attorney.

After she had been with the district attorney's office for nine months she was given a series of related cases to try, cases no one else wanted. It was a high-visibility affair involving militant high school teachers who had closed down their school over some labor issues and had in the process broken the law in a number of ways. "They were only misdemeanor cases," Tipton said, "but because they were in the news and politically sensi-

Eileen Franklin, age seven.
(Collection of the author)

The Franklin children in 1970. From left: Diana, Kate, Eileen, George junior, and Janice. *(Collection of the author)*

George Franklin.
(Collection of the author)

After the birth of Eileen's daughter, George Franklin visited often. *(Collection of the author)*

Eileen was always her father's favorite. *(Collection of the author)*

Barry and Eileen on a trip to Europe in 1984. *(Collection of the author)*

Eileen and Jessica. *(Collection of the author)*

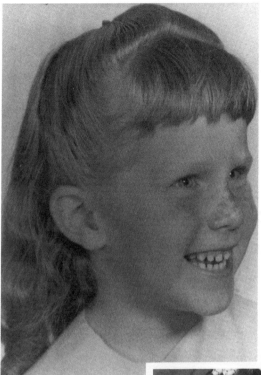

Jurors in the trial of George Franklin gasped when shown the photos of the victim, Susan Nason *(above)*, and Eileen's daughter, Jessica Lipsker *(right)*. *(Collection of the author)*

George Franklin underwent a marked transformation during the time between his arraignment in November of 1989 *(top)* and the preliminary hearing in May of 1990 *(bottom)*. *(Vern Fisher)*

When Eileen testified at the preliminary hearing, her father (with white hair) stared at her impassively. *(William Wright)*

George Franklin's attorneys, Douglas Horngrad and Arthur Wachtel. *(Vern Fisher)*

Below: Detective Bryan Cassandro *(left)* and Assistant District Attorney Martin Murray escort Margaret and Shirley Nason into the courtroom. *(Vern Fisher)*

Assistant District Attorney Elaine Tipton, who prosecuted the case, speaks to the press just after the verdict. *(Vern Fisher)*

Throughout the trial Detective Robert Morse provided strong support to Eileen, as shown here just after the verdict. *(Vern Fisher)*

tive, I was under heavy scrutiny from both my office and the public. I won the cases and was elated, because I knew I had done all right. I knew I could handle myself in court." In her twelve years as a prosecutor, Tipton had developed a courtroom style that was forceful and combative without any loss of her femininity.

At the time she took over the Franklin case, Elaine Tipton was eight years older than Eileen. She was a good-looking blond woman of medium height and slender build, with fine features and a tentative, almost breathless quality that belied her courtroom toughness. One element of glamour slightly incongruous with her no-nonsense courtroom demeanor was the white Jaguar she drove to work each day. She lived in a comfortable house not far from the courthouse that was furnished with family antiques and china that she treasured.

The main focus of her personal life was her family—she was particularly close to her two sisters—and a small group of intimate friends. Unlike many in her field, she did not see prosecution work as a step to public office. She loved being a prosecutor, and had won convictions in a number of important cases. In one, she had won the death penalty in a child molestation–murder case. The trial of George Franklin would be the high point of an already distinguished career.

Tipton's first impression of Eileen was more favorable than Eileen's was of her. With her family's emphasis on education, Tipton found it hard to believe that Eileen had never finished high school. "I thought she was not just bright or street-smart, but intelligent, articulate, insightful." This good opinion only grew as they came to know each other over the months ahead and as Tipton began to wonder about the terrible childhood traumas that had caused "a woman of Eileen's innate ability to drop out of the mainstream." She would eventually say how rare it was to find a witness like Eileen. "Her ability to comprehend," Tipton later said, "to pick up nuances, to know what turn of phrase might be problematic—you can't teach those things to a witness."

On more than one occasion in the dialogue between Eileen and Tipton in the following weeks, Tipton asked if it was possible that Eileen had remembered the murder all along, but for good reasons had chosen not to come forward. Tipton emphasized that, if this was the case, it was nothing Eileen should be ashamed of. There would be no punitive consequences, and the case could still proceed. "We didn't tell her it was a better story or a worse one," Tipton said. "We told her we could work with it. Never hesitating, Eileen took the position with us: 'Here it is. This is what happened. I can't explain it. You deal with it.'"

As Tipton and her team threw themselves into building their case, Morse and Cassandro spoke with everyone connected to the story—the Nasons, the Franklins, Foster City neighbors, the legions of law-enforcement people. At one point, the two detectives flew to Philadelphia to interview Eileen's Aunt Jean.

Tipton set out to build a psychiatric structure to support what she felt was her case's biggest hurdle, the twenty-year repression. All the physical evidence gathered by the police from Susan Nason's murder had been meticulously preserved. This was now subjected to painstaking examination in the unlikely chance that some hair or fingerprint might link the crime to George Franklin and remove the burden of proof from Eileen. Tipton knew this was the sort of evidence Eileen had been so eager to learn if they had.

Throughout the spring of 1990, Eileen continued to receive calls from every member of her family, each with his or her own agenda for damage control. Once, when George junior was on the phone with a suspiciously detailed list of questions, Barry suddenly said, "Why are you asking Eileen these things, George? Are you working for the defense?" To their astonishment, and—for his candor—to his credit, he answered that he was. Hearing this, Barry yelled that he didn't want George calling there anymore, and hung up. Smarting under what she saw as an underhanded betrayal, Eileen was incredulous that her younger brother, who had suffered so much at their father's hands and who feared him more than any of the others, was working against her and aggressively working for their father's acquittal.

Eileen

In the middle of 1989, when I was thinking more seriously about contacting the police, I wanted first to have my prostitution conviction expunged from my record. I was eligible for this, since more than five years had passed since the conviction, with no further arrests. I had been told I could then erase all record of my arrest and conviction, even to law enforcement. I got things moving through the attorney who had handled my case. In August 1989 I received a court document ordering the conviction expunged. I was tremendously relieved to close that chapter of my life.

In November, when I gave my first statement to Inspectors Morse and Cassandro, I asked them if they had run a police check on me. Bob said that they had, and that my record was clean. I was overjoyed. The police would not judge me about my past! I was not going to be publicly humiliated! I could proceed, untainted, in seeking justice for Susan! I felt I had won a tremendous legal victory.

Some time after my father was arrested, Martin Murray called me to say that my father's lawyers had requested a rap sheet on me and other witnesses. Unconcerned, I told him to go ahead and supply one. The worst they'd find, I thought, was a speeding ticket or two. Several days later, Marty called me and told me that the rap sheet had shown my misdemeanor conviction and the defense would surely want this information.

I was devastated. This is it, I thought. I have ruined my children's lives. I will be shunned at their school and asked to step down as room mother of the kindergarten. I will no longer be able to conduct business, because no one will respect me. I will be cast out from the Lipsker family, who will be disgraced by my presence. The newspapers are going to love this and prey on me, all because I witnessed a murder.

Marty told me that he would inform the defense in a letter only that a police check had been run on me and that there had been one misdemeanor conviction many years before, which had no bearing on my honesty or veracity as a witness. The nature of the conviction would not be provided in the letter, and, should the defense lawyers wish to pursue the matter, a judge would decide if my conviction was admissible in court.

For the time being, the defense attorneys would not know the nature of my offense, which meant that the press would not know. I was supposed to feel relieved, but I felt awful. How could a person's record be clear one day and show an arrest a few days later? Damn computers, I thought.

Many months later after Elaine took over the prosecution and the trial was approaching, she explained that my conviction would be the topic of a pretrial motion hearing. Elaine said that the hearing would determine whether one misdemeanor conviction by a witness, not relating to honesty or veracity, would be admissible in court. She said that the hearing would not be about me by name, but simply about "a witness." The possibility that my conviction would become public knowledge seemed to be increasing, and I was frightened by that.

When the judge, before the trial, ruled in our favor, Elaine told me that she considered this her most significant victory to date with the case. She could not discuss it with others, however, because of my desire for privacy. I felt guilty robbing Elaine of her victory, but not so guilty that I wanted anyone to know what she'd been victorious about. I was also tremendously relieved, not just that Elaine had won her motion but that she was on the same side as I was.

The preliminary hearings that California holds on felony cases serve the function of grand juries in other states. The primary difference is that they are held in open court rather than in secret. They are truncated run-throughs of cases' basic elements that enable judges to determine whether sufficient evidence exists to bind cases over to trial, or whether circumstances exist to invalidate their viability. The hearings are not exhaustive weighings of the evidence, as in trials, but quick overviews to seek out crippling gaps in the assembled evidence, or legal flaws that might render significant portions of the evidence inadmissible.

If judges drop their guard, determined defense attorneys can turn preliminary hearings into life-sized replicas of the trials to come, with parades of marginal witnesses, and piles of mildly relevant evidence. The preliminary hearing in the Franklin case began on May 21, 1990, and was presided over by Judge James Browning, Jr., who had been the prosecutor in the Patty Hearst trial. The hearings focused on two main issues: Was Eileen a credible witness, and had her memory been elicited through hypnosis? The latter point was crucial, since her entire eyewitness account would have been inadmissible evidence in the state of California (although not in all states), and the case would have collapsed had she in fact been hypnotized.

A former firefighter friend who had become a lawyer recommended to George Franklin for his defense a criminal attorney named Douglas Horngrad, of the San Francisco firm of Horngrad and Wachtel. Horngrad was a tall, pleasant-looking man in his late thirties. Horn-rimmed glasses and a slight bend in his posture, perhaps to lower himself to a more reasonable conversational level, gave him a professorial air. His partner, Arthur

Wachtel, was below average height and had a thick and unwieldy head of steel-gray hair that in no way lessened a springy, boyish quality that belied his thirty-eight years. Throughout the preliminary hearings, both Horngrad and Wachtel presented a dour, charmless demeanor to the court, their only flashes of personality, particularly in Horngrad's case, being a testy combativeness. Later, at the trial itself, his style would change dramatically. He would become conspicuously civil to everyone, exuding an easy amiability, and would often be quite funny.

A major issue to be resolved before the preliminary hearings began was whether or not to admit the press and the public. Since inflammatory and highly damaging allegations would be made against Franklin, he asked his lawyers to try for closed hearings. Not only was that disallowed, but the judge ruled that a pool television camera would be permitted to record the proceedings. Few had expected this in a trial that would necessitate such excruciating personal testimony from reluctant witnesses. At the subsequent trial, the presiding judge would not allow a camera in his courtroom; all the footage of the principals testifying that was later shown on television was from the preliminary hearings.

The biggest surprise at the outset of the hearings was George Franklin himself. The change that had been worked on his appearance was so extreme that people who had been following the case and who had seen him at the arraignment, shots of which were shown on the NBC piece, were unaware that the nondescript-looking man sitting at the defense table was, indeed, the defendant.

In the six months since his arrest, Franklin had lost forty pounds, converting his figure from burly to average. His unruly gray hair had been cut short and parted neatly. His ferocious beard had been shaved to reveal a benign face excessively lined for his fifty years. Steel-rimmed glasses concealed his one strong remaining feature, thick eyebrows that met over his nose in a perpetual scowl. With a gray suit and a timorous blue tie to complete the de-villainization, they had succeeded in converting an alarmingly wild-looking brute into someone who resembled the mousy principal of a junior high school, far more Jekyll than Hyde. Throughout the days ahead, even at some highly dramatic moments, Franklin would sit silently, with a pleasant expression just short of a smile fixed permanently to his face.

The main points Elaine Tipton hoped to establish in the preliminary hearing were that Susan Nason was indeed murdered, that Eileen Franklin had witnessed it, and that Eileen could identify the murderer. Tipton also brought in subsidiary witnesses to testify to a number of tangential points that added no further proof of Franklin's guilt, but that reinforced Eileen's version of the crime.

An example was Margaret Nason, now a thin, fragile, middle-aged woman who countered one of the defense's alternative explanations of Susan's death by testifying shakily that her daughter would never have gone off in a car with a stranger. Also, a number of police and forensic experts testified, in gruesome detail, to the manner of death and the condition of the body when it was discovered.

As Eileen prepared to fly up from Los Angeles to testify, she was determined that Sica and Aaron be kept unaware of what was taking place. Anyone discussing the case with Eileen in the presence of her children was told to refer to her father as "the defendant." As a precaution against their learning of the trial inadvertently, Eileen had requested a meeting with the two top administrators of her children's school so that she could tell them herself what they would probably learn through gossip or from the press.

The women had been sympathetic, and had suggested that, in case one of the children said something in class, it might be best to discreetly inform the other teachers. Eileen agreed. She was very gratified when, some days later, a teacher approached her and said that her husband was in police work and admired Eileen's courage in coming forward.

Eileen

The morning I was scheduled to testify, Bob Morse picked Barry and me up at the airport and drove us directly to the Hall of Justice in Redwood City. I met with Elaine and expected that I would be taken to the hotel to register, relax a moment, and change my clothes. Elaine and I went through some of my statements, but primarily she helped me stay calm and focused on testifying. As the time came closer for me to appear in court, we realized that it would be impossible to get to the hotel and back in time. I would have to dress in the ladies' room of the district attorney's office.

Bob got my suitcase from his car, and we found that my

suit was badly wrinkled. I discovered that the San Mateo County District Attorney's Office did not keep an iron and an ironing board on hand for their witnesses. Elaine, always resourceful, sent Bob to her home, which was not far, for hers. Coming back into the building carrying an ironing board and iron, Bob made quite a spectacle. He took a good bit of ribbing from the people who knew him.

His courthouse buddies would have gotten an even bigger kick from seeing him set up the board and start to iron my suit. He had taken off his jacket, so his service revolver was in plain view. As I saw him ironing away, I protested that he shouldn't do that; I knew how to iron. Bob smiled and reminded me of his earlier claim: "You wouldn't believe the things we do for our witnesses."

After I had dressed, I went into the ladies' room to fix my hair, but my hands were shaking so badly I couldn't control the direction of the braid I was trying to make into a bun. Elaine came into the ladies' room and took a couple of hairpins that I had set out and got my hair in place. She talked soothingly to me as she worked, and I was reminded of the days when my sisters and I had helped each other dress. I was really lucky to have ended up with Bob and Elaine.

TWELVE

On the first day of Eileen's testimony, journalists and television cameramen, about to get their first glimpse of the remarkable accuser, clogged the courthouse corridor. Tipton told a stunned Barry that she wanted Robert Morse to escort Eileen into the courtroom. Since Barry and Eileen had arrived in San Francisco that morning, the prosecution team agreed that Barry was adding to Eileen's anxiety, telling her how she should testify, how to outsmart the defense lawyer, criticizing and complaining about the prosecution's strategy. Exasperated, Tipton resolved to separate Barry from Eileen and keep him from her throughout the day. Barry was furious.

Manipulating Barry was not easy, but Tipton got her way by simply keeping Barry out of her office while she had a last-minute conference with Eileen. Then, as he sat fuming in the waiting room, Robert Morse and Cassandro spirited Eileen out another exit for the walk across the street to the old courthouse where the hearings were being held. Eileen would never have thwarted Barry to such a degree on her own, but on this particular morning she was relieved others were doing so.

As a result, Barry missed Eileen's spectacular entrance into the jammed courtroom, and into the public eye, where she would remain for some time to come. As television cameras and reporters followed her across the street and to the second-floor courtroom door, she looked frightened and tense but lovely. She wore a navy blue suit with white trim—businesslike without being severe—pearl and gold earrings, a strand of pearls, and a pearl clasp in the bun at the back of her head.

On the witness stand, she handled herself admirably, despite her stage fright and the taut hold she clearly had on her emotions. As soon as she was sworn in, Horngrad challenged her

174

competence as a witness because of the hypnosis issue. The judge told the opposing counsel to argue that point immediately. By both Horngrad and Tipton, Eileen was taken through the two instances of having told others she had been hypnotized, and she gave her reasons for having lied about this and stated categorically that she had never been hypnotized.

Saying he would reserve his ruling on the point, the judge told counsel to proceed with the main body of the witness's testimony. With the television camera on her, and some twenty reporters writing rapidly, Eileen described all the events she could remember of the murder. Arriving at the moment when she saw her father about to crush Susan's head with a rock, Eileen raised her hands over her head in demonstration. Newspapers throughout the United States ran this striking picture, a young woman showing a courtroom full of people how her father had bludgeoned her best friend to death. In his cross-examination, Horngrad asked countless questions about the circumstances of her recollection, and far fewer about the murder itself.

During the lunch recess, Barry, who was not allowed into the courtroom because he was scheduled to testify several days later, gained admittance to Elaine Tipton's office when Eileen and the prosecution team returned from the courtroom. In front of Eileen—whose life, for the moment, was in the hands of the two lawyers—he berated Martin Murray and Tipton for having kept him from his wife. He needed to talk to her, he said, to get her to commit to one of the film offers. All the frustration that had been building on both sides poured out until the mild-mannered Murray was screaming that Barry, with his constant interference, his statements to the press, his "fucking book and movie deals," was jeopardizing the entire case. "Things were boiling at such a high level," Tipton later said, "we told him he was doing everything conceivable to upset Eileen, to undermine the integrity of the prosecution."

Far from daunting Barry, the criticism only angered him further, and he yelled back that Murray's office had lied to Eileen, that they were mishandling the case and were not treating him with respect. (Barry was sufficiently worried that Murray might have a point about the deal-making, so he immediately retained a top criminal attorney for an independent opinion. He was assured that, under these unusual circumstances, a book and a film would not hurt the prosecution.) Whatever the rights and wrongs of the two sides, and while

both believed they were guided by a concern for Eileen, a
high-voltage fight between the people closest to Eileen in her
ordeal was, for her, an additional nightmare and, in the eyes of
most observers, an unnecessary one on this nightmarish day.

A friend of Eileen's and Barry's stepped out of the courthouse during the recess on the first afternoon of Eileen's testimony, and found Barry pacing up and down on the empty
sidewalk, dressed in his business suit and tie, his garment bag
over his shoulder. He spotted the friend and asked for a lift to
the airport. "I'm getting out of here," he said. "I won't be
treated like a child. They don't want me to be with Eileen? Fine!
Let them do whatever they want. Fucking lawyers! I can't stand
any of them!" The friend convinced Barry that if Eileen learned
he had left town, it would upset her even more.

After court adjourned the first day, Barry, somewhat calmed,
got Eileen something to eat at their hotel near the airport.
Then, with a friend, they took a drive around Foster City,
which was only a few minutes away. As they drove past the
house on Harvester, Eileen remarked on how the color had
been changed, then fell silent. Pointing out the apartments
where Eileen had worked and Barry was living when they met,
she brightened and they both grew nostalgic.

"Do you remember feeding the ducks, Barry?" Eileen said.
He reminded her of the boating events. He pointed to a building
where a friend had lived. Eileen said he was wrong; it had been
a different building. They argued, mildly at first, then fiercely.
Over the next few days, such disputes broke out frequently,
always about inconsequential discrepancies between his recollection and hers. An outsider might have wondered at the trivial
facts from their past that could send Barry, but especially Eileen, into prolonged dogfights. Others realized that this was a
woman for whom getting her memories right was terribly, terribly important.

While the press coverage was not a hundred percent behind
Eileen—some reporters made their skepticism evident in their
pieces—no one implied she was crazy, as she had feared. On
the second day of her testimony, she wore her hair down and
a simpler outfit. She seemed considerably more relaxed, even
to the point of trading barbs with Horngrad. When she said she
had not discussed a certain matter with George junior, Horngrad asked if she was angry with her brother. She said yes.
Looking directly at Horngrad, she added, "If you had anything

you wanted to know, you could have asked me yourself. You didn't have to send my brother in as a spy."

On the final day of testimony when Horngrad asked if she believed her memory was limited, she replied that she believed *all* memory was limited. Angrily, Horngrad said, "We are not talking about all memory, but about a murder scene." But Eileen had won that round. Just before dismissing her, Horngrad asked, "Did you love your father?"

Quietly and not looking toward Franklin, she said, "I think I have always loved my father."

Eileen later asked a friend in court how her father had reacted when she said that. The friend replied that he had shown no change of expression. Indeed, throughout Eileen's testimony, even as she described her father bringing the rock down on Susan's head, Franklin sat at the defense table, not ten yards from her, gazing at her with rapt interest, more a proud parent watching a loved child performing well than a man being accused by that child of a heinous crime. When Eileen mentioned having once considered hypnosis as a way of losing weight, Franklin smiled broadly and appeared to be trying to catch her eye. As she would whenever she was in the courtroom, she avoided looking his way.

The defense had promised that Janice would provide the defendant with an alibi. This turned out to be that in her 1984 statement to the police accusing her father of Susan's murder, she had said that she encountered her father in their house "around four o'clock." Since Susan did not arrive home from school until after three, this would not have allowed him enough time to drive up Route 92, molest and murder her, and return home by four.

On the stand, Janice told Horngrad that she had been wrong in her earlier statement to the police. She now thought the time had been closer to five or five-thirty. She took advantage of this correction to do further damage to her father: Because of the physical, verbal, and sexual abuse inflicted on all of them by the defendant in the home, she said, she always stayed out as late as possible. Leah also got across what a monster George Franklin had been to live with, but testified that she could remember nothing out of the ordinary about him at the time of Susan's murder.

Barry, who had been called as a witness for the defense, had been looking forward eagerly to taking the witness stand. He welcomed a chance to make a monkey out of Horngrad and

Wachtel and get in some shots at his father-in-law. When an opening for the latter did not present itself, Barry forced in the information before an objection could stop him. The questioning had been about the rough conditions in the Franklin home. In a lightning non sequitur, Barry blurted that Eileen's father had once held her down so a friend of his could rape her. The courtroom was stunned. Naturally, Barry's verbal hand grenade led that day's news stories.

During his direct examination by Wachtel, Barry had made several misstatements and said other things vulnerable to twisting by the defense. Tipton later told a friend, "The usual way to deal with that kind of witness is to go in on cross-examination and clean things up, undo some of the damage he has done on direct. But when Wachtel finished his direct examination, I said, 'No questions.' I didn't want to give Horngrad another crack at Barry on redirect. I just wanted him out of there."

Although Barry was a problem for Tipton, her overall appraisal of him was not all negative. "While he's up on the stand spouting out one problem for me after another, I'm sitting there thinking to myself—Barry, Barry, Barry, when will you learn? The answer? Never. There isn't a force on earth that can get him to change. Barry will do what Barry will do. He's one in a trillion.

"But I believe," Tipton continued, "that of all the husbands on this planet—most of them more nurturing, more supportive, more sensitive to their wives' needs—faced with the situation that faced Barry and Eileen, eighty percent of them would have said to their wives, 'I believe you, I love you, and I want things to be right for you, but I don't think you should put yourself through this, it's going to be too hard on you, it will be too hard on us as a family. We'll get him some other way, but I don't want you to come forward because it will destroy our lives.' Barry didn't do that. His agenda was to expose George Franklin for the evil person he is. Even if Barry feared George Franklin coming after his family, he could have laid low. He could have urged his wife to remain silent. Instead he did the right thing."

Since neither Eileen nor Barry was needed anymore in court, they headed home to Canoga Park. A friend, who had been in court and was now driving them to the San Francisco airport, said to Barry, "That was some bombshell you dropped in court about Eileen's rape!" When she learned that Barry had trumpeted the story in open court, Eileen completely fell apart, crying and screaming at Barry that he had totally betrayed her.

Why was she upset, he asked. Wasn't the idea to put George Franklin in jail? To show the world what a monster he was? "But that was something that happened to *me*," she cried. "I don't want the whole world to know about it. If it had to be told, it was for *me* to tell, not you." She would not be mollified.

Later, in the airport, waiting for their flight to be called, Barry and Eileen were standing at opposite ends of a long magazine rack thumbing through magazines. Two men in business suits stood browsing between them. "Hey, Eileen," Barry called out brightly. "You made *Time* magazine this week." The two businessmen both turned to look at Eileen.

"Barry," she said, spitting her words, *"SHUT UP!"*

Judge Browning had grown increasingly impatient with Horngrad as the hearings went into their second week, eventually warning him before the introduction of his next witness that too many of his witnesses produced nothing helpful, and that the next one had better be significant. When Horngrad finally finished, he had raised the specter of a suspicious character who had been seen in Foster City at the time of Susan's disappearance, he had pointed up discrepancies between Eileen's testimony and Janice's, he had alluded scathingly to Eileen's book and movie deals, which she did not deny were in the works although nothing was signed, and he had raised the possibility that Eileen had been hypnotized. None of it persuaded Judge Browning that the state's case was flawed or inadequate. On June 1, 1990, he ruled that George Franklin be bound over to trial.

Eileen

After the preliminary hearing, I decided I would try to put an end to the torment of returning memories. The prosecution had won its first round in the courtroom; I would win a personal victory over my memory, to purge myself of other memories I might have repressed. I decided to see if I could force open the locked doors in my mind that I knew were still there, doors that blocked me from remembering so much of my childhood.

I had been wondering if it might be possible for me to

manipulate my mind into not repressing but remembering. I was curious to experiment with my mind, hoping to unlock the past. There were areas of my childhood that terrified me when I started to think about them. When I approached them, a siren went off in my head, screaming, "BEWARE. DO NOT ENTER!" I thought that by trying to get past these deep feelings of fright or terror locked inside me, I could bring back specific events, thus lessening the vague feeling of terror that dominated my life. I wanted to grasp the memories and bravely confront them. I thought that unassisted I could resolve them, file them away discarded in my mind as "normal" memories.

I thought very carefully about the ramifications of my making an effort to remember events I had never before recalled. Horngrad's hostile questioning had been unnerving for me, and I did not want to prolong any future contact with him by doing something that he might construe as legally questionable. I was also afraid of doing anything that might endanger the prosecution of the case or cause Elaine Tipton to question my credibility or good sense.

Unfortunately, at the time I was feeling ambitious and strong, so I decided to try remembering. I prepared myself intellectually for the cleaning-out process, but neglected to brace myself emotionally for another hellish incident with my father that was unrelated to Susan's murder. I soon realized that the pain hidden within was better left shielded from my consciousness. Ironically, in an effort to heal and strengthen myself, I initiated new pain.

As I tried to reenter the frightening areas of my childhood, I began recalling memorable places. I could easily remember being at home and at school, with the constant noise of other children and the oppressive fear. I searched through my mind for the familiar feeling of overwhelming terror, the feeling that shadowed so many benign memories, causing me to shy away from them. It was the feeling of terror that coursed through me when I thought of the sound of Susan's murder, the momentary and disorienting fright that overrode all other senses for an instant, telling me that "X marked the spot" and I was at X.

I decide to take a mental walk through the house at 678 Harvester. To my thinking, that house of horrors, with its constant violence, can hold no secrets and is a safe place to begin my experiment. I imagine walking through the entire house. The family room with the ugly brown linoleum, the kitchen windows facing the neighbors' house on one side and the courtyard on the other, the stark living room. I imagine walking toward the hallway, past my parents' bedroom. As I turn down the hallway, I am mentally stopped. I can walk no farther. A hint of terror washes over me.

I can't determine why I have stopped, so I force myself to continue. As I mentally pass the bathroom next to my parents' bedroom, my fright looms. Because the bathroom is what frightens me, my memory will not budge from the hallway. I tell myself there is no sense in trying to remember, if I am going to run scared at the slightest fear. I become more terrified, yet more intrigued with vague, frightened feelings. Now my curiosity draws me into the terrifying room.

What do I remember? I remember being in the bathtub with my father. I am very young, because my hair is short. He is holding me under my arms, bouncing me up and down, playing with me. I am happy, laughing. While he bounces me, he occasionally tickles me under my arms. He is talking reassuringly and playfully. We are both smiling and laughing. But what I am feeling is something hard in his lap.

No, I decide, I do not want to remember this. I try to convince myself that nothing else happened. I am certain that I do not want to remember this. Why had I ever mentally walked through that door? Sadly, I know I cannot live with the unresolved fear of that bathroom. I must explore further.

I ask myself, "If nothing else happened, why am I suddenly sick at my stomach and terrified?" I decide to try to remember a bit more, praying that nothing else happened, that I'll be left with a wonderful memory of my father.

He's playing with me, the water is warm, and the bath is full and bubbly, the way I like it. I am sitting in his lap, and he pushes my shoulders forward, moving my hips toward him. The hardness presses firmly against my bottom. I say, "Ow," or make a noise. He responds with more tickling. It hurts. He continues to press. . . .

No. I do not think I should remember this anymore. My stomach begins to hurt. I become scared. Beyond my control now, the memory comes. The strength and logic that might have prevented the memory are overwhelmed by fear, pain, doubt, and curiosity.

I remember the feeling of the pressure, which is searing. I yell—no, I yelp like a wounded animal. With my cry, he suddenly pushes my shoulders forward, putting my head underwater. When he lessens his force, I lift my head from the water. I am choking, sputtering, gasping for air, and sobbing. My mother walks in and asks what has happened. He dismisses her by saying something like I have gotten soap in my eyes.

Once the memory had returned completely, I felt very alone. Unprotected and betrayed. This was how I always felt when memories returned. Now that the memory was back in my mind, I desperately wanted to talk to someone. I should not have ventured back into that bathroom alone.

Because of the legal ramifications of what had just come back to me, my feelings of isolation were compounded. I knew I could not discuss this with anyone under subpoena. I could not talk to Barry; he too was under subpoena, and in any case he'd tell me to forget it. Not a word to my mother, she would not want to know this. I would like to have told Janice, but in her compassion she'd feel my pain, which she didn't need right then. I could not call Kirk Barrett, though he knows how deeply my memory can frighten me, because he is testifying. Sharon, Denise, Lynn, and Lea are all out of the question. How can they possibly understand the violation and fear, so fresh in my mind, yet from so long ago? Elaine, my tower of strength, my final hope—I fear she would have to tell Horngrad, as the law required, her professionalism overruling her compassion.

There was no one I could call. Everyone I cared about was subject to subpoena, or too normal to understand the extensive violation of my body and mind. I was alone and scared. I'd been violated. The upcoming trial rendered me silent. After more than two decades my father had gotten away with another crime. He was the victor. I was voiceless.

Barry's plan to move his business to Switzerland was stalled while he was waiting for a commitment from one of the firms that had expressed interest. Friends who knew Switzerland had warned him that the Swiss, even when favorably impressed, look over foreigners for a year before deciding whether or not to do business with them. Barry said he would give it six months. If by then he did not have at least one firm client, he would give up his studio in St. Gallen, sell his car, and resign himself to the smog and crime of Los Angeles—until another idea turned up.

The six months had almost elapsed when not just one but two important companies offered him a contract. He and I flew into action. The main thing was to find a house big enough for us all, plus a school for the children. With Barry stationing himself in Switzerland, I commuted between St. Gallen and Canoga Park, trying to be a mother and close up a large operation on one continent, then jump on a plane to house-hunt on another. Hanging over all of my frenzied activity was the specter of my father's trial, which had been scheduled for October.

My sense of myself had changed drastically over the past months. Since testifying at the preliminary hearing I felt tired —worn out on life. I looked the same, only sadder. I was an echo of my former self. As I thumbed through my Canoga Park closets, trying to find an outfit for dinner and a trek on the beach with friends, I realized that all of these clothes belonged to someone else. I was no longer the person who bought them.

A July night out in southern California should be fun and relaxing, but I felt awkward trying on my summer clothes. Soft, feminine, and mildly sexy outfits that I had worn with relish in the past seemed wrong, as if I did not belong in this skin anymore. I was no longer comfortable being soft, feminine, or sexy. I knew that this was a result of *The Case*. I tried to tell myself that this was what happened when one approached thirty. Everyone changes. But I knew the truth.

When I tried on a filmy strapless dress, it made me feel too vulnerable. A dress with a laced-up bodice and a short skirt made me realize I was no longer comfortable having sex appeal. I had been robbed of my femininity. I had always enjoyed the attention of men, but now I felt uneasy wearing anything that might make men notice me.

My vulnerability, sex appeal, and femininity, which were reflected in my clothing, had died. The painful days spent on the witness stand in Redwood City had altered me, killing an area of my emotions where I once felt at peace with myself, where I felt safe. I was now afraid to wear anything that would call attention to me. I had had too much attention. I felt raped by the press.

I could discard the clothes, but that wouldn't solve the problem, since I had no idea what clothes would suit me now. It would make more sense to discard the mind that made these clothes irrelevant, but you can't do that. Too bad. Just how the hell would I go forward with my life now?

My outlook improved after Elaine scheduled a series of appointments for me over a two-day period in San Francisco with Dr. Lenore Terr, who coincidentally was the psychiatrist who had appeared on the NBC piece about my case. The understanding was that Dr. Terr would testify at the trial about how memory works. Elaine wanted me to meet with Terr to give her an opportunity to discuss my memory. Bob Morse met me at the San Jose airport and presented me with an adorable teddy bear. The police were looking better all the time.

Since we had several hours to kill, Morse cheerfully agreed to take me to the department stores around Union Square where we bought children's clothes and I picked out a tie for him to wear in court. He drove me to the office of Dr. Terr. I knew little about her except that Elaine said she was a top expert on childhood trauma and had written a book. I asked her about herself—Bob had told me that I always ask more questions than an investigator. When she told me the title of her book, *Too Scared to Cry,* I replied that she was the right person for me to talk to.

My meetings with Dr. Terr were very interesting. She knew how to ask questions that made sense to my memories. I was amazed because she truly seemed to understand how they had returned and continued to evolve. Dr. Terr never looked at me as if I were peculiar, even when I told her about making myself invisible as a child, forgetting a rape and a murder for two decades, and being a former drug abuser.

I wished that I could have more time with her when the trial was over, so that I could understand my mind as well as she did. When I left her office I felt completely "normal." Dr. Terr had not doubted my sanity or my thought process; she seemed to accept my repression as a natural phenomenon. The visits, which had been initiated as a piece of prosecution strategy, had given me a stronger belief in myself and more hope for my future.

PART THREE

The Trial

THIRTEEN

THE FRANKLIN CASE HAD BEEN ASSIGNED TO JUDGE THOMAS McGinn Smith, whose courtroom was on the second floor of Redwood City's Hall of Justice, a large, nondescript, postwar building that stood across the street from the venerable domed courthouse where the preliminary hearing had taken place. Both the sheriff's office and the district attorney's office were also in the newer building.

The entire fourth floor was the county jail, where as many as five hundred men—women were placed elsewhere—served their sentences, if less than a year, or awaited trial. One man charged with murder had been there for three years while his lawyer kept winning continuances. Throughout the trial, George Franklin commuted between his cell on the fourth floor to the courtroom on the second. Tipton's office was on the third floor.

Judge Smith's courtroom was not large; four rows of cushioned theater seats could accommodate sixty spectators. This was meager seating for a trial that had attracted national attention, especially when that number would have to include newspaper reporters, television producers and writers, two book authors, and one screenwriter. A number of seats would also be claimed by a brace of courtroom artists; cameras had been banned from the courtroom in a ruling that NBC was appealing, unsuccessfully as it turned out. An additional number of seats, generally six, were set aside for those close to the case—Susan Nason's parents, for example, who would be at the trial most every day. Standees were not permitted, so reporters assigned to the case groaned when they found out they would have to arrive early each day to be assured seats.

The seating problem was lessened somewhat by the trial

across the hall of Ramon Salcido, who was accused of having
gone on a cocaine-induced rampage and killed his wife, two
daughters, his wife's mother, the wife's two sisters, a coworker,
and four other people. The trial, now entering its final stages,
had caused a sensation and was given daily coverage by the
press. Owing perhaps to the higher body count, or to the fact
that it had gotten a head start, Salcido competed with the
Franklin trial as a lure for the thrill-seeking courthouse regulars.

A modern feature of the Franklin courtroom was the placement of the witness box at the center of the facing wall; the
judge's bench was at an angle in the left front corner, which
allowed the judge a view of the witness, the jury, and the counsel tables. George Franklin would sit with his two lawyers at the
defense table on the left, as far from the jury as possible.

Between the defense table and the judge's elevated bench was
the desk of the court clerk, an expressionless, middle-aged
woman named Peggy Gensel. During even the most riveting
testimony, she would sit shuffling her papers, oblivious to the
exciting drama unfolding across the top of her desk. A three-
month calendar hung on the wall behind the witness box. Prior
estimates of the trial's duration were four to six weeks, but
during prolonged, aimless stretches of testimony, the three
months hung there ominously and, at the slowest moments,
seemed to glow like a mute overtime alarm.

In the pretrial motions, a major issue was whether or not to
permit other conduct of George Franklin to be introduced into
evidence. This conduct consisted of acts, statements, and items
found on Franklin at the time of his arrest that would establish
his sexual interest in children. Tipton was anxious to establish
that Susan Nason had been molested before being murdered; in
that way, a conviction would automatically be first-degree,
under California's felony-murder rule. To do this Tipton hoped
to be allowed an exception to the rule that prohibits introducing uncharged conduct of a defendant.

Horngrad, equally anxious to block such damaging testimony about his client, was willing to stipulate that whoever
killed Susan had molested her first. The judge ruled against
Tipton, which her colleagues thought was a major setback.
Tipton, however, managed to introduce through another opening a small but potent amount of Franklin's other damning
misdeeds. The conglomerate of rules and ordinances governing
trials is like a masonry structure protecting the crime under

adjudication from extraneous or prejudicial information. But it is, as Tipton knew, a structure with numerous doors and windows.

Under the discovery laws, Tipton had informed the defense that "one of her witnesses" had been arrested on a misdemeanor charge. Horngrad argued that he should be allowed to introduce this in testimony, saying, "what if hypothetically the witness with a record was Mrs. Franklin-Lipsker?" Judge Smith ruled in favor of Tipton, disallowing any testimony about the criminal record of the witness, whoever it was. Since the discovery laws apply only to the prosecution, Tipton was unsure how much Horngrad knew, but scored her victory high among the items about which she should remain super-vigilant, and resolved to spring to her feet at the merest hint that Horngrad might be sneaking in a reference to Eileen's arrest.

Waiting anxiously in Zurich for word on this motion, Eileen was enormously relieved, but the sense of disaster averted was quickly buried in the avalanche of other anxieties. A reporter from the *San Mateo Times,* Janet Parker Beck, writing either from a misinterpretation of Horngrad's hypothesis or from inside information, wrote that a misdemeanor conviction of Mrs. Franklin-Lipsker was ruled inadmissible since "the underlying conduct [leading to the witness's conviction] does not and would not relate to the credibility of the witness." In the rush of events as the trial approached, little notice was given Beck's scoop.

In the complexity of their assembly, criminal trials are similar to symphonic concerts. A number of people come together—lawyers, clerks, investigators, researchers, witnesses—to offer up a meticulously constructed piece of work for the consideration of a diverse audience. Many in attendance have been drawn by nothing more than an enthusiasm for the genre; others might have a specific interest in a particular trial. Among those present are a handful whose appraisals, like those of music critics, are of primary importance—these are the judge and the jury.

The proceedings begin with jury selection, an often rambling, inconclusive prelude in which opposing counsels establish both their own characters and the mood of what is about to unfold. Behind the repetitive and tedious questioning of the panelists, the trial's major themes begin to emerge. With the lawyers' opening statements, the device of hint and suggestion is abandoned and the trial's dominant themes are announced with unadorned clarity. The assertions that both sides will seek to prove and disprove are laid on the table and enunciated in a manner that allows for no confusion as to purpose.

At the conclusion of these declarations, the laborious process of development begins—a parade of witnesses and evidence that may address only a small aspect of the major themes of guilt or innocence, or that might illuminate the overall concept. There will be digressions into areas of great contrast to the central points, and there may be climaxes in which one of the developmental points is taken to exciting heights. The underlying themes, however, will always be revisited, and, with the clamorous finale of the closing statements and the final chord of the jury's verdict, resolved.

With the opposing counsel at their tables, George Franklin, accompanied by an armed and uniformed bailiff, entered the courtroom from the right-hand door of the facing wall and strode diagonally across the open space to the defense table on the left. In one arm he carried a folder of papers; the other arm swung with a jauntiness that would have seemed inappropriate even in a more neutral situation. Seated at the table, Franklin removed his glasses and rubbed his eyes. He looked even older than he had at the preliminary hearings—the dark brows were still heavy and pronounced, but they were the strongest element of his features, and when he concealed them by putting his spectacles back on, he once again appeared bland and nondescript. His face, while still maintaining its blockish masculine shape, now appeared more furrowed than lined, making him look a good deal older than his fifty-one years. Even more unflattering to him, the room's fluorescent lighting brought out a slight yellowish pallor that had not been apparent in the sunlit courtroom across the street.

A Foster City friend of the Franklin girls who attended the first day's hearing telephoned Janice later in the day and commented on her father's arm-swinging entrance. "He always had a cocky walk," Janice replied. The friend went on to describe his sickly complexion. "He had jaundice a few years ago," Janice explained, then added, "Can you imagine how alone he must feel now? He's so used to being in complete control. Now he's in prison with no control at all, and his life will be at the mercy of twelve strangers. It's got to be the worst moment in his life!"

Judge Smith, a handsome middle-aged man, established himself quickly as unassuming and low-key by allowing the court to rise to its feet only at his first appearance each day. Even then, he slipped so quickly into his chair from the door immediately to its rear that spectators had time to do little more than clutch purses and newspapers, preparing to rise, before he was already seated. Once seated, Judge Smith's manner was calm and courteous; his low-pitched, soft voice was free of any hint of authoritarian bombast. Jury selection was about to begin.

Before turning the interrogation of individual jurors over to counsel, the judge directed a few general questions to each in turn. What have you heard about the case? Where do you live? What newspaper do you read? Did you hear about the case on TV? Have you or any of your family ever suffered child molestation? Had dealings with psychiatry? Will serving on the jury for four to six weeks be a special hardship for you? Would you listen to other jurors, even if you disagreed with them? Do you have any problem with presumption of innocence until proven guilty?

After a number of panelists had been questioned and the tedium of the *voir dire* process was well established, a whimsical side emerged in Judge Smith. He asked a well-spoken engineer from Lockheed if he had any friends in law enforcement. When the man answered that he did not, the judge then asked in a sympathetic voice, "Do you have any friends?" Few settings are more welcoming to comic relief than courtrooms, and with the judge's joke, the courtroom erupted in laughter. Throughout most of the trial, however, it was not Groucho-like hyperbole but kindliness and benevolence that emanated from the bench.

After a few minutes of questioning, the judge turned each juror over to the attorneys whose interaction had changed considerably from the preliminary hearing. Gone was Horngrad's abrasive, somewhat haughty posturing of a man indignant that his client was undergoing prosecution in the first place. Instead one saw a well-mannered lawyer addressing each juror in soft, persuasive tones.

The change of style was not only limited to the prospective jurors. In exchanges with Elaine Tipton before court was called to order and during breaks, the prickliness had vanished and was replaced by amiability and smiles. Tipton momentarily seemed taken aback by this change and the dynamic between them began to take on the rhythms of a Doris Day–Rock

Hudson adversarial mating dance—a worrisome portent for those hoping for fiery confrontations.

Horngrad's questions to the jurors alternated between establishing the jurors' overall fairness and questions specific to the case. Have you ever been a victim of a crime? Have you taken psychology courses? Would you have a problem assessing and scrutinizing a witness's testimony? One question Horngrad returned to with increasing regularity was: "Would you necessarily believe a witness just because he or she said they saw something happen?" and a variant: "Is it possible for someone to believe something is true that is not?"

With this seemingly guileless challenge to eyewitness testimony, jurors' minds were set off in quest of other possibilities, and the specters of liars and the deluded were released into the courtroom to hover over the proceedings until the trial's end, six weeks later.

Horngrad elaborated on his theme of false memory with a folksy anecdote. A father and a son attended the World Series in 1970. The father leaped to his feet along with everyone else to see an historic winning home run hit 425 feet across the centerfield fence. The crowd rose to its feet and the son, too small to see beyond the people in front of him, missed it entirely. "The kid didn't see it at all," Horngrad said imploringly, "but twenty years later, telling about the incident, *he says he saw it.*"

While Horngrad had chosen to amplify the more polite of his two points, that witnesses, with the passage of time, can believe they have seen things that they never saw, he had also introduced a dangerous ancillary point, one to which he would return later, when his psychiatric experts were attacked by the prosecution. While the boy's memory may have been flawed, causing him to misrepresent his involvement in the event, the central fact was undiminished: a home run had, in fact, been hit that day. Horngrad was establishing that people may garble the past, but they still get the central facts right. He had no anecdote for his other point, that witnesses sometimes lie.

Some of Horngrad's questions aired his worries that the horrendous photos of the murdered Susan Nason would inflame the jury against his client. "The question is not *if* Susan was brutally murdered," he asserted, "but *who did it?* As a juror, would you be inclined to take your anger out on Mr. Franklin?" In furtherance of his invitations to the jurors to disbelieve Eileen Franklin, he asked, "Can you assess a witness's credibility?" "Do you accept or do you *scrutinize* the testimony?" "Do you think the mind can play tricks?" "Can children reconstruct events in a way so that they make sense of them?" "Would you consider as factors whatever motivations a witness might have? Is it possible that one would have a motive to lie? Revenge, for example?" With little subtlety, Horngrad was preparing the jurors for the worst sort of treachery from the state's star witness.

When each panelist was interrogated by Elaine Tipton, her manner was matter-of-fact, almost brusque. "Have you ever encountered repression?" "How do you feel about it?" "Do you think the nature of the event can affect whether or not it is repressed?" "Is a repressed memory automatically less accurate because it has been repressed?" "Do you think anyone who repressed a memory has mental problems?" (To this question, one juror said yes, and was dismissed.) "Do you think repression is possible?" "Do you think a child can be an accurate witness?" "Were you ever friends with a woman who was molested?" Horngrad objected to this last question on the grounds that Tipton's specifying women as the only ones molested was prejudicial. The judge agreed.

As the interrogations proceeded through several panels, a number of jurors were dismissed for cause. An alarming three panelists in a row claimed there had been child abuse in their families. Demographically the panelists seemed more consistently middle-class than a selection of prospective jurors in a large city would be. More than half of this cross-section of suburban San Francisco had attended college, and most of the others spoke well and seemed generally informed.

As they were interrogated one by one, and asked to describe their feelings about such abstruse phenomena as child molestation and repression, it became apparent how carefully they had to tread between normal attitudes and ones so forceful or skewed as to brand them biased. One man flatly announced that he found it hard to believe anyone could forget something as important as a murder for twenty years. Another admitted having difficulty believing that a father could abuse his own child.

Constantly lurking beneath the questions and answers was the unspoken awareness that jurors can quickly deduce the "wrong" answers and offer them up as a way of avoiding four to six weeks immersed in the brutal murder of an eight-year-old. One reason this may have remained unspoken was the disinclination of lawyers on both sides to try their case before jurors who were strongly opposed to serving. If all a panelist had to say to be dismissed was that he or she did not believe repression was possible, it would not take long for other jurors to concoct their own passports to freedom.

Judge Smith emphasized if any of the questions became too personal, he would protect the jurors' privacy by clearing the courtroom. Two jurors took up the judge's offer. One of them, a young medical intern named Alger Chapman III, with the well-bred good looks to match his patrician name, told the court that a member of his family had been molested as a child. Whatever elaboration he offered on this in the closed chamber apparently relieved the defense's understandable concern, and Chapman later emerged as a juror and, eventually, foreman of the jury.

As the repetitive process droned on for days, it became apparent that the prosecution was most anxious to avoid jurors who were skeptical about the phenomenon of repression or resistant to twenty-year-old testimony. The defense wanted none who would believe without reservation the sworn testimony of a self-proclaimed eyewitness. It was not a complex basis for screening, and neither side subscribed to one of the jury-profiling services that claim to be able to forecast the way a given set of jurors will decide, given a few basic demographic and personal facts.

After five days, a jury was empaneled and sworn in. Although the defense could have been excused for fearing women jurors because they might experience a more visceral revulsion against a man who would be shown to have sexually abused his daughters, the jury was made up of eight women and four men. Two of the men appeared to be still in their twenties, and the fourth was a banker in his upper sixties. The women ranged in age from thirty to sixty.

On the morning of the trial's first day, October 31, 1990, a large crowd of spectators and press gathered outside the second-floor courtroom of Judge Smith. Television camera crews, relegated to the corridor, had to content themselves with photographing the entrance into the court of the opposing legal teams and the victim's recently divorced parents, Donald and Margaret Nason, their surviving daughter, Shirley, and Donald Nason's mother.

The press recognized the older Nasons, but Shirley Nason,

an attractive young woman with the short bobbed hair and lithe good looks of a *Brideshead Revisited* aristocrat, remained a puzzle for several days until one reporter, when asked a question by Donald Nason's mother, seized the opening to establish that the young woman with her group was Shirley. Reporters often did not hesitate to approach spectators about whom they were curious and ask them outright who they were, but most sensed the shield of pain that surrounded the Nason contingent, and left them alone.

At five minutes past nine, Elaine Tipton began her opening statement in the State of California's case against George Franklin. She started out in the lulling tones of a bedtime story. Walking in front of the jury, she said quietly, "I want you to meet two little girls. They were playmates, the best of friends. On September 22, 1969, one of those girls was molested and brutally murdered by the other girl's father, George Franklin." She turned toward the defendant, who looked steadily at her, showing no emotion. "Twenty-one years later we are brought together in this courtroom to relive that horror."

Tipton then led the jury through Susan's last day. She spoke of the friendship between Susan and Eileen, of the Franklin family, and of Eileen's favored status with her father, which made it not unusual for him to take her along on an errand or a jaunt. She described father and daughter setting off in the Volkswagen van, seeing Susan, picking her up, and heading up into the hills west of Foster City and San Mateo. The girls, Tipton said, had played on the mattress in the back of the van, full of "innocent childhood excitement, two friends in the company of one friend's father in what would be the last hours of one's life."

Tipton told of the highway pull-off, of Franklin joining the girls in the van's rear, of Eileen moving to the front seat and looking back to see her father on top of Susan, holding both of her hands with one of his, his pelvis moving up and down. "Stop, no," Tipton said, her voice rising only slightly. "The last touch Susan felt was not of love and affection, but of lust and perversion.

"When the molestation ended," Tipton said, "Susan Nason went out of the van and was on the ground, crying and making a fuss. When George Franklin heard her cries, he knew his act would not be kept a secret; he knew that when she got home, she would report him." With so many elements of the story repeated over and over in first the preliminary hearing and shortly in the trial itself, this would be the only reference to the motive the prosecution ascribed to George Franklin until the closing statements a month hence.

As Tipton went on to describe the crime, both Margaret and Shirley Nason closed their eyes and held them shut. Tipton said that as George Franklin raised the rock above the little girl's head, "Susie raised her own hand in a childlike attempt to protect herself. The next thing Eileen saw and heard, particularly heard, was her father crushing her best friend's skull. . . ."

Donald Nason, his bull-like neck pressing against his tight sport shirt, flushed, his already ruddy complexion turning a darker red. For anyone conjecturing what must have been in his mind at that moment, the wooden rail separating him from George Franklin must have looked frighteningly inadequate. From the defendant's table, Franklin gazed impassively at Tipton as though he were hearing her describe an interesting trip she had just taken to Bali. Once Tipton left the story's ugliest moment, the rock coming down on Susan's skull, the relief in the courtroom was palpable. The Nason women opened their eyes.

Her voice now low and sad, Tipton said, "Susan's terror ended at that moment. Eileen's had just begun." She told of Eileen's horror, her attempt to run, how her father caught her, pulled her to the ground, then "began planting the seeds of silence." He began terrorizing her, telling her it was over, that there was nothing to be done. "It was your idea," he said, "to get Susan into the van. If you tell what happened, no one will believe you. They'll lock you up, just like they locked up your mother. And then, finally, if you tell, I'll have to kill you."

Tipton then shifted from Eileen's account to the physical evidence. It shows that he moved the body to a more secluded area of the ravine, where he used a bedspring and brush to cover the body. Eileen remembers him doing something with a brown object. He placed a rock near the body to make the death look accidental. Eileen remembers seeing several cars drive by and wondering what these people would think if they knew what had just happened here.

From such a sophisticated, adult point of view, Tipton returned quickly to her theme of childhood terror. "Eileen was full of the distress only a child can understand. She knew something very terrible had happened. She knew Susie had been left alone, that as it got dark she would become cold and frightened. . . ." And then the first linking of Eileen's astounding story to the testimony of another: Janice remembers that when Eileen got home that evening, Eileen was shaking and sweating. Janice took her into bed with her. Concluding the first phase of the story, Tipton said, "Eileen would bury deep in her mind what she had seen that day."

Tipton then switched to the realization by Margaret Nason that her daughter was missing, the mounting panic, and the final county-wide search for Susan. With the accused sitting so conspicuously at hand, this part of the tale took on greater resonance as Tipton added to his crime the enormous trouble, expense, and anguish the search had caused hundreds of people —all of which could have been spared had he anonymously reported the body's location. Tipton, who didn't hesitate to offer Franklin's motives for his alleged actions, spared the jury the probable reason behind this silence—that a fresh corpse is more likely to yield clues than a weathered one.

"No one had seen Susie's disappearance. No one except one terrified and traumatized child and the man who had murdered her."

As Tipton described the discovery of the body and its decomposed condition, Susan Nason's grandmother held her hands clasped in front of her as if in prayer, shaking her head slightly from side to side. In gruesome detail, Tipton described the coroner's findings. Then, quietly, she said, "All that was left of Susan Nason was her skull, her skeletal remains, and a small amount of mummified skin. There was nothing left of this child's body to identify." She went on to say that Margaret Nason had identified her daughter—giving the courtroom another reminder that George Franklin had brutalized others besides Susan.

Tipton's voice rose as she said, "For twenty years this terrifying event remained buried deep in the mind of Eileen Franklin. For twenty years the defendant lived his life pretending to know nothing about Susan Nason's death." Since the possible innocence of the accused should always be in a jury's mind, Tipton was making sure they entertained the other possibility: that Franklin had lived a free man for two decades when he should have been immediately and permanently isolated from society.

"Eileen Franklin had significant gaps in her memory of her own childhood," Tipton said. "She had to cope with memories of verbal, physical, and sexual abuse." The jury, having just been told, with no uncertainty, that George Franklin had coolly murdered an eight-year-old girl, now sat impassively as they learned that he had also sexually abused his own daughter. They did not yet know that this second accusation, enough to repulse most people, would not be contested, while the accusation of murder would be fought ferociously for the next month. "There was a complex relationship between father and daughter," Tipton said, "one based on fear, violence, and love. Behind the closed doors of the Franklin House, there was violence and abuse."

Tipton jumped ahead to 1989 and Eileen's recollection of the murder. She told of Eileen's fear and panic at the terrible realization, of her inability to confide it to anyone for months, and, finally, of her decision to tell a member of her family, choosing her brother George and telling him that the memory had come through hypnosis by her therapist. Surprisingly, Tipton did not offer Eileen's explanation for lying to George about this.

Tipton described Eileen's tortured path to her decision to tell the police what she now knew, her fear of both her father and of authority itself in having allowed so much time to pass before offering her testimony. "She was assured, if she would disclose her information, the authorities would take appropriate steps to protect her." Tipton was omitting nothing that might suggest to the jury what a dangerous and menacing man —even to his own daughter—was sitting there before them.

Making the point that Eileen knew her coming forward would thoroughly disrupt her life, Tipton said that Eileen would tell the jury two things that had led to her decision: first, that she felt the tragedy was her own fault in that it never would have happened if she hadn't asked her father to bring Susan along in the van; second, that she owed it to Mr. and Mrs. Nason to conclude their daughter's tragic story and bring justice to her killer. Tipton said that the prosecution's case did not depend exclusively on the testimony of Eileen Franklin, that the jury would hear evidence from pathologists, forensic scientists, and officials present at the discovery of the body, twenty years ago. "All will corroborate what Eileen Franklin says."

Everything said so far had been brought out at the preliminary hearing and had been reported in the press. Tipton, however, had saved some surprises for the final phase of her statement. She said that the jury would learn of statements and conduct by the defendant that would substantiate his guilt. "A few days after Susan's disappearance, George Franklin gave his wife, Leah, a bloodstained shirt to launder, and said he had hurt himself while painting."

Those familiar with the testimony were startled by this fresh evidence and wondered, if it came from Leah, how she could have neglected to mention it at the preliminary hearing. Tipton quickly moved on to another phase of Leah's involvement, that she had once accused her husband of having killed Susan and "he did not deny it."

Tipton's next piece of new evidence had a similar ring of television-drama plotting. Explaining that it is routine for police to stake out the graves of unsolved murder victims on anniversaries of their deaths, she said that this had been done on the first anniversary of Susan Nason's death, and that George Franklin had come to the site of her grave.

For her final piece of damning evidence, Tipton had saved Franklin's words when he was arrested: "Have you talked to my daughter?" Obviously, Tipton hoped this would fix in jurors' minds that Franklin, on learning the police were finally aware of his murder of Susan, had blurted out what he knew to be the one way they could have traced him.

"For twenty years the Nasons have lived with the horrible unanswered question of who killed their daughter." Now, Tipton said, with the case she was about to place before them, that question would finally be answered and the jury, she felt confident, would find the defendant guilty. Her opening statement had taken an hour and forty minutes.

After a fifteen-minute break, Douglas Horngrad began his statement by saying it was an obligation of the prosecution to "outline a skeleton" of what they hoped to prove, but that, by the same rules, Mr. Franklin was under no obligation to make an opening statement. He went on to talk for two hours. "We all agree," he began, "that Susan Nason's death is tragic. My client, however, *did not do it.* There is no physical evidence to link Mr. Franklin to this charge, nor is there any circumstantial evidence. The jury will hear a story from Eileen Franklin that is constantly changing to meet the evidence and to meet the requirements of law. She told different versions to different people. The one consistency is that she hoped to persuade the listener of the truth of her story. She also admits to telling things that are not true—lies."

Horngrad then proceeded to the backbone of his defense, an attack on Eileen's behavior in the months following her alleged recollection. He first threw into question the fact that Eileen had waited three to five months before telling anyone; that during these months she had been seeing a therapist, Katherine Rieder, but had not told her, although she *had* discussed another repressed memory with Rieder; that she had told her recollection to another therapist, Kirk Barrett, in either *March or May,* and said she had told him that she had immediately remembered her father as Susan's murderer. Barrett, Horngrad said, told a different story: that she had told him she could see the murder, but not the murderer, that she could not make out the face. "Somebody's lying," Horngrad said darkly.

He proceeded to Eileen's conversation with George junior, in which she had told him the recollection came to her during hypnosis. Unlike Tipton, Horngrad offered Eileen's explanation, that she had lied to her brother because she wanted him to believe her. A month later, Horngrad said, she had told her mother, who is an attorney, and who told Eileen that hypnotic testimony was inadmissible.

Later, on the witness stand, Leah would deny having told Eileen this, but Horngrad stated this not unreasonable assumption as fact. As soon as Eileen learned this from her mother, Horngrad said, she dropped the hypnosis story. She also told another (Barry, the testimony would claim) that she "had lived with the memory for all these years." When Barry had called the police with his wife's story, he had made no mention of repression.

"Barry is a powerful figure in Eileen's life," Horngrad said. "You may not hear from Barry, however, because for reasons best known to himself he chooses not to come here to testify." Horngrad glanced toward the prosecution as though surprised Tipton did not object to the slur on the goodwill of one of her players. Slowly, Tipton obliged with an objection, which was sustained.

Horngrad turned his sights to another of Eileen Franklin's support group, her sister Janice. His voice only slightly sarcastic, he told the jury that in 1984, Janice, with no evidence, had told the police she suspected her father of killing Susan Nason. On the afternoon of the murder, she told investigators, she had come home at four-fifteen and seen her father. Since Susan had been seen close to that time, Janice then changed her story and said she had come home later.

Turning up the derision a notch, Horngrad said to the jurors, "Janice is somewhat ubiquitous in this case." Then, translating, he added, "She's everywhere in this story." Janice said, he went on, that she never told Eileen about going to the police until *after* Eileen herself had contacted the authorities in 1989. Eileen is firm that the conversation with Janice happened in 1986.

While this inconsistency was sinking in, Horngrad paused, then said, "Janice is important in many ways." In Eileen's first version of her story, she and her father were alone in the van. After Janice moved in with Eileen and Barry in 1989, the story changed to Janice being in the van also, that she had gotten out when Susan had gotten in. Horngrad hammered away at Janice's fluctuating involvement in the case as the faulty joist that would cause the structure's collapse.

"When Barry spoke on the phone to the police in November of 1989," Horngrad said, "and told them he had a witness to Susan Nason's murder, he emphasized two points: one, that his witness knew things that were not in the press; and, two, that there was a second witness [i.e., Janice]."

As for Eileen's account of the crime, Horngrad said it was simply not true that she knew things that had not been in the papers. "The crushed ring, the clothing Susan wore, the head injuries, the mattress over the body, the surrounding trees . . ." He spoke slowly, with heavy emphasis. *"It was all in the public domain."* Adding that there had been no second witness, he said, "So both of Barry's claims to the police were untrue."

He then focused on Eileen's story. In the first version, he said, she recalled it happening in the morning. Then there was the press attention after her coming forward and "The Today Show" interview, all of which established the time of day as afternoon. By the preliminary hearing, the morning was out, the afternoon in. For the preliminary hearing, Janice was out of the van. The bumpy road becomes Highway 92, the woods are a pull-off, and the secluded woods are now near a highway, with cars whizzing by.

The mattress found over Susan's body, Horngrad continued, was not a mattress, but an old wooden box spring. It could not have fit into the van. So she had changed this to a vague memory of him trying to get *something* out of the van. For the kill, his voice rose as he said, "All of her changes comply with the known facts."

Why is she changing her story, Horngrad asked. By now, Eileen is a celebrity. She is on "The Today Show," she is offered book deals, movie deals. She hires a Beverly Hills entertainment attorney to screen the offers. There is now a book and movie deal. If he is guilty, it is worth a half million dollars to her. If he is not convicted, it's worth nothing.

Those in the courtroom who knew the facts were surprised by Horngrad's misstatement of the truth in this and in many other assertions. He had subpoenaed the book contract and knew, or should have known, that it contained not a word regarding the trial's outcome. The book would be written regardless of conviction or acquittal; the publisher was obliged to pay her the same amount either way as was the film company.

When questioned about this later, he dismissed it as a technicality. "If Franklin is acquitted," he said, "Eileen's publishers will not be nearly so keen to publish, will they?" He was unmoved by the argument that the lack of any such stipulation in the contract was strong evidence that her publishers would publish either way, since publishers are not known for gambling large sums on heads-or-tails deals. Inexplicably, Elaine Tipton, who was highly concerned about the damage done to her case by Eileen and Barry's two commercial deals, never corrected this untrue and damaging allegation against her star witness, an allegation that would later be repeated on national television as hard fact.

Signing to write a book about an extraordinary experience, a unique family drama, is one thing; quite another thing would be to sign a contract that depends on a conviction in a trial in which you are a star witness. Horngrad saw no distinction. Neither, it appeared, did Elaine Tipton. Perhaps it was an example of the inability of two such skilled attorneys as Tipton and Horngrad to emerge briefly from their subjective concerns and realize that to some people, even some who were closely involved, the trial's outcome was not a matter of great importance. Even this early in the trial, it appeared that both lawyers had an emotional involvement in the case, one that went beyond the purely professional and egotistic urge to win.

Horngrad concluded the book-and-film portion of his statement with a family vignette: "Right now Eileen and Barry are in Switzerland arguing over how much of this money goes to the Lipsker family, how much they will keep." This was a reference to an announcement that Eileen planned to give a good portion of her earnings to charity.

Returning to various witnesses' changes of story, he told the jury that Eileen had telephoned George junior and said she had not been hypnotized, and that she had also informed the district attorney that she had told a couple of people she *had* been hypnotized. Her mother had never told anyone about a bloody shirt. At the preliminary hearing, Leah had said that there had been *nothing unusual about that day*. She also remembered that, during a fight when she was married to George Franklin, she had said to him, "I think you killed Susan Nason." He had replied, "Leah, you always think the worst of me."

"That's their *admission!*" Horngrad said with amazement. And then added, "As for the visit to the grave one year later, *that never happened!*"

The prosecution, he said, would bring forth psychiatrists to testify that repressed memory was possible. They would also say it was possible to harbor a false memory. Eileen Franklin's memory stemmed from 1969, when Foster City was saturated with news about Susan Nason's disappearance and, later, the discovery of her body. A massive investigation had revealed that a neighborhood child, Ann Hobbs, had been lured by a man into a blue car. The police had been flooded with calls from neighbors saying they had seen a man in a blue car. The man was never caught.

Having established an alternative scenario, Horngrad moved toward his conclusion. "The prosecution will bring you no physical evidence against Mr. Franklin, and no second witness. Eileen Franklin's testimony stands alone. And all the facts she presented to the police are in the public domain. You jurors will have a choice. One, she is lying. Two, she had a repressed memory. Three, her mind is playing tricks. You cannot accept Eileen Franklin's testimony as proof that her father committed this crime. You will, therefore, find him to be not guilty."

Eileen

In a few days I would have to fly from Zurich to California for the trial. I felt I had to explain to my children's school why I would be gone for so long, and tell them exactly why I was going, so that they would be prepared in the event that news of the trial got as far as Zurich. My worst fear was that something might be blurted out in school in front of my children. I wasn't looking forward to telling my grim story to these foreign women, so I waited until the last moment.

I had sent notes to each teacher asking for a meeting. I cried as I wrote the notes. I dreaded having to explain, yet again, about the trial, about my strange life. I requested a meeting with both teachers at the same time, since I did not think I could explain twice. I received a note in reply confirming a three-fifteen appointment in the preschool classroom.

I was rather nervous, addressing these two British women, hoping that I would not say something about these delicate matters in American English that might be misinterpreted in the King's English. Throughout the day I rehearsed what I would say, but each time the effort brought me close to tears, so I stopped. I imagined that the teachers probably assumed I was coming to announce an imminent divorce. How I wished it were that simple.

In the preschool classroom, three grown women perched on tiny children's chairs, I prefaced my speech by saying I wished there were a way I could avoid this conversation. I told them that I was returning to the States the following morning to testify in a criminal trial. I would rather not go into a lot of detail, I said, but I had to give them some.

I started by telling them I appeared to suffer from a psychological phenomenon called repressed memory. Both teachers nodded understandingly. Jessica's teacher said that she had heard of this. So far, so good.

I plunged on. "Twenty-one years ago, when I was eight years old, my best friend, who was also eight, was murdered." In my pre-court paranoia I felt I had to be cautious of time frames in case these women were ever called to testify about what I had said to them. "Approximately a year and a half ago," I added, accentuating the word *approximately,* "I began to have memories of having witnessed this murder. Approximately one year ago my husband and I decided to go to the police with this information. The end result was that my father was arrested for this murder, and I must return to California to testify. Unfortunately, the press has taken quite an interest in this whole event. Since I know that most of the Americans here read *USA Today* and the *International Herald-Tribune,* and watch CNN news, I am afraid that someone, perhaps one of the schoolchildren, is going to see me in the news, and I must protect my children, who know nothing about this whole business."

At this point Jessica's teacher stopped me to say, "Jessica was crying quite a bit this morning." She explained that Jessica had expressed concern that her mommy was going to court and that she was afraid "the bad man" I had told them about might hurt her mommy. I thought that I had protected my kids and prepared them well for my absence. I had believed they would express their doubts or concerns to me. I had given a lot of thought to how I should handle this to avoid worrying them. I felt I had failed.

Jessica's teacher said she appreciated my telling them. She could now help comfort Jessica appropriately. I told them that if any parent or child should mention this to my children, they would be kept at home for a few days. They said they understood. As I left the meeting I felt glad that I had overcome my discomfort and told the teachers. I was reassured that my children would be looked after with sensitivity.

FOURTEEN

ELAINE TIPTON BELIEVES THAT THE FINAL DAYS BEFORE THE start of the trial are the most anxious. "You think of all the things you wished you'd done and worry about the many more things you should have done but forgot or didn't even know about." Another prosecutor told her a conviction in the Franklin case was unlikely, adding, "There are a hundred ways to shoot you down." Tipton felt that was true when she inherited the case. "By the time we went to trial," she said, "there were a hundred and ten ways to shoot me down."

Involved as Elaine Tipton was in the case, she was constantly aware that Eileen had far more at stake than she. Either a father Eileen had loved would be put away forever, or, if exonerated, he would be a permanent threat to society, but more particularly to the safety of Eileen and her family. Eileen would be publicly branded as a scheming and lying monster, an abomination among daughters.

Having come to care for Eileen, Tipton felt sharply her responsibility in having encouraged her to proceed, assuring her they would win. Now, like any good lawyer with a good case, she had to face the prospect of not winning. And while prosecutors and defense lawyers live with this reality, they rationalize about the law of averages: For every case you lose that you should have won, they know, you will win one you should have lost.

Such cosmic balancing works for a career involving scores of cases. The difficulty arises from the principal players of each one, for whom a case may be the central drama of their lives. These are people to whom prosecutors often grow attached. For Tipton, losing the Franklin case would be a blow to her pride, a blow to her faith in the criminal-justice system, a blow to her moral sense—but, most particularly, it would leave her feeling that, not only had she let down someone for whom she cared very much, but she had made a complete mess of that person's life.

At noon on October 31, 1990, Elaine Tipton called her first witness, Mary Jane Larkin, a short, dark-haired woman who had been Susan Nason's fourth-grade teacher, and who confirmed that Susan had wanted to take Celia Oakley her shoes, and that teachers warned students not to talk to strangers. In cross-examination, Arthur Wachtel spent some twelve minutes challenging the firmness of Larkin's recollections and trying, unsuccessfully, to induce her to admit the possibility that school let out later than 3:00 P.M. that day. All who testified about this would agree that this sometimes happened earlier, but never later.

Margaret Nason was the next witness. As she took the stand, she was as composed and steady as she had been at the preliminary hearing. She described in detail Susan's arrival home from school, her leaving to return Celia's shoes. She told of her concern at about four-thirty when Susan had not returned, and said that she had phoned the Oakley house, waited a little bit longer, then set out on her bicycle to look for her daughter. After six, she went to the Oakley home and ran into Celia on the walk in front of her house. "I was devastated," she said, "to learn Celia had not been with Susan." Her voice broke, and Tipton asked her if she needed a minute.

"I'm okay," she said and straightened herself in the witness chair. The courtroom was very still.

Tipton led her through the events of the evening of September 22, 1969, most of which, Nason said, were a blur to her now. She told of the extortion letters that came to their house in the following weeks, one saying that if they didn't pay a certain amount, one of Susan's fingers would be cut off and sent to them. Tipton asked what her state of mind was in those weeks. "It is almost indescribable to have a child missing, the pain of it. . . ."

"Were you thinking clearly in those weeks?"

"No, definitely not."

They then discussed the discovery of Susan's body and Margaret Nason's identification of her daughter, and Tipton verified that the crushed ring found with the body had not been crushed when Susan left home. Tipton asked her if she had ever discussed details of the body's condition and the scene of the crime with neighbors and friends. Nason assured her she had never done so.

During Wachtel's cross-examination, the pathetic information emerged that, in the period after Susan's disappearance but before her body was found, the Nasons had posed for a newspaper photo preparing for Susan's birthday. After questioning Margaret Nason about her daughters' friendship with the Franklin girls, Wachtel asked if she had ever suspected anyone in the neighborhood of killing Susan. Tipton immediately objected and was sustained. As she came off the stand, Margaret Nason gave a sad smile toward family members. After a recess, she sat next to her husband from whom she was recently divorced.

With the parade of witnesses from Foster City in the next few weeks, it began to appear that the community produced specimens of every level of American social class. A series of witnesses, all having grown up on identical streets, attending the same school, playing together in the same parks—would emerge as examples of a wide range of choices—blue-collar, professional, scholarly, patrician. Or maybe it was that Foster City produced social blanks on which later would be written the class trappings picked up elsewhere. In 1969, the period under discussion, because Foster City had almost no stores, residents had to drive to San Mateo to shop; they may also have had to leave the neighborhood to find an identity.

The next witness, Celia Oakley, fell somewhere between the academic and patrician categories. A nice-looking young woman, she told the court in well-bred accents that she was getting a Ph.D. in engineering at Stanford. Her recollection of the day in question was hazy, but she remembered Susan bringing her shoes to her; she didn't think they had played after that, but was not sure. No, she did not remember anything unusual happening that day. She recalled nothing that might have scared her. Wachtel's cross-examination brought out that Oakley wasn't sure she had gone outdoors when Susan came by. "So you wouldn't have noticed if anything unusual happened, would you?"

With the events surrounding Susan's disappearance fixed in the jurors' minds, Tipton proceeded to witnesses involved in the discovery of the body. Forewarned by the prosecution of grim details, the Nasons stayed out of the courtroom. She called to the stand Ephe Bottimore, the water department groundskeeper, now retired, who had found Susan. He seemed pleased to testify about what was surely the most momentous happening in his life. Some people win the lottery, others father quadruplets, and a few stumble on the bodies of missing girls. Bottimore described the site as well as the placement and condition of the body.

Much of Bottimore's testimony, and that of the sheriff's department officers at the scene who followed him, was aimed at foreclosing various defense suppositions, such as that her body might have been thrown from a passing car, or that she might have died in a fall. Jurors learned that the body, which was mostly skeletal, was found thirty-five feet from the road, lying on its left side, the left leg curled underneath the outstretched right leg. A rat's nest was discovered forty-three inches from her head, and a rock with hairs on it was found by her head. One brown shoe was found approximately ten inches from her right foot. About five to ten feet away, a child's white sock that matched the one on Susan's left foot was found hanging on a bush. Her other shoe was never found. The ring on her right hand was "broken"; the one on her left hand, a gold-colored ring with blue stones, was intact.

A number of photographs were introduced into evidence: various shots of the murder site, some from above, at the pullout, looking down the bank; others close to the box spring; and, most gruesome, photos taken through the box-spring coils of rusted metal covering the skeletonized remains. The image was powerful: a child's skull, not fully denuded of flesh, hazily but unmistakably visible through the twisted coils of rusted metal. Below the skull, in the confused welter of bones and springs, tatters of cheerfully printed blue dress fabric were poignant reminders of the animated innocence that this pitiful and disgusting pile of debris had once been.

As the photographs were passed slowly from one juror to the next, a stillness fell over the courtroom. There were none of the whispered conversations that usually broke out when no one was addressing the court. Tipton introduced the two rings as well as photographic blow-ups of them. She also introduced the two rocks found at the scene. The one that had hair on it was small, a scant five inches long and, at its widest point, perhaps three inches wide. As it was passed to the defense table for inspection, George Franklin examined it with the respectful curiosity of a metallurgist examining an ore sample. His emotions must have been complex if the stone he held in his hand was indeed the weapon with which he had crushed Susan Nason's skull twenty years before.

When Dr. Peter Benson, the coroner who had performed Susan Nason's autopsy, was called, heads craned to see if the Nasons were in their customary front-row right seats. To everyone's relief, they were not. The courtroom was treated to graphic descriptions of the skull and the decomposed body. Benson described two large "defects" on the skull's right side, both with radiating fracture lines. Tipton produced a model of a skull with the areas of the fractures painted a dark red. George Franklin examined this grotesque artifact with his usual scholarly impassivity. Susan's white underpants and two white socks, all in self-sealing plastic bags, were also entered into evidence.

The main point Tipton sought to establish with Benson was that the skull's "defects" were consistent with two lethal blows to the head from an irregular object such as a rock. More than two blows were unlikely, Benson testified. It was also unlikely that the murder instrument was a smooth, man-made object. In a clump of hair that still adhered to the skull, a fingernail was found.

An additional point of Benson's testimony was particularly gruesome. The tips of Susan's right-hand fingers were missing, while the bones of her left hand were intact. Although the bone fragments might have broken off in the normal process of deterioration, they could not have disintegrated altogether in the ten weeks the body had been exposed, and would have been found in the exhaustive search of the immediate area. They must have been carried off. The absence of these parts, Benson said, suggested that the hand had been wounded; animals such as rats and mice are more quickly attracted to wounded parts of bodies than to healthy ones.

Wachtel, after establishing that Benson testified more frequently for the prosecution than for the defense, said that while Susan's injuries suggested they were caused by a defensive movement, it was also possible they were not. Benson admitted this was true. Wachtel also attacked the size of the rock. Wasn't it too small to have caused those fractures? Not if applied with enough force and speed, Benson replied.

Eileen

To make sure I got over my jet lag before having to testify, I flew to Los Angeles several days before I was to be called, and hid out at the home of my brother- and sister-in-law, Lee and Denise. I told almost no one where I was, not even my sisters. My dear friend Sharon Nelson, who stood by me through the preliminary hearing, would do the same at the trial. She knows what I am going through, and suggested it might help if I tried writing some of it down. I took her advice.

October 30: Five days before I was to testify, and I'm scared. No, I'm terrified. I'm terrified of the press when I enter the courtroom. At the preliminary hearing, they scared me so much that I could feel my face turn white. My heart pounded in my chest until I felt a tightening, almost crushing pain. I had to hold my breath to make it stop.

I hate the thought of a jury just sitting there staring at me. I've always thought my profile looked so sad. Why does the jury have to see my worst side? They'll think me ugly and of questionable sanity. Not the most comforting thought.

I don't want to testify. I don't want to testify. As I read the preliminary-hearing transcripts, I concluded that I sounded like a jerk. Horngrad wouldn't leave me alone about the exact dates of telephone calls. I should have kept a journal documenting each call, the return of each memory, each conversation. I should have had the foresight to keep records. I never knew what the witness stand would be like. Now that I know, it terrifies me.

November 1: I am truly fortunate to be at Lee and Denise's house these few days before the trial. Their kids provide a nice diversion. I love to cook, so have taken over in the kitchen, which suits them fine, since they both work. Lee and Denise are nonintrusive, yet loving and supportive. I have no desire to socialize with Los Angeles friends. I am happy just to be holed up in a home where I feel loved and protected.

It is stupid for me to be this terrified. I have not slept since two-thirty this morning, and I am afraid to try to sleep, because it will give my mind idle moments to think about the trial. Denise was worried about me tonight, because she heard me crying. I want to get the tears out now so I can remain stoic on the witness stand. For so many months I haven't been able to cry. My tears have returned, but for a long time they wouldn't come. A headache a few nights ago got so intense, I let go. That one good cry seems to have reopened my tear ducts.

Over the past months I have forced myself not to give in to the pain and sense of loss that surround the murder and the trial. It has left me in an emotional void. I may have won out over tears, but I grew an ulcer instead. Lee offered me an analogy. He compared what I am going through to the way a bullet wound heals. He explained that a bullet wound must receive constant cleaning and redressing. If it gets that kind of attention, it heals well. I suppose Lee thinks I am capable of healing from this experience. I don't know if I am.

I wish I knew how to get back to God. He probably wants me to come to him right now, but I don't know how. Prayer doesn't guide me back. I feel like my soul has died. I feel like my inner life is gone and that maybe I don't get another one. My ulcer is churning, which means my stomach is as scared as I am. My forehead hurts so much of the time, thinking about all of it hurts. I wish I could get some sleep. I feel so inept and so very lost.

November 2: I must stop by Katherine Rieder's office to get the dates of my visits before I head up to the Bay Area. It looks as though I was wrong about one more little thing —these dates. Elaine tells me it's important we give the jury the right dates. Horngrad is going to make me out a liar. He's out for blood. I asked Elaine if we were going to win. The doubt had come over me strongly yesterday and I couldn't shake it. Elaine said, "I won't promise, but I think we have a real good shot at it."

Last spring I had assured Elaine that if she "held me up" during the months before the trial, I would not lean on her during the trial because I knew she needed all her energy for that. Still, I told her I wanted to say something to her, but because of my promise not to lean, I would only say it one time. I told her that I was terrified, that I have never felt such an intense emotion. What startles me, and I tried to convey this to her, is the intensity of the fear I feel. It is an absolute terror which I can't shake. She said she understood, that it was natural, and tried to bolster me.

Before leaving Los Angeles for the Bay Area, I spent some time with Barry's parents. I had a resistance to being with them since returning to the States. It reminded me that I didn't have a set of intact, loving parents.

As usual, my in-laws were very kind to me. Lea told me that some of her friends in the Bay Area had asked her about the trial, knowing that I was her daughter-in-law. I felt sorry for Lea, having to deal with her friends' inquiries about me. But she was not feeling sorry for herself. She said that whenever anyone asked about the case, she and Aaron always spoke about me with admiration and respect, because they believed what I was doing was right and because I was their daughter.

I felt such love for Aaron and Lea. They were telling people they were proud of me. As with everyone, I am afraid that they will reject me when they learn all the horrible details and know how physically and sexually damaged I am. The time is near for everyone to find out, and I did not want to lose another set of parents.

I planned to drive to the Bay Area, thinking it would be therapeutic. I love driving my Mercedes-Benz; it's big, alluring, customized, and my favorite color, green. I feel like the queen of the road. With the sunroof open and a stack of new CDs, I hoped that four hundred miles of highway would allow time to sort my thoughts before testifying.

I needed to resolve my conflicting feelings about my sisters and brother. I wanted to love them, but I did not feel love. I also needed to accept the possibility that my father might not be convicted. I dreaded the idea. The journey from first memory to trial had been too mentally costly and emotionally draining. I wanted so badly to believe in the American justice system, but I knew that it did not always work, and that this could be one of those times.

As I drove, I thought about Kate and Mike. I decided that I should ignore my anger at them. To me, they are despicable and a waste of any emotion. I am ashamed to have known, respected, and trusted both of them. I wondered how Kate could live with herself, now that she was a mother. Did she not yet understand the value of a child? It frightened me that I had nearly told Kate about the murder first. If I had done that, where would I be now? I did not want to waste time mourning the loss of Kate in my life. Mike had shown his true colors years ago, and I felt no loss. I would have to accept her absence as a positive contribution to my mental health, but I felt truly sad that Kate was not the person I thought she was.

I drove across central California, which was extremely dry and drought-stricken. I had made the trip many times before, but had never seen the Central Valley so parched. I thought about George junior, and decided to make no firm decision about him. Surely he would understand the truth when it came out during the trial. If not, he could live his life in denial. I was not going to crusade for George to accept the truth. After the parental examples we grew up with, his fierce denial was not surprising.

George had become hostile *after the arrest,* not when I had told him of the memory. I wondered what had so suddenly turned him against me. If he thought that I was lying, why hadn't he said so before the arrest? Why had it taken several months and the arrest of our father for him to reject what I was saying?

I knew that it would be a waste of time and energy to try reasoning with him. George had made it clear during our telephone conversations that he did not want to listen, but only to show me his anger. He did not want all the facts, but only the information that would permit his off-the-wall opinions. The possibility that George and I would never again have a relationship was very real. What I had learned about him in the past year left me with little desire to win back his friendship.

I thought about my mother, and how devastating an acquittal would be for her. I was worried about her health and emotional state during the trial. I was concerned that her husband would know of no way to help her through this ordeal. I wondered whether her law practice would survive if she had a convicted murderer for an ex-husband.

I was worried about my closeness to Diana. She would have to make her own decisions about our future. She knew that George junior and I were at odds. She had said that when the trial was over she would decide which of us was telling the truth. Her indecision and friendliness to George junior had strained our relationship badly. Also, Diana had casually and inaccurately attributed statements to me. I was nervous she might do it again. She did not seem to understand the importance of quoting me accurately or not at all. I wanted to see Diana when I was in the Bay Area, but I was afraid she would report a garbled version to George junior, who would then relay *his* version to Horngrad.

I feared that Diana, too, would not be a part of my future. She vacillated between supporting me, defending George junior, and trying to remain neutral in a situation too heated for neutrality. I wanted Diana and me to be close again after the trial—but I also wanted a loving father, a supportive brother, and an honest sister and brother-in-law—none of which life was giving me.

As I drove, I thought about my father. I wondered why he was continuing with his farce. I felt angry that he was willing to subject his entire family to a public and painful trial when he knew that he was guilty. As I had for months, I tried to understand why he had not killed me that day. If he expected silence, he should have assured it, not forced an eight-year-old to be his confidante. I hated living with the memory of a murder he had no right to commit or to allow me to witness. I was convinced that he knew many more details of the murder than I did, but that he would never reveal them.

I wanted to go to my father and plead with him to fill in the holes in my memory. I wanted to go to him and demand that he tell me everything he had done in front of me, or to me, so that I wouldn't have to go through the traumas of remembering things one at a time. He was the only one who could unlock all of the horrible repressed memories. I wanted to tell him that he owed me my life back. I wanted to force him to tell the truth. But I knew he could not be forced to tell the truth. Or to face it.

I listened to a CD by the Neville Brothers, particularly a song called "Fearless." Each time I listened to the song, I became more convinced that I could be fearless. I was committed to facing my father without fear. He would be the victor if I was still the terrorized child he had made me into.

As I approached Redwood City, I noticed that Crystal Gayle was singing a concert. When I saw Bob Morse, I mentioned that it might be a way to take my mind off what lay ahead in the next few days. Bob couldn't go, but said he would arrange for someone from his department to take me. The date Bob arranged turned out to be Michael Dirickson, the son of the family for whom I'd baby-sat who was now an investigator on the case! I had told Bob I'd had a crush on Michael. I was pleased, but a little embarrassed. Michael is still good-looking, still nice, and we had a pleasant time talking about each other's kids. At that anxious time, it was welcome to be presented with a pleasant memory from my past.

As agreed, the Saturday morning before I testified, Elaine and I met in her office. During the past few months I had come to respect and admire Elaine very much. I had no doubt about her competence and intelligence; they were obvious. Through months of telephone conversations I discovered that she also was compassionate, sensitive, insightful, kind, and funny. She had been my primary source of strength in the past months, but I was afraid to lean on her now because I knew that the trial was terribly demanding of her.

We began by discussing everything except my testimony. I wanted to put off getting into the facts of the case, and Elaine seemed to sense my need to discuss topics other than the trial. I told her about Switzerland, my new house with no furniture, my children and their adjustment to school, how Barry and I were adjusting to life abroad, my blessed anonymity in our village outside of Zurich.

It was wonderful to have a leisurely time with Elaine. I had kept my feelings and thoughts bottled up for so long, I was afraid I might break down and start crying, never stopping, if I touched the surface of my pain. Because all of my family was under subpoena, she had forbidden me to discuss my memory with them. A therapist might get subpoenaed as well. Except for Elaine, I was on my own.

She told me that I had to discuss with her the rape and the other sexual abuse, because I was going to have to testify regarding these incidents. Also, she wanted to cover the difficult or confusing areas of my preliminary-hearing testimony with me. I knew that Elaine and I needed to cover my testimony, but I dreaded it. We continued to discuss everything except my testimony and my memory.

We started going over the less emotional matters. I asked Elaine if at some point during the day I could have a break to get my hair cut. I had avoided my hairdresser in Los Angeles for fear the trial would be mentioned. Elaine told me that she also wanted a break in the afternoon, because she had a manicure scheduled. She would take me with her to the salon, and I could get a trim at the same time. I thought it was kind of Elaine to make this offer. I had worried that because of the notoriety of the case, she might be ashamed to be seen with me in public.

Since the news coverage of my rape during the preliminary hearing, I was embarrassed to be seen in public in the Bay Area. Whenever I was recognized, I felt certain, probably irrationally, that the person was thinking solely of the rape, viewing me as damaged. Or they might think I was what Horngrad implied—a woman who would put her father in jail for life with a lie in order to make money.

At the beauty shop in San Carlos, the owner, MaryAnn, was asking Elaine about the trial which she had been following in the newspaper. I soon realized that the woman cutting my hair had no idea that I was the person being mentioned across the room. It felt good to be anonymous.

Back in Elaine's office, I knew that the time had come to discuss the subject I dreaded, the rape. I was jealous that Elaine could be unemotional and distanced, that she did not have to feel the pain. We shared the same goal, but, ultimately, disclosing the details of each event was going to be torture for me and simply work for Elaine.

I wanted Elaine to understand how my memory worked, and how it felt for me to experience memories and to live with them. I hoped that if she could understand the way I felt and thought, she could make the jury understand. I also felt a tremendous need to talk to her and clear away the barriers I had built up during the months when I had not been permitted to talk.

I explained to Elaine how fresh the emotions that came with the memories were for me. They didn't feel twenty years old, but new. I had not had twenty years to heal; for me the memories were only one year, or six months, or two days old. I was trying to fit the memories of an eight-year-old into the mind of a twenty-nine-year-old. As an adult, trying to merge the terrifying and violent memories of a child into my existing memories had been very difficult. My feelings of outrage, helplessness, and loss of identity had been great. I explained to Elaine the terrible frustration that I felt knowing that I didn't have a mind like other people. I told Elaine how I hated having memories come back to disrupt my life, scar me more deeply, and make me afraid of still more memories yet to come.

I told her how I hated the thought of the press sitting and listening to the painful details of my life, how frustrated I was that I had no right to privacy, how I hated the thought of an audience of detached, disinterested journalists observing me and forming judgments as I testified.

I told Elaine how confused I felt about my sexuality and my womanhood now that I had to incorporate a rape and other sexual abuse into my identity. Rape counseling, which I felt I deserved, was not available to me now because of the trial. I did not know how to think about or respond to sex now that I knew how painful, terrifying, and frightening it could be. As a woman, how much more damaged could I be? Could I or would I ever feel "normal"? I felt extremely vulnerable and confused, two more emotions that I did not need, this near to testifying.

I talked to Elaine about the terribly high price of the whole trial. It had snipped the threads holding my family together. I felt so ashamed when people knew private information about me and my family. The past year had been devoted to my memories, the terrible events of my past, the upcoming trial, and staying sane—not to enjoying my children's development, my life in a new country. My sexuality, a year of my children's life, my siblings, my mind, my privacy—how much more could my father rob from me?

I expressed to Elaine my fears about appearing in court. I knew nothing about the jurors, yet they knew about me and would make a judgment based upon their view of me. How could these jurors possibly understand what I was remembering? *I* did not understand what I was remembering. As I explained, I began to feel that Elaine understood.

I told her how scared I would be if my father was not convicted, scared for me and for my children. I told her I felt that people at their school probably thought I was a bad mother because I had left my kids right after moving to Switzerland. I told her how hard it had been to have no one to talk to. Everyone was off limits; I felt all bottled up inside. I could not have an open relationship with anyone because I had to pretend that I was fine, when in fact I ached so badly from loneliness, fear, and despair.

Finally, I couldn't avoid it any longer, so I told her about the rape. It was the first time I had ever discussed it in detail. I described how my legs were restrained so I could not close them, and had stopped struggling to close them because it was futile. My father had covered my mouth with his hand, roughly turning my head to the left. He had held my left shoulder down. Just talking about the rape made that shoulder hurt again.

To discuss the rape, I have to think about it in detail. When I think about it, the memory of the pain overrides my ability to describe it well. Mostly, I want to run screaming from it. I want to run away from the memory, from the pain, from the shock of remembering, from the betrayal by my father. I want to flee, to lose the memory, but my mind runs as fast as I do. There is nowhere to go that I can leave my mind behind.

I must sit unemotionally and describe clearly what happened. I am supposed to explain calmly the sequence of events, what it felt like as a young girl to be raped by an adult male. What my father did, what my godfather did. What it felt like to struggle futilely. What it felt like to get up from the table after the rape, how badly my little body ached. No one was there to help me get dressed. I felt so damned alone. I was left alone in the room afterwards, but I could faintly hear the men's voices in another room. As I bent to put on my shoes, my lower abdomen and bottom hurt terribly. When I walked I could feel a stickiness between my legs, but I had no idea why.

In order to discuss it without being disabled by the memory of the pain, I must be distanced—mature, I suppose. What matters is not that I was horribly violated, but that I must be ready to testify about it in court. The pain of the rape will not go away if I sob, or scream, or run. The fact that it happened will never go away. But I don't have the time to deal with my reaction; the trial will not be won if I sob at each pain.

Very gently, Elaine asked me, "Did anyone say anything?" Suddenly the memory of voices came back to me. My God, I thought, I don't want to remember more! Just as with my other returning memories, I felt panic, fear, and a desire to cry. I felt a flash of betrayal; I had trusted Elaine, yet she was asking a question that evoked yet another memory and more pain. She knew I didn't want to remember more!

I looked across at Elaine. Her face looked so soft, so concerned. I knew she must have a reason for asking this. I tried to tell her, but I choked for a second. Then I described the voice to Elaine. My godfather said, "She's gonna like this, huh, George?" My dad cackled, his evil laugh was a cackle. Again, I feel betrayed by God. He didn't have to make it come back. I did not need to remember this.

I started to cry as I described the rape. I avoided eye contact with Elaine, trying to be invisible. When I looked across the desk at her, she was looking down; she too was crying. I had told Barry, Leah, and George junior but for the first time it felt as though someone cared that I had been raped. At last I did not feel all alone in my suffering. I knew that even if we did not win the trial, someone understood what I was living with.

Now I had yet one more horrible detail to live with, the words that were spoken, but for once I hadn't crossed the chasm alone. This time Elaine had been there. She looked at me so kindly and tenderly. She said, "I'm going to convict that bastard!" Sadly, I hoped that she was right. It would not diminish my pain, or nullify the rape, but it was the only justice available.

I told Elaine about the bathtub incident and the time that my father put his finger in my vagina in our living room when I was about seven years old. Elaine gave me a wonderful present. She called each event by its legal name. Everything that my father had done to me was "uncharged conduct," a nice, bland heading for a dreaded file in my memory. The bathtub incident was "attempted sodomy," the living room incident "digital penetration"; the rape had a number assigned to it. Everything could be mentally filed under the heading of uncharged conduct, which helped me to distance myself from the emotions and focus on the facts.

One of the most difficult things that Elaine asked me to do was to describe the sound of the murder. I begged her not to make me discuss it. I hated having to think about that horrible sound, which gave me a choking sensation and a jolt of terror. I had been quite shaken when I was pushed, nearly forced, to describe the sound to Dr. Lenore Terr. I did not want to describe the sound to Elaine or to the jury. I told Elaine that she had the psychiatric evaluation report by Dr. Terr, so she already knew what it had sounded like. Elaine and I went back and forth regarding my reluctance to describe it. She was right about the legal necessity, and I agreed reluctantly.

Sunday morning, Elaine and I went to mass together in Menlo Park. I had wanted to go to church, and Elaine had planned to attend mass, so she invited me to come with her.

We lit candles together, before returning to her office for more work. I had a pretty good idea that Elaine's prayer was the same as mine.

I had read my preliminary-hearing transcript—nearly four hundred pages—quite thoroughly. I had also read my statements to Morse and Cassandro, and the telephone conversation transcripts. We had a lot to cover. During the preliminary hearing, Horngrad had pounced on inconsistencies, yet as we went through the transcripts the surprising thing to me was the significant number of *consistent* statements. Horngrad had taken many of my statements out of context, twisting and turning their meanings in an attempt to misdirect and confuse me.

Several times I said to Elaine, "See, this is exactly what I said! Horngrad turned it around to discredit me with it later!" One example is that I had initially said that my father had driven us out "towards" the woods. Horngrad repeatedly stated that I had said that my father drove us "into" the woods, a significant difference since my version was accurate and his wasn't. On the witness stand you can't combat that sort of thing unless you are absolutely certain of every last preposition, adjective, and verb of your previous testimony.

After going through the preliminary-hearing transcript, Elaine played the audio tapes of my anonymous conversations with Inspector Etter. I felt like crying as I listened to them. In the tapes I sounded so frightened, distrustful, and nervous. At one point in one of the tapes I expressed a fear that I was going to be the one on trial if an arrest ensued; sadly I realized that my fear of one year ago had proved accurate.

I hoped that Elaine would play the tape in court so that Horngrad's claims of inconsistent statements by me could be swept away. As I listened to the tapes, I thought, my God, that voice sounds scared, but very concerned and honest. The jury has to hear this!

At one point Elaine asked me if I still felt connected to my father. I told her sadly that his insistence that he be publicly tried instead of telling the truth had finished off any feeling I had left for him. Shyly I asked her how my father looked, and if he was well—contradicting what I'd just said. I mentioned something about the visit to my father in jail. For the first time she and I discussed that meeting, then she said to me, "You don't mind if I ask you about the visit in court, do you?" I trusted Elaine and said I didn't.

When I left Elaine's office I felt very confident that she and I both knew what we were doing. Aside from telling the truth, it was important that I listen carefully to the wording of each question asked. If Horngrad attributed a statement to me that I did not believe I had made, I should ask to see the transcript. Elaine advised me to pause before answering any questions in case she wanted to make an objection, although we both had noticed at the preliminary hearing that I naturally paused before speaking in court.

When Elaine and I finally finished, I left her and settled in for the night at the Sofitel Hotel. The next day I would testify that my father was a rapist and murderer. The next day might be the beginning of justice for Susan Nason.

The night before my testimony, my fear was as strong as ever, but I was comforted by the feeling that I was being well looked after. I was confident that Elaine could handle the legal issues; Bob Morse would chauffeur, guard, and feed me; Sharon would give me moral support; and Barry would be awaiting my calls in Zurich. I knew I'd have trouble sleeping. Several friends had suggested I take a valium. They don't understand that ever since my involvement with drugs, I refuse to take anything like that.

I did get some sleep but arose early and took a long walk along the edge of the lagoon behind the Sofitel Hotel. I wanted to feel the cool Bay morning and smell the new day. I wanted all of my senses to be functioning well, to be in balance. I did not want my fear to overpower my healthy feelings. I did not want to become like a caged animal, aware only of my immediate surroundings. I wanted to feel the cold air shock my lungs so that I would know I was alive. I wanted to walk in the morning as I have walked countless other mornings, so that I could maintain my normalcy. I wanted to live a few anonymous moments before I was judged by a jury and a courtroom full of strangers.

I crossed over the lagoon and walked through an office complex until I reached the Bay's edge. On a boat dock opposite the hotel I started talking to God. I reminded him that I was here and that I was prepared for the day. I asked him to make me fearless. I asked him to watch over me from a distance. I told him that I was counting on him to bring me through this trial. I asked him to ready my heart and mind if there was not a conviction. I told him, as I stood on this dock in the water, that I was here, that I was trying to do what he would want me to do, but that I needed guidance.

As I walked back to the hotel I passed an office building where the morning newspapers were stacked up outside. I thought, "Soon I'll be in those newspapers and have my privacy totally violated." The thought made me very sad.

I concentrated on being aware, feeling healthy, not being overwhelmed. I wanted my ulcer to be calm. I breakfasted on melon, potatoes, and peppermint tea. Once again I talked to God. I talked to myself. Then I talked to Barry.

I put on an emerald green dress with a pretty ivory yoke. I wanted my clothing to say, "I am feminine and soft. I am vulnerable. In this setting I am not powerful." I wanted the jurors to see beyond my face, my clothes, and my life-style and see a plain woman, a woman who had been a young girl with a best friend. I wanted the jury to understand that I was in court to tell the truth, not to impress them with beauty, fashion, or sophistication.

When Bob Morse rang up my room from the lobby, I rode down in the elevator with a lawyer-like man carrying flexible files and a briefcase. When the elevator doors opened, Bob greeted both of us and chatted momentarily with the man, who turned out to be the prosecutor in the notorious Salcido multiple-murder case. "Another white hat," I thought.

As we prepared to leave the hotel, an older couple recognized Bob and greeted him. When they looked at me, I wasn't sure whether their smiles were of recognition of me or of catching Bob leaving a hotel early in the morning with a young woman.

As he escorted me to his car, Bob was so gentle with me, it made me feel fragile. I noticed he was not wearing the necktie I'd helped him pick out at Macy's to wear in court. I was disappointed, and feared this might be a bad omen. When I asked him where the tie was, he said he would wear it tomorrow. This actually turned out better, because that was the day of my cross-examination and I needed reassurance even more.

Sharon met me at the courthouse. On a sheet of pink notepaper was written: "Isaiah 54:17: 'No weapon formed against you shall prosper and every tongue which rises against you shall be condemned. This is the heritage of the servants of the Lord.' " To which she had added, "That's you!"

When the time came to leave Elaine's office and take the elevator down to the courtroom, I felt as if I were being led to my death. Was I ever frightened. I hate to be stared at, yet I knew they would all stare. I had no idea who was on the jury, and that was unsettling.

Before the trial could proceed, I had to testify in closed court about my father's abuse in our home, so that the judge could rule on the admissibility of previous sexual and physical abuse of me. Janice and Diana had already given in-camera testimony about this to the judge. The press, jurors, and spectators would be barred.

I walked alone to the witness stand, sat down, and stared at my father. Because this testimony was to be limited to his treatment of his own children, I found myself ready to confront him. I wanted him to know what he had done to me. I wanted to rip his denial away. I wanted to strip away the protective shell that enveloped him, the armor plate that had permitted him to beat and have sex with his children. I wanted him to know that regardless of what he wanted to believe, that no matter how well he lied to himself, the things he did to me and so many others were wrong and painful and damnable.

The issues the judge was to rule on for admissibility were my recollection of having been digitally penetrated, the attempted sodomy in the bathtub, the rape by Stew Smith, the physical abuse. The brief testimony I gave in the closed courtroom was both strengthening and cleansing for me.

What the jury didn't see, what the press didn't know, was that I looked my father directly in the eye as I recounted these abuses. I was telling him that I remembered. I was showing him that I was unafraid. I was confronting him in a most personal, intimate manner as I spoke directly to him with all the vehemence and anger I felt. When I was finished testifying, I think he knew that his violation of me was wrong. I think he knew that I found it unconscionable and horrific.

When I finished this portion of my testimony, I was completely wrung out. The anger, betrayal, pain, and humiliation of what he had done to me were out in the open. I wanted him to know that it had hurt me so terribly badly. I wanted him to know how senseless and sadistic his beatings had been. I wanted him to know that, by telling the truth about him, I had triumphed over him and I was freeing myself from him.

Though I had yet to begin my trial testimony, I was spent emotionally after this brief preliminary testimony. I had confronted the child abuser, the rapist, the pedophile. The only thing left was to confront the murderer and the liar.

It was later reported in the press that I had not looked at my father in the courtroom. They did not know that in the closed session, when I spoke about his crimes against me rather than those against Susan, I looked him directly in the eye and told the truth, and that my confrontation with him was over. Later that day, after I had testified in open court, Keith, the law student who was assisting Elaine, told me that he liked my first testimony in the closed courtroom better because my anger was more obvious. Elaine also said it would be okay for me to show emotions on the witness stand, that it was totally appropriate to show the pain, humiliation, confusion, and fear I felt.

They did not understand how raped I felt by the press, producers, tabloids, news shows, and others waiting to exploit my terrible experiences and the pain they had brought me. When I testified about being sexually abused, I could hear writers and journalists scribbling furiously on notepads. The sound of the pencils and pens of the press echoed in my ears as I recounted rape, murder, abuse, and humiliation. It was as if I were telling an interesting story. In front of them, I wanted to show as little as possible. When it counted, to my father, I let all my feelings show.

On Monday morning, November 5, word had gone out that Eileen would be testifying, and the crowd outside the courtroom was as large as on the day of the opening statements. Some reporters had been lined up since seven-thirty. Because of her ulcer, Eileen was fifteen pounds lighter than when she had testified in May. Her green silk dress, with its large, biblike collar of ivory antique lace, looked aggressively prim but contrasted prettily with the long, luxuriant red hair that fell over her shoulders. Taking the witness chair, she smiled slightly as she responded to Tipton's "Good morning, Miss Franklin."

On direct examination, Tipton led Eileen through her school days and her friendship with Susan, and asked her, with what seemed questionable relevance, what she looked like in fourth grade. Eileen smiled and said, "I was a goofy-looking kid—red hair, lots of freckles, bucked teeth." The jurors contemplated the stunning woman before them as if straining to picture her as "goofy-looking."

When they got to the day of Susan's disappearance, Tipton asked Eileen if it was normal for her father to take her in the van and not the other children. She said it was. Tipton then asked, "What kind of relationship did you have with your father at that time?" Horngrad objected on the grounds the question was vague. Judge Smith overruled.

"I was his favorite. I spent more time with him than the others."

After a few more questions about her childhood, Tipton asked if Eileen's father was in court. Eileen said he was. "Could you point him out?" Eileen turned her head slowly toward the defendant and, looking straight at him with a pained look, pointed to him with a quick gesture of her hand. He gazed back at her with no expression.

She described in detail everything she remembered about the events leading up to the murder—seeing Susan on the street near her house, her getting into the van, the two friends playing on the mattress in the back of the van, her father drinking a beer, driving them up past Crystal Springs Reservoir, pulling over, getting into the back with the two little girls. . . .

The jurors, having just seen the alleged results of this outing —the crushed skull, the fragments of a child's dress, the rotting body that had been concealed under an old box spring—sat engrossed as they learned of the lighthearted, innocent expedition that had preceded it: a father, his favorite daughter, and her best friend out on a lark in the beautiful coastal range above San Mateo, playing hooky from their customary routines. As she spoke, Eileen's voice was even and pleasant. When her narration was interrupted by an objection and she was forced to sit silently, a sad expression came over her face, replacing the evenness with which she told her story.

"We were still playing in the back of the van when the ground became bumpy and then we stopped. My father got out. He was drinking a beer and smoking a cigarette. I remember seeing him in the distance. He got in the back of the van by the sliding door on the side and began playing with us. At first I stayed in the back, then I got up and walked up between the two front seats to the passenger seat. I turned around and was on my knees looking over the back of the seat. I could see Susan lying, my father on top of her. He had her little arms above her head. Her legs were dangling, not reaching the floor."

The defense, in one of its more strained attempts to impeach Eileen, would later point out that if she was really remembering this from the point of view of an eight-year-old, she would not have said "little arms" but simply "arms."

"Her arms were up like this." Eileen raised her arms above her head and crossed her wrists. "He was holding her wrists with one hand. He was pushing his pelvis against her, back and forth between her legs. Her dress was up. I saw something white. I recall his pants were on, but I later saw him zip up his zipper."

Donald Nason, sitting like a stone monument, betrayed the volcanic rage inside him by turning a near-purplish color that looked as if it presaged an arterial explosion. Tipton asked, "What was Susan doing with her arms?"

"She was struggling, whimpering. She said, 'No, don't.' He said, 'Now, Susie.'"

"How many times did he say this?"

"I don't know how many times," Eileen said, her voice growing strained, at the point of tears.

"Then what happened?"

"I walked back between the two seats." Her voice grew very quiet. "I crawled up in a ball behind the driver's seat."

"I'm sorry," Tipton said, "I couldn't hear you."

"I crawled up into a ball on the floor!" she repeated, her voice angry and overloud as she broke into a sob. She paused a minute to compose herself, then continued with her former quiet, "I was scared. . . ."

Tipton handed her a cup of water, which Eileen took and held to her lips. Having gotten through one repugnant crime, Eileen, and the rest of the courtroom, immediately had to address the other. "I saw Susie walk down a decline, she was walking very cautiously, not sure-footedly. My father was off to the left. I was next to the van, next to the passenger door. He was below me to the left."

Perhaps feeling the story was unfolding too quickly for the jury to digest fully, Tipton had Eileen pause to describe the area, the "clutter" and "odd things" she recalled seeing down the slope, and whatever else she could remember about the setting. She then had Eileen go to a large white tablet hanging on the wall behind her and draw an aerial view of the van, then indicate where she and Susan had been playing, then the spot to which she had moved, and from which she had seen her father on top of Susan, and then the place where she had curled up into a ball.

"Susan was sitting on the ground in a hunched position, her knees up to her chest."

"How far was she from you?"

"Perhaps twenty feet from where I was standing, but I don't like to guess. She was crying. My father approached her with his hands over his head holding a rock. I screamed. . . ." The courtroom was totally still. A juror closed her eyes.

"Susan's hands flew up to her head." Eileen brought her own hands to her chin level. "He started to come down with his arms. I turned away. I heard two blows. It sounded like a crack. I heard two sounds."

Tipton interrupted a second time, perhaps again to allow contemplation of the moment. She got up and went around from behind the prosecution table and brought Robert Morse with her. She asked Eileen to position them both as she, Susan, and her father had been positioned. With no comment, Tipton played Susan's part. Eileen's recollection was that her father and Susan had been down the slope, but not directly below her. Susan had to turn her head to the left to meet Eileen's glance.

"After I heard the blows, I next remember seeing Susan slumped over. I went down to where she was and looked at her head. I saw blood, some detached hair, and something whitish, something that was also bloody. I turned away. I next saw her hand; it was also bloody. I saw Susan's silver ring that was smashed. I wanted to turn my head away. It was so horrible, too horrible for me to look at. I started to run away from Susan. My father grabbed me, knocked me to the ground.

"He said, 'It's over now. You've got to stop this.' I was screaming. He lifted me, put me on his knee, and said I had to forget all about this. If I told anyone, they would blame me. He said they wouldn't believe me, they would put me away. He said if I didn't stop crying, he would have to kill me. I was terrified. I absolutely believed him.

"I went up to the van. He took a shovel or a trencher from the van and I could hear him digging to the left of Susan. Then my father came back to the van and was pulling something from the back. He wanted me to help. I remember him saying, 'God damn it, Eileen.' He rarely called me Eileen, usually he called me 'Pooh' or 'Pooh Bear.' His right arm was extended, he was moving something bulky. I could see the road and cars going by. I remember thinking, if they only knew what was going on. I felt completely alone.

"Once I got into the van, I wasn't watching him. I looked one time. The only thing I remember was him crouching over Susan's body, putting rocks on her. He said, 'I'll make it look like she fell.' I thought I saw him put this thing over her body. . . ."

Eileen spoke of arriving home, of her frightened, emotional state, of being comforted by Janice, and of never having been questioned by the police. She talked about the difficulty she began having in school. She said she had never again thought about the murder. Tipton questioned her about the violence Eileen had experienced in her home. Her voice growing shaky, Eileen said that her home had been a very violent, very scary place. "Who was violent?" Tipton asked.

"My father, occasionally my mother." Eileen started to weep, but stopped herself. When asked to elaborate, Eileen spoke first about "the everyday violence," her father whacking them on the head with a serving spoon at the table, shoving them through a door if he felt they were not moving fast enough. It was not punishment for breaking rules, she said. "We never knew when it might happen or what had caused it."

Tipton asked if there had been more extreme violence. "Yes. He beat us. He would become angry about something and punch me." She closed her fist. "He might hit anywhere in the body. He did it to all of us, but [to] Janice and George junior the most." She described in detail some beatings of Janice and her brother; she talked about the drinking, the fights with Leah. About Leah, Tipton asked, "What was her level of mothering?"

"Nonexistent, to my recollection," Eileen said.

She recalled that after the murder her father had almost stopped beating her, but not the others. She could only recall one time when he had hit her. Tipton got her to relate other unusual aspects of her childhood. Eileen told of her fondness for hiding in various places in the house, of pulling out patches of her hair when she felt bored or nervous, of counting her fingers over and over on the long walk home from school. She spoke of attempting to kill herself when she was fifteen, "with Seconals, I think," and of not finishing high school.

With Eileen's skewed development fresh in the jurors' minds, Tipton got back to what many might see as the cause of her dysfunctioning, namely the sexual abuse. She asked Eileen to describe the first occasion when her father had abused her. Up to now, the sexual abuse of Eileen and her sisters had only been alluded to publicly in general terms. Knowing they were finally about to get details, journalists leaned forward.

The first occasion she could recall was when she was five. She described the episode in the bathtub that had come back to her only several months before. She then described the rape by Stew Smith: her father holding her arms with one hand, his other hand over her mouth, the two men laughing as Stew Smith said, "She's going to like this, huh, George?" Eileen broke down, but Tipton pushed ahead.

"What orifice did he penetrate?"

Eileen, still weeping with her head lowered, her long hair falling over her face, said quietly, "I don't know." Then, slightly louder, "It was the most excruciating thing to have happen. It was so painful, I can't associate it with anything but pain." Years later, she testified, she ran into Smith at an Alateen meeting in San Mateo. When she greeted him, he looked at her in shock and backed away. The scene suggested a social pitfall of repression: the ability to be civil to someone you would like to see castrated.

Tipton then discussed the way in which the memories returned. They did not come all at once, Eileen said, but more often in short bits, over a period of months. Eileen related how the memory of the murder had come back to her in her Canoga Park family room. At the end of the detailed account, Tipton asked her if she had tried to remember more details about what she envisioned.

"Absolutely not," Eileen said forcefully. "I was trying to *stop* thinking about it. I did not want it in my mind. I did not want it to be part of me." There was then a lengthy discussion of her visits to therapists, her reasons for going, her reticence to tell them of what she had remembered. This reached a climax when Eileen said she had been afraid to tell them. Tipton asked why. Her voice rising as if in anger, she replied, "Because I was afraid maybe I was a little bit crazy and would have to be locked up like my mother. I also thought the therapists might be legally bound to report it to the authorities."

Tipton then led her through her having told her brother, then her mother. Her reasons for lying about having been hypnotized were thoroughly explored, and culminated with her saying emphatically, "I've never been hypnotized in my life." By way of explaining her feeling a need to bolster her story to George junior, she said, "He was willing to accept that I had seen [the murder], but rejected that I had forgotten it." Horngrad immediately objected to this effort to convert one of his star witnesses into a prosecution witness. Judge Smith told the jury to disregard any comments made to the witness by her brother.

Eileen told of consulting an attorney to see if she could make her accusation anonymously, and of the other courses she had considered: that before she had told Barry in November of 1989, she had decided to go to the police, but that she had wanted to wait until after the holidays and after her daughter's birthday. At the reference to Sica, Eileen broke down, but quickly recovered.

She testified at length about her first contacts with the police, her fears for herself and her family, her fears of being bumped from department to department, her fears that her testimony would not be sufficient for a conviction, her fears that the case would be mishandled. Tipton bravely confronted Eileen's phone call to George junior in which she had told him not to mention anything about hypnosis, but later in the same conversation had said, "Screw it. Go ahead and tell them so we have nothing to hide." She described the press onslaught when her name got out, Eileen's dismay on learning that anyone could write about her, her decision to do one interview with NBC and, later, acquiescing to book and film deals.

"What was your understanding about the degree of control you would have with the book and film?" Tipton asked.

"It was not just that I had control, but rather that I could choose people who would not distort and tell untruths. I never affirmatively desired anything to be made about this."

When asked how much she had received from the book agreement, she replied that she had received $45,000, part of which went to attorneys' fees. Of the $10,000 she had received for the film, $5,000 had gone to Children of the Night, an organization that helps teenagers get out of prostitution. The rest was given to the Children's Home Society. Curiously, Horngrad would allow these modest figures to stand. While alluding in his cross-examination to "more money she would receive down the line," he never spelled out the exact figures, which he knew were far greater. Picking up this distortion, a newspaper ran a story with the headline, "Eileen Franklin Makes Book Deal for $50,000."

After establishing that Barry had a lot to do with Eileen's financial deals, Tipton asked, "Is the subject of money something that you and your husband have agreed on?"

Horngrad objected, saying that Tipton was trying to make Barry a witness. She shifted and asked Eileen how she felt about the deals. Her voice choking, she said, "I think it's wrong to make money on this. It's putting a price on the truth. It's putting a price on Susan's life, on my relationship with my father. It never occurred to me they would make a movie about this when I came forward."

Going into her close, Tipton elicited from Eileen her feelings about her father. "I felt I loved him," she said. "I worried about him. I was afraid of him. I felt sad for him. What he did was so wrong, I had to divorce myself from the fact that he was my father. It was as if he was someone else. If I'd seen anyone else do this, I would have gone to the police without hesitation. I felt I owed it to the Nasons to tell the truth. As a mother, I could imagine how terrible it would be to go years and years without knowing who had killed your child. Even if nothing came of it, I'd know I had made the right decision."

For her final bit of testimony, Tipton got Eileen to describe her visit to the jail concluding with him pointing to the Conversations May Be Monitored sign when she asked him to tell the truth. Tipton went on the attack. "Did he indicate an unwillingness to see you?"

"No."

"Did he accuse you of falsely accusing him?"

"No."

"Did he ever insist you withdraw your false accusation?"

"No."

"Did he ever show anger or outrage at what you had done to him?"

"No."

"Did he ever deny having killed Susan Nason?"

"No."

"What did he say to you?"

"He asked if I would come to see him again."

Tipton said she had no further questions.

Whatever sympathy for the defendant may have been raised by the last exchange, it in no way matched the harm done him by his failure to deny the crime or denounce Eileen. The one way for him to refute this was to take the witness stand, which was far too dangerous for him to do. The minute he said anything that suggested he was a man of good character, Tipton could then bring in "a parade of witnesses to prove he was not." Horngrad later had other explanations for his client's silence on the jail visit, but did not attempt to dispute Eileen's characterization of the form and content of the dialogue.

After seeing the effect of Eileen's jail visit on the jury, Horngrad changed his mind about having gone along with this testimony in the first place. Tipton had phoned him the night before and told him she intended to introduce the jail visit. "Do you have any objections?" she had asked.

"Not me," he said, then added, "but I don't know why you would want to use that. It does you more harm than good."

Now he made a motion and argued passionately to disallow all of Eileen's testimony about the visit, even admitting his dereliction in not having objected sooner. "I must have been asleep, Your Honor," he said genially.

Tipton later explained why she had not called Horngrad about this testimony until the night before; although she knew of the visit, she had not thought to ask what had been said. It is a strong example of the burgeoning complexity of such an apparently simple case—that of a daughter saying she had seen her father murder her friend—that two such astute lawyers as Tipton and Horngrad would miss the potential impact of the conversation between Franklin and his accuser. In the flow of events from the moment of accusation, every exchange, every comment—and, now, every failure to comment—could have telling repercussions and had to be weighed and analyzed as to its effect on guilt or innocence. Because both lawyers confronted enormous amounts of material requiring such inspection, an episode as revelatory as Eileen's visit to her father came close to being overlooked by both of them.

That Eileen had gone to see her father at all was in itself extraordinary. The jury may have realized that a false accuser would have had little motive to make such a visit, and many obvious reasons to avoid it. Since no one would consider it obligatory for an accuser to face privately the accused she would shortly be facing in court, she could have stayed away without fear of negative appearances.

For Eileen to have gone for no purpose other than her naïve hope to persuade her father to confess, and thereby spare everyone the long ordeal of a trial, bespoke a confidence in the rightness of her cause that could not have escaped the jury. Her action was too bizarre to be calculated strategy, too potentially painful for vindictive satisfaction. While her explanation of why she had gone made borderline sense to outsiders, it made considerably more to people who knew Eileen.

Eileen

The long talk I had with Elaine Tipton the weekend before I testified was wonderfully strengthening. Because I had been told not to discuss trial-related topics, it was the first opportunity in almost a year to relieve myself of the terrible memories. They simply swim around in my head, eating away at me as I stifled any sign of emotion from fear of upsetting the children.

As I related the horrible story of my rape to Elaine, I felt the purging of my pain. When I finished, I felt raw, as if I had been scoured internally. The compassion I could feel from her made it okay for me to have been raped.

On the witness stand, when Elaine asked me to describe the rape and the molestation to the court, I was once again speaking directly to her. No one else was in my awareness. Though I knew that notes were being taken by the press, that Horngrad was scribbling away, that the jury was watching and listening intently—only Elaine Tipton existed for me. I could not tell anyone else. It hurts too badly to think about it. By mentally talking only to Elaine, I could block out having to parade my innermost pain in front of a roomful of strangers.

As she led me through direct examination, Elaine asked me to tell the jury what part of my father was hard when we were in the bathtub. I couldn't believe she was asking me that. I replied, calmly yet with disbelief at her question, "Do I have to say it?"

My fantasy that Elaine and I were having a private conversation was shattered. Suddenly not only the jury but the entire courtroom was there. The judge. Twelve jurors. Three alternate jurors. Media and strangers looking at me. Mr. Nason, too. I could see the faces of friends among the strangers—Carol, Sharon, Terrilynn, and Lynn. After they heard what my father had done to me, they continued to care for me. I expected them to reject me, I had been so damaged, so tarnished. I am not your equal.

I don't know which shames me more, the fact that I was an object of my father's sexual perversion, or the fact that I have had no memory of events for two decades. I don't know where to go for that answer.

FIFTEEN

As Horngrad began his cross-examination of Eileen, he and she made a striking pair of adversaries. The criminal-justice system had brought face to face in a public arena this young man and woman, both of them with full lives that had nothing to do with George Franklin, to utilize whatever intelligence both possessed—as well as their mental agility, knowledge of the law, shrewdness, charm, nerve, powers of persuasion, and, above all, stamina—in a fierce battle over the life of one man.

Each had an enormous stake in the contest, but the primary result of their struggle would devolve on George Franklin, who sat—mute, powerless—watching his remaining life being decided by this man and this woman, one of whom he had fathered, the other whom he had just met, but whom he was paying to save him. Technically, the overall conflict was between Horngrad and Tipton, but everyone knew the decisive battle was between Douglas Horngrad and Eileen Franklin.

His first questions explored Eileen's close relationship with her father, enumerating the many trips they had taken together. He emphasized the 1978 trip to Mexico, during which they had slept together in the back of Franklin's van. Horngrad would later produce psychiatrists to testify on the unlikelihood of a traumatized victim willingly getting into a van with her victimizer, even if the trauma had been repressed.

He then questioned her accusingly about having withheld the name of Katherine Rieder when her therapeutic history was subpoenaed. Eileen rightly claimed the subpoena asked only for records of therapists she had visited. She had no records of Rieder but subsequently volunteered her name. After establishing that Eileen had seen Rieder *after* having her recollection, he asked why she had not told Rieder about it, even though they

had discussed both Susan's murder and another repressed
memory. His other point on this subject was that, although
Eileen admitted having touched on a returning memory with
Rieder in December of 1988, she had expressed bafflement
about repression to Kirk Barrett seven months later, when she
first told him of her recollection. Eileen sought to make a
distinction between *forgetting* an incident of molestation and
repressing witnessing a murder.

At the end of the day's session, two reporters, both young
women, were excitedly discussing George Franklin. It seemed
that during breaks and other lulls, he had turned and tried to
stare each of them down "in a most unpleasant way," according to one. They had seen him do it to other women in the
courtroom.

"Maybe," said one, "he's practicing up to scare the jurors."

The next morning Horngrad asked why Eileen, five months
after her recollection, had told Kirk Barrett it had come to her
one week earlier. Eileen said she didn't recall telling him that;
she had probably said "recently." "Is five months 'recent' to
you?" Horngrad snapped, in his first show of hostility. She said
she thought it was when you were talking about something that
happened twenty years ago.

He then moved on to her second divulgence, to George junior, during his visit to Canoga Park in the summer of 1989.
After going over the circumstances again and again, he asked
why she had been so concerned about her brother's reaction.

"I felt that forgetting the murder was really peculiar and
strange."

That Horngrad spent so much time on Eileen's having told
her brother she had been hypnotized, then denying it, suggested
that the defense considered this one of its strongest points. It
certainly had the double benefit of questioning the legality of
Eileen's testimony and establishing that she could lie. He tried
to show that at the preliminary hearing Eileen had denied asking George junior not to tell anyone she had mentioned hypnosis, but then had admitted she had done so. Horngrad had
framed his question in a way that had been impossible for
Eileen to answer correctly. Off the stand, she had explained this
to Tipton, who had informed Horngrad. He now attempted to
make it appear that Eileen had changed her mind about denying something she had done. He asked if it was true she had not
mentioned the hypnosis story to the prosecutors until May of

1989, the time of the preliminary hearing. She said she had wanted to tell them, but had been forbidden by the district attorney to make statements at random, and cautioned that she should follow proper procedures. Irritated by her goody-goody answer, he snapped, "You didn't tell them till May. True or false?"

When, for the tenth variation of the same question, Horngrad asked if she had told her mother she had been hypnotized because she was afraid Leah wouldn't believe her, Eileen paused a long time, then said, "I don't think that is accurate. I told her I'd been hypnotized because I could not explain why I'd had no memory of this for twenty years."

"Didn't Kirk Barrett explain it to you?"

Exasperated, Eileen said, "I didn't know if I was the third person or the three-millionth to have this happen to them."

"Why did you think hypnosis was a better story?"

"I thought *anything* was a better story than that I was this freak of nature who had this memory. . . ."

Since Eileen had admitted to having lied to her brother and mother about having been hypnotized, it was hard to see where Horngrad was going with such prolonged questioning about it. Perhaps his motive was just to keep the damaging episode in front of the jury as long as possible. Many observers felt that one of the hardest parts of her story to accept was that she had been lying when she told her mother and brother that the recollection had come to her through hypnosis. If jurors also had difficulty believing this, it might lead them to conclude that her testimony was legally tainted, but not that Franklin was innocent. This was one of a number of places where the law and common sense appeared at odds and took the case into areas of abstruse legal nuance, the kind of dilemmas that make judges' instructions to juries so important.

For the next two hours Horngrad asked question after question aimed at Eileen's changes in her story from earlier statements: the hypnosis–no-hypnosis episode was followed with Janice in or out of the van, her father pulling a mattress from the back of the van or pulling "some large object," the bumpy road changing to a pull-off, the time of day changing from the morning to the afternoon. He also grilled Eileen about the frequency of her meetings with Tipton and the number of phone calls between them, and her meetings with the two criminal lawyers she consulted.

In connection with the change about the mattress, Horngrad asked if she had seen "The Today Show" piece on the case. She said she had seen only a few seconds of it. Hadn't she seen 1969 footage used in the piece that showed the murder site and a rusty box spring that was found over Susan's body? No. And as for the change of time of day in her recollection, wasn't she aware that the piece had opened with Chuck Scarborough saying, "In early afternoon, Susan Nason came home from school and was never seen again?" Hadn't that changed her recollection about the time of day? No. She said that when the segment had aired, Barry had called out from another room, "Eileen, you're on." She had stuck her head into the room to see how she looked on television. That was all. Horngrad registered incredulity that the video of the NBC piece had sat in her house for four months and she had never watched it.

"I had been strongly admonished by Martin Murray not to."

"But weren't you curious?"

Her voice rose in anger. "To watch an interview about my best friend being murdered? *No!*"

Horngrad discussed the folder of news articles Barry kept in their home. Had she looked at them? No. He followed with a number of questions along similar lines, then summed up his thesis. "It wasn't your exposure to reporting that may have changed your recollection?"

"No, it wasn't."

The next day, Horngrad returned to the period immediately following the murder.

HORNGRAD: Did you go to school the next day?

EILEEN: I don't remember.

HORNGRAD: At the preliminary hearings, did you say you stopped remembering the murder when you looked down and saw Susan's bloody hand?

EILEEN: That's not exactly what I said.

HORNGRAD: What did you say?

EILEEN: When I looked at Susan's head and knew what had happened was so terrible, I fixed my gaze on her hand and blocked out the rest of what had happened.

HORNGRAD: That night when you were in bed with Janice and you were shaking, did you remember the murder?

EILEEN: I don't know.

HORNGRAD: Until January 1989 the memory did not return?

EILEEN: Yes.

HORNGRAD: Do you recall the first thing you said to Inspector Etter in the phone conversation of November twenty-first?

EILEEN: Not exactly.

HORNGRAD: [reading from transcript]: "After the body was found, I was afraid for a while, but then had to get on with my life. . . ." Why did you say this?

EILEEN: I felt strange, but not connected to what had happened. It was very peculiar.

HORNGRAD: But why did you say, "I had to get on with my life?" Why did you say, "I had to continue functioning in order to keep the lie going"? What was the lie, Mrs. Lipsker?

EILEEN: I guess that everything was fine.

A short time later Horngrad asked her why, when she first spoke with Etter, she had never mentioned that the memory had been repressed. She answered that she had assumed Barry had told them, and she "had gone into the conversations believing that they knew." Why on "The Today Show" had she told Chuck Scarborough it had taken her "many weeks" to tell her husband when in fact it had taken her ten months? She replied that she hadn't thought it was any of Scarborough's business.

"But you didn't say that. You said it took you 'many weeks.' "

"I think ten months is many weeks."

This kind of fencing went on until Horngrad returned to Eileen's account of Franklin's molestation of Susan. Putting as much contempt for her story as possible in his voice, Horngrad said, "Can anyone besides you tell us what he was doing in the back of that van?"

"Yes," Eileen said calmly.

Startled, Horngrad said, "Who?"

"I think my father could."

Horngrad threw up his arms, then leaned on Peggy Gensel's filing cabinet and was silent for a few moments. Eileen later said she was delighted to have been given such an opening, but also felt resentment that her father was being given such poor representation. "I wanted to win," she said, "but not by default."

Horngrad switched to another well-worked subject. "Isn't it true that you never shared your suspicions with anyone until you told your brother in August?" Elaine Tipton rose angrily to her feet. "Objection, Your Honor. Counsel misstates three days of testimony. They were not 'suspicions.' " The judge sustained her and Tipton returned to her seat, shaking her head in disgust. Both sides agreed to the word "image" to describe Eileen's memory of the murder.

Changing tack, Horngrad then devoted considerable time to the episode of the buried diary. He asked when Eileen had first remembered her father burying something. In December of 1988, she said. Where were you when you had this memory? In one of her more prolonged displays of irritation, she snapped, "On the Winnetka Avenue on-ramp onto the 101 Freeway in Los Angeles!" Unperturbed at her anger, Horngrad showed her the transcript of her May testimony, in which she said she had remembered the burying incident "in the last two or three months." Since she now claimed to remember her father burying something *before* she had her recollection of the murder and a year before she learned of the diary from her Aunt Jean, it appeared Horngrad felt there was something suspect in her having remembered her father burying an object *after* she heard about the diary.

"It occurred to you that you might find corroboration of your story in the diary, isn't that true?"

Eileen did not answer. He showed her the transcript. Many in the court were puzzled by this badgering over the diary. Since the whole business was worthless to the prosecution unless a diary containing incriminating entries was found, and none was, what was being established except that Eileen and the prosecution were eager to find corroborating evidence? Not only was it hard to see anything wrong with that, but it tended to confirm Eileen's sincerity; a person perpetrating a hoax would not expect to find self-incriminating entries written in the hand of one falsely accused.

As with so many thrusts of the defense, primarily efforts to catch Eileen in inconsistencies, they promised a small gain—in this case, mixed-up dates and a keen desire to convict her father—while threatening a bigger setback: that Eileen was telling the truth or at least believed she was. While Eileen did not appear damaged by the line of questioning, it appeared to upset her as much as had any other of Horngrad's tactics. Rather than being told about a diary by her aunt, he now said accusingly, Eileen testified that she "had remembered it."

"Didn't I go on to explain?"

"I'm sure your attorney will do that," Horngrad said sarcastically. The judge sustained Tipton's angry objection and told the jury that Mrs. Lipsker was not represented by an attorney, and that the jury should disregard counsel's remark.

Eileen, now very emotional, asked, "How can I answer this if I can't go on to explain my answer?" She broke down. There was a bench conference during which Eileen sat with her head lowered in her hand. Then, having regained control, she straightened, turned away from the bench, and looked at the jury.

Horngrad led Eileen through a prolonged review of her childhood, then returned to the now-familiar areas of her discrepancies and omissions: her failure to give the name of Katherine Rieder, her original description of the site as "woods" (which wasn't true; she had correctly said they had driven "*towards* the woods"), her telling Inspector Etter that she and her father had picked Susan up in "a car," not a van, her visit to a criminal lawyer, which Horngrad implied was for coaching.

Horngrad plunged into the rape by Stew Smith, homing in on Eileen's first having said she thought the rapist was a black man. Her explanation was that there had been a Jimi Hendrix poster on the wall close by as it was happening, and she remembered seeing an Afro hairdo during the rape.

"You merged a true event with a poster on the wall?" Horngrad said, pleased that Eileen had offered this demonstration of the suggestibility of her memory.

"Yes," she said quietly, her head down.

"What changed your mind?"

Horngrad would have done better to leave the inflammatory subject while he was ahead. Eileen was silent for a prolonged moment, then said, "I couldn't live with the memory of this terrible pain. I realized that was not an effective way to deal with the pain, to push it down, try to stop it from coming into my mind."

George Franklin sat gazing at his daughter with a pleasantly rapt expression, as though listening to her describing the new decor of her living room. She explained that when she forced herself to concentrate on the rape, she saw that the edges of the Afro in her memory were iridescent, as in a sixties poster. Also, when she thought hard about it, she knew her father had no black friends. After concentrating on the face over a period of time, she saw Stew Smith clearly.

Horngrad returned to her conversations with Barry about the murder, and asked if she had told Barry that she had followed Susan's death in the newspapers. "I don't know," Eileen snapped. "Why don't you subpoena him and ask him?"

She had been on the witness stand for almost two days, and her cool composure was weakening. George Franklin had a reputation among firefighters as a smartass, cocky and impertinent. With the strain of the prolonged testimony, these qualities of her father were starting to break through in Eileen's witness-stand performance.

Other matters were delved into, but as soon as the judge declared a recess and the jurors had left the courtroom, Horngrad asked to plead a motion concerning Eileen's snide remark about getting Barry to testify. In asking him why he didn't subpoena Barry, Horngrad said, the witness had opened the door to a forbidden subject. She knew, Horngrad argued, that he had sent two registered letters asking Barry to come, offering to pay his way. Barry had answered that he was unable to come.

Horngrad said that if the witness knew of the defense's efforts and asked him in front of the jury, "Why don't you subpoena him?" it sent a message to the jury that Horngrad had been derelict, when in fact there was reason to believe she had persuaded him not to come. These were grounds for a mistrial, Horngrad argued; at the very least he should be permitted to question her about her husband's reasons for not coming.

Judge Smith said this was a perfect example of "a bootstrap argument," that if she had had a conversation with Barry about testimony, that was something the jury should hear, but not about whether or not to come to America. If, Horngrad countered, she'd persuaded her husband not to return, it went to the heart of her state of mind and the jury should know about it. The judge said, "If the world were not round . . ."

After a recess and before the jurors returned, Horngrad formally argued for permission to ask Eileen if she had ever discouraged any witness from testifying. Horngrad elaborated on his reasons for wanting to bring before the jury the issue of Barry's absence. Tipton countered that Eileen had left two small children home with her husband, who was starting a new business in Switzerland. There had, she said, been no attempt to circumvent due process that no subpoena had been served. Horngrad sputtered a few more words and the judge cut him off, saying, "I am ready to rule, and the answer is no."

When the jury returned, Horngrad zeroed in on every piece of Eileen's memory of the murder that had come to her after the original recollection: seeing clutter at the site, seeing her father putting a rock by Susan to make her death appear an accident, seeing her father throwing something, the changed time of day, and so on. With each altered or added fact, Horngrad asked if she had testified to the new fact in her statement of November 25, and the answer each time was no. When did she first remember it? Had she heard something similar in the newspapers, on television, from the DA's office?

When Horngrad asked her about her previous testimony, Eileen often said she didn't remember. Horngrad would then ask the dread courtroom question: "If I showed you the page in the transcript, would it refresh your recollection?" With the already creeping pace of the questions, this routine brought things to a standstill as the appropriate page was found in the enormous transcript books. On a number of these occasions, Horngrad could not find the earlier statement he claimed was contradictory, or, even worse, when he found it, discovered Eileen had not testified as he claimed.

Jurors were visibly pleased when Horngrad again asked if a glance at the transcript would refresh her memory, and Eileen snapped *"No!"* By now she was clearly exhausted. Shortly after her defiant and angry outburst, she started to break down in tears at another question she was unable to answer: When had she first remembered her father throwing the shoes? Horngrad asked if she needed a moment. In control again, she said, "No, I'm fine."

For his final area of attack, Horngrad returned to the book and movie deals. Inexplicably, he listed the many film companies that had contacted Eileen, thereby confirming her contention of an onslaught. Turning to her contract, he went over the details of the agreements with a relish more appropriate to the agent who had made the deals. Once again he curiously neglected to establish the far larger amount of money that would eventually come to Eileen for the book than the $50,000 already testified to. Since he was trying to leave in the jurors' minds the suggestion that she might be falsely accusing her father of a capital crime in order to make money, the amount of money would seem highly relevant.

He concluded his cross-examination with a salvo of accusatory questions:

"Can you assure this jury that there will never be any changes in your memory?"

"Objection!"

"Sustained."

"Can you assure this jury that there will never be any changes in your different versions?"

"Objection!"

"Sustained."

"Are you sure that there will be no more changes. . . ."

"Objection!"

"Sustained."

"No further questions, Your Honor."

Although it was approaching four-thirty, the usual time for ending the day's session, Tipton called another witness, a short, dark-haired woman in her forties. After giving her name, Carolyn Mount Adams, and saying she lived in Nevada, she told the court that she had had a romantic relationship with the defendant for four years and had lived with him during that time.

"Was there something said to end the relationship?" Tipton asked.

"Yes."

"And what was that?"

"He said he had had sex with his daughter."

"And what was your reaction to that?"

Horngrad objected and was sustained. Tipton said she had no further questions. Only half rising from his seat, Horngrad said, "No questions." Carolyn Adams left the stand after approximately four minutes.

It was a brilliant piece of prosecutorial orchestration. For three days the jury had listened to Eileen Franklin talk of her father's physical and sexual abuse of his children, how he had assisted in the rape of his daughter, how he had molested and finally murdered Susan. Jurors' heads had been force-fed with a mind-boggling catalog of evil perpetrated by the mild-looking man sitting silently before them. All of these repugnant accusations could be dismissed, if the accusing daughter could be written off as deluded, lying, or deranged.

Eileen was barely out of the courtroom when the prosecution brought in a woman in no way connected to Eileen—from another state, in fact—who testified that Franklin had admitted having committed incest with one of his own daughters. It was a lesser crime than the one he was charged with, to be sure, but it deftly branded George Franklin with a rare amorality that set him apart from most other males. It was, in effect, saying to the jury, "This daughter you have been listening to for three days is not vindictive, delusional, or crazy. She is telling the truth about an evil and ruthless man whom you must now judge." Carolyn Adams's few minutes of testimony punctuated and, to a degree, validated Eileen Franklin's hours and hours of diffuse incriminations. To conclude the work's first movement, Tipton had jolted the courtroom with a succinct and clarion chord.

Eileen

For so many months I had dreaded being cross-examined by Horngrad. Only a few moments into it, I knew it was going to be rough. He mentioned my daughter's date of birth within a moment of mentioning my wedding date, hoping the jury would notice I had not been married when I had Sica. I thought to myself, He's going to play dirty. But then I had a different thought: My father is paying him to discredit me, and if that is all they have to discredit me, it's not going to work. His tactic made me so angry it served to toughen me up for our battle.

In the corridor outside the courtroom afterwards, Elaine told me that she was going to put me back on the witness stand for redirect. She had explained to me earlier that if I was put on the witness stand for redirect, Horngrad could cross-examine my redirect statements. I was exhausted and did not have the mental energy to wrestle again with Horngrad. I was afraid I would say something wrong.

She said she had only three questions for me, but they were important. One was about my constant childhood belief that I would be murdered. Elaine knew that this was one of the embarrassing topics that I did not want to disclose on the witness stand. I felt absolutely defeated.

I hated the thought of telling this to the jury, and especially to the press. By this time I knew that my thought processes as a child had been pretty odd, and each admission was a fresh humiliation. I thought that the more I disclosed, the more everyone would think I was a freak.

After speaking with Elaine, I took a brief walk with Sharon. I was feeling sad, violated, and exhausted, and I was yawning constantly. As we walked I thought back to the first time I had ever verbalized my belief that I would inevitably be murdered. It had been in Kirk Barrett's office. The topic had come up when Kirk asked me if I could remember, as a child, what plans or thoughts I'd had for my future.

I had not thought about this before, but I realized with a shock that I had always considered my mortality tentative, assuming that my life would end in murder. I had told him that I was not merely afraid that one day I might be killed, nor was I afraid of death, but I actually waited, living and planning my life around what I believed was the unavoidable day when I would be murdered. I never questioned whether this thought was "normal"; it was such a consistent belief that I accepted it without question.

After I had discussed this with Kirk, we both laughed, he in his kind, supportive way. He assured me that after what I had witnessed and survived, this thought process was perfectly logical. Somehow I didn't think that was what the jury and press would think.

But Elaine felt that bringing it out was important, so I agreed to her questioning me about it. For her, I was willing to expose yet another piece of my oddity—and expose myself another time to Horngrad's hostile barrages. I thought, It's a good thing I believe so much in Elaine, because this stinks.

Back on the witness stand, Elaine asked me what my hopes, dreams, and plans for the future had been as a child. I thought, There is no way the jury is going to understand this. Then I spoke the humiliating words: "I always expected to be murdered." I could tell this made a strong impression on the jury.

On his recross, Horngrad made a final attempt to discredit me by pouncing on Tipton's reference to my "dreams." Tipton objected, and Judge Smith sustained it. I was finally finished. That one final probing into my weirdness had been a small price to get out of there.

"I'm so glad it's over," I said to Sharon as we walked out of the courtroom. She smiled.

"I'm so glad it's over," I said again.

Sharon laughed and held my hand. I wanted to feel alive again, but I needed to believe that the trial was over for me first. When I got back to Zurich, I had time to reflect on my court experience, especially having to discuss in public the rape, my most private humiliation.

The first night I was home, Barry pulled close to me in bed, obviously aroused. I tried to respond, but I felt like a plastic person. Having discussed the rape in detail for the first time that week had left me feeling newly aware of the encounter, and newly raped.

As Barry continued in his attempt to seduce me, the words from the rape echoed in my head, *"She's gonna like this, huh, George? She's gonna like this, huh, George?"*

I wanted Barry to make it go away. When the memories come back, I feel so helpless. Barry was the only other person in the room, yet pleading for help would sound irrational. No words could make it go away. The feeling of betrayal. The feeling of terror. And something rare for me—a feeling of sexual confusion.

How can the pain that was inflicted on me possibly have brought pleasure to my father and godfather? How did two decades of repression allow the memory to return so clearly? How can this memory be so fresh and real while my present life is so vague and all but inoperative?

Even though I wanted to tell Barry why I could not respond, I didn't believe he would understand my explanation. I wanted to say to him, "Don't you see I was raped again last week?"

SIXTEEN

WHEN EILEEN FRANKLIN HAD FINISHED TESTIFYING, THE NUM-
ber of spectators in the courtroom dropped off abruptly. For
the next days there would be a handful of press regulars, a
larger group of press irregulars, and a small contingent of curious citizens. The spectators who frequent criminal courtrooms
are a curious mix. Some are lured by the aroma of lawlessness
that permeates courthouses, of maverick humanity that has
broken the barriers of acceptable behavior. Often they are simply retired people looking for distraction, or lonely people
eager to join the conversations that spring up among strangers
after a jolting piece of testimony. Occasionally they are people
who have had similarly intense dramas in their lives, or think
they have, and hope in the charged atmosphere of a criminal
trial to find an opportunity to tell someone, anyone, their stories. They see the courtroom as a communal campfire around
which outlandish tales are told; if they wait patiently, they
believe, they will be given their turn.

Whatever their motives for attending trials, the courtroom
groupies should be congratulated. As theater, criminal prosecu-
tions can reach levels of emotion that staged works can never
match. No matter how brilliant a play's writing, acting, or
directing, it can only approximate the dramatic intensity that
was constant while Eileen Franklin testified against her father
—not actors struggling to simulate the feelings, but a real
daughter and her real father who was sitting forty feet from her.
Equally searing was the tension hanging in the courtroom air
between Donald Nason and the man he was convinced had
molested his daughter, then crushed her head with a rock.

All of the accusations, revelations, verbal thrusts, and horrifying details are played out against the electric atmosphere of

real-life and real-death adversaries confronting each other in an enclosed, controlled space. Well-crafted film or stage works can focus on and illuminate ideas and insights into the human dilemma. They can have a shape and an intellectual cohesiveness that criminal trials, with their unwieldy configurations, interruptions, and often baffling digressions cannot achieve. For connoisseurs of undiluted human emotion, however, the difference between a vivid courtroom struggle and the best-crafted theater piece is the difference an art lover would feel between a bona fide Van Gogh and a copy so meticulous as to be undetectable except by microscope.

After Eileen's testimony, several forensic experts from the FBI crime lab in Washington were called to provide more details about the condition of the ring and other evidence from the crime scene. With their usual thoroughness, Morse and Cassandro had located George Franklin's van. Photographs of it were introduced, along with samples from the van's carpet and seat covers; the prosecution was going to great lengths to establish that exhaustive examination of the van's present interior could turn up no evidence of Susan Nason having ever been in it, but at the same time Tipton's experts established that finding such evidence after so many years was highly unlikely. Bryan Cassandro was called to report the time it took him to drive from the corner where Susan was picked up to the turnoff on Route 92: seventeen minutes.

After lunch on Thursday, November 8, Janice Franklin was called to the stand. She had flown up from Los Angeles the day before and had spent several nerve-racking hours with Elaine Tipton, who saw her as an area of vulnerability for her case in that Janice had been quoted giving differing versions of whether or not she had been present when Susan was abducted.

Perhaps the biggest problem that Janice represented for Tipton was that in her 1984 statement to the police she had said she thought the time she had encountered her father at home was around four o'clock or four-fifteen. If accurate, this would provide George Franklin with an alibi, since it would not have given him time to commit the murder.

The Janice Franklin who had waited outside Foster City Elementary School to settle scores with bullying boys now relished the chance to go several rounds with Horngrad. Tipton, however, discouraged her from engaging the defense lawyer in swordplay, impressing on her the pitfalls into which such banter could lead. By the time she reached the witness stand, Janice was nervous, and had lost all relish for the contest.

The Franklin women's concern with their courtroom appearances was evident in her outfit. She was perhaps the most elegant of the sisters and looked stunning in a vivid violet dress of a simple cut that showed off her figure. The benign interest with which George Franklin contemplated witnesses doing their best to keep him in jail now disappeared and he glared coldly at Janice.

After asking her to identify the defendant, Tipton inquired about her recollections of the day Susan disappeared. She said she had gone out to play, but did not recall where. She had a feeling she might have been playing tetherball with a friend named Terry Dalmau. Had she contacted Terry Dalmau recently? Yes, to ask if she remembered their having played. She didn't. Tipton moved on to Janice's arrival home the evening of the murder. Janice said that she always stayed out as late as she could. She had been barred from giving the reason for staying out that she had proclaimed at the preliminary hearing: to avoid the physical and sexual abuse from her father. She now limited herself to saying that she had arrived home at five-thirty or six o'clock and encountered her father in the living room. He had said hello to her. It had taken her aback, since he usually greeted her with a sarcastic or abusive remark.

"Saying hello to you was unusual?" Tipton asked.

"Very," Janice said meaningfully. This too was considerably softer than the description of this encounter that she had given in May, when she had said he had greeted her in a strange voice that frightened her. With the judge's ruling barring testimony about Franklin's other crimes against children, Horngrad had succeeded in toning down Janice's powerful testimony of what went on in their home. Through Tipton's questions, Janice told of Eileen crying, trembling, and sweating that night when she went to bed. She told of speaking to the police and of her father kicking her in the base of her spine when she went to the phone to answer more police questions.

After Susan was found, Janice had been called to the school principal's office to identify Susan's two rings. Tipton then asked Janice about her having contacted the police in 1984 to accuse her father of Susan's murder. Her mother also had the same suspicion, she said. She related her conversation with Sergeant Richie, who had made an effort to pinpoint four-fifteen as the time she had encountered her father. "He seemed to favor four or four-fifteen, so I finally let him."

"Was that your time or Sergeant Richie's?" Tipton asked.

"Sergeant Richie's."

"Was it a certainty for you?"

"No."

"In 1984, did you know what time you came home the day Susan disappeared?"

"No."

Horngrad began his cross-examination of Janice by grilling her about the recent recollection of having played with Terry Dalmau on the day Susan disappeared. When this led nowhere, he moved to the subject of Susan's rings. Yes, she had identified them and later discussed them with Eileen. Horngrad pounced. "Don't you consider the rings as part of the facts in this case?" She did. "Didn't you tell me you had not discussed the facts of the case with Eileen? Were there any other conversations with Eileen in the time you were living with her?" Objection. Sustained. "Did you discuss any other facts of the case with her?" Tipton objected again, adding, "He's throwing around the word *facts* so loosely."

"Have you talked to Eileen about any evidence in this case?" Horngrad persisted. Tipton objected again and was sustained. Later, when Horngrad was asking about various statements Janice had given to the district attorney's office, he said, "As a Franklin girl, it bothered you that Susan's murderer was never found, isn't that true?"

Scathingly, Janice replied, "It didn't bother me 'as a Franklin girl,' but it bothered me." There was a big laugh. During a break, Tipton, who had been looking increasingly anxious during Janice's cross-examination, said to her, "You're letting your wit show through too much."

Back on the stand, Janice was asked why, in her statement three weeks before the preliminary hearing, she had said she had never told Eileen about going to the police in 1984, then testified in the preliminary hearing that she *had* told her? She had forgotten. Had she discussed her suspicions with Eileen before that? Yes. When? She had no idea.

"You told her about your suspicions, but didn't mention going to the police?"

"I might have," she said.

"Then, on August first of this year, you told Detective Morse in a phone conversation that the first time you mentioned your suspicions to Eileen was August of 1989, three months before she came forward. . . ."

All of these dates and differing versions of conversations, statements, and testimony were undoubtedly confusing for the jury. On the assumption they were able to perceive Horngrad's line of reasoning, they still had a number of conclusions they could draw. Janice was confused. Janice and Eileen were confused. Janice had stated a fact, then reconsidered. Janice had lied and thought better of it. Janice was altering the facts to aid the prosecution. Janice and Eileen were in collusion.

If they leaned toward the last conclusion, they would also have to acknowledge it was probably the sloppiest collaboration in the history of conspiracies. The most minimal rehearsal would have resulted in a more cohesive story than the differing versions that were unfolding. But one aspect of their story—that they had never discussed the case while living together for many months—was believed by almost no one who heard it.

Tipton would later explain her interest in Janice's hazy memory of the day twenty years ago. "I think it is likely that Janice was present in some way. She may have come across the lot and seen her father with Eileen and Susan in the van, she may even have gone up to the van. Neither sister can remember exactly what the contact was, but both sisters had impressions of Janice seeing them set off in the van."

To Tipton it was important and incriminating to the defendant. "How else," she asks, "can you explain why George Franklin was so anxious to intimidate Janice? Kicking her in the back when she walked to the phone to talk to the police? Giving her the evil eye when she came into the house that day?" George junior and others would later ask why Franklin, if he had murdered Susan Nason in front of Eileen, had not also killed Eileen to ensure silence? If Tipton's theory was correct, that he believed he could guarantee the silence of one daughter with a scowl and a kick, it was more credible that he believed he could silence Eileen with the threat of killing her.

Horngrad tried to establish that Janice and Eileen, even as children, read newspapers, that Janice had seen the "Today Show" piece and other coverage of the case, that she had discussed her recollections with Barry. He finally came out with his main allegation: that she had put her story together with Eileen's *before* Eileen went to the police. Janice replied that Eileen and Barry had talked to the police behind closed doors, that she was unaware they had done it. Had Eileen ever asked her if she had seen Susan get into the van? No. "In all the time you lived together, she never asked you that?"

"Not to my recollection." Janice also denied ever having discussed with Barry her feeling that she might have seen Susan getting into the van. Horngrad was zeroing in on Barry's having told the district attorney's office in his original phone conversations that there was another witness. If he could establish a related conversation between Janice and Barry, it would again suggest conspiracy. All he could establish with any certainty, however, was that Janice had vague recollections about the day of Susan's disappearance, which she may or may not have discussed with Eileen and Barry.

While Horngrad was trying to enhance the likelihood of communication among the three, he was also establishing that there had been no effort whatsoever to get their stories straight. Like so many defense ploys, his line of questioning, in attempting an advance of a few inches, risked the loss of a few yards. With nothing helpful to the defense having been said, Janice left the witness stand.

Tipton's next witness was a deputy fire chief of San Mateo County, Jerry Johnson, whose sole purpose was to ascertain that George Franklin had not been at work on the afternoon of September 22, 1969. Johnson's familiarity with the log books would later come to the rescue of the prosecution when Horngrad produced a last-minute surprise.

The next morning, at ten o'clock, Eileen, still in her nightgown, was rushing around her room at the Sofitel trying to pack, worrying how to get cash, and deliberating what to do with her car. She was desperate to return to Switzerland to see her children. Elaine had told her she might be recalled, but not for at least nine days—enough time, Eileen thought, to justify the $1,500 round-trip ticket. Elaine had also told her she might not be needed again, so she might be able to go home for good. But there was no question in Eileen's mind that she had to be in Redwood City for the verdict. She would not hesitate to fly from Zurich to a California courtroom to hear one word spoken.

But now she wanted to get home. "Sica is having a slumber party," she said in anguish to a friend who had come to help her check out. "And those two Los Angeles kids are seeing their first snow. I'm missing all that! I am definitely going home."

They talked about her testimony and the questions she had

had to answer about her brother, George. "He'll be furious," Eileen said, breaking into a big smile, "when he hears I called him 'Georgie' for two hours."

"Did you do it to needle him?"

Eileen turned serious. "No. I wouldn't do that. I'm not playing politics with this thing. I did it to distinguish him from my father." Now, smiling again: "But he'll freak!" In the midst of the deadly courtroom battle, Eileen had momentarily become one of a family of cutups who felt she had gotten off a good one.

As Eileen packed, she and her friend talked about the jury. "I noticed this one man," Eileen said, "the guy with the beard in the front row on the far end? He looked at me so intently, with such a sympathetic look on his face, it gave me confidence, made me feel good." The friend said that the jurors who were taking notes were scribbling frantically during Eileen's direct testimony, but during the cross-examination they stopped.

"Really?" Eileen said, delighted. "That's great!"

Eileen said that one juror, an older woman, seemed to be nodding off. "Made me feel my little tragedies are boring," Eileen said. The friend said the bailiff would clear his throat to wake her up, but now had a new technique—he would send a cup of water down the row to her.

"To throw on her?" Eileen asked.

"She gets the idea, but only stays awake for a few minutes. It's getting to be a real bucket brigade. I've heard the judge has met with the attorneys about it and the juror might be dismissed."

The phone had rung **three** times in a row. The last time had been Barry with a list of things for her to buy. When the phone rang a fourth time, Eileen snatched at it in irritation. Then, gently nestling the receiver in her shoulder, her red hair falling over it, she said softly, her irritation gone, "Hi, Elaine." She listened, then cried out, *"No! That can't be!"* Putting her hand over the mouthpiece, she said to the friend, "Horngrad's got a witness to testify the platform and mattress were not in the van when Susan was killed!" Then she said to Elaine, "It's simply not true. I'm sure you can deal with it, Elaine."

Over the weekend, Elaine Tipton had begun to feel ill, and by Tuesday morning, as she was preparing to call her principal psychiatric expert, Dr. Lenore Terr, she had a full-blown case of flu. The trial was not yet half over, but Tipton would go through the rest of it feeling rotten, on some days with laryngitis, but determined not to delay things by asking for a recess. Everyone around her knew what she was enduring and tried to make things easier for her. Morse and Cassandro made trips for cough drops and medicine, her law clerk made regular runs to the basement cafeteria for hot tea and lemon, and friends would cook casseroles and leave them at her front door. On this first day of feeling terrible, she was glad her witness was an articulate expert, experienced at testifying, one who would not require too much effort on Tipton's part.

Horngrad requested that the judge disallow Dr. Terr, or at least impose a limiting instruction on the grounds that the jury might regard her testimony about repressed memory as buttressing the truth of Eileen's memory. Tipton argued that the prosecution was entitled to combat the myth that forgetting such a memorable event as a murder would be impossible. Horngrad responded that no such "myth" had been entered in testimony, and that jurors who held such opinions were excluded for cause. The judge denied his request, but would not allow any mention that Eileen had been examined by Terr to bar any implication of substantiation.

If trials offer much in terms of stimulation, they also serve up generous helpings of tedium, such as establishing the credentials of expert witnesses. The room sits frozen with boredom while doctors, psychiatrists, and forensic scientists are encouraged to toot their horns endlessly—rattling off degrees, awards, professional societies, all evoked in the somewhat touching belief that such badges and labels raise the likelihood that these individuals are speaking the truth.

The credentials of Dr. Lenore Terr, the only psychiatrist to be called by the prosecution, ran longer than most to establish that she was one of the nation's foremost experts in traumatized children. Her special field of interest was the effect of trauma on children's memories. She had recently published a book on the subject, titled *Too Scared to Cry,* which focused on the school-bus full of children kidnapped at the California town of Chowchilla.

Dr. Terr, an attractive, youthful-looking woman in her early fifties, answered Tipton's questions in a direct, no-nonsense manner that was mercifully free of the jargon with which so many experts try to clobber their audience into respecting their fields and themselves. Tipton elicited from her a succinct lecture on the subject of memory. Since the beginnings of psychiatry in the 1880s, Terr said, memory has been an important area for study. Five principal types of memory have been identified: The first is immediate memory, such as is involved in remembering a sentence just spoken. The second is knowledge and skill memory, the mental storage of basic tools like math and spelling; people with other memory problems can still possess these skills. The third is "priming" memory, which enables one to learn other skills. An example would be learning to ride a tricycle, which in turn permits learning to ride a bicycle.

"And next . . ." Dr. Terr said with her usual easy assurance, then paused. After an awkward silence she said, "I'm afraid I'm blanking on this one." Her memory lapse was funny enough to arouse suspicions of a planned gambit aimed at endearment. The courtroom roared. Elaine Tipton was having no lapses of memory, or anything else, and came to the rescue.

"I believe I may ask you this," she said. "Are you familiar with *associative* memory?"

"Oh, *that's* it," said Dr. Terr, somewhat giddily. "That would be opening car doors, curtsying to the queen, things that are remembered by an association." Back on track, she proceeded. "Then there is episodic memory, remembering the things that happen to you, the experiences that stick with you. . . ." With the basic types of memory on the record, Terr arrived at the subject of repressed memory. For an event to come back into consciousness after having been buried for years was a well-known phenomenon, she said, and had been well known for a long time; repression was different from forgetting in that it was an active process in which one actively kept a particular memory down—a defense mechanism, a coping mechanism. She cited several examples of repression from her own experience.

Tipton asked how reliable recovered memories were. Memories could be altered in details, Terr said, but then so could unrepressed memories. They were no more or less reliable because they had been repressed. When asked what sort of conditions led to repressing a memory, Terr said it was more likely to be an ongoing situation rather than a single trauma.

This was a crucial point for Tipton to establish, since she used it as the "back door" through which she won admittance for Franklin's sexual abuse that Horngrad, with his stipulation that Susan Nason had been molested, had succeeded in blocking in the pre-trial motions. Because Terr had stated repression was more likely to occur in a child who had experienced repeated trauma, the judge allowed a certain amount of testimony about other traumas Eileen had experienced, not to expand on Franklin's villainy, but to substantiate the prosecution's claim of repression. In the many victories Tipton would have over Horngrad, this was one of the most ingenious.

Children can forbid themselves to think about certain things. When they anticipate they are about to think of the forbidden subject, they might hide, think themselves invisible—all kinds of mechanisms can be called into action to turn off the memory. Threats could cause children to repress memories, Terr said. A parent might threaten to beat them, kill them, or simply frighten them by saying that if the parents went to jail there would be no one at home to take care of them. Shame and guilt were also important parts of repression, Terr said; it was common for children who had suffered trauma to feel themselves to be less than human. They would see other children in control of their lives, avoiding the kind of trauma they had faced. The traumatized children, on the other hand, would see themselves as having allowed things to get totally out of control. When kids took on part of the responsibility for terrible things happening, it made them feel more in control. But it also led to greater guilt.

Tipton asked about the triggers or conditions that could lead to recovering repressed memories. Most important was that the person must feel safe, Terr replied, that they wouldn't be destroyed if the memory was allowed to surface. Independence could be a factor; they had moved out of the home and were no longer dependent on the person they feared. The memory might be triggered by seeing something similar to what had happened to them—"a person, a place, a look on someone's face. . . ."

That Terr had examined Eileen extensively had been barred from testimony but at times her detailed knowledge of Eileen's case came dangerously close to the surface. Not that everything she was saying wasn't valid and as sound as her science could get, but since the classic film *Spellbound,* in which a murder was recalled by a fork being pulled over a tablecloth, it has been widespread psychiatric lore that *anything* can spark a dormant memory. From all the millions of possible causes, to single out "the look on someone's face" made Terr appear to be tailoring her testimony to fit Eileen's story in too obvious a way. It was also unnecessary, since Tipton was doing a good job of shaping the testimony with such questions as the one she asked next: "Can having children the same age as you were when repression occurred trigger a memory?" Terr assured her it could.

anticipation of the cross-examination, Tipton introduced the subject of false traumatic memories, a phenomenon that, according to Terr, occurred with far less frequency than valid memories. How can you tell them apart? "True memories are accompanied by signs and symptoms," Terr said. "A child might have fantasies about wishing someone dead, they might have fears of growing up, they might have fears for their future or feel they have no future." (Eileen again.)

Terr gave vivid examples of signs and symptoms in patients who had repressed a traumatic memory—a boy who had seen his brother shot in the head and had then lost his hair in the same spot; another boy, who had repressed being abused, and who could not feel his body and so might be hurt playing and not realize it. Such things would not happen to people experiencing false memories. People with false memories rarely offered details. For example, a young girl said her psychiatrist was a satanist and had forced her to have sex. When asked what kind of sex, she looked blank and said, "Just sex." Such a vague answer suggested a false memory, which it turned out to be.

With valid memories there should be accompanying emotion. Terr went on to tell a horrible story about a small child being eviscerated by the drain in a wading pool in front of two sisters. A third sister who was nearby did not see the tragedy, but came to think she had. When, years later, she described the scene to Terr, she showed none of the emotion her sisters had shown in describing the memory. Also, she did not offer personal details of her own, only saying things that her sisters could have told her.

To conclude her direct examination, Tipton asked Dr. Terr if repression would be more likely to diminish or enhance a memory. It might enhance it, Terr replied, if there had been no input to adulterate it. Terr had earlier given an example of a man who had repressed having been in a disastrous flood, a notorious event in his town, about which he surely had heard much over the years. She acknowledged the possibility that, with some repressed memories, alterations from external input were a strong possibility, but of course, in Eileen's case, since there were no other witnesses, it was not.

Launching into his cross-examination with unusual vigor, Horngrad wanted to know how often Terr ran across a repressed murder. Terr said she had dealt with others. Horngrad then questioned her extensively on various case histories in her book aimed at establishing that some repressed memories could never be confirmed as real or false if there was no corroborative evidence, that traumatized children would probably resist entering into situations similar to the ones where traumas had occurred, and that post-traumatic effects could spread to others who were not traumatized. It was clear that both Horngrad and Tipton had combed Terr's book for any scrap that might reinforce either side's position. When he had hold of such a scrap, Horngrad worried it with repeated questions, none of which shook Terr's standard for distinguishing real and false memories.

At one point an exasperated Tipton jumped to her feet and said, "Your Honor, I object to the same question being asked five times." Disingenuously, Judge Smith said, "I only heard three times."

After many more questions that dealt with repression in a general way, Horngrad brought his line directly back to Eileen in discussing a person's feeling of safety as being conducive to retrieving a repressed memory. "How about," he asked, "a person going through a divorce action, who was filing an affidavit about child support, who was worried that her spouse was running off with all their money, who was scheduled to go to court the same month and was worried about fighting a custody battle? Would such a person feel safe and secure?" Tipton objected on the puzzling grounds that the question was not relevant. She was overruled.

"Would a person feel safe with all that on their mind?" Horngrad persisted.

"Probably not," Terr said, "unless they had you as an attorney." The courtroom laughed and Horngrad smiled.

He cited more examples of distorted memories of traumatizing events in Terr's book. Among the most helpful to his thesis was the story of a young Chowchilla girl who remembered one of her kidnappers as a blond woman, while all of the kidnappers had, in fact, been male. She had had a fight that morning with her mother, who was blond. Later, Terr countered this implication with a hypothetical situation: If the courtroom ceiling were to collapse right now, one of us might recall the wall as green rather than brown, but that wouldn't mean the ceiling didn't fall. This would be the running rebuttal to the considerable testimony Horngrad would introduce on the tricks the mind could play with memories.

That would be true, Horngrad said, except when the entire memory was false. Terr said again that false memories were extremely rare. Horngrad asked if there were any studies on the subject. Impatiently, Terr burst out, "You can't do a study on it. It would be like doing a study of the giraffes in Ohio. There are not enough of them."

It was interesting that Terr, who was being paid a fee for her testimony (approximately $4,000) but who otherwise had no involvement in the case, would display anger at the implication that Eileen's memory was false. In a later interview she said that after having done the psychiatric evaluation of Eileen for the state the preceding August, she was convinced Eileen had witnessed Susan's murder. But she was not being asked to testify to this opinion—in fact she was forbidden to do so. Her annoyance may have been triggered by the doubt cast on her skill at evaluating patients, but it came across in the courtroom as an unscientific partisanship.

There were a number of questions about dreams; these were high on Terr's list of signs and symptoms, particularly with her Chowchilla victims. This line was aimed at Eileen's having testified that she experienced no dreams. Terr emphasized that while dreams sometimes occurred after one had repressed a trauma, they were by no means inevitable.

On her redirect examination, Tipton struck out repeatedly at Horngrad's implication that, based on the examples in Terr's book, it would be unlikely for a traumatized child who had repressed a trauma willingly to get into a van and take a trip with the perpetrator of that trauma, a reference to Eileen's trip to Mexico with her father. She emphasized the distinction between the Chowchilla children fearing the perpetrators who were strangers and fearing a father who was loved by the child. Tipton got Terr to reiterate that dreams were not always present in cases of repressed trauma.

In his recross-examination, Horngrad asked if Terr would agree with the Freudian proposition that children susceptible to repression were also susceptible to suggestion. Terr said she knew of no studies to suggest that. Did she reject Freud's findings? "He was not modern," replied Terr, repeating the word she had used to characterize her own school of psychiatry. Then she added condescendingly, "Some of his early papers are valuable, the early studies of his patients."

"But isn't it true that there is a school of psychiatric thought that believes the hysterical personality who is susceptible to repression is also susceptible to suggestion?"

"I suppose those who have bought into Freud's ideas might

have some ideas like that," Terr replied, making Freudian analysis sound like a fringe movement of dubious respectability. Then, perhaps feeling she was being overly harsh about the founder of her discipline, she added, "Freud was not interested in trauma. The modern way of looking at it is that people really do suffer these things and have ways of coping with them."

Horngrad returned to the prevalence of dreams in post-traumatic repressions, and after four o'clock he said he had no further questions. The psychiatric portion of the prosecution's case had taken up most of one day.

SEVENTEEN

IF LENORE TERR HAD SOUGHT TO PROVIDE THE PROSECUTION'S case with its intellectual and scientific underpinnings, Tipton's next witness, Eileen's mother, brought it back to the emotional entanglements. At four-twenty, Leah Peluffo entered the court and started toward the witness stand. She looked handsome in a loose black jacket and a gold blouse, her black hair falling to her shoulders and framing her good features. She looked sensitive, attractive, and at least ten years younger than her fifty years.

With the jury still out, the judge asked Tipton why this witness was being called. What was her testimony? Tipton responded that Leah had suspected her husband of having murdered Susan, and she had confronted him with her suspicions in the late 1970s. She would also testify, Tipton said, to the atmosphere of hostility, violence, and abuse in the household as it related to George Franklin and Eileen. The jury would not hear the most flagrant examples of his physical and sexual abuse.

Horngrad said that flat-out character evidence was not admissible and would inflame the jury. "We do not contest that she confronted the defendant with her suspicions," Horngrad said, but as for the rest of her testimony about the atmosphere in the household, "it says nothing about his guilt or innocence." Tipton replied that Leah would establish the verbal and physical violence that constituted the kind of continuous trauma for Eileen that was conducive to repression.

"That doesn't mean he's guilty of murder," the judge said reflectively.

"If," Horngrad said, "it's only to show Eileen's state of

mind, I would ask the court to limit her testimony to what happened to Eileen." The judge agreed.

As Leah was being sworn in, she gave her last name as Franklin rather than her present married name—an effort, later used as well by her daughter, Kate, for maintaining as much anonymity as possible. Tipton first asked Leah about the VW van. "Was there a platform and mattress in the back in 1969?"

"Yes," Leah replied.

Leah described George Franklin's off-hours, his housepainting business, the equipment often carried in the van; she stated that Eileen was his favorite, and often accompanied him on errands and jaunts. Asked about the atmosphere in the home, she said, "It was very stressful, there was much physical and verbal abuse." Her voice grew thick with emotion. "It was living in terror. I did not feel safe in my own home." She started to cry. "I wasn't safe, and my children weren't safe. The verbal abuse was constant, the physical abuse sporadic."

After asking a series of questions about the time of Susan's disappearance, Tipton played her trump card. "Did anything unusual occur after Susan Nason's disappearance regarding a laundry item?"

"Yes. My husband gave me a shirt with bloodstains on it and asked me to wash it."

"How did you know they were bloodstains?"

"He told me. He said they came from a painting accident."

"What was your reaction?"

"I later thought that the stains couldn't have been from a painting accident. You use a screwdriver to open a can of paint and a hammer to close it. There was too much blood."

Horngrad leaped to his feet. "Objection! She's drawing a conclusion." He was sustained.

Tipton rephrased her question. "In what way was his explanation unusual?"

"There was more blood than there would have been from a normal, minimal accident." Horngrad did not object to the rephrasing.

There followed a discussion of Leah's reasons for not having mentioned the shirt before. Leah said the recollection had come to her during her testimony at the preliminary hearing, but she had left the courtroom without mentioning it to anyone. She had later told Detective Morse.

Tipton struggled to make Leah's bombshell believable. It

was hard enough to believe that Franklin, shortly after Susan's disappearance, when her body could be found at any moment, would have brought such a suspicious and potentially incriminating item to the attention of anyone, especially his adversarial wife. As Horngrad pointed out, Franklin knew how to operate the washing machine and could have laundered the shirt himself. He also could have discarded it.

But even if one could accept that Leah had been given a shirt with "too much blood on it" by a husband she knew to be violent, it was hard to believe that when Susan's battered body had been found ten weeks later, Leah made no connection with the suspicious shirt. Twenty years later, when her husband was charged with the murder, she still didn't remember it in several conversations with her daughters and with the authorities. Not until the preliminary hearing did she recall the shirt, and she did not speak of it publicly until the trial itself, perhaps the last opportunity to put her ex-husband in jail permanently.

Many people in the courtroom, hearing this startling and incriminating bit of testimony for the first time, did not believe it. Oddly enough, Leah's daughter Janice and her sister, Sue, neither of whom had much favorable to say about Leah, believed her without question. Janice summed up her feelings: "Leah may be many things, but she's not a liar." Her sister believed the shirt story on the grounds that George was too arrogant to think anyone would suspect him, and too much a male chauvinist to wash the shirt himself.

Tipton asked Leah if she recalled having an opinion about the defendant and Susan Nason's death. She responded that she had. Once in the late seventies when he had come to her house on Beach Park, she asked him if he had murdered Susan. He had responded something to the effect of, "Oh, Leah, why do you always think things like that of me?"

"Did he ever say he didn't do such a thing?" Tipton asked. "No."

Tipton asked Leah if Franklin had told her about his diary. She replied that he had, adding, "I remember wondering what anyone at age thirty-eight had done that was worth writing about. He told me he had wrapped the diary in a plastic bag and buried it on Star Hill Road. I wondered why."

She spoke of one or perhaps two conversations she had had with Janice about suspecting her husband of having killed Susan. In a subsequent conversation with Eileen, she said shortly afterward that she had advised her to consult a criminal lawyer, but denied having told Eileen that testimony derived from hypnosis was inadmissible.

"I didn't know anything about that," Leah said.

"Did Eileen later ask you to keep secret her having mentioned hypnosis?"

"No."

As Horngrad began his cross-examination, he asked her whether, in the phone conversation in which Eileen had told her about witnessing the murder, she had asked if Leah remembered any changes in her afterward. "On the second call, on October twenty-sixth, 1989," Horngrad continued, "did Eileen say she had been hypnotized?"

"No. She told me three things," Leah said, her voice starting to quaver. "She told me that her father had sexually abused her. She said that he had held her down while someone raped her. She said that he had murdered Susan Nason." Leah broke into sobs and was given a minute to recover.

"What was your reaction?"

"I was shocked. I asked her what I could do to help her."

Horngrad tried unsuccessfully to pinpoint when Eileen had mentioned hypnosis, then returned to Leah's reaction to Eileen's news. "I felt like someone dropped a bomb. Here I could see that she needed me, and I didn't know where to begin to help her. I'd always been there for her." Her emotions rose again, and, almost crying, she said, "I thought, How can she tell Barry? How can I tell my husband?"

Horngrad said, "I have no further questions at this time."

As Leah walked toward the courtroom door, Margaret Nason got up from the first row and the two women walked out together. Todd Kirk, Eileen's high school friend, was in court that day, and commented in the corridor about what he had just heard in court. "That was typical of Leah. Turning everything to herself. The poor victim. 'What will I tell my husband?' As if that's the big issue when your daughter sees a murder."

After an employee of Skylawn Cemetery established the location of Susan Nason's grave, Tipton called to the stand William Hensel, a retired Foster City law-enforcement officer who had conducted much of the investigation into Susan Nason's murder. He recounted the entire police involvement, starting with the first phone call at 7:45 in the evening of September 22, 1969. He remembered interviewing "a Franklin daughter" but did not recall which one. He spoke of the search, of the many false leads, of interviewing all sex offenders in the area, and of the assumption that the perpetrator was a stranger.

Tipton then asked if he had attended the funeral. When he said he had, she asked why. "First, because it was Susan. . . ." (According to Margaret Nason, Hensel had become obsessed with the case.) "Second, we wanted to see who attended." Tipton asked what action the police had taken on the anniversary of Susan's disappearance. Hensel replied that he and a colleague had staked out Susan's grave to see who drove past it. Tipton asked why.

"From our training at the police academy and from our training with the homicide unit—" Horngrad cut him off with a vociferous objection. The subject of why they had gone to the grave was abandoned.

In a later interview, Detective Bryan Cassandro would talk about the police experience with grave visits that Judge Smith had not allowed. It was common, he said, for murderers to visit the graves of their victims, particularly on various anniversaries. "They might go and do nothing. Sometimes they desecrate the graves. Sometimes it's a sexual thing. I've even heard of a guy pissing on the grave of his victim."

Hensel testified that he and a colleague remained in their car and wrote down the license number of every car that passed the grave, which was in an isolated and remote area of the cemetery. He had turned the list over to his superiors and suggested they check the license numbers with the Department of Motor Vehicles. When Tipton showed him a list, he identified it as the list he had submitted. It was dated October 13, 1970, three weeks after the anniversary of Susan's murder.

"Is the license number VXJ707 [Franklin's license number] on the list?" Tipton asked.

"Yes."

Horngrad flung himself into his cross-examination. "Did you personally get the teletype back?"

Hensel replied that he had not gotten it back.

"You gave the list to your superiors, and they sent it?"

Hensel said this was what had occurred.

"You never saw it again, right?"

Hensel affirmed this.

"Why was there a three-week gap before the list was sent off?"

"I don't know."

Franklin's alleged 1970 visit to Susan Nason's grave had not been mentioned at the preliminary hearings and was, along with Leah's bloody shirt, one of the prosecution's two startling pieces of new evidence to corroborate Eileen's story. In his opening statement, Horngrad had trumpeted that this visit never occurred, but now, with the man who claimed to have witnessed it on the stand in front of him, he did nothing to damage the testimony—except perhaps to show some inefficiency in police procedures. It would later develop that Horngrad was still preparing a counterattack that would demolish this claim and shake the underpinnings of the district attorney's case.

Horngrad asked about the incident in which a Foster City child, Ann Hobbs, alleged that a strange man had tried to get her into a blue station wagon three days before Susan disappeared. Horngrad seized upon the fact that the blue station wagon was mentioned in a police lookout flyer about Susan as proof that the police considered the station wagon a strong lead in the Nason case. Hensel and subsequent witnesses took the position that they had been desperate and had grabbed at any possibility, regardless of how remote.

The last witness Elaine Tipton introduced for the prosecution was Detective Robert Morse, who would produce the prosecution's third piece of corroborative evidence: Franklin's remark on being arrested. Morse told of going to the defendant's apartment in Carmichael, California, and telling him that he wanted to question him about Susan Nason's murder, upon which Franklin had said, "Have you talked with my daughter?" Having saved this for their final salvo, the prosecution clearly felt the remark to be highly incriminating.

Horngrad's cross-examination of Morse brought out the interesting information that Bryan Cassandro disagreed with Morse about what Franklin had said regarding his daughter. (In a closed hearing Cassandro had testified that he thought Franklin had asked Morse if the police had been speaking to his "daughters," in the plural. That the partners would return from Sacramento with such a discrepancy in so significant a statement bespoke an impressive level of scrupulousness.) Horngrad then moved to a statement Morse had made shortly after taking a deposition from Eileen, in which he said, "I have examined news articles of the time, and they do not mention Susan's hand being damaged or that her ring was crushed." Horngrad emphasized that Morse had referred to *articles* in the plural. Morse now said he had seen only one.

Horngrad asked Morse if, in reviewing the Nason file, he had learned that Janice had identified Susan's crushed ring. Tipton objected and was sustained. He rephrased. Had Morse said that Janice had identified the ring in 1969? Morse said he didn't recall. "Of what you know now," Horngrad said expansively, "what is known to Eileen Franklin about the murder that was not in the public domain?" Tipton objected and was sustained. Horngrad said he had nothing further. Tipton rose and said, "The prosecution rests."

Because of the holiday and the four-day work week the judge had established, the prosecution's seven days of testimony had covered two weeks. In that time, Tipton had placed before the jury the story of a bloody shirt the defendant had given his wife, the information that he had not denied killing Susan when Leah accused him many years later, nor had he denied it to his daughter when she visited him in jail, or in any way reproached her for having accused him. He had, in fact, asked police coming to arrest him if they had talked to his daughter.

Tipton had established that the home in which Eileen had grown up was a nightmare of physical and sexual abuse, and that in spite of this she had a close and loving relationship with her father. Tipton had presented expert psychiatric testimony that explained the repression mechanism and the symptoms, many of which Eileen showed, that accompanied real memories as opposed to false ones.

But, more than anything else, the prosecution had offered an eyewitness to the crime who appeared sound and rational, who didn't collapse under rigorous cross-examination, and who never revealed any attitudes that might suggest a motive for a false accusation, primarily vindictiveness toward her father or a desire for the fame and money her notoriety was bringing her. The defense would try to throw into question many of these prosecution assertions, but above all they had to destroy the credibility of Eileen Franklin.

EIGHTEEN

THE FIRST WITNESS FOR THE DEFENSE WAS JAY JAFFE, THE BEV-
erly Hills criminal lawyer Eileen had consulted for advice on
how to proceed. Jaffe was a dignified, conservatively dressed
young man in his late thirties, who looked as if he would
explode ferociously if anyone touched his BMW. Horngrad
asked a series of questions all aimed at discrediting Eileen, both
her motives in having made her accusations and her believability as a witness. Had she ever told Jaffe the memory was lost?
Jaffe didn't recall. That it had bothered her for some time? No.
Had she told him about having had this image, this so-called
memory? Tipton objected and was sustained.

The one thing Eileen had recalled about the incident, Jaffe
said, was the crushed ring. He had asked her if she had read
about it or had been told by someone. She said neither had
happened, that it was her memory. Horngrad asked if Jaffe had
informed her what would make her testimony invalid? He
hadn't been worried about her credibility, he said, but had tried
to assist her in a traumatic decision. Had Jaffe discussed the
inadmissibility of hypnotic testimony? He might have. After a
few more questions, Jaffe apologized for his faulty memory
about the conversation and said that, had he known he would
later have to testify about it, he would have taken notes.

In her cross-examination, Tipton asked if Eileen had expressed reluctance or sadness about coming forward. Maybe
reluctance, but not sadness, Jaffe said. Had she said she wanted
to wreak revenge on her father? Jaffe replied that he never had
that sense. Had she expressed fears for her safety? Yes. Horngrad objected and was overruled. Had Jaffe told her she must
not get information about the crime from other sources? Yes,
Jaffe replied, and was dismissed.

The second defense witness was a key figure in the drama, Eileen's therapist Kirk Barrett, who was the first person to whom she had told her recollection. Barrett was a pleasant-looking man in his forties with the soft, kindly delivery of a priest. After reviewing the time frame of her visits, Barrett told how Eileen had first mentioned Susan's murder without offering any information about who had done it. After establishing that Barrett practiced hypnosis, Horngrad asked if he had ever discussed that subject with Eileen. Only once, he said, when she had asked him about it in connection with post-partum weight loss. He had never hypnotized her.

Eileen's initial mention of the murder had begun by her telling him of disturbing "images" she had been having. The first of these was of a pile of dirty clothes on a sidewalk; the next was of a mangled metal ring. She had also told Barrett about a van like her father's figuring in these images. The pile of clothes was never explained to Barrett. As for the other image, he was vague about the evolution of her revelations to him. Tipton objected to the use of the word *evolution* and was sustained.

Eileen, Barrett continued, had gradually told him more and more, until she finally told of seeing her father bring a rock down on Susan's head. The whole story had come out gradually between the first part of June and July 18, 1989, but he couldn't remember exactly what she had told him and on what date.

"Did she tell you the [recollection] happened a few days before she told you?"

"I recall thinking that," Barrett said in reference to his erroneous preliminary-hearing testimony, "but not her telling me that."

"Before telling you that her father was involved," Horngrad said, "she told you she saw images but no person, isn't that true?"

"No," Barrett replied, "she said she saw a person but could not tell who it was."

It is curious that Horngrad made so much of Eileen's delay in telling anyone of her recollection, and also that he would attack the piecemeal way in which she had finally done so. She had always maintained that her two primary reasons for waiting so long to tell her memory were her fear she would be thought crazy and her fear of unleashing legal repercussions that would quickly get out of her control. When she did decide to tell, she did so very gradually, to get a sense of whether or not the listener thought she was unbalanced or might take some precipitous action, as Barry indeed had done. According to Eileen, her delay had been a gradual mustering of her courage and resolve; Horngrad hoped to make it appear a gradual fabrication and refinement of her tall tale.

Barrett said Eileen, after telling him, was puzzled that she could forget something so important as a murder. Referring to her having told Katherine Rieder that she only recently remembered being molested, Horngrad asked, "Did she tell you she had discussed the same thing with another therapist?" Tipton's objection of his renewed effort to establish that Eileen had known about repression was again sustained.

Horngrad asked if, when Eileen had first told Barrett about a crushed ring, she had associated it with Susan. He did not believe so, Barrett said. Had she mentioned that Janice had told her about identifying Susan's rings in 1969? Tipton objected and was sustained. Judge Smith agreed that Horngrad's juxtaposition of questions pointed the jury toward a conclusion.

Many of the questions Horngrad asked succeeded in painting a picture of Eileen's emerging recollection as vague, splintered, and not etched clearly in her mind. While Barrett's testimony was not completely damaging to her story, it could have been a lot more helpful had he recalled that Eileen had made a clear, unwavering description of her murder recollection. That Barrett did not do this helped to alleviate suspicions he might be in collusion with Eileen to combat a much more important problem: whether she had been hypnotized by him.

Her testimony that Barrett had not hypnotized her was one of the shakiest parts of her story, if only because she herself had told two family members that she had been hypnotized. The only corroboration for her changed story was Barrett himself, a therapist to whom she felt very close and who might conceivably have agreed to deny having hypnotized her after learning how ruinous to her case such an admission would be. That his testimony now was so much less supportive of her story than it might have been helped to dispel the specter of collusion.

Horngrad elicited from Barrett that Eileen had never reported any dreams about her father, never expressed fear of entering his van (although Eileen testified at preliminaries that she had told Barrett of fearing the van). "Did Eileen ever tell you," Horngrad asked, "that she was holding back and purposely not telling you who the assailant was in her recollection?" No, she did not. Horngrad turned his witness over to Elaine Tipton.

"Is it a fair statement," Tipton began, "that Eileen never said 'I'm not going to tell you who the murderer is?' " No, Barrett said, she never did. "Do you know if she knew who the murderer was?" No, he did not. Horngrad objected on grounds the question called for a speculation, but was overruled. Tipton inquired whether there was anything unusual in a patient withholding information from a therapist, but Horngrad objected to this line and was sustained.

Tipton concluded her cross-examination by asking a series of questions designed to establish that Barrett found nothing unbalanced about Eileen, but rather that she fit the pattern of a post-traumatic stress victim. Clearly upset at this effort to use one of *his* witnesses to prove Eileen sane, Horngrad leaped to his feet and asked question after question of his witness aimed at demolishing any suggestion that Barrett was a bona fide expert in either psychology or psychiatry. Had he a Ph.D.? No. Had he published? No. Was he a member of professional societies? No. Was he licensed in clinical psychology? No. Had he ever qualified as an expert witness in any court? No. Turning to the judge, Horngrad said, "With all due respect, Your Honor, I ask that Mr. Barrett not be qualified as an expert witness in this case." The jury looked baffled.

With the mists of southern California gurudom still swirling around Barrett, Tipton asked him a few more questions to leave firmly in jurors' minds that Barrett, whatever his credentials, had not hypnotized Eileen.

Of all the witnesses to testify in the trial of George Franklin, perhaps the most puzzling was the defendant's son, George Franklin, Jr. In his preliminary meeting with Elaine Tipton, he had made no secret of his contempt for this prosecution, and had boldly accused her of railroading his father to further her own political ambitions. He later refused to allow his statements to be recorded, saying that Tipton would doctor the tapes.

In light of how little George junior knew about both Tipton and the case, it was a remarkably strong charge and a desperate effort to wrench the proceedings from a quest for the truth about a crime and to redeposit the criminality on those very people who were sworn to seek justice. While such corruption surely exists, his allegation was apparently based on nothing more than his belief, which he had expressed to Eileen, that such ruthless and felonious behavior was endemic in law enforcement.

When Bryan Cassandro came to the witness room to escort George junior to the courtroom, he ignored Cassandro's attempts at conversation and insisted on walking behind him rather than alongside, as most witnesses did. On the stand he was bristly and arch with Horngrad, blatantly hostile toward Tipton. His determination to show his outrage at the proceedings was hard to fathom. If he believed that his father was innocent and that corrupt district attorneys had seized on his sister's innocent delusion to further their careers with a sensational conviction, he might be expected to be as persuasive as possible to combat his sister's charges. The only explanation for his anger was a belief that collusion between Eileen and the prosecution to frame an innocent man made a monstrous injustice unavoidable.

George was dressed in a light gray suit, a white shirt, and a neutral tie. It was the civilized and unobtrusive getup of one who knew nothing of violence, abuse, or dysfunctional families. At twenty-seven, he spoke like an elderly academic. His clipped and precise tones had an exasperated edge, like a college professor addressing an uncomprehending class. His choice of words was bookish and, at times, florid. He referred to Eileen's "spectrum of therapies," but then undermined the effect of offhand literary swagger by repeating this arresting phrase a few minutes later.

Horngrad got George junior to describe his visit to Eileen's Canoga Park house in August of 1989, and a conversation they had had there about their family. "She was very disapproving of our parents," he said, "and gave examples of their shortcomings." George described Eileen's comparison of their upbringing with the way she was raising her own children—the private schools, the medical care, the playrooms full of toys. She was angry, he said, that she had recently been diagnosed as being allergic to dairy products. When she was a child, no one had been interested enough to discover this. She talked to her brother about her therapy, and spoke of their family as "dysfunctional."

"Did she tell you of having had an image of your father committing a murder?" Horngrad asked.

George said that on the evening of the second night of his visit, she had told him of a memory of their father killing Susan

Nason. "She told me," he said, "that while she was under hypnosis the memory had come out." After their father was arrested, she had phoned him to say the memory had not come to her under hypnosis, and that he was not to tell anyone she had said it had. "I told her I would not lie."

In a later phone call, near Christmas of 1989, she had accused George of speaking with the defense. Then, having established that she no longer trusted him, he said that she had told him the memory had come out during psychotherapy.

As Elaine Tipton began her cross-examination, George stiffened and his answers became more clipped. When Eileen had told him their father had murdered Susan, Tipton asked, was his reaction disbelief? Yes. Had George discouraged her from going forward? No. Had he encouraged her to do so?

"She was about to go to Europe. I told her to go, then call me when she returned and we'd decide where to go from there. I said I'd go back through the local newspapers, do some research, then we could decide what to do."

"Did you say you would 'poke it with a stick'?"

"Yes."

"What does that mean?"

"That we would keep a safe distance from it."

"Isn't it true that your sister left you feeling very uncomfortable and unsettled?"

"Somewhat."

"Didn't you describe what she told you as a 'revelation'?"

"Yes."

"Was that your word?"

"Yes."

Returning to the subject of hypnosis, Tipton asked her next question in the form that connotes suspicion of doctored testimony: "Do you consider hypnosis important in this case?" Horngrad objected and was sustained. After referring to his new assertions about the memory coming back through therapy and nightmares, Tipton said, "Did you hold back information when I questioned you on May fifteenth, just prior to the preliminary hearing?"

Franklin's voice seething, he said, "I was attempting to answer your questions, Miss Tipton."

She asked if, prior to May 15 when she interviewed him, he had refused to speak with the prosecution. Yes. And hadn't he spoken with the defense? He had. She took a long pause, permitting the jury to digest his bias. Then she pushed away at his having not mentioned before that Eileen had told him her memory had come during therapy.

"When I left your office, I believed I had answered your questions to your satisfaction, *Miss Tipton*." He all but spat her name.

She snapped back, "But I didn't know what you knew, did I, *Mr. Franklin*?" giving the same snide emphasis to his name he had given hers. She paused to allow both their tempers to cool, then asked, "You testified that Eileen told you her memory had come to her in a nightmare. When did she tell you that?"

"February, I believe."

"When did you last talk with her?"

"I think it was in February," he replied, then added scathingly, "It was the same day she went on 'The Today Show.' "

"You're very bitter about that, aren't you, *Mr. Franklin*?"

Horngrad objected and was sustained.

Tipton went on, "Did you disclose to law enforcement about her telling you of nightmares?"

"I don't know. You have the transcript, Miss Tipton."

She indicated there was *nothing* in the transcript about nightmares. He said that he had mentioned them in a discussion with her prior to the formal interview. Tipton did not dispute that, although it indicated that he had, in casual conversation, introduced a highly significant new bit of testimony that she had failed to pursue in her formal interrogation of him. If true, this would have been a singularly uncharacteristic piece of carelessness on Tipton's part.

"When Eileen told you she had not been hypnotized, she told you she had said that only to make [her recollection] more believable for you, didn't she?"

"Yes, she did."

"When she disclosed her recollection, your reaction was one of disbelief, isn't that correct?"

"Yes, but internally."

George was not going to yield an inch of corroboration of Eileen's story unless forced to. Tipton asked if he had visited his father in jail. Yes, he had, perhaps three times. She asked how long had it been since he had seen his father before the arrest. Four or five years, he replied.

"Weren't you telling the defendant everything Eileen said to you?"

"I was telling him anything relevant to the case. Anything personal I kept to ourselves."

Tipton asked a few more questions to emphasize his degree of assistance to the defense, then said, "You have a hope or expectation about the outcome of this case, isn't that true?"

He answered to the effect that he was naturally concerned.

On redirect, Horngrad asked what he had meant when he had said 'internally.' "

"I did not show my disbelief."

"Did you want to testify today?"

"No."

"By way of preparation, how much time did we spend together?"

"Twenty minutes. Ten yesterday, ten today." Horngrad concluded by bringing out that George had requested that his statement to the district attorney's office not be taped, but that Horngrad had later requested that it be taped. When Franklin was dismissed, he stormed out of the courtroom, almost stamping his feet in one final and startling display of anger. It had been an extraordinary performance.

Until now, the trial had seen a few angry flare-ups, but the proceedings generally had been marked by civility. The atmosphere had been one of a good-faith effort to determine the truth of a serious allegation. Others who had testified—particularly Eileen, Janice, and Leah—had had reason to be pained and deeply emotional about the highly personal matters being so publicly aired. But before George junior, no one had challenged the state's right to inquire into this family's grim secrets.

The jury did not know, nor, indeed, could they be expected to deduce, the base and corrupt motives young Franklin had ascribed to the state in going after his father. The net result of his studied prickliness was not, as he probably hoped, to throw the entire prosecution into question, but rather to present himself as a disturbed if not unbalanced young man. As his anger permeated the courtroom, many of those watching were simply baffled by his strained rudeness to Tipton. Others who knew of this man's battered childhood felt a chill as they watched the pent-up rage of this product of child abuse who was now close to the age his father had been at the time of the murder.

The next defense witness was the youngest Franklin daughter, Diana, who was, with her large, dark eyes, slim figure, and abundance of auburn hair, the most striking of a good-looking quartet. After establishing that Diana had been unwilling to cooperate with the defense, Horngrad asked only one question. Did she recall a conversation in the hallway during the preliminary hearing when she had told him and Tipton that Eileen had phoned back George junior to withdraw her hypnosis story *the next day* rather than the weeks later Eileen had testified to?

Diana replied, "That's what *I* said, not what *she* said."

On cross-examination Tipton asked why she had misspoken. In her reply, Diana spoke for most witnesses in most trials. "I said 'the next day' out of nerves. I'm not used to having every word I say being picked apart. Those were my words, not Eileen's." Tipton had no further questions and Diana left the stand.

NINETEEN

In an effort to prove there had not been enough time for George Franklin to have killed Susan, Horngrad introduced a number of witnesses who had had contact with her the day she disappeared. If he established anything beyond any doubt on this point, however, it was how vague and uncertain, if not totally wrong, all of these witnesses were. Most knew they had seen Susan sometime between three o'clock, when school let out, and six, when most of them had to be home for supper. To Tipton's question if their encounters might have been earlier than the three-thirty or four o'clock they had originally said, they all replied that it was possible.

Horngrad had a second objective with this set of witnesses: to bring out the reports of the mysterious blue station wagon that had been seen around the neighborhood in the days preceding and just after Susan's disappearance, and whose driver had allegedly tried to abduct Ann Hobbs three days before Susan vanished. Horngrad had reason for hope along these lines, as one woman, Susanna Banks, offered elaborate testimony that came close to confirming that alternate scenario for Susan's murder.

Sue Banks, now remarried and no longer living in Foster City, was a heavyset, middle-aged woman with bleached blond hair and glasses. In September 1969 she had lived at the corner of Balclutha and Matsonia. Shortly after three o'clock on the day she disappeared, Susan had stopped at her door and asked if this was the Oakleys' house. Mrs. Banks had taken her partway down Matsonia and pointed her toward the right house. As she was walking back to her house, Banks saw her daughter, Linda, playing in the lot across the street and told her it was time to come home.

She then noticed an unfamiliar car parked at h car was either "white, green, or blue." When she house she heard her dog barking. She looked fro window. Through the slats in the fence that separa̲ḻ̲ḏ̲ ḥ̲ḇ̲r̲ ̲ṇ̲ọ̲ṳ̲s̲e from her neighbor's, she saw the head of a child in the driveway. She could not recognize the features, but the child had reddish-blond hair. She thought it was Susan. The dog continued barking and "trying to get out to the car." The car took off.

When Tipton asked her if she had told all of this to the police at the time, Banks said, "I must have told them." Courtroom protocol forbids counsel or anyone else yelling, "That's a lot of hooey," and counsel must leave fanciful tales hanging in the air and in jurors' minds, often for many days, before they have the opportunity to demolish them. For Tipton in this case, the wait was ten days, at which time she brought in Inspector William Hensel, the retired police officer who had interviewed Banks in 1969. Hensel was firm in testifying how eager the police had been for any leads, and that Banks had said nothing to him about these suspicious circumstances.

Tipton would further demolish this tale with photos showing that the boards of Banks's fence touched one another, allowing nothing to be seen through them ("I saw what I saw."), that it would have been impossible to see as far as the Oakleys' yard from the Bankses' kitchen window, that no other people in the area heard a barking dog.

One line of Tipton's questioning of Banks was revealing of the way in which memories were affected by the subsequent information that flooded Foster City regarding this notorious happening. Banks testified that when she had seen Susan outside her kitchen window, she thought, "What are you doing there? It's your birthday. You should be home." Tipton got Banks to admit she had not then known it was Susan's birthday; she learned that later. She admitted she "must have gotten mixed up" on that point.

Banks's daughter, Linda, testified immediately after her mother, and corroborated much of what she said. When Linda was playing in the lot, she saw her mother walking Susan up Matsonia. After Mrs. Banks called to Linda to come home, she passed a man in a parked car who tried to talk to her. Under cross-examination, her corroboration collapsed when she admitted having said in earlier statements that she was uncertain how much of her knowledge of that afternoon was actually

.rom her memory and how much drew on what her mother had told her.

Many hours of court time had been taken up by the two Banks women. Horngrad had worked hard to put across their stories and give his client hope for a different explanation of Susan's murder, a provocative set of scenario fragments just plausible enough to plant reasonable doubt in the jury's minds. Until Tipton had time to refute this testimony, jurors' heads would be filled with this image of a frantically barking dog and a would-be child-abductor in the vicinity of an unaccompanied Susan minutes before she disappeared forever.

Equally disruptive testimony came from a young woman with the unlikely name of Penny Stocks, who said she had been a playmate of Shirley Nason's. Her story, also shown later to be false, was a case study for armchair psychoanalysts in that she had twisted the events of the day of Susan's disappearance in her own memory so that, not George Franklin, not the stranger in the blue station wagon, but *she* was responsible for Susan's grim fate.

On the afternoon of the disappearance, Stocks testified, she and Shirley Nason had been playing football in the vacant lot on Balclutha. Susan had passed by and asked if she could join them. In an earlier statement, Stocks had placed the time she had seen Susan at around five o'clock, which explained the defense's interest in her guilt-heavy story. She now amended this to "about four," which would still be most helpful in exonerating George Franklin.

Showing pain at the recollection, Stocks said that she and Shirley had told Susan to go away because they didn't want to play with her. Their heartless rejection had caused Susan to wander off to her destruction. For twenty years, Stocks said, close to tears, she had felt guilt about this. Her lifelong anguish over a minor cruelty provided telling contrast to the cocky aplomb of the defendant, who, aside from whether or not he had murdered Susan, did not deny a catalog of crimes almost as heinous.

When asked what color dress Susan had been wearing, Stocks replied, unhesitatingly and incorrectly, that it had been black and red with a little white line, then added jarringly, "I went to twenty fabric stores looking for a similar fabric to bring to court today."

In her cross-examination, Tipton established Stocks's confused memory by pointing out that she was in a different school at the time than the one she had testified to. Embellishing her story of guilt, Stocks said that her friendship with Shirley Nason had ended that day because Shirley also had held Stocks responsible for her sister's death. Tipton brought out that in 1969 Stocks had said she wasn't sure if the day she had been playing with Shirley was the same day Susan disappeared. Asked why she had said this, she replied, "I was scared."

Stocks provided another test of Tipton's forbearance. To impeach Stocks, she had to wait over a week until Shirley Nason took the stand and testified that she had not played with anyone that day, and that she had never known anyone named Penny Stocks. With that, the bottom dropped out of the Penny Stocks market.

The attempted abduction of Ann Hobbs had been alluded to so often by the defense, it had become a constant minor theme. It was a surprise then, when the legendary Ann Hobbs took the stand to say she did not recall an incident with a blue station wagon, she did not recall giving a statement about it to the police, she did not recall the day Susan disappeared, nor did she recall anything unusual happening in September of 1969. When she was shown the transcript of her reporting all of this to the police, she said that it did not refresh her memory. She was excused. Tipton later speculated that Ann Hobbs was herself a victim of repression.

Horngrad continued to flail the Ann Hobbs story with a number of witnesses who had spotted blue station wagons around the time of Susan's murder. Horngrad called Eileen's mother back to the stand and asked questions aimed at establishing the newspapers and other media that were available in the Franklin household, and which Eileen might have seen. He tried to get her to admit that her divorce from Franklin had been bitter, and also that there was some confusion over the condition of the back of his van in 1969. Leah succeeded in avoiding his implications at every turn until another line of questions threatened her reputation as a mother. With that, her answers became exactly what Horngrad wanted and did damage to one of the conditions Dr. Terr had specified as conducive to repression.

"After Susan disappeared, was Eileen a happy child?"

"I thought so," Leah replied.

Having scored a small victory, Horngrad turned to the piece of Leah's testimony for the prosecution that threatened him the most, the bloody shirt. "Do you recall that at the preliminary hearing you were asked if there had been anything unusual about George Franklin the day Susan disappeared?" She did. "You said, 'Unusual like what?' and I said, 'Like a bloody shirt or something like that.' You said no." This raised an intriguing new possibility. If Leah had invented the bloody shirt to ensure her hated husband's conviction—a dirty punch to reinforce Eileen's principled attack—Horngrad's question suggested that he might have provided the inspiration.

Leah admitted having denied any recollection of the bloody shirt when she'd been asked directly about it, but during subsequent questioning on different subjects, it had come back to her. She then added cryptically, "The memory came, then went away." Horngrad stepped up his attack. She had said nothing about the bloody shirt until September 24, 1990? Right. Four months after the preliminary hearing? Yes. Over ten months after George Franklin's arrest? Yes. And three weeks before the start of this trial? Yes.

"Yes," Leah said, "I remembered the explanation the defendant gave me at the time about why there was so much blood on the shirt."

"Isn't it true you've been approached by movie and book folks?" Tipton objected and was sustained. Having allowed to stand unchallenged Horngrad's untrue assertion that the various commercial deals depended on a conviction, Tipton was now watching a second of her witnesses be impugned by the falsehood and be stigmatized with a motive to give false testimony.

In her cross-examination, Tipton drew on Leah's hatred of Franklin. She asked Leah if she could tell the jury of things that might have affected her ability to observe what was going on in the household in the late sixties and early seventies. Leah said that at that time she was living in a marriage that had turned into a nightmare. Her parents had been happily married for forty-five years, her background was Catholic, and she saw marriage as something to work at. The defendant could get away with whatever he wanted. It had been "a careening kind of existence. I'd get it even after there had been violence, then there'd be an even greater outburst of violence."

Tipton reviewed her explanation for the delay in having reported the bloody shirt. Horngrad had a few more questions about the van, and Leah was dismissed. As she came down from the stand and headed for the courtroom doors, she passed close by Donald and Shirley Nason, who were in their usual seats in the front row. She gave them a small wave—the sort one would give the next-door neighbors upon running into them at a movie house.

After halfheartedly trying to establish a third scenario for Susan's murder, involving a blue chambray work shirt found at the scene, Horngrad moved on quickly to what would be his most strenuous effort, focusing on his psychiatric experts, who would contradict Lenore Terr and attempt to cast doubt on Eileen's story of repression.

Expert testimony has become big business in the criminal-justice system. Psychiatrists like Dr. Lenore Terr routinely charge their hourly consulting rate for their efforts on behalf of one side or another of a litigation. What makes testifying so lucrative is that when they charge a patient this fee, it is for a one-to-one session for which there might have been additional hours of unpaid research, reflection, or other forms of preparation. Even though an expert might spend less than an hour on the witness stand, prosecutors and defense lawyers must pay for preparation time as well, making a bill for twelve or fifteen hours the norm rather than the exception. Fees of three to five thousand dollars are routine and can be much higher. Lawyers would be the last people to protest such gouging, and it is understood among those in the business of freeing the innocent and jailing the guilty that if you want an expert to testify on your side, it will be expensive. Since these eminent doctors and other scientists often get little more than ten thousand dollars to write a full-length book, the testifying game provides an alluring adjunct to their annual incomes, rather like speaker's fees for congressmen.

Since an expert rarely testifies without the opposition producing a comparable expert to undermine everything he or she has just said, the experts invariably cancel each other out, enriching themselves but leaving the prosecution and defense where they were before the display of arcane knowledge. Unless, of course, a given expert makes more sense, is more persuasive, or clobbers his opposition in the credential department.

The knight sent in by the defense to topple Terr and drive her from the field was Dr. David Spiegel, a psychiatrist who informed the court he had been on the staff of the Stanford University Medical School for fifteen years, was an associate editor of two psychiatric journals, and had written many articles about his specialty, dissociative disorders.

When his testimony began, the chest-thumping continued. His responses were laden with convoluted expressions and distance-establishing constructions. He spoke about the therapeutic effort to retrieve repressed memories so that the patient can place them in "a new cognitive framework." Such jargon inspired yearnings for limp but clear valley-girl clichés such as, "So the patient could deal with it." Spiegel had none of Terr's ingratiating amiability; in fact, he seemed to be striving to show his distaste for participating in the sordid proceedings.

Post-traumatic stress victims usually display three categories of symptoms, he said. First, they have intrusive recollections of the trauma, sometimes reliving it. Second, they suffer from detachment; they no longer enjoy things they formally enjoyed. Third—and because of Eileen's close relationship with her father after Susan's murder, this was the one Horngrad wanted— they are stimulus sensitive. They avoid situations similar to those of the trauma and might even show symptoms when they find themselves in such situations.

He defined *dissociation* as an inability to integrate aspects of one's life that are normally integrated. One's memory ceases to be a continuous flow. In one state the dissociative person is unable to recall what he did in another state. This leads to multiple personalities. "There is increasing evidence that physically abused kids have associative disorders," Dr. Spiegel said. "We now see dissociation as a way of protecting oneself from trauma. It becomes a mental habit."

Horngrad asked Spiegel to list other symptoms of post-traumatic stress. Spiegel replied that victims might suffer from an inability to trust others, have memory lapses, block out specific events of the past and near-present, feel inappropriate guilt, and experience emotions unrelated to their present lives. Would they have dreams or nightmares, Horngrad asked. Yes, that too. And the lack of nightmares? "That would not be consistent with post-traumatic stress syndrome."

Horngrad then asked, "And a normal, happy life after the trauma—how does that fit in with post-traumatic stress syndrome?"

Tipton objected and was sustained. Both psychiatrists who had testified so far had been careful to say the symptoms he denoted were generally apparent, but not invariably. Even with that loophole, the defense would have to struggle to establish that Eileen had had a happy childhood. Eileen's mother was the only witness to have testified that she "thought" Eileen had had a "normal, happy life" after Susan's murder. But Leah had also testified that they were all terrorized in their own home, that their lives were an ongoing nightmare. ("Maybe that's Leah's idea of normal and happy," Janice said when she learned of Leah's statement after the trial.) With not one but two wobbly foundations, Horngrad seemed to be straining for inconsistencies, but then there was always that other potential benefit if logic failed—confusing the jury with "expert overkill." Enough confusion can in itself produce reasonable doubt.

When he delved into the likelihood of a traumatized person willingly reentering the situation of the trauma (Eileen's trip to Mexico with her father in the van), he used a hypothetical example of someone undergoing a trauma in a private plane at the hands of the pilot. Would the victim willingly get back in the plane to take a long pleasure trip with the same pilot? In spite of his imaginative plot outline for a sadomasochistic film, Horngrad was ignoring a major difference between his hypothetical perpetrator and the defendant: the pilot was a stranger to the trauma victim, the defendant was her father.

Horngrad asked Dr. Spiegel how easy it was for a psychiatrist to distinguish a real memory from a false one. Although Tipton had asked Dr. Terr the same question several times, she now objected to Horngrad's asking it and was overruled. Spiegel said it could be difficult, especially if one only had the patient's word. Even with the best will, a patient's memory could be garbled by outside factors. Children who had been repeatedly traumatized were more likely to have a false memory. This contradicted Terr, who had said that repeated trauma was conducive to repression, not to false memory.

In discussing the ways buried memories could be unearthed, Dr. Spiegel repeated Terr's assertions that memory was most likely to return when there was a stimulus, when the person felt safe and secure and was no longer fearful. He then added something to reinforce Eileen's claim: the recovery could be quite sudden. As he ran out of steam, Horngrad put a number of questions to Dr. Spiegel that seemed to establish that the mind was unpredictable and tricky and that there were a large number of peculiar people out there.

On her cross-examination, Tipton first established that Spiegel was not a child psychiatrist, while *her* expert was a nation-

ally known authority on traumatized children. Having attacked
the relevance of his expertise, she then took swings at the field
he and Terr shared, eventually getting him to admit that, as a
science, psychiatry was "a somewhat softer body of knowledge
than other branches of medicine." Tipton induced him to tell
the court that it was possible to repress a memory without
having a dissociative disorder.

She went on to note that Spiegel's experience was primarily
with extreme cases of dissociation, which diminished his relevance to Eileen's much milder symptom, repression. He had, in
fact, never worked on a case of repression. She then made an
effort to elicit more precise definitions of his terms—suppres-
sion, repression, dissociation—but it was a little like trying to
force giant puffballs into tiny pillboxes. Perhaps embittered by
her exertions, she concluded by revealing that Spiegel was being
paid three hundred dollars an hour for his testimony, most of
which could have been offered by anyone who had watched a
few television dramas on shock or trauma. When Spiegel estimated he had spent about twelve hours on the case, she asked
if he would then earn between three and four thousand dollars
on the case.

He answered wryly, but with the language purist's bugaboo,
"Hopefully."

On redirect, Horngrad got off one of his better sallies: "Keeping that rate in mind, I will be brief."

After trying to salvage the reputation and relevance that
Tipton had slurred, Horngrad got his witness to attest that a
symptom such as a sense of futurelessness can come from any
number of causes; it cannot be used as proof of a particular
trauma. In this and other questions he was, perhaps inadvertently, undermining not just *some* psychiatric testimony helpful
to the prosecution, but *all* of it—both for and against Eileen's
claim of repression. Various symptoms and lack of symptoms
might point toward or away from certain conclusions about a
post-traumatic stress victim, but they never proved or dis-
proved them.

For his final question, Horngrad returned to his favorite
theme, the common knowledge of all of Eileen's remembered
details of the crime; this time, however, he arrived at his most
persuasive form for the question: "In assessing the validity of
a memory of a traumatized person, wouldn't you be suspicious
if they only remembered things that were in the public domain?"

Tipton shot to her feet, and her objection was sustained. On recross she asked if "a person gave a multiplicity of details, some in the public domain, some not"—Horngrad objected to the last two words, and the judge instructed the jury to disregard them—"would that substantiate her story?"

"No. Sheer numbers of details mean nothing. People can tell elaborate stories about false memories."

The entire afternoon—and four thousand dollars—had been spent batting the psychiatric puffballs back and forth, in the process instilling much confusion in the jurors' minds. The few gains the defense had made were nullified by commensurate gains for the prosecution.

The first witness the next morning, November 19, would present the surprise testimony that had so shaken Eileen when she heard it alluded to in her hotel room over the phone from Tipton. He was Bill Mann, a dark-haired, amiable-looking man who had become a friend of George Franklin's after he joined the San Mateo Fire Department in 1969. Franklin had been the company cook, and had done the food shopping. Mann had helped unload groceries from the back of his van "about twenty times." Emphatically, Mann said there had been no platform or mattress in Franklin's van at that time. He also said that he had visited Franklin in jail on one occasion.

Tipton all but threw herself at Mann for one of her most bravura turns. After establishing that Mann had conferred with the defense team but had not answered the prosecution's phone calls, Tipton then zeroed in on the time frame. Mann had started as a firefighting trainee in mid-October of 1969, a few weeks after Susan's murder, but he said he had never ridden in the van until ten years later, but only removed groceries from it. "Why is the interior of someone else's van so memorable to you twenty years later?" It was just something he remembered, he replied.

"Did you keep records or notes of the modifications to Mr. Franklin's van?" No.

"Did you look at photos of Mr. Franklin's van?" No.

"Is there any reason why you would have a personal interest in Mr. Franklin's van?" No. But Mann recalled Franklin's having put the mattress in some time later, when he went on a trip. Tipton pursued Mann's degree of friendship with Franklin and his familiarity with the van, then sprang her I-know-you're-lying question: "Are you aware of the significance of the mattress in this case?" He had read some things about it. "But you know the presence or absence of a mattress is significant in this case?"

"I don't. . . ." Mann began. "I'm not aware of degree of significance. No."

"But you know the case is about a child molestation on a mattress?" He did.

"When did you first give thought to the interior of George Franklin's van?"

"When I first saw it."

"And have you been thinking about that interior for the last twenty-one years?"

"I've always had a recollection of that van. It's something you just know, like the front room in your house."

"Your front room or *my* front room?" Tipton snapped with contempt. Horngrad's objection was sustained, and Tipton said she had no further questions. There was no doubt that Mann's assertion had seriously shaken Eileen's story. If a major element of her recollection—a mattress on which she and Susan had played, and on which Susan was later molested—could be shown to have come into existence well after Susan's murder, it would go far toward substantiating the defense's claim that her memory was pieced together with details she had learned later. The setback, however, proved to be little more than another test of prosecutorial patience.

An air of expectation surrounded the next witness, Katherine Rieder, a psychological therapist whom Eileen had been seeing shortly before she started seeing Kirk Barrett. Horngrad had referred to her many times in his interrogations, so it was clear that the short blond woman in her early forties who took the stand was important to him.

His questions homed in quickly on her main relevance to the case: Eileen had started seeing Rieder in the spring of 1988, six months before the same month she said she had her recollection, but in some twelve one-hour sessions over that period, Eileen had never mentioned to Rieder her shocking memory. Equally significant to Horngrad was that Eileen had told Rieder of a different memory that had recently surfaced, that she had been molested by her father when she was six or seven.

When Eileen had been on the stand, Horngrad had asked her with manifest skepticism how she could express bafflement to Kirk Barrett in June about the return of a repressed memory, when only a few months before she had discussed a forgotten memory. Horngrad had incorrectly implied that Rieder had explained the phenomenon of repression to her in December of 1988.

Eileen had made a distinction between losing the memory of something in the very distant past and repressing a more traumatic occurrence that happened when she was older. She also knew that there were far greater possible repercussions in telling anyone about a murder than in telling a therapist about a hazy sexual episode with her father.

In her cross-examination, Tipton asked if Rieder had any way of knowing if a patient was holding something back. She didn't. Was it unusual for patients to hold back topics from discussion? Not at all. Did Rieder have any way of knowing when Eileen Franklin may have recollected seeing Susan Nason killed? Horngrad objected, saying the question assumed facts not in evidence.

"They *are* in evidence, Your Honor," Tipton said angrily, and Horngrad was overruled. She now pushed on with greater vigor. Did Rieder have any way of seeing what patients were holding back? No. Was she a mind reader? No. Rieder was doing little for either side. But Tipton made a final stab at winning some benefit from her opposition's witness: "Are you trained to detect signs and symptoms of mental disorder?" "Yes." "Did you see any such signs and symptoms in Eileen Franklin?" "No."

Dr. Elizabeth Loftus was one of the nation's foremost authorities on memory, and Horngrad introduced her to the court with the flourish of a Barnum unveiling his Jenny Lind. A genial, dark-haired woman in her early forties, Loftus presented a stupefying array of credits that included faculty posts at the University of Washington, Harvard, Stanford, and Georgetown. She had been a president of the experimental psychology division of the American Psychology Association. She had written fourteen books and more than two hundred articles. When asked if she had received any honors, she said, "I'm not sure where to begin."

Dr. Loftus's main area of interest was the way in which memory could be affected and distorted by external variables. Her experiments tended to stay close to one format. Showing a reenactment of a shocking event like a car crash, usually on film, she then questioned the subjects after giving them incorrect information about what they had seen—perhaps erroneous newspaper accounts or confused testimony of other eye-witnesses—to appraise the degree to which this outside input affected their memories.

With a quick series of questions, Horngrad got Loftus to depict the human memory as exceedingly suggestible and unreliable. Loftus had an endless supply of examples of garbled memories—people willing to swear that a blue car had been white, a Yield sign had been a Stop sign, and so on. Some of her examples were more subtle, such as when she asked subjects who had seen a film of a car speeding down a highway, how fast they estimated it was going when it passed the barn. There had, in fact, been no barn, but when questioned about the film later, many insisted they had seen a barn. In her testimony it was never made clear how much she was measuring memory rather than human powers of observation, but for Horngrad's purposes it was sufficient that Loftus was depicting *Homo sapiens* as a species incapable of remembering events accurately.

In her cross-examination, Tipton established that of Loftus's 150 to 175 participations in criminal proceedings in the past fifteen years, all had been for the defense. Tipton then went into a prolonged examination of Loftus's experimental methods, revealing, as she had with the other expert witnesses, a thorough knowledge of the witness's writings. She brought out that Loftus's studies dealing with identifications never involved *relatives* of the subjects, and, even more tellingly, that her studies never involved *repressed* memory.

This line was building to one of Tipton's finest moments in the trial. Discussing a study in which some six hundred subjects were shown a man robbing a store, Loftus indicated the wide variations in the retellings of the scene. It was clear that Loftus could be a valuable witness in a trial in which the identification of a stranger was crucial, or the identification of an automobile seen only fleetingly. But the case at hand involved a witness identifying her own father and a van she had been in hundreds of times. By proving that details of a memory often change, Loftus, rather than helping the defense, was explaining and justifying the small errors Eileen had made in her story. Tipton cut right to the heart of Loftus's irrelevance to Franklin's defense by saying, "But none of the six hundred reported that they had seen nothing at all, did they?"

"No."

"The question might be 'Which hand was the gun in?' "

"Yes."

" 'Did the man have a beard or no beard?' "

"That's correct."

" 'Gloves or no gloves?' "

Almost inaudibly, "That's right."

"You never had a response when a subject saw a man at bat at a baseball game rather than robbing a store?"

At this point Loftus switched sides and agreed with Tipton that it was only in details that viewers varied, and sometimes they even reported the details accurately. Unmoved by Loftus's cooperation, Tipton finished her off by asking how much her testimony would cost the defense. At $250 an hour, Dr. Loftus expected her bill for her efforts on behalf of George Franklin to be about five thousand dollars plus expenses.

After Loftus was dismissed, the problem of the dozing juror came to a head, and a conference was called in the judge's chambers that resulted in the juror's dismissal. For various reasons three of the alternates had now been pressed into active duty, leaving only one for the remainder of the trial. If it should happen that two more jurors were unable to remain until a verdict was reached, the judge would have to declare a mistrial.

TWENTY

IF THE PSYCHIATRIC EXPERTS PROVIDED THE GEORGE FRANK-
lin trial with its intellectual meat, members of the Franklin
family provided the emotional juice. They also provided considerable confusion. Two had sided with Eileen in the prosecution—Janice and Leah; one, George junior, was aggressively
helping the defense; Diana was aligned with neither side. But all
of them had changed their testimony substantially from earlier
sworn statements. The explanation was put forth in part by Dr.
Loftus, who memorialized the fragility of human memory.

But befuddlement or carelessness could not fully explain the
altered testimony. There was reason to think that the Franklins,
all of whom cared passionately about the trial's outcome, were
dredging their memories assiduously, perhaps creatively, and
certainly belatedly, for additional evidence that might tip the
judicial scales. It is possible that none of them were aware that
the others were doing the same thing, assuming that each abid-
ed by the court's injunction not to communicate with one another about what occurred in court. The likelihood of their
observing this injunction was strong, since almost none of them
were speaking.

Kate and Leah were completely isolated, speaking to none of
the others or to each other. Even the two closest siblings, Janice
and Eileen, had had a falling out when Janice moved out of the
Lipsker house before the trial; at the moment they had minimal
contact. Diana spoke to George junior, which was enough to
have Eileen not speaking to Diana. Janice was just barely
speaking to Diana, but when, in one phone conversation,
Diana snapped at Janice about something, Janice closed the
iron door on Diana. Perhaps the defendant had had the most

interfamily communication in that he had received visits from Eileen, Leah, Janice, and George junior.

When she took the stand, Kate Franklin made the altering of testimony unanimous. Since she had not testified at the preliminary hearing, few people in court had seen her before. She was short and slightly overweight, but had the unmistakable Franklin good looks, more on the delicate order of Leah rather than the more dramatic features of George Franklin, which Eileen had inherited.

The most startling addition Kate made to the record was that Eileen had told her she had had the recollection in a nightmare. With the hypnosis, the therapy, and the nightmare, the jury had now heard three versions of Eileen's recollection, all different from her sworn version. George junior and Leah had established these, now Kate added a third voice of confusion.

Kate brought into court other pieces of damaging information she claimed Eileen had told her: that Janice was in the van and had been asked to get out when Susan got in, that their father had driven them into the woods, and that, because of her "nightmares that brought the murder back to her," Eileen had returned to therapy. Her testimony had an almost surgical destructiveness about it.

In cross-examination, Tipton all but lunged at Kate. Before tearing into her fresh recollections, however, she puzzled the court by asking about Kate's grandmother-in-law, an elderly woman named Helen Elkins. Hadn't Kate and her husband sent this old lady into court each day Eileen was on the stand to report back everything she said? Kate denied this vociferously. Kate also denied that she had ever discouraged Eileen from coming forward, or that she had said Eileen's action would bring shame on the Franklin name and place a cloud over the head of Kate's child. "She and Barry are adults," she said primly. "I knew that they would do what they thought was right."

Eileen, Barry, and other family members were later stunned by Kate's revisionism. Whether or not she had pleaded with Eileen not to come forward—and all of them had heard her do so—would not have much effect on George Franklin's fate. And many could understand anyone trying to talk one family member out of accusing another of murder twenty years after the fact, even if she thought he probably was guilty. But once the decision had been made and the state had taken over the case, to go into court and to deny with such sangfroid actions by her that had been witnessed by many made her a dangerous witness indeed.

None of Kate's conversations with her family revealed an interest in whether or not her father had committed the crime. It seemed to be her feeling that whatever had happened was in the past, a period in which they all had suffered enough to justify any action or omission that would lead to as tranquil and problem-free a present as possible. If this indeed was Kate's reasoning for compromising herself in court and thereby perhaps assisting a murderer to go unpunished, it bespoke additional long-range damage of child abuse.

More than any other witness, Kate had placed herself in direct opposition to Eileen's statements—which was the basis, of course, for Tipton's questions—leaving no room for any conclusion but that one of them was lying. The contradictions were so strong and they countered such recent statements that they precluded the explanation of fuzzy memory that so plausibly explained other discrepancies within the family.

At a point when Tipton's questioning grew heated, Kate said in a patronizing tone, "We all share the same objective, Elaine, to see the truth come out." Just as George junior had contemptuously snapped out the formal "Miss Tipton," Kate now used Tipton's first name sneeringly, as if to say, "You may be a big-deal prosecutor around here, honey, but I know you are only one of the girls."

"In May of 1990," Tipton asked, "when you were interviewed by me and Inspector Morse, you told us nothing of dreams. Correct?" Yes. "Or of Eileen returning to therapy?" Yes. "Or of driving into the woods?" Yes. "Or Janice being in the van?" Yes. "Inspector Morse asked if there was anything else you could think of. You said no?" That's right. Tipton asked Kate if she had told Eileen as Eileen had said that the Nasons had probably forgotten about Susan after so many years? No. Why had she given her name as Franklin and not her married name? Haughtily she said, "I wish to protect my privacy and will continue to do so."

And then Tipton's I-know-you're-lying question: "Do you consider the nightmare testimony an important fact in this case?" She did not.

When Eileen had first told Kate of the murder, what had her reaction been? "I was in shock, I didn't know what to think. I was appalled. I thought I would throw up." Then she added, "I was pregnant at the time, and things went to my stomach."

This last statement suggested that learning her father was a child-murderer was just one of a series of irritations that made for trying days. Tipton reviewed the catalog of new information Kate was belatedly producing: Eileen had told her of Susan getting into the van, that Janice was in the van, that they drove to some woods, that she had had the memory in nightmares, and that she had returned to therapy.

"Do you have a good memory?" Tipton asked. Kate said she did. "Did you tell authorities that you had no memory of your childhood before your eighteenth birthday?" Kate answered that she had said she only remembered a few things.

George Franklin, who had sat through this testimony as impassively as he had been sitting through the rest of the trial, now let out a sigh that sounded like exasperation, but that members of the Franklin family might have taken for relief.

On redirect, Horngrad asked why she had not reported these facts earlier. Kate said those areas had not been touched on in the interview. "You didn't think it would be appropriate?" Horngrad prompted.

"Appropriate is not the right word," she said. "I didn't see the relevance."

Although Kate may not have known it, she had now joined her mother and George junior in admitting to having withheld major information on the grounds that it was insignificant or, in her stronger variation, irrelevant. None of them could have known the effect this pattern of forgetfulness was having on the jury. While each Franklin might think it understandable to have omitted a piece of information from a statement to the authorities a year earlier, for them *all* to have done so, and with such highly potent facts, had a seriously undermining effect on the testimony of each.

If individually the family members weren't aware of how, taking the stand one after another, they were making themselves sound like a chorus line of apocryphiers, Horngrad and Tipton had to have been. Perhaps because one witness was Tipton's (Leah) and two were Horngrad's (George junior and Kate), neither attorney was too concerned about the damage to credibility done by the string of tardy recollections. As for the Franklins, they may have reasoned that if Eileen could forget a murder for twenty years, they should be allowed to forget for one year such things as nightmares and bloody shirts.

* * *

After Kate was excused, Horngrad produced his most impressive piece of defense legwork. It would not only destroy, as promised, the allegation that Franklin had visited Susan's grave on the first anniversary of her death, but it raised questions about the prosecution's methods in their campaign to convict George Franklin.

Four witnesses were presented to testify that they were owners of cars whose license plates were on Detective Hensel's list. (In California, license numbers remain with cars when they are sold.) All of them had been in Skylawn Cemetery on the day of Susan's funeral: none had been there, or could have been there in most cases, on the first anniversary, the date the prosecution claimed the list was taken. One witness, the owner of a used-car lot in Watsonville, California, had purchased one of the cars on the list and produced a certificate of nonoperation covering the period when the car was said to have been seen, along with Franklin's car, passing Susan's grave. The previous owner lived in Foster City and may well have attended Susan Nason's funeral. The others had equally unequivocal stories.

The list of license numbers that had been introduced in court as sighted at the cemetery one year after Susan's murder was proven beyond question to be a list of numbers taken ten months earlier, at Susan's funeral. Since this was the one day when George Franklin's car was sure to have been in that area, it raised suspicions as to how such a mistake could have been made. Since these witnesses were in no position to throw light on the mistake, they were useless to Tipton on cross-examination. She would have to wait for her rebuttal to dispel the dark cloud that had drifted over her case.

Another advantageous bit of timing for the defense, undoubtedly planned, was that court was about to break for Thanksgiving recess. Jurors, who by now were crammed with dates, times, names, and conflicting stories, would have five days to mull over the bogus license-number list that the prosecution had flourished as one of its most dramatic pieces of corroboration of Eileen's allegation.

In the corridor outside the courtroom a journalist made the suggestion to Horngrad and Wachtel that the false license list looked suspiciously like evidence rigging. Horngrad, still basking in the stir his sleuthing had caused, seemed surprised, then dismissed that possibility. "No," he said with a smile, "it's just good old human error." Wachtel was even more shocked at the suggestion, and said, "If that were the case, the trial would be over and we could all go home."

It was odd that Horngrad, whose defense was predicated on the implied dishonesty of the prosecution's main witnesses, would reject the possibility that evidence had been deliberately falsified. In open court he had made clear his belief that not only was Eileen lying but that Janice and Leah were too. His frequent question, "When did you first have this recollection?" when asked again and again, had come to be interpreted as, "When did you decide to change lie number one and replace it with lie number two?"

Having implied that the prosecution's witnesses were lying, he somehow seemed to find unthinkable the suggestion that anyone on the prosecution team might have falsified evidence. The distinction seemed to lie in the fact that Tipton and her team were law-enforcement officials; Eileen and her family were private citizens. Falsifying evidence or testimony was serious business for either, but Horngrad knew it was far more serious for the officials. His attitude seemed to be, "Civilians might wander in and lie under oath, but we professionals in the game wouldn't dream of such a thing."

To start off the trial's final week, Horngrad first recalled William Hensel in an unsuccessful attempt to resurrect the Ann Hobbs incident. He also called another former police official who had worked on the Susan Nason case, Eugene Stewart, who had issued statements to the press on the case at the time. Horngrad coaxed him to say that the police had not withheld information from the public, as the prosecution now asserted, that everything they knew about the case was passed along to journalists.

A question that had been hanging over the trial for some time came to a climax as Horngrad argued to be permitted to read from Barry Lipsker's preliminary-hearing testimony, on the grounds that he had shown due diligence in attempting to get Lipsker to return from Switzerland to testify, but Lipsker had thwarted his efforts with evasions and hollow excuses. He had written two registered letters, and offered to wire-transfer $1,500 or whatever was needed for the fare. "Mr. Lipsker," he said sniffily, like the hostess of a flop tea party, "clearly doesn't care to be with us."

With Tipton's flu showing little improvement, the pressures of the trial were beginning to weigh on her. She came back to her office after a particularly tense morning in court to find a large basket of flowers waiting for her at the receptionist. She carried them into the office and read the note. The flowers were a gesture of support from her two sisters who had written a loving couplet from the song "Sisters" sung by Rosemary Clooney and Vera-Ellen in the film *White Christmas*. Tipton closed her door, put her head on her desk and cried.

"I had just had a big dose of Eileen's sisters," she said in describing this moment some months later, "maybe it was one of the curves Kate had thrown. Sometimes those women can be supportive of each other, but most of the time, they have their own problems, their own agendas. I sat there crying and thanking God I had been born a Tipton sister rather than a Franklin sister."

Tipton kept a photograph of Susan Nason inside her desk drawer where no one else could see it. Many prosecutors keep at hand some such reminder of the crime or the victim they are avenging. Tipton felt a strong sense of obligation to Eileen. She felt her star witness's high moral courage in coming forward deserved the best possible prosecution, the most vigorous effort on her part. "I had enormous respect for what she had done and for what she was going through, but I felt that my main obligation was to Susan Nason."

Eileen

After my week at home with Barry and my children, I had scheduled a morning flight and had said good-bye to my children before sending them off to school. When Barry went down to the car with my luggage, he saw a car parked in our driveway. As our house is by a meadow at the end of a small road in a tiny town, this was surprising. I watched a woman approach Barry and ask him if he was Barry Lipsker.

When Barry said he was, the woman handed him a subpoena from Horngrad and Wachtel. She apologized for coming at such an early hour, then started to leave. Barry looked at the document, then stopped her. "You know," he said, "this isn't a legal document here in Switzerland." She replied that indeed she did know it, but that she was being paid to deliver it anyway.

For weeks Barry and I had expected to be summoned by the Swiss court to comply with international subpoena procedure. The fact that Horngrad and Wachtel had hired someone to deliver a worthless piece of paper showed a disregard of the law and was a waste of their client's money. As Barry had said all along, he would testify at the trial if he were legally served a subpoena. After all, he had asked me, why should I miss work and leave the kids if Horngrad can't even figure out how to serve a subpoena?

Tipton and the Lipskers seemed to have outsmarted Horngrad on this point. To serve a subpoena to an American outside the United States is a costly and time-consuming process. It appeared that Horngrad may have assumed Barry would accompany Eileen to California where he could serve his subpoena and avoid the costly international process.

Another possibility was that Horngrad did not want Lipsker to return and was making a show of exerting "due diligence" to get him back in order to meet the court's requirements for reading prior testimony. It was unlikely that Barry, after months of reflection and badgering by Eileen and the prosecution, would be as helpful to the defense as he had been earlier.

The problem with reading from the transcript is that it affords no opportunity to underscore certain remarks, as one can with a witness. Counsel cannot raise his voice, affect incredulity, rephrase a question four times, or any of a score of tricks for highlighting a statement to ensure that it registers with the jury. The few things Lipsker said on the stand in May that eroded his wife's account were buried in reams of testimony that bolstered her. A listener had to be thoroughly knowledgeable about the case and pay close attention in order to pick up the bits that Horngrad hoped would discredit Eileen's account of the murder itself and her recollection of it.

When Horngrad won permission to read from the transcript, Tipton forestalled any possibility of underscoring by insisting that an entire section be read, not just the bits that served Horngrad's purposes. The testimony was from Barry's cross-examination by Arthur Wachtel, and was read in a flat voice by the court stenographer.

It began with Barry's account of Eileen's telling him of the recollection, and his original phone call to the police. He said that she would not discuss details of the crime with him. He admitted having said he would like to murder George Franklin. When asked if he had told the police "she couldn't live with it anymore," Barry replied that that was his interpretation, not her words. Wachtel asked Barry if he had said he didn't know why it took her so many years to come forward. Barry replied that he may have.

Had Barry said that Eileen knew all the details of the case because she had followed it in the media? He had been very nervous at the time, he said, and he had been putting words in Eileen's mouth, then added, "She wasn't sitting there telling me what to say." Wachtel asked what her relationship with her father had been. Incongruously, Barry said, "Her physical relationship? Well, she told me he once held her down while a friend raped her in exchange for drugs."

After much rambling testimony about matters the jury had already heard many times, Wachtel asked Barry if he had told a reporter from station KCBC that Eileen started having her recollections "a few weeks ago." Disarmingly, Barry replied that "apparently some of my facts were not correct." Had he said she had "flashbacks"? It had been his word, not Eileen's. Had he said Janice and Eileen "put their stories together"? Barry did not recall.

For all the many pieces of testimony that were in conflict with Eileen's account, Barry had offered plausible explanations, usually that he was speaking from nerves, false assumptions, or misunderstandings of what Eileen had told him. The testimony also painted a picture of a man deeply disturbed by the crime his wife had described to him, and concerned as well about the jeopardy into which his wife would be putting herself if she came forward.

When Eileen arrived back at her Aunt Sue's house in the Portola Valley, she got a call from Elaine Tipton asking her not to speak with any members of her family who were on the witness list. One of them, she wouldn't say which, might be recalled to the stand, and Horngrad could make trouble if she had spoken with this person. Eileen called her grandfather and asked him to explain to Leah that Eileen could not call her.

Helen Elkins, the eighty-eight-year-old grandmother of Kate's husband, was put on the stand to state that she had never attended this trial, denying Leah's testimony that Elkins was reporting each day's testimony to Kate. So absurd, in fact, was the likelihood of this frail old lady being pressed into spy duty, and so definite was Leah's assertion that Elkins was Kate's spy, that it raised the suggestion that Kate and her husband might have told this to Leah for no other reason than to embarrass her in a courtroom situation.

As Helen Elkins left the stand, she walked toward the defendant, who looked startled, and mouthed "Hi." The trial had gone on for five weeks. Each of Franklin's five children had testified, as well as his ex-wife, an ex-lover, and a number of former colleagues and neighbors. Not one of them had ever greeted him by so much as a nod. Now this elderly woman who had probably met Franklin once in her life and who had just denied attending his trial made a highly conspicuous point of greeting him.

Before resting his case, Horngrad made a last plea for permission to introduce newspaper articles about Susan's disappearance and the discovery of her body. He hoped to show that everything Eileen knew was in the public domain. Tipton argued that *all* eyewitness testimony could be thrown out if opposing counsel merely had to show that an eyewitness could have learned his or her facts in the media. She was ignoring the fact that other eyewitnesses didn't wait twenty-one years to come forward, and that prosecutors didn't always argue, as Tipton had, that their witnesses possessed information that *only* could have been known to an eyewitness, so Horngrad's point seemed to have merit.

With greater subtlety, Tipton also argued that the press reports were full of both accurate and inaccurate information. That Eileen had not picked up any of the bogus facts could be taken as proof that her recollection was uncontaminated by press exposure. Judge Smith was disinclined to allow the evidence, on the grounds that "its probative value is outweighed by the possibility of confusing the jury," and ruled against Horngrad.

The last witness for the defense was Cinde Chorness, an attractive blond reporter for the *San Mateo Times*. She turned out to be another Horngrad attempt to introduce testimony from Barry Lipsker, in that she had interviewed Lipsker and reported statements damaging to the prosecution. Chorness tried to evade Horngrad's thrust, but finally admitted Barry had told her that "Eileen and Janice put their stories together."

"Did he tell you that Janice was with Eileen and Susan Nason that day?"

"Yes."

"No further questions."

Tipton leaped to her feet. "You heard this from Barry?" Yes. "Not Eileen?" Yes. Tipton also seized the opportunity to paint for the jurors a sketch of Barry. "Did you find Barry to be talkative?" Yes. "Eager to share his opinions, whether asked or not?" Horngrad's objection was overruled.

"Yes," Chorness responded. "He seemed eager to talk."

"Did he ask his wife's permission to give this interview?"

"I have no idea."

"Did he interrupt you and start talking?" Tipton seemed ready to continue her portrait-by-question indefinitely.

"I don't recall."

At 2:05 P.M. on November 26, the defense rested.

In her rebuttal, Tipton first called Margaret Nason to lambast the Banks women and their mysterious car and barking dog. Margaret Nason testified that when she went to the Bankses' house looking for Susan, Mrs. Banks had said nothing about a dog, a suspicious car, or having seen Susan in the driveway behind her house. Horngrad asked if Nason had any recollection of Shirley going out to play with another girl that afternoon. She did not. He showed a 1969 police report in which she had said Shirley had gone out to play. It did not help her recollection. Former police detective Gordon Penfold was recalled to say that when he had interviewed Banks at the time, she had said nothing to him about the suspicious circumstances.

Next was William Hensel, making his third appearance on the stand, to try to dispel the dark cloud of the erroneous license-number list. Hensel was willing to take the blame for the mistake, saying that owing to the October 13, 1970, date on the list, he had mistaken it for a list of cars at the grave on the first anniversary of Susan's murder, September 22, 1970. Horngrad flew at him. How could this happen? Hadn't Hensel taken down the numbers and turned them over to his superiors, who, in turn, he assumed, had sent them off to the Department of Motor Vehicles for the owners' names? He had. As for what had happened to the correct list, Hensel never saw it again. (No one could produce it, or anything else—no assignment sheet, no report, no notes—to prove that Susan's grave had indeed been staked out on the first anniversary of the murder.)

Horngrad asked why anyone would want the list of attendees at the December 9, 1969 funeral in October 1970? Hensel did not know. Horngrad grew indignant and expressed incredulity that Hensel would misidentify such an important piece of evidence based simply on the date's being only three weeks after the date in question.

"Sir, you came into court," Horngrad said, his voice rising, "and positively identified that as a list of numbers taken on the anniversary of Susan Nason's murder, when it was, in fact, a list taken ten months earlier, when my client was known to be at the cemetery?"

Hensel stuck to the prosecution's story that it had been an innocent mistake. In a later interview, Tipton took the blame for failing to discover Hensel's mistake. She stated that she had accepted Hensel's recollection that this was the 1970 list rather than the 1969 one, though he was relying only on his memory and the date at the top of the list. When asked if it made sense to have a list of license numbers without some indication of what the list was and when it was taken, she could only shrug and say that in the far-off period in question, police work was not exemplary. The question also arose as to how it emerged from deep within twenty years of police records and made its way into the evidence scrapbooks of the Franklin case without some effort to establish the list's relevance and authenticity. Tipton admits that she should have run a check on the list's other licenses. Had she done so, she later said, she would have discovered the mistaken date and the list would not have been introduced.

Tipton next called Robert Morse to testify that the fence at Sue Banks's house was six feet tall and too solidly built to see the head of a little girl on the other side. George Franklin, Jr., returned to the stand and, with conspicuous civility, appeared to have rethought his first, abrasive performance. Tipton asked about his visits to his father in jail. He had been to see him three times. "Did you ask him if he had committed the crime?" Tipton asked.

"Yes."

"What did he say?"

"He denied it."

"He specifically denied having killed this girl?"

"Yes, in so many words."

This innocuous exchange was one of Tipton's most brilliant ploys. She knew that one of the strongest elements of her case was Eileen's account of the jail visit during which Franklin had not said a word of recrimination against Eileen or anything to suggest his innocence. Rather than basking in this victory, Tipton brooded about ways in which the defense might try to nullify the damage to their client. Putting herself in their calculations, she saw a way to do this. Horngrad could put Wachtel

on the stand and have him testify that Franklin's attorneys had
forbidden him to discuss the case. The inference would be
unavoidable: he had not denied the crime to Eileen because he
had been forbidden to.

If Horngrad did this on re-rebuttal, she would not have an
opportunity to counteract the ploy; she knew she must counteract it before it happened. Knowing of George junior's jail
visit and his eagerness to cast doubt on Eileen, she had brought
him back to the stand on the chance he would say his father had
denied the crime to him. Apparently delighted to be offered an
opportunity to contradict Eileen, he had walked into the trap,
and effectively closed the door to a possible defense claim that
Franklin had been forbidden to say a word about the case.

Leah Franklin returned to be asked about a visit she had
made to her daughter Kate on the evening before Leah was
scheduled to meet with Tipton. She stated that she had been
told by Kate that her grandmother-in-law had been in court
every day and was reporting back to her. Learning of Eileen's
testimony, Kate had phoned Horngrad and told him that Eileen was not telling the truth, but Leah did not remember
exactly which of Eileen's points Kate disputed. Leah said that
Kate had been against Eileen coming forward "all the way
through." Kate had taken maternity leave early from her job
because she was so humiliated by Eileen's action. These were
flat contradictions of Kate's testimony, leaving no other possibility but that one of them had perjured herself.

"Did Kate ever say it was unfair of Eileen to go forward
because they all lived in the Bay Area but Eileen did not?"
Horngrad objected, and Tipton made her point about Kate's
superficiality with a rephrasing. Before leaving the stand, Leah
again contradicted Kate's testimony by saying that Kate had
been "adamantly" against Eileen's going forward.

Tipton's primary purpose in calling Assistant District Attorney Martin Murray to the stand was to establish the careful
adherence to proper form to which the authorities had adhered
since the first phone calls from Eileen—providing her with
none of their information about the case and only taking information from her under the most controlled circumstances.
They had impressed on her the importance of not learning
anything from them or from any outside source. Murray affirmed that, from the outset, Eileen had denied having been
hypnotized, and he stated that she had never indicated a desire
to conceal her therapy with Katherine Rieder.

On cross-examination, Horngrad resurrected his Janice-in-the-van gambit by asking Murray if Eileen had told him of that. She had told either him or Detectives Morse and Cassandro, he replied. Had Murray brought up the subject of hypnosis, or had Eileen? He had. At one point Horngrad attained a climactic parody of all the trial's who-told-whom-what questions by asking, "Didn't Eileen tell you that Janice had told Barry that Eileen was upset for weeks after Susan Nason disappeared?"

"Objection," Tipton said, jumping to her feet. "That's triple hearsay."

For weeks now the jury had been struggling to assimilate the Franklin family's numerous exchanges of information about the murder. Eileen told Janice, Leah told Kate, Janice told Barry, Barry told the world. . . . If ever there was a moment when the jury's capacity to trace the flow of information collapsed into total confusion, this was it.

When, in her redirect, Tipton asked if Murray felt that Eileen had gotten her facts right, Horngrad objected and was sustained by Judge Smith, who added, "The facts of this case will be decided by the jury, not by Mr. Murray or anyone else." Tipton asked if Murray had told Eileen she possessed facts unavailable in any way except by her being present at the murder. He said he had. "Did you check newspaper articles of the time," she said, "to see if this were true?" Horngrad, who would shortly argue again to examine this subject in open court, objected and was sustained.

Of all the conflicting versions of events that the members of the Franklin family had given under oath, there was always the possibility of flawed recollection to explain the contradiction. Kate and her mother had now whipped off the mask of civility and were openly calling each other liars. Curiously, their confrontation was over relatively inconsequential matters. George junior's and Kate's alterations of Eileen's story were far more damaging to the prosecution, but they were more equivocal. Eileen, confused and frightened by the sudden return of a powerful memory, had admitted giving a false story about the way in which her memory had emerged. This left room for legitimate disagreements over what had occurred.

Not so with Kate and Leah. Kate said she had never opposed Eileen's going forward. Leah said she had. Leah said Kate had sent Helen Elkins to spy. Kate denied it. The family disagreements had already caused a complete break between Eileen and Kate and between Eileen and George junior. For Kate and

Leah now to clash head-on, each accusing the other of lying, seemed a superfluous border skirmish in the war between Eileen and her brother, and all but irrelevant to the terminal struggle between Eileen and her father.

Because of a scheduling problem, Horngrad was allowed to introduce another witness for the defense, Dr. Paul William Herrmann, a forensic scientist whose main testimony was that all of the forensic evidence presented by the prosecution was inconclusive. His principal point was summed up late in his testimony, when he said that forensic evidence that was "consistent with" a given set of circumstances in no way proved those circumstances, but merely did not rule them out.

" 'Consistent with,' " he said, "is a pretty meaningless expression. It only means that it's one of many things that could have happened. The two skull injuries could have been two blows, but there could have been three if two fell on the same spot. The instrument could have been irregular, but then maybe it wasn't. The smaller of the two rocks, the one with Susan's hair on it, was unlikely to have been the murder weapon, as it was too small. Could it have been? Well, yes, but . . ." And so on until the doctor slipped over the edge into absurdity when he suggested other ways Susan's ring might have been crushed. "An animal might have tried to bite the ring and crushed it, or a bird. . . ." Angrily waving the blow-up photograph of the mangled ring at him, Tipton snapped, "You think a bird did that?" The jurors laughed along with the rest of the court.

In response to Tipton's hypothetical sequence of events that would logically tie all the forensic evidence together, Herrmann's favorite parry, used three times, was that her scenario "makes a nice story, but I don't know if it's true." Tipton said she was appalled, and hoped jurors were, that he would use the term "nice story" to describe the murder of a little girl. The fencing went on and on, with the doctor offering other possible explanations of the crushed ring, until Tipton, waxing melodramatic for the first time since her opening statement, lowered her voice and said, "Wouldn't it be very likely that the ring was crushed when that little girl saw what was coming at her, and tried to protect herself with her hand?"

Smugly he said, as if for the first time, "It makes a good story, but I don't know if that's what happened."

Tipton seemed particularly angered by Herrmann and threw herself into his demolition with unusual gusto. When she finally snapped "No further questions" and he slunk from the stand, Bryan Cassandro turned to Bob Morse and said, "Boy, how would you like to be her husband and come home too late?"

If the erroneous list of license numbers was the prosecution's biggest embarrassment ("I've got egg on my face," Tipton said in her office, "and we've just got to live with it."), the defense was now to suffer a similar debunking. Deputy Fire Chief Barry Johnson was recalled to the stand, where he said he had talked on the previous day with Bill Mann, the firefighter who had insisted there was no platform or mattress in the back of George Franklin's van in 1969.

Reversing his testimony, Mann had told Johnson that he wasn't sure he had brought groceries in from the van in 1969. It might have been in 1974, after he had come to know Franklin better. Johnson had pried this admission from Mann by confronting him with the engine company's log books, which showed that he could only have worked at the same station with Franklin on one day of 1969, not the many days he had testified to. This totally undercut his claim of great acquaintance with either Franklin or his van at the time of the murder.

Some suspected the explanation for Mann's odd performance lay in the mindless solidarity among firefighters that Eileen, since childhood, had suspected and deplored. Whatever it was, Mann's testimony—so certain, so wrong—would remain, like the license-number list and the Banks women's barking dog, one of the enigmas of the case.

If the next witness had been the last of the trial rather than the third from the last, it would have shown a nice sense of symmetry. He was Inspector Charles Etter, the first law-enforcement officer with whom Barry and Eileen had made contact in their original November 1989 phone calls. Since Etter's only function as a witness was to verify that proper procedures had been observed in taping those conversations, paving the way for Tipton to play them in court, his appearance had, for some, the more important function of revealing what a minor but key figure in the drama looked like.

In a light blue suit and a conservative necktie, he was a handsome, fatherly man with a full head of white hair and glasses, who looked as though he might have left a lit pipe in an ashtray outside the courtroom. As a representative of authority, he was far closer to Judge Hardy than Joe Friday, and the sort of kindly father figure that anyone blindly calling the police with a bizarre story would be lucky to draw.

When the final tally of heroism of the case is made, Etter's role should rank high. Considering Eileen's skittish and torn state at that crucial juncture, an impatient, skeptical, or insensitive reaction from the police could have driven her into permanent silence. As the court was about to hear, Etter had deftly and gently coaxed Eileen into following through on her impulse to come forward. Now, on the witness stand, he answered Tipton's prefatory questions, then, to a very quiet courtroom, the tape was played.

Throughout the trial the jurors had heard repeatedly about Eileen's anonymous telephone conversations with the police, which ranked, after her moment of recollection and the murder itself, as climactic moments in the drama. Of those three crucial happenings, however, this one, like the murder and unlike the recollection, which simply came to her, was based on a human decision. Now jurors would hear, not flawed recollections of the moment from different viewpoints, but the moment itself.

Since the jury's main task was to evaluate Eileen's credibility, the sort of person she was took on major importance. Her tone and demeanor in her first contact with hard-edged authority could tell much about her credibility. This would not be the Eileen they had all seen on the witness stand—prepared, rehearsed, under the world's scrutiny—but a person who was invisible, nameless, and dizzyingly uncertain of her legal ground. By introducing the tape of these calls at the trial's end, Tipton was counting heavily on Eileen's persuading the jury of her sincerity as she had at the outset persuaded the police.

There was little doubt that it was her believability on this initial contact that prompted the police to proceed. To be sure, they checked the file on the Nason case and found that most (but not all) of what she told them jibed with existing information. It also appeared that they believed their own frequent assertion that Eileen knew things she could not have known unless she had been present at the crime.

One reason they had never undertaken an exhaustive examination of all the news accounts published in 1969 was their belief that Eileen was telling them the truth. For all the technological wizardry at their disposal—forensic science, lie detectors, data storage and retrieval—police still rely on gut feelings about the people who report crimes. Now Tipton was asking the jury to decide the matter in the same way. This was the case's true symmetry.

While Etter remained on the stand, Tipton played the section in which Eileen described the crime to him. "Can I give it to you briefly?" she asked. When he said she could tell it as she liked, she went on, "Well, I was in the car with the person who committed the crime. We stopped and picked Susan Nason up, she was on the sidewalk across the street from her house. . . ."

"In Foster City?"

"Yeah." As her narration approached the murder itself, her voice became emotional, almost too shaky to continue, but she got through Susan's death and stopped.

Etter said, "Go ahead."

"Isn't that enough?" she replied, a touch of her sassy sarcasm creeping through. When she was asked what Susan had been wearing, she struggled to remember, then said she was sorry, but she didn't want to guess.

At the end of her statement, Etter asked if he might have Eileen's phone number. His tone was casual, as though he feared that if he jerked the line too abruptly, she might swim away. Eileen chuckled and said, "Do you guys trace calls?"

The last exchange Tipton included was Eileen asking what else the police knew about the case. "I'm afraid if there's no other evidence," she said, "it's just my word, and that means nothing." For Tipton this was a bold note on which to conclude this testimony. Even the suggestion that the sole witness's word meant nothing was a dangerous thought to float so close to jury deliberation. The weeks of forensic and psychiatric testimony affirmed only that the case's known facts were "consistent with" her story; they did not prove it.

Still, Eileen's concern about other evidence contained a germ of corroboration. Had she been crazy or bent on vengeance, she would probably not have worried much about what else the authorities knew. Anyone sufficiently motivated to testify falsely is likely to insist on being believed and to demand an immediate arrest. But while Eileen was still anonymous, she showed concern about the adequacy of her testimony and was actually counseling the police against launching a case on her word alone. If that was a strategy calculated to deceive, it was ingenious.

Whatever the jurors' evaluations of Eileen's words might be, they could now hear for themselves the guarded, fearful, shy, and slightly coy young woman whom the police had first encountered. Tipton felt herself to be on firm ground, and the courtroom sat mesmerized throughout the ten minutes of telephone conversation. It was a brilliant conclusion to Tipton's exhaustive prosecution.

Horngrad introduced two final witnesses: Detective Martin Gunderson, in a highly anticlimactic attempt to elicit testimony that Shirley Nason had gone out to play on the afternoon of the murder, and, finally, Kate Franklin, to reiterate her claim that Eileen had told her the recollection had come in a dream, to affirm that her leaving her job was for maternity leave and had nothing to do with the case, and, finally, that she had not sent her ancient grandmother-in-law to cover the trial for her.

On November 14, the defense rested. There would be no further testimony.

TWENTY-ONE

DEVIATING FROM THE CUSTOMARY SEQUENCE, JUDGE SMITH indicated that he would instruct the jury before the closing statements. With the jury still absent, he first invited argument from counsel about the points of instruction he intended to include. He said to Horngrad and Tipton, "Are you ready to talk?"

"Always," Horngrad replied, then switched from jury instruction to a motion to introduce various disputed items into evidence. One was the collaboration agreement for this book. Judge Smith was disinclined to allow it. "But, Your Honor," Horngrad said, exasperation in his voice, "when I tried to elicit certain related testimony, you forbade it, saying the matter was covered in the collaboration agreement. Now I am told the agreement is not to be admitted!"

"I read it through in detail," the judge replied, unperturbed at his own seeming duplicity. "I do not see that it has any probative value. It is confusing. I deny it."

When Horngrad also tried to introduce the erroneous list of license-plate numbers, Tipton was on her feet immediately. "Everyone knows that Detective Hensel made a mistake," she said. "Why put it in the record?" Judge Smith agreed. Horngrad made a final effort to introduce media accounts from 1969 to prove Eileen could have learned her information from them. He quoted several articles that contained some of the details that had given her account credibility. Tipton countered that she, in turn, could go through all the 1969 press accounts and cull out numerous inaccuracies. "One account," she said by way of example, "wrote of Susan's ring being found 'at the scene,' rather than on her hand, as Eileen described."

Horngrad grew impassioned. Introducing these news stories,

he said, "is critical to our case! The jury left the court with the idea that Eileen knows things she could only have known if she were [at the scene]. If it's prejudicial, I haven't heard in what way." Then, in a final burst of anguish, Horngrad said that the decision to bar the news stories was "eviscerating" his case. Judge Smith countered that it had been stated in testimony that Eileen could have learned many of her facts from news accounts and that he didn't want the trial to degenerate into "a battle by newspapers."

Boldly, Horngrad said, "It is *not* covered by testimony, and the jury will wrongfully convict if they are not shown that the facts were public knowledge." Judge Smith remained firm in excluding the newspaper articles. He then read to Tipton and Horngrad the numbers of the listed instructions he planned to read to the jurors. The lawyers both argued for and against certain instructions. As was typical in this sort of horse-trading, Horngrad argued against including a limiting instruction about child molestation that admonished jurors not to take such evidence as proof that Franklin had committed the murder. "Why plant the seed?" he argued. The judge overruled him.

When the instructions to be read were agreed upon, the jury was brought back into court. Judge Smith started by telling them they must follow the law whether or not they agreed with it, and they must not be guided by pity, sentiment, or compassion. They had to weigh the evidence and apply the law regardless of the consequences; they should not single out one point of evidence and ignore the others. The statements made by attorneys were not evidence. Jurors should not speculate on reasons for the objections the lawyers had raised.

Counsels' questions were not evidence. Jurors must not consider stricken evidence, but only the evidence from the trial. No other source might be considered. Jurors must not make any investigation on their own. They must not, for instance, visit the scene. They must not discuss the case with anyone except fellow jurors, and then only when all were present. Circumstantial evidence was evidence that, if found to be true, inferred that another fact was true. Facts did not have to be proved by direct evidence; both were acceptable. Finding the defendant guilty on circumstantial evidence required that it be the only rational conclusion.

If two items of evidence conflicted with each other, jurors must reject the one that pointed to guilt. If one interpretation pointed to specific intent on the part of the defendant and another interpretation pointed to lack of intent, jurors must pick the latter. Certain evidence was admitted for limited purposes, and jurors might accept it only for those limited purposes for which it was admitted. Any testimony entered as evidence from a prior trial must be accepted as though given at this trial.

In evaluating witnesses, jurors must consider the witnesses' ability to see or hear, their character and quality of their testimony, their demeanor and manner, any bias or other motives they might show, their attitude toward the defendant and toward the trial, their consistency, their willingness to admit to untruthfulness. If jurors discovered a witness in a lie, they must reject all of his or her testimony. They must not use the number of witnesses as a decisive factor for one side or the other. While jurors heard evidence of physical and sexual abuse in this trial, this was admitted for limited purposes, and they were not to use it as evidence of whether the defendant did or did not commit this crime. Motive was not an element of the criminal charge, but jurors might use it to determine guilt or innocence. Jurors must not draw inferences from the fact that the defendant did not testify; the defendant's silence on being accused by others must not be used to judge his guilt or innocence.

No person might be convicted unless each element of the crime could have been committed by him. Experts could give testimony, and jurors could evaluate the qualifications of experts and give their testimony whatever weight they felt it was entitled to. The statements of the psychiatric witnesses for the prosecution were not evidence of the truth of the claim of repressed memory. With the failure to prove any one fact, jurors must determine the overall effect.

The defendant was presumed innocent until the contrary was proved. The people had the burden of proof. *Reasonable* doubt did not mean an *impossible* doubt. In the case of the eyewitness testimony received in this trial, jurors should consider the witness's believability, her opportunity to observe, her stress at the time, her ability to provide a description or make an identification, the extent of her certainty, and whether the testimony was the product of her own recollection.

The charge of murder required proof of specific intent. To prove murder, three elements must be present: that someone was killed; that the killing was unlawful; and that there was malice aforethought. Malice could be expressed intent or implied intent. Forethought did not require a considerable period of time or long deliberation; a person's calculated decision could be arrived at in a very short period of time. Three elements were involved in child molestation: there must be molestation; the person molested must be under fourteen; there must be a specific intent to satisfy sexual desire. Bare skin was not necessary for child molestation; the child could be dressed.

Jurors must understand the term *felony murder*. If the murder was tied to a felony, the state did not have to prove intent; it was automatically first-degree murder. The defense had stipulated that Susan Nason was molested; therefore, if the jury found that she was, indeed, killed by the defendant, the verdict would be first-degree murder.

When the jury had been instructed, Elaine Tipton stood to begin her closing statement. She thanked the jury for their attention and patience over the past four weeks. Having launched her case by introducing the jurors to two little girls, Tipton began her finale by adding Eileen's daughter, Jessica, into the drama's principals by referring to "the *three* little girls who had brought us together," reminding jurors that Sica Lipsker had triggered Eileen's recollection. "We're here," she said, "because the defendant chose to murder a little girl rather than be identified as a child molester, and because one of those little girls had the strength and courage to come forward." (This was one of the few references in the trial to a motive.)

Tipton announced that the wealth of evidence she had presented all corroborated the account of the eyewitness. The defense had presented no evidence that in any way detracted from that. Tipton then led the jurors through a review of the evidence that, while detailed, was highly succinct compared to the trial itself. She pointed to Eileen's "grueling two days of cross-examination" and how well she had stood up to it, adding that the defense had never asked one single question about the murder. "Instead," she said, "they asked her about everything but the murder, trying to make jurors believe the case is about media, hypnosis, counseling, psychiatry, factions within the family. . . . Ninety percent of this was red herrings. George Franklin is on trial, not Eileen Franklin."

In describing the murder, Tipton reached an emotional climax when she described the feelings of despair and distress felt by the eight-year-old Eileen at leaving Susie at the murder scene. For the most part, Tipton's recapitulation of her case was straightforward and free of analysis. She lingered over Franklin's strange response to Eileen's jail visit. What would an innocent person have said? 'Eileen, you know it's not true. Why are you doing this to me? Are you sick? Angry? Why are you falsely accusing me?' Had he said any of these things? No. "That alone," she said, "is worth its weight in gold." Tipton explained the concept of adoptive admission, when an accused person passes up an opportunity to make a denial.

She attacked the various "red herrings"—the blue station wagon, the barking dog, Ann Hobbs's would-be abductor. Tipton then asked why jurors should trust Eileen's memory after so long a time. In spite of the defense's attempt to inject an aura of mystery and madness into Eileen's repression, she said, her response was not unusual. She recapitulated the days of psychiatric testimony that reinforced Eileen's claim of buried memory, and threw in such statistics as that in a study of adults who had suffered abuse as children, sixty percent had at some point repressed all recollection of it. Tipton revisited the incidents of Franklin's abuse of his children, including the rape by Stew Smith, pointing out that the defense had not refuted any of this. Franklin was a man who had so defiled the name "father" that he did not deserve to be called by it.

Tipton's case had encompassed a remarkably broad range. It had involved such disparate facets of knowledge as hungry animals' preference for wounded flesh and the work schedules of firemen. Jurors had learned of the psychiatric intricacies of retrieving repressed memory, and of the play routines of Foster City children. But in her peroration she attempted to cut through the welter of facts by focusing on Eileen.

George Franklin, Tipton said, could kill Susan Nason, but he could not kill the spirit of his daughter. He might have crushed a less resilient child, but Eileen had survived spiritually, mentally, and physically by burying the memory, locking it away. By his despicable acts he had tried to prevent her remembering what she had seen. Now he was seeking to capitalize on that by portraying her as either a cunning liar or a deranged person. His strategy relied on doubt that an adult would remember such an event as accurately as she did.

The defense had two arguments—that Eileen had a false memory or that she was deliberately lying. Either was preposterous. The only version that made sense was that she witnessed the murder and, in order to survive, repressed the memory of it. No one would have gone through what she had gone through if it were not true. She'd wrenched her life apart. She'd lost her privacy as well as that of her children and her family. She'd let the whole world know that she was held down and raped while her father laughed. She'd sat through a cross-examination that humiliated and harassed her. Horngrad objected at this point, a rare occurrence in closing statements, and was overruled.

Eileen, Tipton continued, "grew up to be a woman of honesty and courage, and I call on this jury's honesty and courage to bring this killer to justice. Justice will not bring Susan Nason back to life or restore Eileen's childhood. . . . For twenty years George Franklin has been free in society, but a verdict of guilty will establish the undeniable truth that was buried twenty years ago. Your verdict will resolve twenty years of silence and uncertainty. . . . I ask you to hold the defendant accountable for this terrible crime and to find George Franklin guilty of murder in the first degree."

Horngrad thanked the jury and spoke of how emotional the trial had been, how difficult it had been for the witnesses as well as for everyone else in the courtroom and especially for Mr. Franklin, who had been charged by his daughter. He said, "I was struck by seeing Susan Nason's contemporaries who are now adults. It's very eerie to see them on the stand. Susan's life ended at eight and it gives a sense of tragedy for all of us." His tone hardened. "But this case is not about emotion. It's a true test of the jurors' oath to dispassionately weigh all the evidence. The case has emotion on one hand and logic and evidence on the other."

Horngrad then went into a lengthy discussion of the legal terms involved—preponderance of evidence, clear and convincing—leading up to the prime requirement in deciding criminal cases: that in order to convict, jurors must find a defendant guilty beyond a reasonable doubt and to a moral certainty with abiding convictions. After examining these abstract concepts, he moved on to the case itself and listed the undisputed facts. He eventually arrived at Eileen and said, "We'll never know if it was a false memory or if it was repressed memory. We'll never know the thought processes of Eileen's that brought us to court; we cannot travel back twenty years in time.

"We can use rules of law to establish her credibility. . . . I submit she told some lies before she came to court. I submit she told you some lies, too. Other than Eileen Franklin, *there is nothing else*. She lied many, many times. How can we believe what she says happened twenty years ago? She admits she lied to her mother, to her brother, and Kate testified she lied to her as well. She misled her husband and her therapist. . . ." Horngrad then went into discrepancies between accounts Eileen said she gave others and what they claimed they were told. One of these inconsistencies was Kirk Barrett saying she had not told him who the murderer was and Eileen saying she had identified the murderer as soon as she told him. He hit the implausibility of Eileen's claim not to have discussed the murder with Janice, her having had no dreams, the forensic opinion that the alleged murder rock was too small.

He launched into the cemetery visit, which he called a "central part of the prosecution's case." "I'm not suggesting the prosecution was malicious," he said, "but the introduction of that testimony was reckless and irresponsible."

He referred to the failure of Franklin to deny he had committed the crime on two occasions as being "barely worthy of mention." He alluded to Leah's confronting her husband with her suspicions and his replying, "You always think the worst of me." Horngrad said, "To me, that's no evidence of anything."

As for Eileen's jail visit, he excused that by saying that Franklin would naturally be very suspicious of a daughter who had accused him of murder, and would be very reticent to say anything. He pointed to Leah's testimony about the bloody shirt, and dismissed that by saying she was simply not truthful. She had been asked about the shirt several times and had said nothing about it. Nor had she told the authorities about Eileen's mentioning hypnosis to her. Horngrad pointed out that Franklin could have disposed of the shirt. "The shirt incident," he said forcefully, *"never happened."*

Horngrad attacked the prosecution for talking about what a monster, what a bad guy, Franklin was. Why, he asked, were they not talking about the evidence in this case? It was beyond dispute, he said, that to abuse a child was unforgivable. Franklin was not seeking their forgiveness; he wasn't on trial for what kind of a guy he was in 1969.

Horngrad homed in on his favorite point, that the prosecution had never proved that Eileen's story contained details that she could not have learned in the newspapers. "I invite her to come in here, to get up and tell you *one thing* that was in her statement that was not in the public domain. The rules of evidence say that you can't come in and throw newspapers around."

Horngrad went over other changes and inconsistencies in Eileen's testimony, saying that if a fact was not consistent with the known facts, she would change or abandon it. By having come forward, Eileen had become a celebrity. He referred to her denying that she knew how much she would make from the book and movie deals. "Is that credible to you?" he asked.

As he headed toward his conclusion, Horngrad speculated that Eileen's recollection of having been sexually molested when she was five was the genesis of the entire story, suggesting either revenge or confusion. He said that she was entitled to have her pain eased, but it was not the jury's job to ease her pain. "Our job is only to decide whether George Franklin committed this murder. Not by this evidence can we decide. Eileen is entitled to her rage. She's entitled to be comforted, but this is more appropriate to therapy. A courtroom is not a psychiatrist's couch. You cannot decide what happened; you do not have the tools to do that. Whether Eileen made it up on purpose or unintentionally, it's not our job to determine."

After a final reminder to the jury of Eileen's having at first changed the man she said raped her from a black to a white man, he chose Mrs. Nason for the conclusion of his narration. "God knows," he said, "I would not utter a word of criticism against Mrs. Nason, but when she says her child would not get into a car with a stranger, we cannot convict on that." He told the jurors he was sure they would stand by their pledge not to consider the fact that Mr. Franklin did not testify. He then said that a finding of not guilty was not a finding of innocence; it only meant the case had not been proved beyond a reasonable doubt. "If I have offended anyone during the trial, I'm sorry, but I feel confident you will return a verdict of not guilty."

Concluding with the suggestion that his client might not be innocent but wasn't proven guilty was a remarkable shift in strategy from the month of repeated assertions of Franklin's innocence. It almost appeared he was withdrawing his weeks of argument and was falling back on a plea of technical innocence rather than real innocence. He appeared to be asking the jury, as indeed the law does, for a high degree of legalistic subtlety: to acquit a man whose own lawyer did not claim he was innocent.

Taking unabashed advantage of courtroom procedure that allows only the prosecution a rebuttal, Tipton again reaffirmed that most of the arguments jurors had heard in the defense's three-hour statement had nothing to do with the case. George Franklin was on trial, not his daughter. She was an eyewitness, and her testimony had been corroborated. Jurors heard only her failings and shortcomings. What did this say? That she was terrified. How dare the defendant fault her for the manner in which she came forward, when it was he who had put her in the moral dilemma? The case was not about how she had disclosed her memory of the crime; she was not charged with improper disclosure.

Tipton noted how easy it would have been for Eileen to deny having mentioned hypnosis. Although the color of Susan's dress had been reported extensively, Eileen had never claimed to remember the dress's color, but had said only that it was an A-line, which Mrs. Nason confirmed. The second fact easily obtained from news reports was the time of day. Eileen had at first said she wasn't sure about this. If she had constructed the story, one of the easiest things for her to learn would have been that Susan disappeared in the afternoon.

Pointing out that the defense had attacked her side's failure to do their homework, she said, "Let's do the reverse. What homework did they do with Mrs. Banks and her daughter? They trotted them both back in . . . and Bill Mann." Deftly, she had made the score three-to-one in the false-testimony department.

Returning to the murder, Tipton asked how Eileen could have known about the rock, about the dress's design, about her father throwing Susie's shoe. Was it a coincidence that only one shoe was found? There was no evidence that any of that information was obtained outside Eileen's own experience. If it was so natural for the defendant not to deny his crime to Eileen, why had he denied it to his son? She concluded her seven months of dogged work by asking the jury, if they could not convict with this case and this evidence, what would it take to bring a killer to justice?

Tipton had finally countered Horngrad's repeated insinuations about Eileen's errors in describing the crime. For those who saw the mistakes as proof of sincerity rather than the opposite that Horngrad hoped, it was long-awaited relief from a nagging illogicality. Tipton had not exactly met Horngrad's challenge to produce one fact that Eileen could not have known from outside sources. For all the extensive and time-consuming legwork the prosecution had clearly done, to claim categorically that one fact or another was never published was, she claimed, beyond her research capabilities, so she had to limit herself to implying that certain facts like the missing shoe were *probably* not mentioned in the papers. Tipton had, in fact, retreated from her opening claim that Eileen knew things about the crime she could have only learned from firsthand knowledge. Instead she had said that the defense had presented no evidence that Eileen had obtained outside information.

Several of Tipton's arguments were specious, such as when she said that if Franklin was too wary of Eileen to deny his crime to her, he would have been equally wary of his son. To Franklin they were not equal. Eileen, not her brother, had accused him of murder. Still, Tipton had vigorously cut through the defenses's obfuscations and red herrings and placed her case where it inevitably had to rest: on the believability of Eileen Franklin.

At 11:00 A.M. on November 29, Judge Smith sent the jury out to begin their deliberations. They had been on duty for six weeks, listening to evidence for a month. With the four-day weeks and the Thanksgiving recess, jurors had actually sat in court for a total of seventeen days, not a long trial by any standards. They had heard twenty-nine prosecution witnesses and thirty-two for the defense. They had scores of pieces of physical evidence to consider, as well as the transcript of Barry's preliminary-hearing testimony and the portion of tape from Eileen's phone calls to the police.

After the jury was out for a short time, they sent word to the judge that they wanted a copy of his instructions. They also requested to hear again the tape of Eileen's phone calls to the police. Horngrad argued against this unsuccessfully, then suggested a compromise: that the jury be given the tape, but no tape machine. This brought a big laugh from everyone, including the judge. George Franklin, in one of his few visible reactions to anything said in court, laughed along with everyone else, then turned and clapped Horngrad on the back.

In the corridor outside the courtroom, Pauline Canny, a CBS producer who had been attending the trial in the hope of winning Eileen's agreement to cooperate in a piece, stopped Horngrad and asked how long after the verdict the sentencing would be if his client was convicted. Airily, Horngrad said, "The thought had never occurred to me."

Nearby, Elaine Tipton was standing chatting with some friends when Robert Morse came up and slid his arm around her waist. "See how slim she is?" he said to the others. "She used to be 180 pounds." There were comments on how consumed she had been by the trial. "She sure was," Morse said. "I've been doing her housework."

Tipton laughed. "It's like men who won't shave until such-and-such happens," she said. "I decided I wouldn't clean my house until this was over."

When the jury went out, Eileen stayed in her Aunt Sue's house in the Portola Valley, reading and nursing her ulcer, which had flared. Toward the end of the afternoon, the foreman, Alger Chapman, sent word that the jury was breaking for the day. Sequestration had been discussed. Horngrad had been in favor of it, but the judge had decided it was unnecessary; the admonitions to avoid media accounts and private discussions would suffice, he said.

The next day Eileen and her aunt returned to the courthouse and resumed their vigil in the district attorney's offices. Around noon, a message came from some friends of Eileen's asking her to join them for lunch at Figaro, a pleasant Italian restaurant in Redwood City. Even though the feeling now was that the jurors would remain out for a number of days—if they did not return right away, then it would be a long time, was the courtroom wisdom—Eileen was too anxious to participate in a social lunch with friends. She urged her aunt to go. Sue hesitated, afraid of missing the verdict, which Tipton had said could arrive at any time. Then she remembered she had brought her cellular phone. Obtaining a promise from Eileen to phone her at the restaurant if the verdict came down, Sue went off to join the others.

On her way to Tipton's office after a pleasant, tension-reducing meal, Sue passed the receptionist's desk at about one-forty-five. The woman looked up and said to her, "You better get down to the courtroom, there's a verdict in the Franklin trial." A journalist in the waiting room overheard the remark and joined Sue in a dash to the elevator. As they emerged on the second floor, the journalist spotted Horngrad in the phone booth, talking intently with the door closed. He went over and tapped on the glass. "There's a verdict," he mouthed.

"What!" Horngrad exclaimed, and abruptly terminated his call. He trotted toward the courtroom, where Sue and several others had already arrived. When he found the door locked as it usually was when the court was not in session, his composure returned and he said to the others condescendingly, "Looks like we need some rumor control here." Just then the door was unlocked from the inside, and court clerk Peggy Gensel appeared.

"We heard there's a verdict, Peggy," Horngrad said. "Is it true?"

"We'll be needing you," Gensel replied quietly.

Her reply could have meant nothing more than that the judge had received a fresh jury request, one that required discussion, but the fact that Gensel had not answered Horngrad's question was taken by him and the others present to mean that it was true—the jurors, after a remarkably brief eight hours of deliberation, had reached a verdict and it was to be read almost immediately.

Eileen

On Friday morning my Aunt Sue and I went to the courthouse hoping that the jury would bring in a verdict. My aunt went to lunch with some friends while I had lunch with Elaine. When we returned to her office, I excused myself to the ladies' room for a moment. As I reentered her office, Elaine was on the phone telling someone she needed to contact Mrs. Nason. She sounded excited. I asked her if the verdict had come in. Still on the phone, she nodded yes. Mechanically I reached for my dress and shoe bag, which hung on the back of Elaine's door, and went to change in the ladies' room.

As I walked out of Elaine's office, my friend Sharon appeared in the hall, walking toward me. When I told her the moment had arrived, she hugged me. I was so nervous that I started shaking and could hardly speak. Sharon went with me to the ladies' room. My hands were shaking so badly that I couldn't undress. Aunt Sue walked in and told me that she was going down to the courtroom and would see me there. We were both stunned that the verdict was in so quickly.

I was overwhelmed with fear and uncertainty. I was so nervous that I couldn't tell which shoe went on which foot. I tried to put on lipstick, but my hands shook too much. When I tried to clip my hair up, I couldn't even brush through it. Sharon tried to calm my nerves as she brushed my hair for me, but I was too overwhelmed to hear what she was saying.

When I was finally dressed, I walked to the hallway outside Elaine's office, where Bob Morse was waiting for me. He

took both of my hands, which were ice cold, and told me not
to worry. I knew he was right, my part was over. I had told
the truth. It was not my responsibility to get the conviction.
The trial was over. Still holding Bob's hands, I said that even
if the jury found my father not guilty, I had done the right
thing for Susan, and would do it all again. The conviction
was irrelevant; the murder had been solved, the truth had
been told.

When word reached Elaine Tipton that there was a verdict,
she got on the phone. The judge had told her that when a
verdict came in, he would wait ten or maybe fifteen minutes
before having it read, but no longer. Tipton had promised to
call Eileen and the Nasons. Eileen was in her office, and Margaret and Shirley Nason were close-by the courthouse. Don
Nason, on the other hand, was up in San Francisco on business.
He was reached by beeper, but saw that it would be impossible
to get to Redwood City in time.

Bob Morse was eating lunch at Fabbro's, a favorite eating
spot with local government and law-enforcement officials. His
meal had just been placed before him when he was called to the
phone. He told the waiter to wrap his lunch for him to take with
him, and rushed to the courthouse. As he drove to the courthouse, a friend he was with asked him whether, if the verdict
was not guilty, he was afraid Donald Nason might "try anything." Without hesitation, Morse replied, "No. I thought
about that early in the trial, but Don doesn't wear a jacket, just
sport shirts. I could spot a bulge in his pocket right away."

Bryan Cassandro, equally confident that a verdict would not
come during the lunch hour, had taken his daughter to a restaurant called Original Joe's. He was on his way back to the
courthouse when his beeper sounded. Journalists had been
warned that when a verdict was reached, the word invariably
spread rapidly among a category of courthouse personnel
known as "verdict junkies" who dropped whatever they were
doing and sprinted to the courtroom. Such advance notice was
a benefit of criminal-justice work. Aware of this, the media
people were obliged to remain nearby in order to avoid being
shut out of the courtroom by newcomers to the trial. Even with
this apprehension, many journalists were caught off guard and
some important media people found themselves blocked from
the courtroom, which had filled in about four minutes.

The bailiff pointed Eileen to one of the few remaining reserved seats in the first row, which happened to be next to Margaret Nason. Although the lives of the two women were now inextricably bound, witnesses were not allowed to communicate, and Eileen had not spoken with Margaret Nason since childhood, but had received a loving note from her a year earlier praising her for her courage in coming forward.

For the first time since the start of the trial, George Franklin entered without a trace of jauntiness in his gait. Instead, he walked slowly to the defense table, looking somber and ashen. When he took his seat, he reached for a glass of water, but his hand was shaking so hard that he decided against it. Horngrad, who had not noticed this, urged him to take some water. This time Franklin did, but his hand was still shaking so much that getting the glass to his lips was difficult.

It is part of courtroom lore that if the jury, when they enter to deliver their verdict, looks at the defendant, it means they have found him not guilty. Conversely, avoiding him with their eyes means a guilty verdict. The Franklin jurors did not look at the man whose fate they had already decided, but then, as a rule, throughout the trial, they had never seemed to look at anything as they entered the courtroom. When they were in their seats, the packed courtroom was totally silent.

"Has the jury reached a verdict?"

Alger Chapman rose. "We have, Your Honor."

"And what is your verdict?"

Margaret Nason clutched Eileen's hand.

"We find the defendant guilty." A soft gasp went up from the courtroom. Horngrad put his hand on the shoulder of George Franklin, who sat stoically. Margaret Nason fell sobbing into the arms of Eileen, who patted her comfortingly. Eileen's long red hair concealed her own reaction. Bob Morse hugged Tipton, and she, too, began to cry.

The jurors were polled by Peggy Gensel, and one after another they stood to pronounce the word "Guilty." The courtroom was orderly, but surprise and emotion ran so high that among the spectators half-rising from their seats to see the principals' reactions, few were aware of the formalities still taking place. A year to the day after Franklin's arraignment and two years after Eileen's recollection, the ordeal was over.

Eileen

Walking to the courtroom to hear the verdict was worse than walking in to testify. My legs felt like cement, and I could hardly breathe. I felt all color leave my face, my stomach was in knots, and the icy feeling in my hands had moved to my feet. Sharon and I sat down next to Mrs. Nason, and she took my hand. I noticed that a woman seated behind me was sketching my picture on her pad and I turned away. Extra sheriff's officers were in the courtroom, and I wondered whether they expected trouble or just wanted to hear the verdict.

As the jury entered the courtroom, I looked to see if they made eye contact with my father or with me, perhaps an indication of the verdict to come. When the jury foreman read the verdict of guilty, I felt my breath leave my body. Mrs. Nason and I hugged and I fought back all emotions, not wanting to share any more of myself with the press. I heard a sigh, or a sound, something that sounded like relief emitted by the crowd in the courtroom. Shirley Nason entered the courtroom late and sat in the seat near me that was held for her by the bailiff. "It's guilty!" I whispered to her with relief.

Bob Morse arrived to escort me out of the courtroom. As I made my way out, my Aunt Sue gave me a big hug, Sharon hugged me too, and a few of the reporters smiled at me. As Bob pushed open the door to the corridor, he put his arm around my waist and whispered, "Don't smile," as he saw the television cameras. Once in the elevator alone with Bob, I put my face in my hands and leaned into the wall, willing myself not to cry with the relief I finally felt.

From Elaine's office I first called Barry. When he answered, I could tell that he had been sleeping, and I forced out the words, "He's guilty. They found him guilty. It's over!" Barry was quite relieved and asked me to call him back later because he was going to call his parents. I then called my mother at her office. The reality was beginning to set in, and I was able to speak the words more normally. My mother was stunned and told me to stay where I was; she would be right over.

Finally I was able to speak with Shirley Nason. I spoke with Mrs. Nason and the preacher from her church. None of us knew what to say. Shortly after my mother arrived at

Elaine's office, Aunt Sue came in and the two sisters spoke for the first time in years. Bob Morse told me that the press was asking for me and the Nasons. I had nothing that I wanted to say, but I knew I wouldn't be allowed to leave the building in peace unless I made a statement.

There was a big crowd in the foyer of the Hall of Justice. Elaine was surrounded by the media, television cameras focused on her as she spoke. Bob escorted me to a bench several feet away, and I watched her being interviewed. I felt very proud of Elaine, and pleased that the press was focusing on her. She deserved all the attention and praise they would give her.

When the press spotted me and came across the room, I still had little to say. Along with the relief that the trial was finally over came the sadness that my father was going to prison. I had lost both Susan and my father, and I didn't think the media could understand the sadness I was feeling. After saying a few words, I had to leave. Everyone in the district attorney's office was smiling, congratulating Bob, Bryan, Marty, and Elaine. This was their victory. I knew they deserved their celebration, but it was not something that I could be part of. I was no longer a member of the team. For me it was, I knew, the final chapter in my relationship with my father, whom I had loved so much.

That evening I went out for a celebration dinner. I was celebrating the end of the trial and justice for Susan Nason. I felt no personal sense of victory; the trial had taken too much from me. I felt tremendous relief—overwhelming relief—that the truth had been understood and believed. But, oh God, how it hurt to have lost so much of my family and my privacy.

Conclusion

TWENTY-TWO

IMMEDIATELY AFTER THE VERDICT, JURORS FOR THE FRANKLIN trial, having agreed not to speak to the press, were taken out a rear door of the Hall of Justice. For a few days they held to their agreement, but eventually one spoke to a member of the prosecution team. Among many observations, the juror said they had been affected by the courtroom appearance of George Franklin, Jr. They were struck by his anger and hostility, seeing it as unfounded and menacing, and made the connection that he was now close to the age his father had been when Susan was murdered. If George's demeanor was indeed a factor—other jurors would stress other issues—it was a gloomy irony, since he had shown more sympathy for the defendant and worked harder on his behalf than anyone who wasn't paid to.

Peter Aaronson, a writer for *The Reporter,* the Bay Area's legal daily, managed to speak to three of the jurors and learned that most of the body's deliberations centered around Eileen's believability. On a chalkboard they had listed the details of the crime she probably could not have learned elsewhere: that Susan had raised her hands to protect herself, the A-line dress, her father throwing something, his placing a rock near Susan's body. They viewed the pain and anxiety she revealed on the witness stand and in the taped phone conversations with the police as evidence of her sincerity. One juror, a young man, said her obvious anguish convinced him she was not "putting herself through this for money."

As for the discrepancies in Eileen's accounts, one juror, a nurse in her early forties, said, "I know it's very important when a witness comes forward, and they need validation. I think she made mistakes in order to be believed, but I know that is a factor in coming forward." Other jurors said they were influenced by Franklin's question on being arrested: "Have you talked to my daughter?"

All were impressed with the preparation and performance of both Tipton and Horngrad, but most felt more comfortable with Tipton. By the end of the first day, ten of the jurors were ready to vote guilty. The foreman, Alger Chapman, who was convinced of Franklin's guilt from the outset of deliberations, argued patiently but persuasively with the two undecided jurors; by the middle of the next day, they too were ready to vote guilty.

Eileen

Anxious as I was to return to Zurich and my children, I wanted to spend a few more days in California to let the whole thing settle in. I had agreed to appear with Elaine on "Good Morning America" the following Monday. I was glad that Elaine would get national recognition for her terrific prosecution.

The extra days in the Bay Area allowed me to say good-bye properly to a number of people I had met through the case, also to say good-bye inwardly to a time and place that would no longer be a part of my life. On Saturday morning, which was sunny and mild, I drove up to Susan's grave, then to Foster City to take a last look. As I passed my Harvester Drive house, I was happy to discover that seeing it no longer produced fear in me. I decided to visit Rae and Aimee Alotta, but found no one home. I walked around the corner toward the Nasons'. This is the neighborhood, I thought, this is where it happened. It looked as harmless now as it did then. I saw Mr. Nason getting out of his car. He looked up as I approached, but didn't recognize me.

"Aren't you going to let me say good-bye?" I said. We talked for a while, he said nice things, and I asked him what he would have advised if I had come to him after first having the recollection, as I had once intended.

"I would have told you to go ahead," he said, "only I would have gone ahead with you."

On Sunday I went to church with Margaret Nason. When we talked afterward, Mrs. Nason again expressed her appreciation and admiration for what I had done, then told me about the work she was doing with the Center for Abuse Prevention. "You know," Margaret Nason said, "the center's abuse education costs only ten dollars per child. When you think how much this trial cost . . ." I was amazed that Mrs. Nason, with the cost to her of this crime, could think about the cost to the state of California.

We discussed the book I planned to write. "I hope it will have an educational value," she said, "that it will alert other parents to the dangers lurking in their safe neighborhoods, the possibility of deranged yet normal-appearing people stalking their children. I hope Susan's story will make people more aware. It should inform parents how to teach their children to recognize and stay away from inappropriate behavior. We have to look out for one another and care for one another. Perhaps nothing could have been done, but the more aware people are, the better the chances of preventing crimes like this."

In speaking about the grief we both felt, she said, "You think that you can share your grief with others, that it helps to be with others experiencing the same loss. But you find that it doesn't. You are on your own."

When I was on "Good Morning America" with Elaine, I was asked if my coming forward and the resulting trial had devastated my family. I answered without hesitation, "I'm not the one who devastated my family, my father devastated my family." Elaine spoke well, but seemed uneasy. She is not a glory-seeker, and I think she feels uncomfortable when fame comes to her.

After the interview, I began allowing myself to feel that maybe it was all over. I had met all my obligations and could now put the entire ordeal of the trial behind me. I could think about heading home and proceeding with my life. This fantasy was shattered when I learned that the police officer who had arrested me for prostitution had given an interview about this episode, the smear on my past that I was so thankful had not come out in the trial.

I could not imagine why anyone in law enforcement, knowing about my involvement in the trial as this person did, knowing about all I had gone through to help the police do their job, still chose to give this sort of hurtful interview. What would motivate a police officer to speak out in such a mean, unnecessary way against a witness? Couldn't he see that I had done the legally correct thing in an extremely difficult situation?

As my trust in Bob Morse had grown, it had tempered my distrust of the police. I was willing to believe that there were some true "white hats" out in the world, men and women working toward justice, deserving of respect. But now I felt my old dislike of the police returning.

At a time when I should have been feeling happy that the trial was over, that I had done the right thing, I was again made to feel violated. Sobbing, I called Barry in Switzerland. I tried to speak with my mother, but was unconsolable. I spoke to Elaine a few times. Knowing how badly I had wanted my past to remain buried, she was extremely sympathetic. She understood how truly irrelevant my earlier mistake was to the conviction of a murderer.

I was finally sobbing hysterically—probably my outrage at this man's viciousness mixed with all the tears I had wanted to shed over the past year, but hadn't. I had an impulse to phone him and ask why he would do such a thing. Angry as I was, I was deeply saddened that I was made to pay yet another price for seeking justice. Even worse, it was the price I had dreaded most of all and the only one I thought I had managed to escape paying. Who says the truth sets you free?

The sentencing of George Franklin had been scheduled for January 28. Three days before, Horngrad belatedly filed his motion for a new trial. Since this is often asking a judge to rule that the trial he presided over has been unfair, it is usually little more than a formality that must be observed prior to an appeal. Most often, the grounds cited are a preview of the grounds that will be used with a higher court.

Among his points, Horngrad charged prosecutorial misconduct in introducing the jail visit. For the prosecution to have flaunted the defendant's failure to deny Eileen's charges was, Horngrad said, in direct violation of his right to remain silent. He also claimed the court had made errors in law, primarily in disallowing the introduction of newspaper articles about Susan's disappearance.

Horngrad had alluded to having turned up a mystery witness who would rock the conviction. It turned out to be one Jeff Munson, a friend of Eileen's from her single days whom she and Barry had taken in when he was down on his luck and with whom she later quarreled. According to Horngrad, Munson would testify that Eileen had voiced suspicions that her father had murdered Susan Nason long before her recollection. Tipton was not in the least troubled by Munson, who had no good reason for not having come forward earlier and who could be shown to have ill will toward Eileen. Tipton was confident Munson would quickly be filed away with Sue Banks and Penny Stocks, people who for a variety of reasons seek to insinuate themselves into other people's dramas.

While damaging information about George Franklin in the prosecution's possession had been prohibited from the trial unless it related to the murder of Susan Nason, it was assembled by the Probate Department and laid before the judge for his consideration prior to sentencing. The results of the search of Franklin's apartment were described in detail—the child pornography, the nude photos, the ads and books with references to sex with children, the sexually explicit letters. A particularly salacious item was a photo of a partially nude Franklin proudly posing in front of his collection of thirty-seven dildos. There was literature from the Renee Gallon Society whose motto was "Sex before eight or it's too late." There were many references to father-daughter incest in the letters and publications, often circled or highlighted in some way. The Probation Department had also invited statements from people who had known the defendant, and had turned up a number of letters pro and con. Eileen, Janice, and Leah had all written eloquently about the suffering George Franklin had inflicted on them, and had stated their hope that he would be kept in jail forever. All of them referred to his having lived a free man for twenty years after ending Susan Nason's life when she was eight.

Anticipating that her father's friends would write on his behalf, Eileen said, "I'm sure that my father has friends who will try to influence and encourage his parole. Chances are, none of these people have been savagely beaten by him. My father did not commit rapes and murder in their presence. George Franklin's friends did not have their best friend murdered by him. Or their daughter."

About what his actions did to her, Eileen wrote: "I live with memories that no one would want. . . . I know of no way to escape the prison of these memories. My father sentenced me to a life of mental imprisonment for the crime of being a little girl that he could control. I did nothing to deserve the life sentence I now serve."

Margaret Nason wrote: "I cannot comprehend how Franklin could do this. I can only think of him as pure evil. He took so much away. Susie was so full of the joy of life. I can still hear her laugh as she made up little dances to do for us, and I hear her voice as I'd tuck her into bed, telling me, 'Mom, you're so comfortable.' I have many memories of her, but the loss of her is so painful, I have to push them away. Time has eased the grief, but any parent that has lost a child can tell you that the pain lasts a lifetime and words are never adequate to express that pain.

"My other daughter suffered so much from this loss. She went into depression that it took her years of therapy to overcome. The scars for her will last a lifetime also. Life continues as life will, but none of us are the same. . . .

"The Franklins—a nice large family with five children— how wonderful. Cute kids, freckled faces—living close by, friendly. Who would ever suspect the terrible trauma going on inside the home. We never did. My heart aches for those children and their mother. . . ."

She wrote of the horror of her daughter's last minutes of life: "In my mind I tell her to run. 'Run, Susie, run.' But she can't and I can feel the blows of the rock as Franklin brings it down on her head."

Donald Nason declined to write anything, saying he would never be able to find the words to express the devastation he felt. He said he had barely been able to work the first two years after Susan's murder. The interviewer from the probation office wrote, "It was readily apparent that he is still deeply suffering." Shirley Nason wrote that for years she "had nightmares trying to rescue Susan, help her, save her." At the end of her letter she said, "[Franklin's] behavior during the trial and some of the testimony given proves that he sees nothing wrong with what he did. . . . Instead he had a proud cockiness as if to clearly say, 'Prove it. You have to prove me guilty! Eileen, I dare you to!' "

A number of letters from friends and relatives of George Franklin attested to what a decent man he was. All commended his having overcome his alcoholism, a fact that suggested the letter-writers were people he had met in AA. Obviously unaware of the sexual arsenal the detectives found in his apartment, and maybe unaware of the perversion behind it, all wrote that there was no evidence of anything askew in Franklin's sexuality.

Franklin's mother, Hattie Jarrett Franklin, in a handwritten letter, told the basic facts of her son's early life, but gave no indication of what kind of boy he had been or man he had become. She concluded, "I love George dearly and I think he is innocent. I pray for George and his family. I know only God can heal a broken heart." His sisters and a brother-in-law wrote of their shock at his conviction and their belief in his innocence.

For the first time in her twelve years as a prosecutor, Elaine Tipton availed herself of her prerogative to write a letter against a defendant. She climaxed a catalog of Franklin's evil by saying he "represents the worst specimen of pedophile and child murderer. It is sad commentary that such heinous conduct could be qualified, but such has been my experience in prosecuting hundreds of child molesters and numerous child murderers. They do come in different variations, and George Franklin is the most despicable and dangerous."

On January 28, 1991, when George Franklin entered Judge Smith's courtroom to hear his sentence, he was smiling and as jaunty as on the first day of the trial. At the defense table he chatted and laughed with Horngrad. All of the Nasons—but none of the other Franklins—were present in the full courtroom. Horngrad argued for leniency, stressing his client's lack of a criminal record. Tipton pointed to the absence of remorse in Franklin and the twenty-one years of "parole" he had already enjoyed.

Judge Smith asked Franklin if he had anything to say. He stood up and, with a strange Southern accent and a muffled voice not once heard in this courtroom over the past six weeks, said, "Yes, Your Honor. I'm not guilty of the crime with which I've been charged." There was a silence while Judge Smith glowered at him. Slowly the judge said, "You are a wicked and depraved man. If it were not for the anomaly of the law in 1969 [the absence of a death penalty], you would be receiving a different sentence. As it is, you are to be remanded for life into the custody of . . ."

Afterward, in the corridor outside, Aimee Alotta hugged Shirley Nason. Elaine Tipton told reporters that Franklin would go to San Quentin to await reassignment to another prison, probably one in northern California. She admitted that her office was currently investigating other crimes. When she emphasized that there was a six-year statute of limitations on child molestation, some reporters took it as a hint that the crimes were more serious.

After telling reporters that Franklin would be eligible for parole in seven years, Tipton added, "You can be sure I will be there to argue that he should not be paroled." That evening, relaxing with friends, Tipton said facetiously "Where are the good old days when child molesters used to get beaten up by other prisoners? You know, by the murderers and kidnappers who found molesters morally repugnant?"

Eileen

Shortly after the conviction, my mother observed how differently the case had been handled now from the way it would have been handled twenty years ago, mainly because there were a large number of powerful women involved who would not have been involved two decades earlier: Elaine Tipton, the prosecuting attorney; Dr. Lenore Terr, the expert witness on repression; and Leah Franklin, an attorney.

I added names of other professional women who had helped me: Lynn Loring, my friend and the president of MGM Television; Audrey Davis-Levin, a sensitive woman and successful television writer hired for the movie; my literary agent, Helen Brann, who kept the wolves from my door, even when I was willing to open it; and Betty Prashker, an impressive woman and my publisher at Crown/Random House.

I felt tremendously grateful to the women of preceding generations who refused to be oppressed, who made way for the powerful women of my adulthood. I also felt grateful to the women who, in years before me, so bravely testified about their own violations, forging a path for me to follow as a rape and sexual-abuse victim.

Though I have met some fine men through this process, I feel it is difficult for any man to understand what I have been forced to endure in the way that a woman can. I am deeply grateful that my memory returned at a time when women could help me down the path I had to take.

After the conviction, Elaine and I were able to talk about things that were off limits during the year from arrest to conviction. Elaine pointed out that whenever I discussed the events of September 22, 1969, I always referred to it as the day of the murder. She said that other people called it "the day Susan disappeared" or "the day Susan was kidnapped." She said that I referred to it only one way, as the day of the murder, because that was what I knew it to be.

She surprised me by saying that, from the beginning, she

had decided that she and I should not grow too close, and
that she had made a big effort to maintain a professional
distance. She certainly was professional. I always got the
impression she was looking very hard for reasons to believe
or disbelieve me. I always felt her decision to believe me was
based on facts, not friendship or emotion. I take this as a
comment on her integrity as well as on my credibility.

When I was ready to leave the Bay Area a few days after
the conviction, I went to the Hall of Justice to say good-bye
to Elaine. I had once told her it was unfair that when the trial
was over, she could walk away from it, but that it was my life
and I could not walk away. As Elaine rode down with me in
the elevator to see me out, I realized that I could now say
good-bye to a building that had been the center of my existence for the past year. The courtroom, Elaine's office, and
the sheriff's department—I could walk away with a new
respect for our criminal-justice system, leaving behind only
my testimony in the court records.

Outside on the entrance steps, as men and women with
briefcases passed in and out of the building on either side of
us, around us, Elaine and I said good-bye. A man called out
to her, congratulating her on her victory as he approached to
speak. He didn't seem to recognize me, and I realized that I
could make an escape. I kissed Elaine quickly and ran off
without looking back. We would remain friends, but it would
never be as it was during the war we fought together. As I
walked away from the building toward my car, I thought of
the father I was leaving behind in a cell on the fourth floor,
probably reading one of his beloved Civil War books. The
thought made me very sad.

I was so glad to return to my family and the beauty of a
Swiss winter. My semitropical children believed they had
invented snow as a special surprise for my return. Barry
treated me like a returning hero for a few minutes, but then
reverted to the Barry I had grown used to. Now he wanted
me to push Elaine to charge Kate with perjury. I agreed with
Barry that Kate's behavior had been outrageous, but I had
no enthusiasm yet for another fight. I was also very upset to
learn about George junior's strange testimony which I found
difficult to understand.

I wondered if I'd been too hard on Leah. For all our
problems, and her misgivings, she did come in strongly on

my side in the case and was supportive through the whole ordeal. Looking back on our relations as I was growing up, I've come to realize that if you give in to the anger you feel toward the parent who has victimized you, it makes you more of a victim, it perpetuates the victimization. I'm sure that is one reason you take out your hostility on the other parent. It dissipates the blame and, at the same time, the rage you feel. In a strange way, blaming the other parent reduces the hold over you of the one who actually mistreated you.

Quickly my days settled into the routine I had looked forward to for so many months. Cooking up vegetarian creations, driving my kids across Switzerland each day to their wonderful school, watching videos together at night, shopping, getting our house organized. The routine kept me so busy that I had less time to think about anything, at least nothing farther away than the distance Aaron could throw something.

With one exception. Our house is the last one on a road that continues climbing a small mountain for another hundred yards past a cow pasture, then dead ends. A broad dirt trail continues up the slope into deep woods. Each day I would slip out of the house to walk up into this beautiful pine forest, sometimes to jog, other times simply to be alone and enjoy the forest's lush beauty and breathe the moist, acrid air. Jogging up the hill is hard work, and my mind is given over to the effort. Coming down is more dangerous for me as I have a chance to think.

I think a lot about God, but not in a way that would please religious people. I had been quite religious before the memories started coming back, then I asked myself what kind of God would make people with memories like this. I became very angry. Maybe it's because I can't get angry enough with my father that I became angry with God. Yet I know that in the past months when I called upon him deep in the night— please give me strength to get through this—I felt very much a hypocrite asking God to guide me when I was so angry at him.

My therapists and others have read books and have an intellectual understanding of repressed memory. I don't have that. What I understand is what it's done to my life. And I become very angry about it. I feel betrayed by God. And even if I did get back my faith, I couldn't pray to God. He might get subpoenaed by Horngrad.

BOUT THE AUTHORS

een Franklin lives in Switzerland with her husband and two
ldren.

illiam Wright is the bestselling author of *Lillian Hellman, The
n Bülow Affair, Pavarotti,* and *All the Pain That Money Can
y: The Life of Christina Onassis.* He lives in New York City
d Bucks County, Pennsylvania.

Not only have I lost my religion, but so many of the beliefs that held me together have unraveled. I used to believe that parents loved their children unconditionally. There goes that belief. I thought I was a good parent, but now I know I am overprotective. Because of what the trial did to my relationships with my siblings, I now see all relationships as tentative; at any time the person I trust most can turn against me.

And my father? Do I now have to accept that he never loved me? I don't believe that. It's easy to listen to Elaine and Bob and agree with the scathing things they have to say about him. They are probably trying to reinforce my belief that I did the right thing. It's not necessary. I know I did the right thing, that my father is as bad as they say. But I know a man they don't, one who could be charming, fun, kind, caring, loving—and who gave me the few happy moments of a horrible childhood—which he also gave me.

But looking back with what I now know about him, I am incensed at his reentering my life after the birth of Jessica. Because of his sexual interest in little girls, his reappearance takes on a sinister cast, not the gesture of support I assumed. He knew, but I didn't, that he had no right to be with me and my infant daughter.

I think a lot about the memories that have had such an impact on my life. They always have a strong emotion associated with them—terror, pain, confusion. The emotion precedes the memory by just a second. When I began having the memories, as soon as I had such feelings, I would try to stop them, because I was aware that a new recollection would only disrupt my life more.

It takes me about three days to accept a frightening new memory. They are like little building blocks that each fits in a place. I don't know how many blocks there are or how many blocks are missing from my memory. Most recently I remembered my father having sex with me. It came in two pieces, the first piece carried the feelings of fear and confusion, so I made myself stop remembering. The second piece snuck up on me a few days later. I was tired, my guard was down. It completed the first memory, or did it?

It's as if I should carry a calling card identifying myself. Below my name it would say Witness to Murder, then below that Sexually Abused Child, then Rape Victim. Now, with this latest horror, I have to add Incest Survivor. What ugly titles my father has given me.

Ever since he denied murdering Susan when I visited him in jail—or to be exact, refused to confess to it—it has been an all-out battle between us, and the battle is not over. To other people, the guilty verdict may appear a big victory for me in our struggle, but I know it is only the first step. The control he had over me is far from exorcized.

He had the power to close down a big part of my mind. He still has the power to keep me wallowing in misery. If I don't achieve mastery over all he has done to me, if I allow part of my memory to remain repressed, my father wins. I must bring out and successfully put to rest all kinds of horror before I can truly say I have beaten him. If I live my life terrified of remembering more, he has won.

I look in the mirror and compare the face I see with photos taken of me before the recollection. In many ways I appear the same, but I can see a major difference: all the joy has left my eyes. If I force myself to think about it, I know it has left me, maybe for good. But it is even sadder to think this shows in my face.

As I jog, all of my memories are not bad. In fact, some connected to the case are wonderful. I think of Elaine and Marty, of meeting Helen Brann and Bill Wright over a lunch at New York's Four Seasons, Connie Chung at our house in Switzerland teaching Jessica how to play Cat's Cradle. I remember Bob Morse, his gun hanging on his side, ironing my blue suit for the preliminary hearing. I remember a birthday party Lisa Silverstein gave during the trial for me with Todd, Aimee, and other high school friends. I remember the unhesitating love and support Barry and his family gave me. I remember the look on Horngrad's face when on the stand I said yes, there was someone else who saw the murder: my father. I remember Mrs. Nason's crying in my arms as the jury said, "Guilty."

But now I have to concentrate on my recovery. Having the memories was like having a six-point earthquake inside of me. Everything shifted, and I have to realign it all. They say that getting these buried memories out into the open puts me on the path to recovery. Maybe, but walking the path is a bitch. Or jogging it.

The downhill memories are the ones that are going to finish me off. It would be okay if I only had to deal with the memories that have already come. Bad as they are, they are out now and, I hope, bearable. But I know there are others,

will be others. I recognize the signs when I am a a visit from an existing memory. There is a di of anxiety to each—Susan's murder, the rape b the bathtub molestation—and I dread each way.

But other rumbles, equally terrifying, annou rors that are forcing their way to the surface, from the deepest pockets of my mind to torment me. I never know what might trigger a fresh a pain. Maybe the bend of a tree on this path, or of the little boy I am about to pass. Any object, can launch new horror in me.

I learned long ago I can do nothing to stop the If they want to come, they will. The other part has no choice but to try not to collapse under th I tell myself they will stop one day. They must.